T0160732

Essential
Korean
Grammar

Acknowledgments

A lot goes into writing a book. This one started with my parents, David and Anita Kingdon, and their emphasis on the value of education and learning, a value I myself have pursued throughout my life. I am grateful for their constant support, as well as that of my brothers, Robbie and Andy Kingdon, and my best friend and surrogate brother, Randal Blandon. Finally, this book wouldn't have been written without the love, support, and constructive suggestions of my husband, Chris Backe; I had wanted to write this for years, but he was the one who finally inspired me to get it started, and kept me supplied with enough encouragement to stick with it once I'd started.

Of course, I also have to thank Tuttle Publishing for their work in publishing this book, not to mention the many other books they've published that have been of use to me in my own language studies. Regarding this book in particular, I am grateful to Eric Oey for getting the ball rolling, to my editors Sandra Korinchak and Nancy Goh, to Mike Page for marketing, to Terri Jadick for general assistance throughout the process, and to all others who worked behind the scenes to make the book a reality. My Korean editors Sanghyun Ahn and Hannah Han were instrumental in making sure all the Korean in the book was correct, and I also have to thank my former Korean tutor Kyehyun Park and all my professors at Yonsei for their instruction.

Finally, I'd like to thank Gordon and Ruth Kingdon, Bill and Joan Brown, Murray and Christine Brown, Beth Lloyd, Euen Moore, Bruce McAuley, Becky Strople, Dave Cook, Jan Barkhouse, Mark Currie, Jon Watts, Carolyn Watts, Lisa Wadden, Ed Charlton, Ian MacKenzie, Stacey van Dyk, Rachel Davison, Dan and Elizabeth Rolfe, Alex Kennedy, Steve Fehr, Paul Benjamin, Amy Bowler, Bob Adamson, Luke Roberts, Azrael Jeffrey, Debbie Kim, Chelsey Mathews, Aaron Seymour, Bill Carver, Emma Chaitongkao, Holly Sroymalai, Ken May, Matthijs van Rooyen, Christian Frech, Park Chansoon, Lee Kayoung, Peter Daley, Jessica Suchan, JD DeLemont, and everyone else who has supported me along the way.

Essential
Korean
Grammar

A comprehensive reference
for learners at every level

LAURA KINGDON

TUTTLE Publishing

Tokyo | Rutland, Vermont | Singapore

"Books to Span the East and West"

Tuttle Publishing was founded in 1832 in the small New England town of Rutland, Vermont [USA]. Our core values remain as strong today as they were then—to publish best-in-class books which bring people together one page at a time. In 1948, we established a publishing office in Japan—and Tuttle is now a leader in publishing English-language books about the arts, languages and cultures of Asia. The world has become a much smaller place today and Asia's economic and cultural influence has grown. Yet the need for meaningful dialogue and information about this diverse region has never been greater. Over the past seven decades, Tuttle has published thousands of books on subjects ranging from martial arts and paper crafts to language learning and literature—and our talented authors, illustrators, designers and photographers have won many prestigious awards. We welcome you to explore the wealth of information available on Asia at www.tuttlepublishing.com.

Published by Tuttle Publishing, an imprint of Periplus Editions (HK) Ltd.

www.tuttlepublishing.com

Copyright © 2015 Laura Kingdon

All rights reserved. No part of this publication may be reproduced or utilized in any form or by any means, electronic or mechanical, including photocopying, recording, or by any information storage and retrieval system, without prior written permission from the publisher.

Library of Congress Control Number: 2015936092

ISBN 978-0-8048-4431-4

First edition
25 24 23 22 21
10 9 8 7 6 5 4
2109VP

Printed in Malaysia

TUTTLE PUBLISHING® is a registered trademark of Tuttle Publishing, a division of Periplus Editions (HK) Ltd.

Distributed by

North America, Latin America & Europe
Tuttle Publishing
364 Innovation Drive
North Clarendon
VT 05759-9436 U.S.A.
Tel: 1 (802) 773-8930
Fax: 1 (802) 773-6993
info@tuttlepublishing.com
www.tuttlepublishing.com

Japan
Tuttle Publishing
Yaekari Building, 3rd Floor
5-4-12 Osaki, Shinagawa-ku
Tokyo 141 0032
Tel: (81) 3 5437-0171
Fax: (81) 3 5437-0755
sales@tuttle.co.jp
www.tuttle.co.jp

Asia Pacific
Berkeley Books Pte. Ltd.
3 Kallang Sector #04-01
Singapore 349278
Tel: (65) 6741-2178
Fax: (65) 6741-2179
inquiries@periplus.com.sg
www.tuttlepublishing.com

Contents

PART ONE
THE BASICS OF KOREAN

PART TWO
GRAMMAR POINTS

PART THREE
FREQUENTLY SEEN WORD PARTS

How to Use This Book

When I first started studying Korean, I found there were any number of books, blogs, podcasts, classes, etc., available for beginners, and I rejoiced. However, as my studies progressed, the quantity of appropriate materials dropped sharply and while there were still many textbooks, very few of them explained the material in a useful way: for instance, though they would happily explain that 어서 eoseo and 으니까 eunikka both roughly meant "so," there was little guidance as to when it was appropriate to use each form. These books also tended to be poorly organized, with ㄴ다고 해서 dago haeseo in one chapter, ㄴ다고 하니까 dago hanikka several chapters later and ㄴ다고 하는데 n dago haneunde a few chapters again after, even though these are all very similar expressions.

In this book, I have attempted to synthesize all the information gained from my studies into a format that's useful and convenient for others to follow. I am not planning to teach you these expressions for the first time but rather to provide a useful guide to help you make sense of what you've already partially learned and to help you use these expressions more fluently, much like a toolbox to help you form correct and natural-sounding Korean sentences rather than ending every single sentence with the same old 아/어/여요 a/eo/yeoyo.

To this end, I have mainly focused on verbs and adverbs. Constructing Korean sentences is really all about what you do with the verbs, and a whole lot of implications are packed into different verb endings. There's a little about pronouns because contractions are used all the time (just like in English) but rarely taught, and then some information about adverbs at the end because a good adverb can really spice up a sentence (and because I myself find them confusing at times and so I suspect others might as well).

I really haven't focused on vocabulary since you can probably use a dictionary just as well as I can. There are some good vocabulary books listed in the Appendix if you want a little more direction.

There are only a few different ways to attach verbs and endings in Korean and I have summarized these on page 19, which you can refer back to anytime. Each expression comes with its own set of "hooks." For example, every expression starting with "ㄴ/는" attaches to verbs the same way: ㄴ to verbs ending in vowels and 는 to verbs ending in consonants, regardless of tense or any other factor. This seems daunting at first, but with practice it will become second nature.

Because this book is intended to take you from beginning to advanced Korean, I recognize that my readers will be at somewhat different levels and will know or not know different things, so I've summarized what I consider to be the basic points of Korean grammar in "The Basics of Korean" for you to check if you need a little help. I haven't spent much time on them because it's not terribly difficult to find good-quality materials on basic Korean grammar. If you find you're not quite ready for this book yet, I've listed some useful beginning Korean books in the Appendix.

I have also tried to keep the language in my examples fairly simple. When possible, they all end in the 아/어/여요 (polite) form because those are the most useful and I wanted to keep everything consistent for the sake of clarity. Unless I say otherwise, you can use any of these expressions with any level of politeness.

The Rating System
(or, How Important Is This Grammar Point to Me?)

All the information in the section "The Basics of Korean" is material you should know before reading the rest of this book. Material in the appendixes is stuff I think might be useful for you to know, but you don't have to study it if you'd rather not. Beyond that, I've rated everything in the main part of the book according to a star system, which works like this:

★★★★★   Critical; with only the five-star expressions, you can communicate almost everything you need to say, and without them you'll have trouble understanding any more than the most basic of sentences.

★★★★   Very helpful; you should learn this if you want to communicate well in Korean

★★★   Useful, fairly common, and will help you sound more natural and fluent

★★   Not that important; grammar only the TOPIK (Test of Proficiency in Korean) people care about

★   Don't worry about this unless there's some reason you need to know it

Expressions are also rated according to whether or not they're used more in speaking or in writing.

	The expression is:
Speaking > Writing	used more often in speaking than in writing
Speaking < Writing	used more often in writing than in speaking
Speaking = Writing	used as often in writing as in speaking
Speaking	used only in speaking
Writing	used only in writing

Grammatical Terms Used in This Book

I've tried to keep grammatical terms to a minimum here so as to avoid confusion and because, honestly, you don't really need to know what a desiderative auxiliary verb is in order to speak Korean. Here are the absolute bare-minimum terms you should know.

Term	Korean term	Meaning	Examples
Noun	명사 myeongsa	A word that names an object, person or place	책 chaek (book) 사람 saram (person) 동대문 (Dongdaemun—place) 민수 (Minsu—male's name)
Action verb	동사 dongsa	A word that tells you what someone or something does	가다 gada (to go) 하다 hada (to do) 먹다 meokda (to eat) 살다 salda (to live)
Descriptive verb[A]	형용사 hyeongyongsa	A word that describes what someone or something is	아름답다 areumdapda (to be beautiful) 빨갛다 ppalgata (to be red) 중요하다 jungyohada (to be important) 덥다 deopda (to be hot)
Adverb	부사 busa	A word that describes how something is done	조용히 joyonghi (quietly) 빨리 ppal-li (quickly) 그래서 geuraeseo (therefore)
Pronoun	대명사 daemyeongsa	A shorthand for a noun	나/저 (I) na/jeo 너/당신 neo/dangsin (you) 우리 uri (we)
Directional verb		A word that describes the action of going or coming	가다 gada (to go) 오다 oda (to come) 돌아가다 doragada (to go back) 떠나다 tteonada (to leave)
Past Tense	과거 gwageo		했다 haetda (did) 먹었다 meogeotda (ate) 더웠다 deowotda (was hot)
Present Tense	현재 hyeonjae		한다 handa (do) 하고 있다 hago itda (doing) 아름다운 areumdaun (beautiful)
Future Tense	미래 mirae		할 것이다 hal geosida (will do) 할 거야 hal geoya (will do—반말) 하겠다 hagetda (will do)
Passive[B]	피동사 pidongsa	A verb that describes what is done to something else	쓰이다 sseu-i-da (to be written/used) 보이다 bo-i-da (to be seen) 먹히다 meokida (to be eaten)

Term	Korean term	Meaning	Examples
Causative[B]	사동 sadong	A verb that describes the action of making something happen	안기다 angida (to hug) 먹이다 meogida (to feed) 씌다 ssu-i uda (to put something [a hat/glasses] on someone else)
Statement	서술문 seosulmun	A sentence ending in a period that neither orders nor suggests anything to anyone else	이렇게 해도 돼요. Ireoke haedo dwaeyo. It can be done like this.
Question	의문문 uimunmun	A sentence that asks for information and ends with a question mark	어떻게 하면 돼요? Eotteoke hamyeon dwaeyo? How should it be done?
Command	명령문 myeong- ryeong-mun	An order telling someone else to do something	이렇게 해 보세요. Ireoke hae boseyo. Try to do it like this.
Suggestion	청유문 cheongyumun	A suggestion to someone else that they do something	이렇게 할까요? Ireoke halkkayo? Shall we do it this way?

[A] In Korean, adjectives are also considered verbs. In their dictionary form they translate to "to be." For example, 아름답다 means "to be beautiful" and if you want to use it to describe someone, you have to conjugate it appropriately.

[B] For more on passives and causatives, and the mysteries of their creation, see page 33.

Essential
Korean
Grammar

The Basics of Korean

Pronouns and Contractions

Let's start by reviewing the basics here. As you should know by this point, you change your pronouns depending on how much respect you want to give the person you're talking to.

English	Lower	Higher
I	나 na	저 jeo
You	너 neo	당신 dangsin
We	우리 uri	저희 jeohui
This	이것 igeot	이것
That	그것 geugeot	그것
That (over there)	저것 jeogeot	저것

너 is used all the time in 반말 (informal language), but if you want to be respectful, it's far more common to refer to someone you're talking to in the third person: 선생님 seonsaengnim (teacher), 계현씨 gyehyeonssi (polite way to address a person named 계현) or even 민정 엄마 minjeong eomma (Minjeong's mother) or something similar. Although 당신 is technically the polite way to say "you," it's almost never used in spoken Korean and if it is, it often means a fight is about to break out. So be very careful with 당신.

As you should also know, subjects and objects take endings: 은/는, 이/가, 을/를 eun/neun, i/ga, eul/reul are the ones we'll deal with here. Go to page 30 if you need to learn about any of these endings.

Here's a table to show you how to contract each word.

Original word	저 jeo	나 na	우리 uri	저희 jeohui	너 neo	이(그/저)것 igeoseun
+는 neun	저는 jeoneun	나는 naneun	우리는 urineun	저희는 jeohuineun	너는 neoneun	이것은 igeoseun
Contraction	전 jeon	난 nan	우린 urin	저흰 jeohuin	넌 neon	이건 igeon
+이/가 i/ga	제가 jega	내가 naega	우리가 uriga	저희가 jeohuiga	네가 nega	이것이 igeosi
Contraction						이게 ige
+을/를 eul/reul	저를 jeoreul	나를 nareul	우리를 urireul	저희를 jeohuireul	너를 neoreul	이것을 igeoseul
Contraction	절 jeol	날 nal	우릴 uril	저흴 jeohuil	널 neol	이걸 igeol
+의 ui	저의 jeoui	나의 naui	우리의 uriui	저희의 jeohuiui	너의 neoui	이것의 igeosui
Contraction	제 je	내 nae			네 ne	

저걸로 주세요. **Jeogeollo juseyo.** Give me that.

이건 어때요? **Igeon eottaeyo?** How about this?

More Contractions:
이렇다/그렇다/저렇다/어떻다 ireota/geureota/jeoreota/eotteota

As you may know, these mean "to be a certain way." 이렇다 means "to be this way," 그렇다 means "to be that way" and 저렇다 means "to be that way over there" and isn't really used that much. These are very versatile expressions that you'll see. and they are used in all kinds of ways. 어떻다 by itself doesn't translate well, but you'll see it all the time as 어떻게 (how).

The most common way you'll probably see them conjugated is by adding the ending 게, which turns a verb into an adverb. We don't have these adverbs in English, at least not as single words, but if "thisly," "thatly," and "that over therely" were words, they'd be translated this way.

어떻게 **eotteoke** How?   그렇게 **geureoke** Like that.

이렇게 **ireoke** Like this.   저렇게 **jeoreoke** Like that over there.

Let's try making some sentences:

어떻게 하면 돼요? **Eotteoke hamyeon dwaeyo?**
What's a good way to do it? (How can I do this?)

그렇게 하면 안 돼요. **Geureoke hamyeon an dwaeyo.** You can't do it like that.

이렇게 어려운 책을 읽지 못 해요. **ireoke eoryeoun chaegeul ikji mot taeyo.**
I can't read such a difficult book.

And here's how to abbreviate 이렇다, 그렇다, 저렇다, and 어떻다 using the tense markers ㄴ and ㄹ. (See page 235 for more information on tense markers).

Original word	이렇다 ireota	그렇다 geureota	저렇다 jeoreota	어떻다 eotteota
+ㄴ	이렇 + ㄴ	그렇 + ㄴ	저렇 + ㄴ	어떻 + ㄴ
Contraction	이런 ireon	그런 geureon	저런 jeoreon	어떤 eotteon
+ㄹ	이렇 + ㄹ	그렇 + ㄹ	저렇 + ㄹ	
Contraction	이릴 ireol	그릴 geureol	저릴 jeoreol	

이런 헤어 스타일은 어떠세요? **Ireon heeo seu-ta-i-reun eotteoseyo?**
What do you think about this hairstyle?

어떤 헤어 스타일을 좋아하세요? **Eotteon heeo seu-ta-i-reul joahaseyo?**
What kind of style do you like?

<u>저런</u> 헤어 스타일을 좋아해요. Jeoreon heeo seu-ta-i-reul joahaeyo.
I like that kind of hairstyle.

More ways to use 이렇다, 저렇다 and especially 그렇다 are on page 377. For now, let's look at 어떻다 and its unique contractions.

When you add 어떻게 plus 하다, you can keep on using 어떻게 하다 or you can contract the whole thing to 어쩌다. This contraction happens in many commonly used expressions.

- 어쩔 수 없다 Eojjeol su eopda

  A: 저기 버스가 가네요! Jeogi beoseuga ganeyo! The bus is leaving!
  B: 어쩔 수 없죠, 뭐. 다음 버스 타요. Eojjeol su eopjo, mwo. Daeum beoseu tayo.
     Oh well, it can't be helped. Let's take the next one.

- 어쩌면 eojjeomyeon Maybe

  내일 어쩌면 비가 올 지도 몰라요. Naeil eojjeomyeon biga ol jido mollayo.
  Maybe it'll rain tomorrow.

- 어쩐지 eojjeonji Somehow

  A: 저 감기 걸린 것 같아요. Jeo gamgi geollin geot gatayo.
     I think I caught a cold.
  B: 어쩐지, 얼굴이 안좋아보이더라고요.
     Eojjeonji, eolguri an-jo-a-bo-i-deo-ra-go-yo.
     Somehow, your face doesn't look that good.

(Here "somehow" means "in some vague way." And while it's strange to tell people in English that their face doesn't look so good, it's done in Korean all the time.)

How to Talk to People Without Being Rude

반말 and 존댓말 and All Their Permutations

There are seven levels of speech in Korean. There used to be many more, but thankfully they've been greatly simplified. Even more thankfully, most of the seven aren't that commonly used. 반말 banmal is the lowest form, used toward children or people very close to you, and it actually covers five of the seven levels, including all the ones you don't need to worry about. The next two levels are both called 존댓말 jondaenmal. One is what I'll refer to as "informal polite" and is by far the most common and useful level. It's used toward strangers, people you don't know well, or people older than you. The other is super-polite and is used when speaking to people higher in rank or status or when addressing crowds. Just as an example, I use 반말 to my students and informal polite to my co-teachers. I just about never use super-polite, but I hear it all the time in subway announcements. Finally, you don't really use any of the levels in writing, so I'll show you how to end sentences when you're writing, too.

As you may also know, Korean grammar much depends on what kind of sentence you're forming. These can be classified as follows:

1. Statements with action verbs
2. Statements with descriptive verbs
3. Statements with nouns

4. Commands
5. Questions
6. Suggestions

Here's how to end each kind of sentence in each level of speech. Note as well that there are many ways to end sentences—this whole book's worth, in fact. The ones listed here are just the basics. Let's start with the three very common ways of speaking.

Sentence type	Tense	반말 (해체 haeche) (casual)	존댓말 (해요체 haeyoche) (informal polite)	존댓말 (하십시오체 hasipsi-o-che) (super polite)	문어체 muneoche (writing)
Action verb statements ending in vowels	Past	했어 haeseo	했어요 haeseoyo	했습니다 haetseupnida	했다 haetda
	Present	해 hae	해요 haeyo	합니다 hapnida	한다 handa
	Future	할 거야 hal geoya	할 거예요 hal geoyeyo	하겠습니다 hagetseumnida	할 것이다 hal geosida
Action verb statements ending in consonants	Past	먹었어 meogeoseo	먹었어요 meogeoseoyo	먹었습니다 meogeotseupnida	먹었다 meogeotda
	Present	먹어 meogeo	먹어요 meogeoyo	먹습니다 meokseubnida	먹는다 meokneunda
	Future	먹을 거야 meogeul geoya	먹을 거예요 meogeul geoyeyo	먹을 겁니다 meogeul geopnida	먹을 것이다 meogeul geosida
Descriptive verb statements ending in vowels	Past	작았어 jagasseo	작았어요 jagasseoyo	작았습니다 jagatseumnida	작았다 jagatda
	Present	작아 jaga	작아요 jagayo	작습니다 jakseumnida	작다 jakda
	Future	작을 거야 jageul geoya	작을 거예요 jageul geoyeyo	작을 겁니다 jageul geopnida	작을 것이다 jageul geosida
Descriptive verb statements ending in consonants	Past	예뻤어 yeppeoseo	예뻤어요 yeppeoseoyo	예뻤습니다 yeppeotseumnida	예뻤다 yeppeotda
	Present	예뻐 yeppeo	예뻐요 yeppeoyo	예쁩니다 yeppeupnida	예쁘다 yeppeuda
	Future	예쁠 거야 yeppeul geoya	예쁠 거예요 yeppeul geoyeyo	예쁠 겁니다 yeppeul geopnida	예쁠 것이다 yeppeul geosida
Noun statements ending in vowels	Past	남자였어 namjayeosseo	남자였어요 namjayeosseoyo	남자였습니다 namjayeotseumnida	남자였다 namjayeotda
	Present	남자야 namjaya	남자예요 namjayeyo	남자입니다 namjaipnida	남자이다 namja-i-da
	Future	남자일 거야 namja-il geoya	남자일 거예요 namja-il geoyeyo	남자일 겁니다 namja-il geopnida	남자일 것이다 namja-il geosida

Sentence type	Tense	반말 (해체 haeche) (casual)	존댓말 (해요체 haeyoche) (informal polite)	존댓말 (하십시오체 hasipsi-o-che) (super polite)	문어체 muneoche (writing)
Noun statements ending in consonants	Past	물이었어 murieosseo	물이었어요 murieosseoyo	물이었습니다 murieotseumnida	물이었다 murieotda
	Present	물이야 muliya	물이에요 mul-i-eyo	물입니다 mulipnida	물이다 mulida
	Future	물일 거야 mulil geoya	물일 거예요 mulil geoyeyo	물일 겁니다 mulil geopnida	물일 것이다 mulil geosida
Commands ending in vowels	Present	해 hae	하세요 haseyo	하십시오 hasipsio	해라E haela
Commands ending in consonants	Present	먹어 meogeo	잡으세요C jabeuseyo	잡으십시오C jabeusipsio	잡아라E jabala
Questions ending in vowels	Past	했어? haesseo?	했어요? haesseoyo?	했습니까? haetseumnikka?	했나?A haenna?
	Present	해? hae?	해요? haeyo?	합니까? hapnikka?	하나?A hana?
	Future	할 거야? hal geoya?	할 거예요? hal geoyeyo?	할 겁니까? hal geopnikka?	하겠나?A hagenna?
Questions ending in consonants	Past	먹었어? meogeosseo?	먹었어요? meogeosseoyo?	먹었습니까? meogeotseumnikka?	먹었나?A meogeonna?
	Present	먹어? meogeo?	먹어요? meogeoyo?	먹습니까? meokseupnikka?	먹나?A meokna?
	Future	먹을 거야?A meogeul geoya?	먹을 거예요? meogeul geoyeyo?	먹을 겁니까? meogeul geopnikka?	먹겠나?A meokgenna?
Suggestions ending in vowels	Present	하자 haja	할래요 hallaeyo/ 할까요 halkkayo	합시다 hapsida	하자 haja
Suggestions ending in consonants	Present	먹자 meokja	먹을래요 meogeullaeyo/ 먹을까요 meogeulkkayo	먹읍시다 meogeupsida	먹자 meokja

   Now let's take a look at some of the more uncommon forms. You'll most likely never hear these in real life. 하오체 and 하게체 are used only by older people (and on warning signs, in the case of [으]시오), while 해라체 is used by people talking either to themselves or to very young children. You may note that it's very similar to the written style (문어체) listed above: in fact, in most respects, they're the same. You have to show great respect to your audience while addressing a crowd verbally, which is almost always done in the super-polite 하십시오체 form, but none at all while addressing them in writing.

Sentence type	Tense	하오체 haeche	하게체 haeyoche	해라체 muneoche
Action verb statements ending in vowels	Past	했소 haetso	했네 haenne	했다 haetda
	Present	하오 hao	하네 hane	한다 handa
	Future	할 거요 hal geoyo	할 거네 hal geone	하겠다/할 것이다/할 거다 hagetda/hal geotsida/hal geoda
Action verb statements ending in consonants	Past	먹었소 meogeotso	먹었네 meogeonne	먹었다 meogeotda
	Present	먹소 meokso	먹네 meokne	먹다 meokda
	Future	먹을 거요 meogeul geoyo	먹을 거네 meogeul geone	먹겠다/먹을 것이다/먹을 거다 meokgetda/meogeul geosida/ meogeul geoda
Descriptive verb statements ending in vowels	Past	작았소 jagatso	작았네 jaganne	작았다 jagatda
	Present	작소 jakso	작네 jakne	작다 jakda
	Future	작을 거요 jageul geoyo	작을 거네 jageul geone	작겠다/작을 것이다/작을 거다 jakgetda/jageul geosida/jageul geoda
Descriptive verb statements ending in consonants	Past	예뻤소 yeppeotso	예뻤네 yeppeonne	예뻤다 yeppeotda
	Present	예쁘오 yeppeuo	예쁘네 yeppeune	예쁘다 yeppeuda
	Future	예쁠 거요 yeppeul geoyo	예쁠 거네 yeppeul geone	예쁘겠다/예쁠 것이다/예쁠 거다 yeppeugetda/yeppeul geosida/ yeppeul geoda
Noun statements ending in vowels	Past	남자였소 namjayeotso	남자였네 namjayeonne	남자였다 namjayeotda
	Present	남자요 namjayo	남자이네 namja-i-ne	남자다/남자이다[B] namjada/namja-i-da
	Future	남자일 거요 namja-il geoyo	남자일 거네 namja-il geone	남자일 갓이다/남자일 거다 namja-il gasida/namja-il geoda
Noun statements ending in consonants	Past	물이었소 mulieotso	물이었네 mulieonne	물이었다 mulieotda
	Present	물이오 mulio	물이네 muline	물이다 mulida
	Future	물일 거요 mulil geoyo	물일 거네 mulil geone	물일 것이다/물일 거다 mulil geosida/mulil geoda
Commands ending in vowels	Present	하시오 hasio	하게 hage	해라[E] haela
Commands ending in consonants	Present	잡으시오[C] jabeusio	먹게 meokge	먹어라[E] meogeola
Questions ending in vowels	Past	했소? haetso?	했나?[A] haetna?	했니? haetni?
	Present	하오? hao?	하나?[A] hana?	하니? hani?
	Future	할 거요? hal geoyo?	할 건가? hal geonga?	할 것이니?/할 거니?[D] hal geosini?/hal geoni?

Sentence type	Tense	하오체 haeche	하게체 haeyoche	해라체 muneoche
Questions ending in consonants	Past	먹었소? meogeotso?	먹었나?[A] meogeonna?	먹었니? meogeonni?
	Present	먹소? meokso?	먹나?[A] meokna?	먹니? meokni?
	Future	먹을 거요? meogeul geoyo?	먹을 건가? meogeul geonga?	먹을 것이니?/할 거니?[D] meogeul geosini?/hal geoni?
Suggestions ending in vowels	Present	합시다 hapsida	하세 hase	하자 haja
Suggestions ending in consonants	Present	먹읍시다 meogeupsida	잡세[C] jabse	먹자 meokja

A These are actually conjugated using the 나/(으)ㄴ가 question forms, which you can find on page 44. Action verbs such as the ones above are conjugated with 나 and descriptive verbs take (으)ㄴ가. So you would say 하나? but 예쁜가?, and 먹나? but 작은가?

B 남자다 and 남자이다 are both acceptable.

C This example was changed from 먹다 to 잡다 because it's impolite to say 먹으세요 and 먹으십시오: you have to change them to 드세요 and 드십시오.

D 거니 is a contraction of 것이니 and is much more commonly used.

E These are conjugated with 어/아/여라, so they actually depend on the vowel in the first syllable rather than whether it ends in a vowel or a consonant.

How to Add Expressions to Verbs

This looks confusing at first, but with some practice it will become second nature to you. The best way to learn it is to learn how different expressions can connect to different verbs, and the good news here is that there are actually only a few ways to do this. First, find the stem of the verb you want to conjugate. That part is easy: just drop the 다, and there's your verb stem. Thus, the stem of 하다 is 하, the stem of 먹다 is 먹, the stem of 모으다 **moeuda** is 모으, and so on. You will never add a Korean grammar expression to a verb including the 다 ending—always use the stem.

Irregular verbs can be tricky, even for advanced students. However, even they are not totally lawless and will always interact with the same kinds of expressions in the same way. Go to the end of the irregular verbs section to find out how to combine them with each type of ending.

Expressions that Don't Change Verbs

Many expressions, particularly those beginning with ㅈ or ㄱ, can simply be added to verbs on their own without any special adaptation. In these cases you won't see anything in parentheses before the expression. Let's take a look at three: 거든, 잖아요, and 지만.

		거든 geodeun	지만 jiman	잖아요 janhayo
Action verbs ending in a vowel	하다 hada	하거든 hageodeun	하지만 hajiman	하잖아요 hajanhayo
Action verbs ending in a consonant	먹다 meokda	먹거든 meokgeodeun	먹지만 meokjiman	먹잖아요 meokjanhayo
Descriptive verbs (adjectives) ending in a vowel	예쁘다 yeppeuda	예쁘거든 yeppeugeodeun	예쁘지만 yeppeujiman	예쁘잖아요 yeppeujanhayo
Descriptive verbs (adjectives) ending in a consonant	작다 jakda	작거든 jakgeodeun	작지만 jakjiman	작잖아요 jakjanhayo

Expressions with 으 or 이 Prefixes

You'll see many expressions in this book that have either 으 or 이 before them in parentheses. In these cases, if your verb stem or noun ends in a consonant, add that 으 or 이 first. Some examples are (으)니까, (으)나 and (이)라서. Normally 으 is used with expressions that are added to verbs and 이 with expressions that are added to nouns.

		(으)니까 (eu)nikka	(으)나 (eu)na	(이)라서 (i)laseo
Action verbs ending in a vowel	하다 hada	하니까 hanikka	하나 hana	
Action verbs ending in a consonant	먹다 meokda	먹으니까 meogeunikka	먹으나 meogeuna	
Descriptive verbs (adjectives) ending in a vowel	예쁘다 yeppeuda	예쁘니까 yeppeunikka	예쁘나 yeppeuna	
Descriptive verbs (adjectives) ending in a consonant	작다 jakda	작으니까 jageunikka	작으나 jageuna	
Nouns ending in a vowel	남자 namja	남자이니까 namja-i-nikka	남자이나 namja-i-na	남자라서 namjalaseo
Nouns ending in a consonant	물 mul	물이니까 mulinikka	물이나 mulina	물이라서 mulilaseo

Expressions with 아/어/여

In these cases, you have to check the last syllable of your verb stem to know how to conjugate the verb.

If that last syllable contains an 아 or an 오, you should add 아. (That includes syllables with 애, 얘, 야 or 요, though I've never seen any verb stems ending in the latter three.)

If it contains any other vowel (어, 우, 으 or 이) then add 어. Again, that includes 여, 유, 에 and 예.

If the verb is 하다, add 여. This makes it 해 plus the rest of the expression; the only time you'll see 하여 is in formal situations, usually in writing. Even in this case, it's not all that commonly used except in the past tense: 하였다.

Let's take a look at 아/어/여서 and 았/었/였이다.

Verb stems ending in vowels can be a somewhat special; see page 26 on how to add 아/어/여 to vowels.

		아/어/여서 a/eo/yeoseo	았/었/였이다 at/eot/yeosida
Verbs with 아 or 오	작다 jakda	작아서 jagaseo	작았다 jagatda
Regular verbs with 어, 우, 으 or 이 (see below for exceptions)	먹다 meogda	먹어서 meogeoseo	먹었다 meogeotda
하다	하다 hada	해서 haeseo	했다 haetda

(으)ㄴ/는, and ㄴ/는

Here's where it gets interesting. First, check the title of the expression carefully to see which of the above sets you should use.

First, we have (으)ㄴ/는. When you see this, you have to go a step further and differentiate between active verbs and descriptive verbs. Descriptive verbs are like adjectives: 예쁘다 yeppeuda, 작다 jakda, 크다 keuda, 조용하다 joyonghada, 중요하다 jungyohada, and so on, while active verbs are verbs that describe actions: 먹다 meokda, 가다 gada, 걷다 geodda, 뛰다 ttuida, and so on.

With (으)ㄴ/는 expressions, active verbs always take 는. Descriptive verbs are conjugated with ㄴ if they end in a vowel and 은 if they end in a consonant. Expressions that are conjugated in this way include (으)ㄴ/는데 and (으)ㄴ/는 탓에.

		(으)ㄴ/는데 (eu)n/neunde	(으)ㄴ/는 탓에 (eu)n/neun tase
Action verbs ending in a vowel	하다	하는데 haneunde	하는 탓에 haneun tase
Action verbs ending in a consonant	먹다	먹는데 meokneunde	먹는 탓에 meokneun tase
Descriptive verbs (adjectives) ending in a vowel	예쁘다	예쁜데 yeppeunde	예쁜 탓에 yeppeun tase
Descriptive verbs (adjectives) ending in a consonant	작다	작은데 jageunde	작은 탓에 jageun tase

Finally, ㄴ/는 is added to verbs which use indirect speech particles; see page 304 on how to conjugate these. Basically, descriptive verbs take 다 plus whatever else you're using in your expression (다고 하다 dago hada, 다기보다 dagiboda, 다면 damyeon) while active verbs take either ㄴ or 는. ㄴ is added to action verb stems ending in vowels while 는 goes after action verb stems ending in consonants.

How to Handle Verbs, Part 1: Changing Their Form

Changing Verbs to Nouns: (으)ㅁ, 기, (으)ㄴ/는 것

■ (으)ㅁ

This can be added to any kind of verb or even to nouns with 이 in case you need to change a noun into a verb and then back into a noun. It's often used in writing and less so in speaking. You're likely to see it on warning signs and other formal notices. There are a few common nouns which always use ㅁ: 꿈 kkum ("dream" from 꾸다 kkuda), 잠 jam ("sleep" from 자다 jada), and 얼음 eoleum ("ice" from 얼다 eolda) come to mind.

While 기 tends to have more to do with activities and appearances, (으)ㅁ is an introvert; it's more concerned with thoughts and ideas.

ㅁ follows vowels and 음 follows consonants. 음 can follow the past tense, but not the future tense.

> 하다 hada (to do) > 함 ham (doing)
>
> 슬프다 seulpeuda (to be sad) > 슬픔 seulpeum (sadness)
>
> 살다 salda (to live) > 삶 salm (life) (irregular)
>
> 믿다 mitda (to believe) > 믿음 mideum (belief)

■ 기

기 gi also turns verbs into nouns and can be added to any kind of verb. It's often used in speaking and there are quite a number of grammar points which demand 기 if you want to use a verb with it. Like (으)ㅁ, some words just like to be used with 기. I'm sure you're all trying to improve your Korean 듣기 deudgi, 쓰기 sseugi, 말하기 malhagi and 읽기 ilggi.

(으)ㅁ is the "quiet, contemplative" way to turn verbs into nouns while 기 is the "extrovert." 기 is normally used more for activities and actions as well as being more common in spoken Korean. It's also used more in proverbs and slogans.

> 하다 hada (to do) > 하기 hagi (doing)
>
> 찾다 chajda (to find) > 찾기 chajgi (finding)
>
> 보다 boda (to see) > 보기 bogi (seeing)
>
> 크다 keuda (to be big) > 크기 keugi (size)

■ (으)ㄴ/는 것

는 것 neun geot is a very easygoing expression. You can use it just about anywhere to turn a verb into a noun. 것 means "thing" and 는 is the present tense marker, but don't think of 는 것 that way; use 는 with any tense and 것 whether you're talking about something concrete or not. Compared to 기 and (으)ㅁ, 는 것 can be used in a greater variety of ways without the same kind of nuances.

하다 **hada** (to do) > 하는 것 **haneun geot** (doing)

찾다 **chajda** (to find) > 찾는 것 **chajneun geot** (finding)

살다 **salda** (to live) > 사는 것 **saneun geot** (living) (irregular)

믿다 **mitda** (to believe) > 믿는 것 **mitneun geot** (believing)

This 것 will often be followed by the subject marker 이 (assuming, of course, that it is the subject of your sentence). In that case it can be shortened to 게. This is used more often in conversation while 것이 is more commonly seen in writing.

Here's a table that shows how to conjugate 는 것. See page 237 for more on 던 **deon**.

	Example	Past	Present	Future
Action verbs ending in vowels	하다	했던 것 haetdeon geot	하는 것 haneun geot	할 것 hal geot
Action verbs ending in consonants	찾다	찾던 것 chajdeon geot	찾는 것 chajneun geot	찾을 것 chajeul geot
Descriptive verbs ending in vowels	예쁘다	예뻤던 것 yeppeotdeon geot	예쁜 것 yeppeun geot	예쁜 것 yeppeun geot
Descriptive verbs ending in consonants	작다	작았던 것 jagatdeon geot	작은 것 jageun geot	작은 것 jageun geot

Changing Action Verbs to Descriptive Verbs: (으)ㄴ/는/(으)ㄹ

(으)ㄴ/는/(으)ㄹ are tense markers and are covered in greater detail on page 235. For now, let's look at how to use them to change an action verb into an adjective. English isn't very efficient about this; if you want to talk about a person visiting your house, you have to say "the person who came," "the person who is coming," or "the person who will come." In Korean, it's much simpler.

ㄴ and 은 are past tense markers. ㄴ goes after verbs ending in vowels and 은 after verbs ending in consonants.

는 is the present tense marker and follows any verb.

ㄹ and 을 are future tense markers. ㄹ follows vowels and 을 follows consonants.

Going back to the visitor we had:

온 사람 **on saram** the person who came

오는 사람 **oneun saram** the person who is coming

올 사람 **ol saram** the person who will come

Who, of course, needs to eat from time to time:

먹은 음식 **meogeun eumsig** the food that was eaten

먹는 음식 **meogneun eumsig** the food that is being eaten

먹을 음식 **meogeul eumsig** the food that will be eaten

By adding (으)ㄴ/는/(으)ㄹ, you can use any verb to describe any noun. Please note that your choice of (으)ㄴ/는/(으)ㄹ depends on the time the action happened relative to the sentence, not relative to right now.

> 올 사람은 김종국이라고 했어요. **Ol sarameun Kim-jong-guk-i-lago haesseoyo.**
> The person who was going to come was called Kim Jongkook.

> 온 사람은 김종국이라고 했어요. **On sarameun Kim-jong-guk-i-lago haesseoyo.**
> The person who had come was called Kim Jongkook.

> 오는 사람은 김종국이라고 했어요.
> **Oneun sarameun Kim-jong-guk-i-lago haesseoyo.**
> The person who was coming was called Kim Jongkook.

Descriptive verbs usually take only (으)ㄴ or maybe sometimes (으)ㄹ. This (으)ㄴ is built into many of them: you've probably talked about things that were 큰 or 작은 or 아름다운. These are all based on verbs (크다, 작다 and 아름답다) that were conjugated using (으)ㄴ.

> 예쁜 아이 **yeppeun a-i** a beautiful child
> 멋있는 남자 **meo-sinneun namja** a handsome man
> 아름다운 여자 **areumdaun yeoja** a beautiful woman

Changing Verbs to Adverbs: 히, 이, 게

■ 게

This is the most common way to form an adverb. You just take the 다 off your verb and add 게.

> 조용하다 **joyonghada** (to be quiet) > 조용하게 **joyonghage** (quietly)
> 즐겁다 **jeulgeobda** (to be pleasant) > 즐겁게 **jeulgeobge** (pleasantly)
> 슬프다 **seulpeuda** (to be sad) > 슬프게 **seulpeuge** (sadly)

In particular, any verb not ending in 하다 should be changed to an adverb using 게. 하다 verbs can always be changed this way as well if you'd like, but in many cases it's more natural to use 히. See below.

■ 히

You can also form an adverb by taking a verb ending in 하다 and changing that 하다 to 히.

> 적당하다 **jeogdanghada** (to be suitable) > 적당히 **jeogdanghi** (suitably)
> 무사하다 **musahada** (to be safe) > 무사히 **musahi** (safely)

편하다 **pyeonhada** (to be comfortable) > 편히 **pyeonhi** (comfortably)

부지런하다 **bujileonhada** (to be diligent) > 부지런히 **bujileonhi** (diligently)

■ 이

This is the rarest of the adverbial forms, and I've seen it only a few times:

~없이 **eobsi** without   ~빠듯이 **ppadeusi** barely, narrowly

밖이 **bakki** outside (as an adverb)   깊이 **gipi** deeply

굳이 **guji** firmly, stubbornly   깨끗이 **kkaekkeusi** cleanly

This isn't a comprehensive list, but it does cover most of the more common 이 adverbs.

Changing Descriptive Verbs to Action Verbs: 아/어/여지다, 게 되다

To change an adjective (descriptive verb) into an action verb, you need to add "become." So "big" becomes "to become big." "Beautiful" becomes "to become beautiful." There are two ways to add this "become," and which one you use depends on whether you're focusing on the situation changing or the fact that the situation has already changed. 아/어/여지다 **a/eo/yeojida** means the focus is on the change itself while 게 되다 **ge doeda** means the focus is on the finished product. In situations where you're using 아/어/여지다 in the past tense (아/어/여졌다), although the change has been completed, the focus is on the situation changing rather than the final result. This is usually not a very big difference.

게 되다 can be added to any verb. 아/어/여지다 follows the same rules as 아/어/여: 아 follows verbs with 아 or 오 as their last vowel, 어 follows verbs with 어, 우, 으 or 이 as their last vowel, and 여 follows 하다.

예쁘다 **yeppeuda** (to be beautiful) > 예뻐지다 **yeppeojida** (to become beautiful)

작다 **jakda** (to be small) > 작아지다 **jagajida** (to become small)

조용하다 **joyonghada** (to be quiet) > 조용해지다 **joyonghaejida** or 조용하게 되다
joyonghage doeda (to become quiet)

Changing Nouns to Verbs: 하다, 이다

A large number, I'd even say most, nouns can be changed to verbs simply by the addition of 하다 **hada**. This is especially true of words derived from 한자 **hanja**. You'll notice Korean has many two-syllable nouns to which you can add 하다 and get a four-syllable word; this is usually two 한자 characters plus 하다. This is also done with many words derived from English.

So if you ever need to change a noun to a verb in a hurry and don't have a grammar reference guide handy, try 하다. It's usually a good guess.

운전 **unjeon** (driving) > 운전하다 **unjeonhada** (to drive)

공부 **gongbu** (studying) > 공부하다 **gongbuhada** (to study)

지각 jigak (tardiness) > 지각하다 jigakhada (to be late)

인쇄/프린트 inswae/peulinteu (printing) > 인쇄하다/프린트 하다 inswaehada/
peulinteu hada (to print)

게임 geim (game) > 게임 하다 geim hada (to play a game)

블로그 beullogeu (blog) > 블로그 하다 beullogeu hada (to blog)

The second way to change a noun is to add 이다, which means "it is." This is necessary for many grammar patterns that will accept only verbs. If you want to sneak a noun in, you can quite often get away with it by adding 이다 to the noun.

학생 haksaeng (student) > 학생이다 haksaeng-i-da (it's/he's/she's a student)

남자 namja (man) > 남자이다 namja-i-da (he's a man)

물 mul (water) > 물이다 murida (it's water)

책 chaek (book) > 책이다 chaegida (it's a book)

Changing Nouns to Descriptive Verbs: 적

Finally, here's how to turn a noun into an adjective. It works with the two-syllable 한자 hanja nouns we talked about in the last section. Add 적 jeok to the end and the result is an adjective. However, these adjectives can't be conjugated like regular Korean adjectives (descriptive verbs); for that, you need to add 이다 ida to the end of them as if they were nouns.

개인 gaein (individual) > 개인적 gaeinjeok (private) > 개인적이다 gaeinjeogida

과학 gwahak (science) > 과학적 gwahakjeok (scientific) > 과학적이다 gwahakjeogida

효율 (efficiency) hyoyul > 효율적 hyoyuljeok (efficient) > 효율적이다 hyoyuljeogida

이렇게 개인적인 질문을 하지 마세요. Ileoke gaeinjeogin jilmuneul haji maseyo.
Please don't ask such personal questions.

이것은 더 효율적인 연료인데요. Igeoseun deo hyoyuljeogin yeonryoindeyo.
This is a more efficient fuel.

How to Handle Verbs, Part 2: Irregular Verbs

Vowels

When a verb stem ends in a vowel and the expression you're adding to the end begins with a vowel (어/아 or 었/았 expressions), you have to combine the two vowels. This isn't difficult as long as you learn how each set combines. In all other cases, ㄴ/는/ㄹ, expressions that have one form for vowels and another for consonants, and expressions that don't change no matter what they follow, you don't have to worry about verbs ending in vowels at all. They're very easy to deal with most of the time.

ㅏ, ㅗ, ㅑ and ㅐ have 아 added to them:

가다 **gada** > 가 > 가 (아 plus 아 = no change)
사다 **sada** > 사 > 사
오다 **oda** > 오 > 와요 **wayo** (오 plus 아 becomes 와)
보다 **boda** > 보 > 봐요 **bwayo**

ㅐ and 야 are based on ㅏ and so are conjugated like 아 verbs.

내다 **naeda** > 내 > 내요 **naeyo**

Verbs ending in ㅓ, ㅜ, ㅡ, ㅣ, ㅕ or ㅔ take 어 and this is added as follows:

서다 **seoda** > 서 > 서요 **seoyo** (어 plus 어 = no change)
켜다 **kyeoda** > 켜 > 켜요 **kyeoyo** (여 plus 어 = no change)
치다 **chida** > 치 > 쳐요 **chyeoyo** (이 plus 어 = 여)
지다 **jida** > 지 > 져요 **jyeoyo**
마시다 **masida** > 마시 **masi** > 마셔요 **masyeoyo**

으 is a meek shy little vowel and prefers to give way whenever it encounters a stronger vowel. This means that it completely disappears from the word, like this:

크다 **keuda** > 크 > 커요 **keoyo**
끄다 **kkeuda** > 끄 > 꺼요 **kkeoyo**

우 has 어 added to it. Some words can be written with the 우 and 어 together or in separate syllables; this is mostly a matter of custom.

태우다 **taeuda** > 태우 > 태워요 **taewoyo**
세우다 **seuda** > 세우 > 세워요 **sewoyo**
주다 **juda** > 주 > 줘요 **jwoyo**
나누다 **nanuda** > 나누 > 나눠요 **nanwoyo**
두다 **duda** > 두 > 두어요 **dueoyo** or 둬요 **dwoyo**

Verbs ending in 에 absorb their 어 like so:

세다 **seda** > 세 > 세요 **seyo**

ㄹ irregular Verbs

Verbs ending in ㄹ and followed by expressions starting with ㅂ, ㅅ, or ㄴ (like ㅂ니다, 세요 or 는) lose the ㄹ altogether.

알다 alda > 알 al > 아세요, aseyo 압니다, 아는, 아시다시피, 아니까, abnida, aneun, asidasipi, anikka ...

> 알아요, 알아, 알면, 알고, 알지만, arayo, ara, almyeon, algo, aljiman ...

When verb stems ending in 알 are changed into nouns using the ending ㅁ (see page 22), it just gets added into the same syllable, like so:

알다 alda > 알 > 앎 alm
살다 salda > 살 > 삶 salm

This doesn't happen with verb stems ending in any other consonant.
Tenses with ㄴ/는/ㄹ look strange with this particular irregularity; see the table below.

Verb	Past Tense	Present Tense	Future Tense
알다 alda	안 an	아는 aneun	알 al
팔다 palda	판 pan	파는 paneun	팔 pal
울다 ulda	운 un	우는 uneun	울 ul

르 irregular Verbs

Verb stems ending in 르 leu are totally regular except when they have to deal with an ending starting with 아/어/여: for instance, 아/어/여요 or 아/어/여서. In these cases, the ㄹ in the verb stem needs an extra ㄹ at the end of the previous syllable with these verbs.

모르다 moreuda > 모르 moreu > 몰ㄹ mol-l > 몰라요 mollayo
고르다 goreuda > 고르 goreu > 골ㄹ gol-l > 골라요 gollayo
바르다 bareuda > 바르 bareu > 발ㄹ bal-l > 발라요 ballayo
빠르다 ppareuda > 빠르 ppareu > 빨ㄹ ppal-l > 빨라요 ppallayo

ㅎ irregular Verbs

These include just about all the color words in Korean, plus 이렇다/그렇다/저렇다 ireota/geureota/jeoreota and 어떻다 eotteota. Other verbs ending in ㅎ are conjugated normally.

놓다 nota > 놓 > 놓아요 noayo
넣다 neota > 넣 > 넣어요 neoeoyo

Color words typically drop their ㅎ and have 이요 added instead of 아요.

빨갛다 ppalgata > 빨갛 > 빨가 ppalga > 빨간, 빨개요 ppalgan, ppalgaeyo
까맣다 kkamata > 까맣 > 까마 kkama > 까만, 까매요 kkaman, kkamaeyo
하얗다 hayata > 하얗 > 하야 haya > 하얀, 하얘요 hayan, hayaeyo

이렇다 ireota/그렇다 geureota/저렇다 jeoreota and 어떻다 eotteota also function like these words.

이렇다 > 이렇 > 이러 ireo > 이런 ireon, 이래요 iraeyo

그렇다 > 그렇 > 그러 geureo > 그런 geureon, 그래요 geuraeyo

저렇다 > 저렇 > 저러 jeoreo > 저런 jeoreon, 저래요 jeoraeyo

어떻다 > 어떻 > 어떠 eotteo > 어떤 eotteon, 어때요 eottaeyo

They're strange enough that, particularly in the case of 그렇다, which is used all over the place, you're better off simply memorizing their permutations. See page 377 for a detailed list of the various ways in which 그렇다 can be conjugated.

Irregular Verbs: Stems Ending with ㅂ, ㅅ or ㄷ

Basically, each of these irregular verbs has two forms: in any instance in which an expression that begins (or can begin) with a vowel is added, the verb will change, while in any instance in which an expression that can begin with only a consonant is added, the verb will be conjugated the regular way. The table below shows how each one changes:

Kind of irregular verb (example)	Verb stem before vowels	Verb stem before consonants
ㅂ (돕다) dopda	도우 dou (ㅂ changes to 우)	돕 dob
ㅅ (짓다) jitda	지 ji (ㅅ disappears)	짓 jit
ㄷ (걷다) geotda	걸 geol (ㄷ changes to ㄹ)	걷 geot

And here are some examples of the verbs in action:

Kind of verb	Example	+ consonant (지만)	+ consonant (는)	+ consonant (고)	+ vowel (아/어/여서)	+ vowel ([으]ㄹ)	+ vowel ([으]면)
ㅂ irregular	돕다 dopda	돕지만 dopjiman	돕는 dopneun	돕고 dopgo	도와서 dowaseo	도울 doul	도우면 doumeyon
	밉다 mipda	밉지만 mipjiman	밉는 mipneun	밉고 mipgo	미워서 miwoseo	미울 miul	미우면 miumyeon
	굽다 gupda	굽지만 gupjiman	굽는 gupneun	굽고 gupgo	구워서 guwoseo	구울 gu-ul	구우면 gu-u-myeon
	눕다 nupda	눕지만 nupjiman	눕는 nupneun	눕고 nupgo	누워서 nuwoseo	누울 nu-ul	누우면 nu-u-myeon
ㅅ irregular	짓다 jitda	짓지만 jitjiman	짓는 jitneun	짓고 jitgo	지어서 jieoseo	지을 jieul	지으면 jieumyeon
	잇다 itda	잇지만 itjiman	잇는 itneun	잇고 itgo	이어서 ieoseo	이을 ieul	이으면 ieumyeon
	붓다 butda	붓지만 butjiman	붓는 butneun	붓고 butgo	부어서 bueoseo	부을 bueul	부으면 bueumyeon

Kind of verb	Example	+ consonant (지만)	+ consonant (는)	+ consonant (고)	+ vowel (아/어/여서)	+ vowel ([으]ㄹ)	+ vowel ([으]면)
ㄷ irregular	낫다 natda	낫지만 natjiman	낫는 nanneun	낫고 natgo	나아서 na-a-seo	나을 naeul	나으면 naeumyeon
	걷다 geotda	걷지만 geotjiman	걷는 geotneun	걷고 geotgo	걸어서 georeoseo	걸을 georeul	걸으면 georeumyeon
	싣다 sitda	싣지만 sitjiman	싣는 sitneun	싣고 sitgo	실어서 sireoseo	실을 sireul	실으면 sireumyeon
	묻다 mutda	묻지만 mutjiman	묻는 mutneun	묻고 mutgo	물어서 mureoseo	물을 mureul	물으면 mureumyeon
	듣다 deutda	듣지만 deutjiman	듣는 deutneun	듣고 deutgo	들어서 deureoseo	들을 deureul	들으면 deureumyeon

It's important to remember that unlike ㄹ, 르, ㅎ, or vowel-based irregularities, which apply to all verbs with that particular spelling pattern, verb stems ending in ㅅ, ㄷ, and ㅂ can be regular or irregular. You just have to memorize which ones are which. Here are a few common ones to get you started:

Regular ㅂ verbs: 입다 ipda, 잡다 japda, 집다 jipda, 씹다 ssipda, 줍다 jupda, 짧다 jjalda, 넓다 neolda, 좁다 jopda

Irregular ㅂ verbs: 덥다 deopda, 쉽다 swipda, 맵다 maepda, 눕다 nupda, 굽다 gupda, 돕다 dopda, 밉다 mipda, 귀엽다 gwiyeopda, 아름답다 areumdapda, 곱다 gopda, 춥다 chupda

Regular ㅅ verbs: 씻다 ssitda, 빗다 bitda, 벗다 beotda

Irregular ㅅ verbs: 붓다 butda, 젓다 jeotda, 짓다 jitda, 잇다 itda, 낫다 natda, 굿 다 geutda

Regular ㄷ verbs: 받다 batda, 쏟다 ssotda, 닫다 datda, 믿다 mitda

Irregular ㄷ verbs: 듣다 deutda, 걷다 geotda, 싣다 sitda, 묻다 mutda

Basic Particles

You should have some familiarity with most of the following particles before using this book. Otherwise you'll have a hard time understanding the example sentences. There are plenty of good beginning books out there that cover this material; see the list of Useful Korean Language Resources in Appendix 2. As reference, here are the basic particles with their general meanings:

이	i	subject particle for words ending in consonants
가	ga	subject particle for words ending in vowels
은	eun	topic particle for words ending in consonants
는	neun	topic particle for words ending in vowels

을	eul	object particle for words ending in consonants
를	reul	object particle for words ending in vowels
에서	eseo	from, at
에	e	to, at, concerning
더러	deoreo	to/from a person (very informal)
에게	ege	to a person (informal)
에게서	egeseo	from a person (informal)
한테	hante	to/from a person (somewhat polite)
께	kke	to a person (super-polite)
께서	kkeseo	from a person (super-polite)
로	ro	through, to for words ending in vowels
으로	euro	through, to for words ending in consonants
부터	buteo	from
까지	kkaji	to, until
의	ui	's (possessive particle)
들	deul	s (pluralizing particle)
씩	ssik	each, at a time
마다	mada	each, every
시	si	added to verbs when talking about people higher in status than you
님	nim	Mr./Mrs./Ms./Miss (very polite)
씨	ssi	Mr./Mrs./Ms./Miss (somewhat polite)
만	man	only
도	do	also, too

All these particles are simply added to the ends of nouns when you want to use them.

Helping Verbs

These verbs follow 아/어/여 verb endings. When added to a verb plus one of those three endings, they mean "to take the result of that verb and do something with it." Here are the more common "helping" verbs:

~가다 gada/오다 oda   to go/to come

~두다 duda/놓다 nota   to keep/to put aside

~넣다 neota   to put

~대다 daeda   to repeat

~가지다 gajida   to carry (in this context, the result of ~ was carried over to something else)

~버리다 beorida	to throw out (in this context, to throw out or to finish/be done with)
~보다 boda	to watch (in this context, to try)
~주다 juda	to give
~내다 naeda	to pay (in this context, it implies accomplishment: ~ was something you did with some effort)

있다 can also follow verbs with 아/어/여, but its use is a little more specialized; see page 255.

As an example, let's try adding these words to 하다 and see the result:

가다/오다 > 해 가다/해 오다 gada/oda > hae gada/hae oda	to do and go/come with
두다/놓다 > 해 두다/해 놓다 duda/nota > hae duda/hae nota	to keep/to put aside
넣다 > 해 넣다 neota > hae neota	to put
대다 > 해 대다 daeda > hae daeda	to do repeatedly
가지다 > 해 가지다 gajida > hae gajida	to do and take
버리다 > 해 버리다 beorida > hae beorida	to do and throw out/get rid of/be done with
보다 > 해 보다 boda > hae boda	to try to do
주다 > 해 주다 juda > hae juda	to do and give/to do something for someone else
내다 > 해 내다 naeda > hae naeda	to accomplish/to finish doing

And let's see one more: 만들다 **mandeulda**, to make.

가다/오다 > 만들어 가다/만들어 오다 mandeureo gada/mandeureo oda	to make and go/come with
두다/놓다 > 만들어 두다/만들어 놓다 mandeureo duda/mandeureo nota	to make and keep/put aside
넣다 > 만들어 넣다 mandeureo neota	to make and put
대다 > 만들어 대다 mandeureo daeda	to repeatedly make

가지다 > 만들어 가지다 mandeureo gajida	to make and take
버리다 > 만들어 버리다 mandeureo beorida	to make and throw out/get rid of/ be done with
보다 > 만들어 보다 mandeureo boda	to try to make
주다 > 만들어 주다 mandeureo juda	to make and give/to make for someone else
내다 > 만들어 내다 mandeureo naeda	to finish making (something very difficult)

Passives and Causatives

Passives

In a passive-voice sentence, make the object of the sentence the subject and don't worry too much about who did the action. For instance, let's take the sentence: "He did his homework." In the passive voice, this would become "His homework was done." Alternatively, let's try "The mother hugged the child." In the passive, it changes to "The child was hugged by the mother."

Korean verbs are changed to the passive voice by adding 이, 히, 리 or 기. Which syllable you add usually depends on the letter the verb ends with; however, there are many exceptions to this rule and you simply have to memorize most of the words.

Having said that, let's discuss the general rules first and common exceptions later.

- Verbs ending in vowels or ㅎ normally have 이 added.

  보다 **boda** (to see) > 보이다 **bo-ida** (to be showing/seen)

  쌓다 **ssata** (to pile) > 쌓이다 **ssa-ida** (to be piled up)

  놓다 **nota** (to put) > 놓이다 **no-ida** (to be put)

  바꾸다 **bakkuda** (to change) > 바뀌다 **bakkwida** (to be changed)

- Verbs ending in ㅂ, ㄷ or ㄱ take 히.

  잡다 **japda** (to catch) > 잡히다 **japida** (to be caught)

  읽다 **ilgda** (to read) > 읽히다 **ilkhida** (to be read)

  먹다 **meokda** (to eat) > 먹히다 **meokida** (to be eaten)

  닫다 **datda** (to close) > 닫히다 **dachida** (to be closed)

■ Verbs ending in ㄹ almost always take 리.

걸다 **geolda** (to hang) > 걸리다 **geollida** (to be hung)

열다 **yeolda** (to open) > 열리다 **yeollida** (to be opened)

듣다 **deutda** (to listen) > 들리다 **deullida** (to be heard)

■ Verbs ending in ㄴ, ㅁ, ㅅ or ㅊ take 기.

안다 **anda** (to hug) > 안기다 **angida** (to be hugged)

끊다 **kkeunta** (to stop) > 끊기다 **kkeunkida** (to be stopped)

쫓다 **jjotda** (to chase) > 쫓기다 **jjotgida** (to be chased)

담다 **damda** (to put something in) > 담기다 **damgida** (to be put in)

When an active verb ends in 하다, you can change it to passive simply by changing 하다 to 되다.

사용하다 **sayonghada** (to use) > 사용되다 **sayongdoeda** (to be used)

활용하다 **hwallyonghada** (to use) > 활용되다 **hwallyongdoeda** (to be used)

이동하다 **idonghada** (to move) > 이동되다 **idongdoeda** (to be moved)

You can also change verbs by adding either 아/어/여지다 or 게 되다; see page 25. For quick reference, here are some examples:

예쁘다 **yeppeuda** (to be beautiful) > 예뻐지다 **yeppeojida** or
예쁘게 되다 **yeppeuge doeda**
(to become beautiful)

작다 **jakda** (to be small)   > 작아지다 **jagajida** or 작게 되다 **jakge doeda**
(to become small)

조용하다 **joyonghada** (to be quiet) > 조용해지다 **joyonghaejida** or 조용하게 되다
joyonghage doeda (to become quiet)

Causatives

If you're an active rather than a passive type and found all that talk of having things happen to you to be unpleasant, you'll enjoy this next part a bit more. This is how to make causative sentences in Korean. In the passive voice, "The child was dressed by the mother"; in the causative voice, "The mother dressed the child."

Just to make things interesting, Korean uses almost exactly the same particles for this as it does for passives. They are 이, 히, 리, and 기. For causatives you also sometimes need 우 and 추.

Just to make it even more fun, the particles sometimes follow the same rules as passives and sometimes not. There are many more exceptions with causative verbs as well.

Again, let's start with the general rules and then move on to exceptions.

■ 이 follows verbs ending in vowels, ㄱ, and ㅎ.

보다 **boda** (to see) > 보이다 **bo-ida** (to show)

먹다 **meokda** (to eat) > 먹이다 **meogida** (to feed)

끓다 **kkeulta** (to be boiling) > 끓이다 **kkeulida** (to boil [something])

죽다 **jukda** (to die) > 죽이다 **jugida** (to kill)

■ 히 follows ㅂ.

입다 **ipda** (to wear) > 입히다 **iphida** (to clothe or to cover)

눕다 **nupda** (to lie down) > 눕히다 **nuphida** (to lay [something/someone] down)

■ 리, again, follows ㄹ.

알다 **alda** (to know) > 알리다 **allida** (to let something be known)

살다 **salda** (to live) > 살리다 **salida** (to save [someone's life])

울다 **ulda** (to cry) > 울리다 **ullida** (to make [someone] cry)

■ 기 follows ㅅ and ㅁ.

숨다 **sumda** (to hide [oneself]) > 숨기다 **sumgida** (to hide [something])

남다 **namda** (to remain) > 남기다 **namgida** (to leave)

웃다 **utda** (to smile) > 웃기다 **utgida** (to make [someone] smile or laugh)

벗다 **beotda** (to take off [someone's clothes]) > 벗기다 **beotgida** (to take off [someone's clothes])

■ 우 isn't actually 우, but rather 이우. It follows verbs ending in vowels.

타다 **tada** (to ride/to burn) > 태우다 **taeuda** (to give a ride/to burn something)

자다 **jada** (to sleep) > 재우다 **jaeuda** (to put to sleep)

서다 **seoda** (to stand) > 세우다 **seuda** (to park)

깨다 **kkaeda** (to wake up) > 깨우다 **kkaeuda** (to wake up [someone])

■ 추 follows ㅈ.

낮다 **natda** (to be low) > 낮추다 **natchuda** (to lower)

늦다 **neutda** (to be late) > 늦추다 **neutchuda** (to delay)

맞다 **matda** (to be right) > 맞추다 **matchuda** (to fit, to make right)

Here are a few common exceptions:

읽다 **ilkda** (to read) > 읽히다 **ilkhida** (to be read)

앉다 **anda** (to sit) > 앉히다 **anchida** (to make someone sit)

맡다 **matda** (to assume, to be in charge) > 맡기다 **matgida** (to entrust)

Like its partner 게 되다 ge doeda, you can use 게 하다 ge hada to make someone do something or to make something become a certain way. It's the active version of 게 되다 ge doeda. See page 205 for how to use 게 하다 ge hada.

Certain other causatives are based on the verb 나다 nada. When changed to causative form, this becomes 내다 naeda. That's true for all variations of 나다 and 내다.

나다 nada (to happen) > 내다 naeda (to make/pay)

끝나다 kkeutnada (to be finished) > 끝내다 kkeutnaeda (to finish)

힘나다 himnada (to gain strength) > 힘내다 himnaeda (to strengthen oneself)

알아내다 aranaeda (to discover)

그 일이 벌써 끝났어요. geu iri beolsseo kkeutnasseoyo.
The work is already finished. (passive)

그 일을 벌써 끝냈어요. Geu ireul beolsseo kkeutnaesseoyo.
I've already finished the work. (causative)

Note that the subject of the sentence changes: for 나다 verbs, the subject will always be whatever was done or whatever happened; for 내다 verbs, the subject should be the person that did the action.

해내다 haenaeda to accomplish (see page 31)

해결해 내다 haegyeolhae naeda to find a solution

Agreement

First of all, most of the time you won't need any special grammar lessons to agree with people in Korean. 응, 네, 예, 그래(요), 당연하죠, 그렇군요/그렇구나, **eung, ne, ye, geu-rae(yo), dang-yeon-ha-jyo, geu-reo-kun-nyo/geu-reo-ku-na** and 맞아(요) **ma-ja(yo)** are all very common ways of saying "Yeah, uh huh, you're right, absolutely, I agree."

However, should you want to agree in a slightly more spectacular fashion, see below:

		Speaking > Writing
~고 말고요 go mal-go-yo	"Of course, ~"	★★★

민수가 오늘도 늦었어요? **Min-su-ga o-neul-do neu-jeo-seo-yo?**
Was Minsu late today as well?

늦고 **말고요**. 민수는 일 때문에 정시에 오지 못 해요.
Neut-go mal-go-yo. Min-su-neun il ttae-mun-e jeong-si-e o-ji mot hae-yo.
Of course he was late. Because of his job, he can't come on time.

Do people ever ask you questions with obvious answers? If so, you'll want to know how to use this expression. It is used to express strong agreement with ~, which is really obvious and beyond doubt. This can be used when replying to a request ("Of course I'll do it!") or when confirming something you think is so obvious that it really doesn't need confirmation.

HOW IT'S FORMED

고 말다 **go malda** is its own expression (see page 232) and it means that something that was expected finally happened. 고요 **goyo** is an expression used at the end of a sentence to add information. Neither of these expressions has much relevance to 고 말고요 **go malgoyo**, which always goes at the end of a sentence.

HOW IT'S CONJUGATED

		Past	Present	Future
Action verbs ending in a vowel	하다 ha-da	하고 말고요 ha-go mal-go-yo 했고 말고요 haet-go mal-go-yo	하고 말고요 ha-go mal-go-yo	하고 말고요 ha-go mal-go-yo 할거고 말고요 hal-geo-go mal-go-yo

		Past	Present	Future
Action verbs ending in a consonant	먹다 meok-da	먹고 말고요 meok-go mal-go-yo 먹었고 말고요 meo-geot-go mal-go-yo	먹고 말고요 meok-go mal-go-yo	먹고 말고요 meok-go mal-go-yo 먹을거고 말고요 meo-geul-geo-go mal-go-yo
Descriptive verbs (adjectives) ending in a vowel	예쁘다 ye-ppeu-da	예쁘고 말고요 ye-ppeu-go mal-go-yo 예뻤고 말고요 ye-ppeot-go mal-go-yo	예쁘고 말고요 ye-ppeu-go mal-go-yo	예쁘고 말고요 ye-ppeu-go mal-go-yo
Descriptive verbs (adjectives) ending in a consonant	작다 jak-da	작고 말고요 jak-go mal-go-yo 작았고 말고요 ja-gat-go mal-go-yo	작고 말고요 jak-go mal-go-yo	작고 말고요 jak-go mal-go-yo
Nouns ending in a vowel	남자 nam-ja	남자이고 말고요 nam-ja-i-go mal-go-yo 남자였고 말고요 nam-ja-yeot-go	남자이고 말고요 nam-ja-i-go mal-go-yo	남자이고 말고요 nam-ja-i-go mal-go-yo 남자일거고 말고요 nam-ja-il-geo-go mal-go-yo
Nouns ending in a consonant	물 mul	물이고 말고요 mul-i-go mal-go-yo 물이었고 말고요 mul-i-eot-go mal-go-yo	물이고 말고요 mul-i-go mal-go-yo	물이고 말고요 mul-i-go mal-go-yo 물일거고 말고요 mu-lil-geo-go mal-go-yo

TAKE NOTE

This expression is used only at the end of very short sentences. If you want to explain yourself further, start a new sentence and do so.

While you can use go 고 말고요 **mal-go-yo** with nouns, it's not very common; people generally prefer one of the expressions listed at the beginning of this section.

고 말았다 **Go ma-rat-da** (see page 233) is not at all the same as 고 말고요. 고 말았다 means that something happened accidentally and/or unfortunately. Likewise, 고 말겠다 **go mal-get-da** (see page 232) is used to talk about definite plans—it has nothing to do with 고 말고요.

EXAMPLE SENTENCES

일을 벌써 끝냈어요? **I-leul beol-sseo kkeun-nae-seo-yo?**
Have you already finished your work?

끝냈**고 말고요**. 다섯시간 전에 그 일을 시작했어요.
Kkeun-naet-go mal-go-yo. Da-seot si-gan jeon-e geu i-leul si-jak-hae-seo-yo.
Of course I've finished. I started five hours ago.

미스 코리아가 예쁜가요? **Miseu koriaga yeppeungayo?** Is Miss Korea beautiful?

예쁘**고 말고요**. 모델이잖아요. **Yeppeugo malgoyo. Moderijanayo.**
Of course she's beautiful! She's a model.

Disagreement/Negatives

Why can't we all just get along? Sometimes you need to object to or disagree with something someone else has said or to state that something is untrue. This section will show you how to do that.

First, however, let's review basic negatives. The simplest way to negate something in Korean is to simply add 지 않다 ji anta to the end of the verb. This works with any kind of verb and after either a vowel or a consonant.

먹다 meokda	to eat	먹지 않다 meokji anta	to not eat
하다 hada	to do	하지 않다 haji anta	to not do
작다 jakda	to be small	작지 않다 jakji anta	to not be small
예쁘다 yeppeuda	to be pretty	예쁘지 않다 yeppeuji anta	to not be pretty

Another option is to put 안 an in front of the verb. This negates the verb. It's not really used much in formal situations or in writing. In common, everyday speech, either 안 or 지 않다 ji anta is usually fine.

먹다 meokda	to eat	안 먹다 an meokda	to not eat
하다 hada	to do	안 하다 an hada	to not do
작다 jakda	to be small	안 작다 an jakda	to not be small
예쁘다 yeppeuda	to be pretty	안 예쁘다 an yeppeuda	to not be pretty

If what you're talking about has to do with capability, 지 못하다 should be used. This is covered on page 297 in the section on Possibility.

Another expression which can also belong in this section is (으)ㄴ/는/(으)ㄹ걸요. It's often used for guesses as well, so it appears in that section on page 149. When used as a negative, it's quite similar to 기는요.

What's with All These 말s?

You'll see a few expressions here and there that look kind of like this:

A(expression) 말 mal (expression) 하다 hada

In these cases the 말 is negating A, so the expression will have something to do with "A or not". The table below summarizes and briefly explains these expressions; I hope it clears up any confusion.

Expression	Page	Meaning	Example
~(으)ㄹ락 말락 하다 (eu) r-rak mallak hada		~ almost, but not quite, happened/is happening	그 사고에서 죽을락 말락 했어요. **Geu sagoeseo jugeullak mallak haesseoyo.** I was hovering on the verge of death after that accident.
~다가 말다가 하다 daga maldaga hada		Doing ~ on and off	운동을 하다가 말다가 하면 근육에 무리가 갈 거예요. Undongeul hadaga maldaga hamyeon geunnyuge muriga gal geoyeyo. If you keep exercising on and off like that, it will be too stressful for your muscles.
~(으)ㄹ지 말지 하다 (eu)r-ji malji hada		I can't decide whether to ~ or not.	운동을 할지 말지 결정 못했어요. Undongeul halji malji gyeoljeong motaesseoyo. I couldn't decide whether or not to exercise.
~(으)ㄹ까 말까 하다 (eu)r-kka malkka hada		I can't decide whether to ~ or not.	운동을 할까 말까 해요. undongeul halkka malkka haeyo. I can't decide whether to exercise or not.
~는 둥 마는 둥 하다 neun dung maneun dung hada		~ almost didn't happen, but ultimately did	비가 오는 둥 마는 둥 했어요. Biga oneun dung maneun dung haesseoyo. It rained just a little.
A 거나 말거나 geona malgeona B		B, whether or not A.	그녀가 예쁘거나 말거나, 저는 그녀를 사랑해요. Geunyeoga yeppeugeona malgeona jeoneun geunyeoreul saranghaeyo. Whether or not she's beautiful, I love her.

~기는요   "~? No, not at all."   **Speaking > Writing**
                                                                    ★★★

A: 오늘 늦었어요? **Oneul neujeosseoyo?** Were you late today?

B: 늦**기는요**. 정시에 왔어요. **Neutgineunnyo. Jeongsie wasseoyo.**
    Late? Not at all. I was on time.

This is a nice way to deny something, especially a compliment. It's often used when you want to be modest such as when you say 안녕 하세요 **annyeong haseyo** to a Korean and are met with heaps of praise for your wonderful Korean abilities.

HOW IT'S CONJUGATED

		Past	Present
Action verbs ending in a vowel	하다	하기는요 hagineunnyo 했기는요 haetgineunnyo	하기는요 hagineunnyo
Action verbs ending in a consonant	먹다	먹기는요 **meokgineunnyo** 먹었기는요 **meogeotgineunnyo**	먹기는요 meokgineunnyo

		Past	Present
Descriptive verbs (adjectives) ending in a vowel	예쁘다	예쁘기는요 yeppeugineunnyo 예뻤기는요 yeppeotgineunnyo	예쁘기는요 yeppeugineunnyo
Descriptive verbs (adjectives) ending in a consonant	작다	작기는요 jakgineunnyo 작았기는요 jagatgineunnyo	작기는요 jakgineunnyo
Nouns ending in a vowel	남자	남자였기는요 namjayeotgineunnyo	남자기는요 namjagineunnyo
Nouns ending in a consonant	물	물이었기는요 murieotgineunnyo	물이기는요 murigineunnyo

TAKE NOTE

As this expression is used to deny something, it's used only when you're responding to something someone has already said. It's normally used in a sentence by itself along with the part that you're not accepting. Then, if you need to explain, start a new sentence.

Keep in mind that since it's used to deny something, you need to add it to the opposite of whatever you think is the truth.

기는요 and (으)ㄴ/는/(으)ㄹ걸요 (see page 149) are both used for similar purposes. They're both gentle ways to contradict what was said. The main difference between them is that when you use 기는요 you have to state the thing you're contradicting, whereas with 걸요 you say the opposite. So if someone says you speak Korean well and you don't think you do (or you know you do, but you want to be modest), you can say 잘 하기는요 jal hagineunnyo.

EXAMPLE SENTENCES

A: 한국은 10월이면 더워요? **Hangukeun shiworinyeon deowoyo?**
Is Korea hot in October?

B: 덥**기는요**. 10월에 시원해요. **Deopgineunnyo. Shiwore siwonhaeyo.**
Hot? Not at all. It's cool in October.

———

A: 한국어를 아주 잘 하시네요! **Hangukeoreul aju jal hasineyo!**
You speak Korean very well!

B: 잘 하**기는요**. **Jal hagineunnyo.** I really don't.

Speaking = Writing
A은/는커녕 eun/neunkeonyeong B, "Rather than A, B" ★★★
 A기는커녕 gineunkeonyeong B

A: 오늘 늦었어요? **Oneul neujeosseoyo?** Were you late today?

B: 늦**기는커녕** 8시에 왔어요. **Neutgineunkeonyeong yeodeolsie waseoyo.**
Not only was I not late, but I was here at eight.

A isn't actually the case. This is usually followed by B, an explanation of what exactly the case is. The expressions above are used in a sentence about something negative, and B is often something easier to accomplish than A but still impossible to achieve.

HOW IT'S CONJUGATED

		All tenses
Action verbs ending in a vowel	하다	하기는커녕 hagineunkeonyeong
Action verbs ending in a consonant	먹다	먹기는커녕 meokgineunkeonyeong
Descriptive verbs (adjectives) ending in a vowel	예쁘다	예쁘기는 커녕 yeppeugineun keonyeong
Descriptive verbs (adjectives) ending in a consonant	작다	작기는커녕 jakgineunkeonyeong
Nouns ending in a vowel	남자	남자는커녕 namjaneunkeonyeong
Nouns ending in a consonant	물	물은커녕 mureunkeonyeong

TAKE NOTE

It's interchangeable with 은/는 말할 것 없다 eun/neun malhal geot eopda.

When speaking, 커녕 is usually dropped. For example, if you want to say 잘 하기는커녕, jal hagineun keonyeong the sentence simply becomes 잘 하기는.

EXAMPLE SENTENCES

A: 한국은 10월이면 더워요?
Hangukeun shiworimyeon deowoyo?
Is Korea hot in October?

B: 덥기는커녕 시원해요.
Deopgineunkeonyeong siwonhaeyo.
Not at all. In fact, it's cool.

A: 한국어를 아주 잘 하시네요!
Hangukeoreul aju jal hasineyo!
You speak Korean very well!

B: 잘 하**기는커녕** 기본적인 표현 밖에 몰라요.
Jal hagineunkeonyeong gibonjeogin pyohyeon bakke mollayo.
Not only do I not speak it well, but I don't know anything except basic expressions.

> **Speaking > Writing**
> ★
> ~(으)면 뭘 해요? (eu)   "What's the point of ~?"
> myeon mwol haeyo?

왜 과속해요? 일찍 가**면 뭘 해요**? 안전이 제일 중요하지요.
Wae gwasokaeyo? Iljjik gamyeon mwol haeyo? Anjeoni jeil jungyohajiyo.
Why are you speeding? What's the point of getting there early? Safety is
more important.

Ever had someone be amazed by something that really wasn't a big deal? Ever want to
bring them down a notch or two? Here's how you can do that. This expression means "What's
the point of ~?" or "So what if ~?" and is usually followed by an explanation of what you
think is more important. For instance, in the example sentence above, you use the expression 면 뭘 해요 to ask "What's the point of speeding?" and then follow it with an explanation of what you think is more important—safety.

HOW IT'S FORMED

면 means "if" (see page 283); 뭘 is 무엇 **mueot** contracted with the object marker 를.

HOW IT'S CONJUGATED

This expression is attached to verbs just like the (으)면 with which it starts.

		Past	Present	Future
Action verbs ending in a vowel	하다	했으면 뭘 해요? haesseumyeon mwol haeyo?	하면 뭘 해요? hamyeon mwol haeyo?	하면 뭘 해요?
Action verbs ending in a consonant	먹다	먹었으면 뭘 해요? meogeoseumyeon mwol haeyo?	먹으면 뭘 해요? meogeumyeon mwol haeyo?	먹으면 뭘 해요?
Descriptive verbs (adjectives) ending in a vowel	예쁘다	예뻤으면 뭘 해요? yeppeoseumyeon mwol haeyo?	예쁘면 뭘 해요? yeppeumyeon mwol haeyo?	예쁘면 뭘 해요?
Descriptive verbs (adjectives) ending in a consonant	작다	작았으면 뭘 해요? jagaseumyeon mwol haeyo?	작으면 뭘 해요? jageumyeon mwol haeyo?	작으면 뭘 해요?
Nouns ending in a vowel	남자	남자였으면 뭘 해요? namjayeosseumyeon mwol haeyo?	남자이면 뭘 해요? namja-i-myeon mwol haeyo?	남자이면 뭘 해요?
Nouns ending in a consonant	물	물이었으면 뭘 해요? murieoseumyeon mwol haeyo?	물이면 뭘 해요? murimyeon mwol haeyo?	물이면 뭘 해요?

TAKE NOTE

The explanation for why ~ doesn't matter often follows ~(으)면 뭘 해요? **(eu)myeon mwol hae-yo?** in a second sentence. It often ends with either 아/어/여야지요 ("you must~"; see page 202) or ㄴ/는데요; see page 69).

EXAMPLE SENTENCES

돈이 많이 모으**면 뭘 해요**? 건강이 제일 중요한데요.
Doni mani moeumyeon mwol haeyo? Geongangi jeil jungyohandeyo.
What's the point of saving a lot of money? Health is the most important thing.

건강에 대해서 계속 걱정하**면 뭘 해요**? 한번 검진 받았으니까 걱정할 필요가 없어요.
Geongange daehaeseo gyesok geokjeonghamyeon mwol haeyo? Hanbeon geomjin badasseunikka geokjeonghal pillyoga eobseoyo.
What's the point of constantly worrying about your health? If you'd just get a checkup, you won't need to worry.

Asking Questions

		Speaking > Writing
나요/(으)ㄴ가요? nayo/(eu)ngayo?	"~?"	★★★★

어제 늦었**나요**? **Eoje neujeonnayo?** Were you late yesterday?

Let's face it: life in Korea can be pretty confusing sometimes, and you'll probably have a few questions about things. You can (and Koreans, more often that not, do) ask questions using standard verb forms like 해요? or 가세요?, but what fun is that? Here's how to sound better when you're actually clueless.

HOW IT'S CONJUGATED

If your question ends in an action verb like 가다 or 먹다 or with a past tense form, you can end it with 나요. If it ends in a descriptive verb like 예쁘다 or 똑똑하다 **ttokttokhada**, end with (으)ㄴ가요.

		Past	Present	Future
Action verbs ending in a vowel	하다	했나요? haennayo?	하나요? hanayo?	할 건가요? hal geongayo?
Action verbs ending in a consonant	먹다	먹었나요? meogeonnayo?	먹나요? meoknayo?	먹을 건가요? meogeul geongayo?

		Past	Present	Future
Descriptive verbs (adjectives) ending in a vowel	예쁘다	예뻤나요? yeppeonnayo?	예쁜가요? yeppeungayo?	예쁠 건가요? yeppeul geongayo?
Descriptive verbs (adjectives) ending in a consonant	작다	작았나요? jagannayo?	작은가요? jageungayo?	작을 건가요? jageul geongayo?

TAKE NOTE

ㄴ가 and 나 reappear later on in expressions such as ㄴ가/나 봐 (see page 138), so they're really useful to learn. They also appear at the end of 뭐 mwo, 언제 eonje, 누구 nugu, 무엇 mueot, and 어디 eodi.

In writing, you'll often see these endings as 나? and (으)ㄴ가? such as in a newspaper interview where a reporter is asking questions:

뭔가 mwonga	Whatever it is/something		
언젠가 eonjenga	Whenever it is/sometime	언제나 eonjena	any time
누군가 nugunga	Whoever it is/someone	누구나 nuguna	anyone
무언가 mueonga	Whatever it is/something	무엇이나 mueosina	anything
어딘가 eodinga	Wherever it is/somewhere	어디나 eodina	anywhere

EXAMPLE SENTENCES

여자친구가 **예쁜가요**? **Yeojachinguga yeppeungayo?** Is your girlfriend beautiful?

아버지가 선생님**인가요**? **Abeojiga seonsaengnimingayo?** Is your father a teacher?

어디로 가야 하**나요**? **Eodiro gaya hanayo?** Where must I go?

쓰레기 봉투가 있**나요**? **Sseuregi bongtuga innayo?** Do you have trash bags?

어제 숙제를 했**나요**? **Eoje sukjereul haennayo?**
Did you do your homework yesterday?

And: Basic Forms

These are all added to the ends of nouns and are fairly easy to use.

		Speaking < Writing
A 와/과 wa/gwa B	"A and B"	★★★★★

Somewhat counterintuitively, 와 goes with words ending in vowels and 과 goes with words ending in consonants. They both simply mean "and" and can also be used to mean "together with," depending on the context. When used to mean "together with," they are often paired with either 같이 **gachi** or 함께 **hamkke**, but you can leave these out, unless you really need to clarify the context.

매운 음식과 짠 음식을 좋아해요. **Maeun eumsikgwa jjan eumsigeul joahaeyo.**
I like spicy foods and salty foods.

홍대와 이태원에 술집이 많아요. **Hongdaewa Itaewone suljibi manayo.**
There are many bars in Hongdae and Itaewon.

친구와 같이 영화 봤어요. **Chinguwa gachi yeonghwa bwasseoyo.**
I saw a movie with a friend.

		Speaking > Writing
A (이)랑 (i)rang B	"A and B"	★★★★★

These have exactly the same meaning as 와/과; in other words, "and" or "together with." They are somewhat more colloquial, but otherwise the same. 이랑 is used after vowels and 랑 after consonants.

매운 음식**이랑** 짠 음식을 좋아해요.
Maeun eumsigirang jjan eumsigeul joahaeyo.
I like spicy foods and salty foods.

홍대랑 이태원에 술집이 많아요. **Hongdaerang Itaewone suljibi manayo.**
There are many bars in Hongdae and Itaewon.

친구랑 같이 영화 봤어요. **Chingurang gachi yeonghwa bwasseoyo.**
I saw a movie with a friend.

		Speaking = Writing
A 하고 hago B	"A and B"	★★★★★

하고 is used the same way as 와/과 and 랑/이랑.

매운 음식**하고** 짠 음식을 좋아해요.
Maeun eumsikhago jjan eumsigeul joahaeyo.
I like spicy foods and salty foods.

홍대**하고** 이태원에 술집이 많아요. **Hongdaehago Itaewone suljibi manayo.**
There are many bars in Hongdae and Itaewon.

친구**하고** 같이 영화 봤어요. **Chinguhago gachi yeonghwa bwasseoyo.**
I saw a movie with a friend.

A (이)며 (i)myeo B	"A and B"	Speaking < Writing ★ ★ ★

This is just another short, simple way to say "and." You can use (이)며 as many times as you'd like in a sentence; just put it after each noun you want to list, including the last one. Since it follows nouns, there's no need to worry about any kind of conjugation. I've changed the third example since 며 can't be used to mean "together with," but can be used for any kind of list. 며 follows nouns ending in vowels and 이며 follows nouns ending in consonants.

매운 음식**이며** 짠 음식**이며** 좋아해요.
Maeun eumsigimyeo jjan eumsigimyeo joahaeyo.
I like spicy foods and salty foods.

홍대**며** 이태원**이며** 갔어요.
Hongdaemyeo Itaewonimyeo gasseoyo.
I went to Hongdae and Itaewon.

민수**며** 가영**이며** 같이 영화 봤어요.
Minsumyeo Kayeongimyeo gachi yeonghwa bwasseoyo.
I saw a movie with Minsu and Kayoung.

~끼리 kkiri	"A group of/among ~"	Speaking > Writing ★ ★ ★

This is not exactly a form of "and," but I'm including it in this section anyway because it combines things in order to make a group and it's very useful to know. It means "a group of ~" or "among ~" and is attached to the end of nouns.

친구**끼리** chingukkiri a group of friends, among friends
우리**끼리** urikkiri our group, among ourselves
학생**끼리** haksaengkkiri a group of students, among students

우리**끼리** 먼저 갈게요. **Urikkiri meonjeo galgeyo.**
Our group will go first.

아이들**끼리** 놀고 있어요. **A-i-deulkkiri nolgo isseoyo.**
The children are playing amongst themselves.

And (So On, and So On...)

Sometimes two is not enough and you want to go on and on—how is this done in Korean?

		Speaking < Writing
A, B 등 deung	"A, B, etc."	★★★★

This is much like "etc." in English. It follows as many examples as you provide (at least two, but you can go on and on if you'd like and if you have patient listeners). After 등, you should go on to explain what A and B are examples of. 등 gets particles added to it just like any other nouns; if you'd normally use a particle after the noun, use it after 등 instead.

종이, 연필 **등을** 시험에 가지고 오세요.
Jongi, yeonpil **deungeul** siheome gajigo oseyo.
Bring paper, a pencil, etc. to the test.

그 슈퍼에서 물, 맥주, 사이다 **등** 음료를 팔아요.
Geu syupeoeseo mul, maekju, sa-ida **deung** eumnyoreul parayo.
That shop sells drinks like water, beer, cider, etc.

이 책을 한국어, 일본어 **등의** 언어로 읽을 수 있어요.
I chaegeul hangukeo, ilboneo **deungui** eoneoro ilgeul su isseoyo.
You can read this book in Korean, Japanese, etc.

		Speaking = Writing
A 같은 gateun B	"Things like A"	★★★★

This one is more like "like, for example." You list your examples before it (A) and put the category they belong to (B) afterward.

종이, 연필 **같은** 학습준비물을 시험에 가지고 오세요.
Jongi, yeonpil **gateun** hakseupjunbimureul siheome gajigo oseyo.
Bring study materials like paper, a pencil, etc. to the test.

그 슈퍼에서 물, 맥주, 사이다 **같은** 음료를 팔아요.
Geu syupeoeseo mul, maekju, sa-ida **gateun** eumnyoreul parayo.
That shop sells drinks like water, beer, cider, etc.

이 책을 한국어, 일본어 **같은** 언어로 읽을 수 있어요.
I chaegeul hangukeo, ilboneo **gateun** eoneoro ilgeul su isseoyo.
You can read this book in languages like Korean, Japanese, etc.

| A (으)ㄹ 겸 (eu)r gyeom B | "A/B" | Speaking = Writing
★★★★ |

This one is a little more complicated. It can be thought of as a slash. If only one example is listed, it becomes more like "and so on." (으)ㄹ 겸 can be used after verbs or 겸 directly after nouns. There is also an expression, (으)ㄹ 겸 해서, which is used to focus on one cause out of many. This is covered on page 95.

아침 **겸** 점심을 먹었어요. **Achim gyeom jeomsimeul meogeosseoyo.**
I ate brunch. (breakfast/lunch)

그는 기자 **겸** 사진사이에요. **Geuneun gija gyeom sajinsaieyo.**
He is a journalist/photographer.

쇼핑도 하고 영화도 볼 **겸**, 명동에 갔어요.
Syopingdo hago yeonghwado bol gyeom, Myeongdonge gasseoyo.
I went to Myeongdong to go shopping and see a movie.

| A 을/를 비롯한 eul/reul birotan B | "B, including A" | Speaking < Writing
★ |

This is a way of listing examples. The 을/를 are object markers; see page 30. The category you're giving examples of shouldn't be too general: for instance, "action movies" is fine, but just "movies" is too broad a category.

카리비안의 해적**을 비롯한** 액션 영화를 봤어요.
Karibianui haejeogeul birotan aeksyeon yeonghwareul bwasseoyo.
I watched some action movies, including Pirates of the Caribbean.

비빔밥**을 비롯한** 한국 음식을 만들어 봤어요.
Bibimbapeul birotan hanguk eumsigeul mandeureo bwasseoyo.
I tried making some Korean food, including bibimbap.

보드카, 위스키, 소주**를 비롯한** 독한 술을 마셨어요.
Bodeuka, wiseuki, sojureul birotan dokhan sureul masyeosseoyo.
I drank strong alcohol, including beer, whiskey and soju.

Linking Sentences: And

Focus: 고

고 by itself is one way of saying "and." You can also put it together with other expressions to get plenty of interesting and unexpected combinations. Here's a quick list if you're confused:

Expression	Page	Meaning	Sample sentence
A고B	51	A and B	민수가 정시에 오고 가영이 늦게 왔어요. Minsuga jeongsie ogo Kayeongi neutge wasseoyo. Minsu came on time and Kayoung was late.
~고요	52	~, too	민수가 늦어요. 음식도 가지고 오지 않고요. Minsuga neujeoyo. Eumsikdo gajigo oji ankoyo. Minsu's late. He also didn't bring any food.
~고 있다	255	Is ~ing	그 아이가 놀고 있어요 Geu aiga nolgo isseoyo. The child is playing.
A고도B	108	Although A, B	서두르고도 늦었어요. Seodureugodo neujeosseoyo. Although I hurried, I was late.
A고는B	–	Because of A, B (unexpectedly) happened	그 책을 읽고는 성격이 달라졌어요. Geu chaegeul ilgoneun seonggyeogi dallajyeosseoyo. Since reading that book, his personality changed completely.
A고서B	280	A, then B	지하철을 타고서 늦었어요. Jihacheoreul tagoseo neujeosseoyo. I took the subway and then I was late.
A고서는B	281	While A, B (can't happen)	신발을 신고서는 집에 들어올 수 없어요. Sinbareul singoseoneun jibe deureool su eobseoyo. You can't come in the house while wearing your shoes.
A고서야B	301	A, then B	우리가 지하철을 타고서야 정시에 올 수 있었어요. Uriga jihacheoreul tagoseoya jeongsie ol su isseosseoyo. We took the subway, and then we were able to arrive on time (at least partly because of taking the subway).
A고 나서B	272	A and then B	저녁을 먹고 나서 담배를 피웠어요. Jeonyeogeul meokgo naseo dambaereul piwosseoyo. I ate dinner and then had a cigarette.
A고자B	229	I plan to A, so B	늦지 않게 오고자 집에서 일찍 출발했어요. Neutji anke ogoja jibeseo iljjik chulbalhaesseoyo. I left the house early so as not to be late.
A고 보니 (까)B	282	I did A and then discovered that B	지하철에 타고 보니 택시보다 더 느렸어요. Jihacheore tago boni taeksiboda deo neuryeosseoyo. I took the subway, but found it was slower than a taxi.
A고 해서B	294	A, so B	열쇠를 잃어버리고 해서 늦게 왔어요. Yeolsoereul ireobeorigo haeseo neutge wasseoyo. I lost my keys (among other things), so I arrived late.
~고 말고(요) go malgo(yo)	37	Of course, ~	늦고 말고요. 민수는 일 때문에 정시에 오지 못 해요. Neutgo malgoyo. Minsuneun il ttaemune jeongsie oji mot haeyo. Of course he was late. Because of his job, he can't come on time.
~고 말겠다 go malgetda	232	I (definitely) plan to ~	이번에는 꼭 정시에 오고 말겠어요. Ibeoneneun kkok jeongsie ogo malgesseoyo. This time I'm definitely going to come on time.

Expression	Page	Meaning	Sample sentence
~고 말았다 go maratda	233	(Unfortunately), ~ happened.	정시에 온다는 것이 결국 늦게 <u>오고 말았어요</u>. **Jeongsie ondaneun geosi gyeolguk neutge ogo marasseoyo.** I meant to come on time, but (unfortunately) I ended up being late.
~고는/곤 하다 goneun/ gon hada	349	Habitually do ~	민수가 대학교 때 자주 수업에 늦게 <u>오곤 했어요</u>. **Minsuga daehakgyo ttae jaju sueobe neutge ogon haesseoyo.** During university, Minsu was habitually late for class.

And: Putting Things Together

The Basics:

> **Speaking = Writing**
>
> A 고 B "A and B" ★★★★★

민수가 정시에 <u>오고</u> 가영이 늦게 왔어요.
Minsuga jeongsie ogo Kayeongi neutge wasseoyo.
Minsu came on time and Kayoung was late.

고 is the workhorse when it comes to combining things in Korean. However, it's a bit of a prima donna, and you can't just stick it in any sentence and expect it to do its job. See the "Take note" section below on how to properly use 고.

HOW IT'S CONJUGATED

		All tenses
Action verbs ending in a vowel	하다 hada	하고 hago
Action verbs ending in a consonant	먹다 meokda	먹고 meokgo
Descriptive verbs (adjectives) ending in a vowel	예쁘다 yeppeuda	예쁘고 yeppeugo
Descriptive verbs (adjectives) ending in a consonant	작다 jakda	작고 jakgo
Nouns ending in a vowel	남자 namja	남자이고 namjaigo
Nouns ending in a consonant	물 mul	물이고 muligo

TAKE NOTE

First of all, the subjects of both clauses, A and B, must be the same you're using one of these three verbs to end A: 가다, 오다 or 일어나다 **ireonada**. In these cases you should use 어서 instead of 고. You can use 가다, 오다 or 일어나다 with 고 if the subjects of both clauses are different from each other.

EXAMPLE SENTENCES

영화를 보**고** 쇼핑을 하러 강남에 갔어요.
Yeonghwareul bogo syopingeul hareo Gangname gasseoyo.
I went to Gangnam to see a movie and go shopping.

그 수업이 재미없**고** 어려워요. **Geu sueobi jaemieopgo eoryeowoyo.**
That class is boring and difficult.

내일 한국어 공부하**고** 책을 읽을 거예요.
Naeil hangukeo gongbuhago chaegeul ilgeul geoyeyo.
Tomorrow I'm going to study Korean and read a book.

민수가 가**고** 가영이 왔어요. **Minsuga gago Kayeongi wasseoyo.**
Minsu left and Kayoung came.

Note that in the last example I used 가다 but changed the subject. If Minsu left and then went to see a movie, you would say 민수가 가서 영화를 봤어요 **Minsuga gaseo yeonghwareul bwasseoyo.**

In all the variations of 고 (고요, 고도, 고서, etc.), the same rules apply: same subjects and no 가다, 오다, or 일어나다 unless the subject of the sentence is different.

		Speaking > Writing
~**고요**	"…and ~, too"	★★★★

민수가 항상 늦어요. 음식도 가지고 오지 않**고요**.
Minsuga hangsang neujeoyo. Eumsikdo gajigo oji ankoyo.
Minsu is always late. He also never brings any food.

Sometimes you say something and then remember something else you wanted to say. In this case, you can add a second sentence using 고요.

HOW IT'S FORMED

고 plus the polite ending 요. Of course, if you want to use this in 반말, you can; just drop the 요.

HOW IT'S CONJUGATED

It's added to the verb at the end of a second sentence, the one where you mention your afterthought.

		Past	Present	Future
Action verbs ending in a vowel	하다	했고요	하고요	할 거고요
Action verbs ending in a consonant	먹다	먹었고요	먹고요	먹을 거고요

TAKE NOTE

You don't have to bother conjugating this expression in the past or future tenses if you don't want to; Koreans often don't. See the last example below.

If you have an object in the second clause (like "Korean" and "a book" in the example below) you should add 도 (too) at the end of it instead of 을/를. It sounds more natural that way.

It may or may not be strictly correct, but I've often heard Koreans use this expression even if the afterthought comes long afterward or is implied. For instance, a teacher will tell her students to "그림 그리세요 **geurim geuriseyo**" (draw a picture) and then five minutes later, "색칠도 하고요 **saekchil do hagoyo**" (also, color it).

EXAMPLE SENTENCES

그 수업이 재미없어요. 어렵**고요**. Geu sueobi jaemieobseoyo. Eoryeopgoyo.
That class is boring. It's also difficult.

내일 한국어 공부할 거예요. 책도 읽**을 거고요**.
Naeil hanguleo gongbuhal geoyeyo. Chaekdo ilgeul geogoyo.

내일 한국어 공부할 거예요. 책도 읽**고요**.
Naeil hangukeo gongbuhal geoyeyo. Chaekdo ilkgoyo.

Tomorrow I'm going to study Korean. I'm also going to read a book.

		Speaking = Writing
A (으)ㄴ/는 데다(가) (eu)n/neun deda(ga) B A 에다(가) eda(ga) B	"B, on top of A/A plus B"	★★★ ★★★

민수가 늦은 **데다가** 음식도 가지고 오지 않았어요.
Minsuga neujeun dedaga eumsikdo gajigo oji anasseoyo.
Minsu was late. He also didn't bring any food.

These expressions are for those who like to cook. They can be used to add one thing to another thing. 에다(가) can be used with nouns to mean "adding one thing to another thing" or "putting something in a specific location."

HOW IT'S FORMED

다가 is a very versatile expression which is explained in detail on page 268. The 에 and (으)ㄴ/는 데 before it simply mark the thing to which something else is being added: there's no other meaning behind it. The 가 part of 다가 is optional.

HOW IT'S CONJUGATED

The difference between the two noun forms is that while 물인 데다가 **murin dedaga** means "It's water, and on top of that…," 물에다가 **muredaga** means to add something to the water.

	Past	Present	Future
Action verbs ending in a vowel	하다	한 데다가 han dedaga	하는 데다가 haneun dedaga	하는 데다가
Action verbs ending in a consonant	먹다	먹은 데다가 meogeun dedaga	먹는 데다가 meokneun dedaga	먹는 데다가
Descriptive verbs (adjectives) ending in a vowel	예쁘다	예쁜 데다가 yeppeun dedaga	예쁜 데다가	예쁜 데다가
Descriptive verbs (adjectives) ending in a consonant	작다	작은 데다가 jageun dedaga	작은 데다가	작은 데다가
Nouns ending in a vowel	남자	남자인 데다가 namjain dedaga 남자에다가 namja-e-daga	남자인 데다가 남자에다가	남자인 데다가 남자에다가
Nouns ending in a consonant	물	물인 데다가 murin dedaga 물에다가 muredaga	물인 데다가 물에다가	물인 데다가 물에다가

TAKE NOTE

The subjects of both clauses should be the same.

The expressions here and (으)ㄹ 뿐만 아니라/더러 **(eu)r ppunman anira/deoreo** have similar meanings, but they are used in different situations. See page 55 for when the 뿐 expressions can and can't be used.

EXAMPLE SENTENCES

■ A ㄴ/은/는 데다(가) **n/eun/neun deda(ga)** B

맛있어 보**이는 데다가** 냄새도 좋아요.
Masisseo boineun dedaga naemsaedo joayo.
It not only looks delicious, but it smells good too.

그는 축구를 잘 하**는 데다가** 농구도 잘 해요.
Geuneun chukgureul jal haneun dedaga nonggudo jal haeyo.
He is not only good at soccer, but also at basketball.

■ A 에다(가) **eda(ga)** B

열**에다가** 스물을 더하면 서른이에요.
Yeoredaga seumureul deohamyeon seoreun-i-e-yo.
Ten plus twenty is thirty.

그것을 트럭**에다가** 실었어요.
Geugeoseul teureogedaga sireo-sseoyo.
He put it in the truck.

큰 그릇**에다** 밀가루와 물을 넣으세요.
Keun geureuseda milgaruwa mureul neo-eu-seyo.
Put flour and water into a big bowl.

		Speaking > Writing
A (으)ㄹ 뿐만 아니라	"Not just A, but also B"	★★★
(eu)r ppunman anira B		
A (으)ㄹ 뿐더러 (eu)r		★
ppundeoreo		

민수가 늦었<u>을</u> **뿐만 아니라** 음식도 가지고 오지 않았어요.
Minsuga neujeosseul ppunman anira eumsikdo gajigo oji anasseoyo.

민수가 늦었<u>을</u> **뿐더러** 음식도 가지고 오지 않았어요.
Minsuga neujeosseul ppundeoreo eumsikdo gajigo oji anasseoyo.

Minsu was late. He also didn't bring any food.

(으)ㄹ 뿐만 아니라 is a very common expression which is quite simple to use, and it essentially means "not just A, but also B". (으)ㄹ 뿐더러 is less common than ㄹ 뿐만 아니라 and not really used these days except by older people, but you may as well learn them together since they're similarly formed and have exactly the same meaning.

HOW IT'S FORMED

We're going to discuss 뿐 later on, on page 337. It's an expression used to limit something: to say that there was only one instance of it. 만 is another limiting expression which means "only." 아니라 is an expression on its own (see page 118) which negates what's before it and asserts what's after it.

HOW IT'S CONJUGATED

		Past	Present	Future
Action verbs ending in a vowel	하다	했을 뿐만 아니라 haesseul ppunman anira 했을 뿐더러 haesseul ppundeoreo	할 뿐만 아니라 hal ppunman anira 할 뿐더러 hal ppundeoreo	할 뿐만 아니라 할 뿐더러
Action verbs ending in a consonant	먹다	먹었을 뿐만 아니라 meogeosseul ppunman anira 먹었을 뿐더러 meogeosseul ppundeoreo	먹을 뿐만 아니라 meogeul ppunman anira 먹을 뿐더러 meogeul ppundeoreo	먹을 뿐만 아니라 먹을 뿐더러
Descriptive verbs (adjectives) ending in a vowel	예쁘다	예뻤을 뿐만 아니라 yeppeosseul ppunman anira 예뻤을 뿐더러 yeppeosseul ppundeoreo	예쁠 뿐만 아니라 yeppeul ppunman anira 예쁠 뿐더러 yeppeul ppundeoreo	예쁠 뿐만 아니라 예쁠 뿐더러
Descriptive verbs (adjectives) ending in a consonant	작다	작았을 뿐만 아니라 jagasseul ppunman anira 작았을 뿐더러 jagasseul ppundeoreo	작을 뿐만 아니라 jageul ppunman anira 작을 뿐더러 jageul ppundeoreo	작을 뿐만 아니라 작을 뿐더러

		Past	Present	Future
Nouns ending in a vowel	남자	남자 뿐만 아니라 namja ppunman anira	남자 뿐만 아니라	남자 뿐만 아니라
Nouns ending in a consonant	물	물 뿐만 아니라 mul ppunman anira	물 뿐만 아니라	물 뿐만 아니라

TAKE NOTE

(으)ㄹ 뿐더러 (eu)r ppundeoreo is not used after nouns.

Since these expressions are used for adding two things together, you can't have a positive statement in A and a negative one in B. Your expressions must either be both positive or both negative. In fact, 뿐더러 can't be used with positive statements at all.

그 애는 예쁠 뿐만 아니라 공부도 잘해요.
Geu aeneun yeppeul ppunman anira gongbudo jalhaeyo. (acceptable)
That child is not only pretty, but she also studies well.

그 애는 공부를 못할 뿐만 아니라 놀기도 못해요.
Geu aeneun gongbureul mothal ppunman anira nolgido mothaeyo. (acceptable)
Not only does that child not study well, but he can't even play.

그 애는 예쁠 뿐더러 착해요.
Geu aeneun yeppeul ppundeoreo chakhaeyo. (ungrammatical)
That child is both pretty and kind.

그 애는 공부를 잘할 뿐더러 놀기도 잘해요.
Geu aeneun gongbureul jalhal ppundeoreo nolgido jalhaeyo. (ungrammatical)
That child not only studies well, but also plays well.

그 애는 공부를 못 할 뿐더러 예쁘지도 않아요.
Geu aeneun gongbureul mothal ppundeoreo yeppeujido anayo. (acceptable)
Not only does that child not study well, she's not even pretty.

There is commonly a 도 after the noun in clause B, and that 도 means "too." See the examples below.

EXAMPLE SENTENCES

맛있어 보**일 뿐만 아니라** 냄새도 좋아요.
Mas-isseo bo-il ppunman anira naemsaedo joayo.
맛있어 보**일 뿐더러** 냄새도 좋아요.
Mas-isseo bo-il ppundeoreo naemsaedo joayo.
It not only looks delicious, but it smells good too.

그는 축구 **뿐만 아니라** 농구도 잘 해요.
Geuneun chukgu ppunman anira nonggudo jal haeyo.

축구를 잘 **할 뿐더러** 농구도 잘 해요.
Chukgureul jal hal ppundeoreo nonggudo jal haeyo.

He is not only good at soccer, but also at basketball.

		Speaking = Writing
A(으)ㄴ/는 물론 (eu)n/neun mullon B	"Not just A, but also B"	★★

민수가 물**은 물론** 음식도 가지고 오지 않았어요.
Minsuga mureun mullon eumsikdo gajigo oji anasseoyo.
Minsu didn't bring any water or food.

물론 means "of course," but not here. Taken as a whole, this phrase is yet another way to express "not just A, but also B." In other words, it's very much like (으)ㄹ 뿐만 아니라 **(eu)r ppunman anira**, but much less common.

HOW IT'S CONJUGATED

		All tenses
Nouns ending in a vowel	남자	남자는 물론 namjaneun mullon
Nouns ending in a consonant	물	물은 물론 mureun mullon

TAKE NOTE

Don't confuse 물은 with 물론 ("of course"). 물론 by itself is more commonly found at the beginning or sometimes at the end of sentences, and is an adverb that stands on its own. You can tell them apart by the (으)ㄴ/는 before 물론 in this expression and by context.

This is interchangeable with 뿐만 아니라 **ppunman anira** and 뿐더러 **ppundeoreo** (see page 55), but it's fairly uncommon.

EXAMPLE SENTENCES

맛있어 보이는 것**은 물론** 냄새도 좋아요.
Mas-isseo bo-i-neun geoseun mullon naemsaedo joayo.
It not only looks delicious, but smells good too.

그는 축구**는 물론** 농구도 잘 해요.
Guneun chukguneun mullon nonggudo jal haeyo.
He is not only good at soccer, but also at basketball.

> **Speaking > Writing**
>
> A말고(도) malgo(do) B,   "Not just A, but B"   ★★
> A외에(도) oe-e(do) B

그는 축구 **말고** 농구도 잘 해요. Geuneun chukgu malgo nonggudo jal haeyo.

그는 축구 **외에** 농구 잘 해요. Geuneun chukgu oe-e nonggu jal haeyo.

He is not only good at soccer, but also at basketball.

I'm putting these two together because they're quite similar. A말고 B and A외에B mean "not just A, but B."

HOW IT'S FORMED

말다 is a verb that means "to not be," and appears in many other expressions such as 할까 말까 (to do it or not to do it). 외 means "outside" and so 외에 refers to the something outside another thing. An equivalent English expression would be, "other than" or "aside from that." The person in the example sentences above is good at soccer (and other than/aside from that) basketball. 도 is used here as an intensifier; see above for how it alters the expression.

HOW IT'S CONJUGATED

		Past	Present	Future
Action verbs ending in a vowel	하다	한 것(이) 말고(도) han geos(i) malgo(do) 한 것(이) 외에(도) han geos(i) oe-e(do)	하는 것(이) 말고(도) haneun geos(i) malgo(do) 하는 것(이) 외에(도) haneun geos(i) oe-e(do)	하는 것(이) 말고(도) 할 것(이) 말고(도) hal geos(i) malgo(do) 하는 것(이) 외에(도) 할 것(이) 외에(도) hal geos(i) oe-e(do)
Action verbs ending in a consonant	먹다	먹은 것(이) 말고(도) meogeun geos(i) malgo(do) 먹은 것(이) 외에(도) meogeun geos(i) oe-e(do)	먹는 것(이) 말고(도) meokneun geos(i) malgo(do) 먹는 것(이) 외에(도) meokneun geos(i) oe-e(do)	먹는 것(이) 말고(도) 먹을 것(이) 말고(도) meogeul geos(i) malgo(do) 먹는 것(이) 외에(도) 먹을 것(이) 외에(도) meogeul geos(i) oe-e(do)
Descriptive verbs (adjectives) ending in a vowel	예쁘다	예쁜 것(이) 말고(도) yeppeun geos(i) malgo(do) 예쁜 것(이) 외에(도) yeppeun geos(i) oe-e(do)	예쁜 것(이) 말고(도) 예쁜 것(이) 외에(도)	예쁜 것(이) 말고(도) 예쁜 것(이) 외에(도)
Descriptive verbs (adjectives) ending in a consonant	작다	작은 것(이) 말고(도) jageun geos(i) malgo(do) 작은 것(이) 외에(도) jageun geos(i) oe-e(do)	작은 것(이) 말고(도) 작은 것(이) 외에(도)	작은 것(이) 말고(도) 작은 것(이) 외에(도)

Nouns ending in a vowel	남자	남자 말고(도) namja malgo(do) 남자 외에(도) namja oe-e(do)	남자 말고(도) 남자 외에(도)	남자 말고(도) 남자 외에(도)
Nouns ending in a consonant	물	물 말고(도) mul malgo(do) 물 외에(도) mul oe-e(do)	물 말고(도) 물 외에(도)	물 말고(도) 물 외에(도)

TAKE NOTE

If you put 도 on the end, the expression changes a little. In this case your B clause should be something very general and broader than your A clause.

EXAMPLE SENTENCES

■ A말고/외에 B

민수가 똑똑하는 것이 **말고** 잘 생긴 것이에요.
Minsuga ttokttokhaneun geosi malgo jal saenggin geosieyo.

민수가 똑똑하는 것이 **외에** 잘 생긴 것이에요.
Minsuga ttokttokhaneun geosi oe-e jal saenggin geosieyo.

Minsu is not just smart, but he is also handsome.

맛있어 보인 것이 **말고** 냄새도 좋은 것이에요.
Mas-isseo boin geosi malgo naemsaedo joeun geosieyo.

맛있어 보인 것이 **외에** 냄새도 좋은 것이에요.
Mas-isseo boin geosi oe-e naemsaedo joeun geosieyo.

It not only looks delicious, but it smells good too.

■ A말고도/외에도 B

민수가 똑똑하는 것이 **말고도** 좋은 점이 많아요.
Minsuga ttokttokhaneun geosi malgodo joeun jeomi manayo.

민수가 똑똑하는 것이 **외에도** 좋은 점이 많아요.
Minsuga ttokttokhaneun geosi oe-e-do joeun jeomi manayo.

Minsu is not just smart, but he has many good qualities too.

맛있어 보인 것이 **말고도** 음식이 많아요.
Mas-isseo boin geosi malgodo eumsigi manayo.

맛있어 보인 것이 **외에도** 음식이 많아요.
Mas-isseo boin geosi oe-e-do eumsigi manayo.

It not only looks delicious, but there's also lots of it.

그는 축구 **말고도** 스포츠를 다 잘 해요.
Geuneun chukgu malgodo seupo-cheureul da jal haeyo.

그는 축구 **외에도** 스포츠를 다 잘 해요.
Geuneun chukgu oe-e-do seupo-cheureul da jal haeyo.

He is not only good at soccer, but also at all sports.

Linking Sentences: Or

A(이)나 (i)na B	"A or B"	Speaking = Writing ★★★★★

This is the most easy, simple, basic way to say "or" in Korean. It goes between two nouns and means "A or B."

커피**나** 차 keopina cha coffee or tea

지하철이**나** 택시 jihacheolina taeksi subway or taxi

야구**나** 축구를 할까요? Yaguna chukgureul halkkayo?
Shall we play baseball or soccer?

가영**이나** 혜진을 만났어요? Kayoungina Hyejineul mannasseoyo?
Did you meet Kayoung or Hyejin?

"스타 워즈"**나** "스타 트렉"을 보고 싶어요.
Seuta Wojeuna Seuta Teurekeul bogo sipeoyo.
I want to watch Star Wars or Star Trek.

If you just use (이)나 by itself after a noun without another noun, it means "or something." You can also use (이)나마 (i)nama, which has the same meaning and implies that whatever is being offered isn't the best choice, but it'll do.

커피**나** 마실래요? Keopina masillaeyo? Shall we drink some coffee or something?

책**이나** 읽고 싶어요. Chaegina ilggo sipeoyo. I want to read a book or something.

책이 없으니까 민수 책**이나마** 보세요.
Chaegi eobseunikka Minsu chaeginama boseyo.
Since you have no book, you can look at Minsu's.

김 선생님을 찾지 못하면 이메일**이나마** 쓰세요.
Kim seonsaengnimeul chatji mothamyeon imeilinama sseuseyo.
If you can't find Mr. Kim, you can send an email or something.

Here are some commonly used expressions with (이)나:

누구나	nuguna	anyone
언제나	eonjena	any time
어디서나	eodiseona	anywhere (used only with 가다, 오다 and other verbs of motion)
어디에서나	eodi-e-seona	anywhere
무엇이나	mueosina	anything
아무거나	amugeona	anything

누구나 갈 수 있어요. **Nuguna gal su isseoyo.** Anyone can go.

언제나 할 수 있어요. **Eonjena hal su isseoyo.** We can do it any time.

어디서나 하면 돼요. **Eodiseona hamyeon dwaeyo.** We can do it anywhere.

어디에서나 하면 돼요. **Eodi-e-seona hamyeon dwaeyo.** We can do it anywhere.

아무거나 주세요. **Amugeona juseyo.** Just give me anything.

		Speaking = Writing
A거나 geona B	"A or B"	★★★★

This is the most basic way to say "or" when you're talking about verbs. Put it after each of two verbs to mean "A or B." You don't need any past tense markers on your verbs; the verb at the end of your sentence tells people all they need to know about when it happened. What you're really doing here is changing a verb into a noun using (으)ㄴ/는 것, adding 이나 (see page 60), and then shrinking the whole expression to 거나.

수영하**거나** 자전거를 타**거나**   go swimming or go biking
suyeonghageona jajeongeoreul tageona

영화를 보**거나** 쇼핑을 하**거나**   see a movie or go shopping
yeonghwareul bogeona syopingeul hageona

커피를 마시**거나** 식사를 하**거나** 할까요?
Keopireul masigeona siksareul hageona halkkayo?
Shall we drink coffee or eat dinner?

지금 은행에 가거나 내일 인터넷 뱅킹을 하거나 해야 해요.
Jigeum eunhaenge gageona naeil inteonet baengkingeul hageona haeya haeyo.
I have to either go to the bank now or log on to online banking tomorrow.

You can use A거나 말거나 **geona malgeona** B to say that whether or not you do A, B will happen.

서두르**거나 말거나** 늦을 거예요. Seodureugeona malgeona neujeul geoyeyo.
Whether you hurry or not, you'll be late.

아이들이 듣**거나 말거나** 선생님은 계속 말했어요.
A-i-deuri deutgeona malgeona seonsaengnimeun gyesok malhaesseoyo.
Whether or not the children were listening, the teacher kept talking.

그녀가 예쁘**거나 말거나**, 저는 그녀를 사랑해요.
Geunyeoga yeppeugeona malgeona, jeoneun geunyeoreulsaranghaeyo.
Whether or not she's beautiful, I love her.

		Speaking > Writing
~(이)라도 (i)rado	"~ or something"	★★★★

This can best be translated as "or something" as in "Do you want to get some coffee or something?" It implies that "something" is not necessarily the first choice, but it will do.

커피**라도** 먹을래요? Keopirado meogeullaeyo?
Do you want to get some coffee or something? (I don't really care if we get coffee or something else.)

이번 주말에 부산**이라도** 갈까요? Ibeon jumare Busanirado galkkayo?
Shall we go to Busan or something this weekend? (I'm not that excited about Busan, but I'd like to go somewhere.)

이거**라도** 주세요. Igeorado juseyo.
Just give me this one. (It's not my first choice, but it'll do.)

It can also be used after question words like 누구, 언제, **nugu, eonje,** or 어디 **eodi** or after 아무 **amu** to mean "any."

누구라도	nugurado	anyone
아무라도	amurado	anyone
언제라도	eonjerado	any time
어디라도	eodirado	anywhere (used only with 가다, 오다 and other verbs of motion)
어디에서라도	eodieseorado	anywhere
무엇이라도	mueosirado	whatever
아무거라도	amugeorado	anything

누구라도 갈 수 있어요. Nugurado gal su isseoyo. Anyone can go.

언제라도 할 수 있어요. Eonjerado hal su isseoyo. We can do it any time.

어디에서라도 하면 돼요. **Eodi-e-seorado hamyeon dwaeyo.** We can do it anywhere.

아무라도 주세요. **Amurado juseyo** Just give me anything.

무엇이라도 주세요. **Mueosirado juseyo.** Just give me whatever.

		Speaking = Writing
A든(지) deunji B 든(지)	"A or B"	★★★★

This goes after nouns or verbs and means that either A or B is fine. It's the same as 거나. When used after verbs, it is always in the form A든지 B든지 and can be used after 았/었/였 if your sentence is in the past tense. After nouns, you should use (이)든지: 남자든지 여자든지 **namjadeunji yeojadeunji** or 물이든지 불이든지 **murideunji burideunji.**

You can also shorten the entire expression to A든 B든 or use A든지 안 A든지, A든지 말든지, or A든지 못 A든지.

커피를 마시**든지** 식사를 하**든지** 할까요?
Keopireul masideunji siksareul hadeunji halkkayo?

커피를 마시**든** 식사를 하**든** 할까요?
Keopireul masideun siksareul hadeun halkkayo?

Shall we drink coffee or eat dinner?

커피**든지** 차**든지** 마실래요? **Keopideunji chadeunji masillaeyo?**
Let's drink some coffee or tea.

비싸**든지** 싸**든지** 사야 돼요. **Bissadeunji ssadeunji saya dwaeyo.**
싸**든지** 말**든지** 사야 돼요. **Ssadeunji maldeunji saya dwaeyo.**
I have to buy it no matter how much it costs. (whether it's cheap or expensive)

네가 가**든지** 못 가**든지**, 내 친구는 나와 있을 거예요.
Nega gadeunji mot gadeunji, nae chinguneun nawa isseul geoyeyo.
Whether or not you can go, my friend will be with me.

Just like 거나 and 라도, 든지 can be added to the end of question words or 아무 to form words that mean "any."

누구든지	nugudeunji	anyone
언제든지	eonjedeunji	any time
어디든지	eodideunji	anywhere (used only with 가다, 오다 and other verbs of motion)
어디에서든지	eodieseodeunji	anywhere
무엇이든지	mueosideunji	anything

누구든지 갈 수 있어요. **Nugudeunji gal su isseoyo.** Anyone can go.

언제든지 할 수 있어요. **Eonjedeunji hal su isseoyo.** We can do it any time.

어디에서든지 하면 돼요. **Eodieseodeunji hamyeon dwaeyo.** We can do it anywhere.

무엇이든지 주세요. **Mueosideunji juseyo.** Just give me whatever.

Speaking = Writing

A(이/으)라/자/(ㄴ/는)다거나   "A or B"   ★★
(i/eu)la/ja/(n/neun)dageona B

This is almost exactly the same as 거나 above, but it's used in situations where A and B are either examples or are about important issues, or are examples used while talking about an important issue. So you can use it to talk about how to solve the city's traffic problem, for example, but it would be strange to use it to talk about your weekend plans. You could, however, use it to give examples of things you normally do on the weekend.

Add an indirect speech particle (see page 304) to 거나, and repeat the particle plus 거나 after every example.

수영**한다거나** 자전거를 **탄다거나**   go swimming or go biking
suyeonghandageona jajeongeoreul tandageona

영화**라거나** 쇼핑**이라거나**   a movie or shopping
yeonghwarageona syopingirageona

소설**이란다거나** 만화**란다거나** 책을 다른 종류를 다 좋아해요.
Soseorirandageona manhwarandageona chaegeul dareun jongnyureul da joahaeyo.
I like all kinds of books like novels or comic books.

패스트 푸드를 끊**는다거나** 운동을 더 열심히 **한다거나** 하면 콜레스케롤 수치를 낮출 수 있어요.
Paeseuteu pudeureul kkeunneundageona undongeul deo yeolsimhi handageona hamyeon kolleseuterol suchi reul natchul su isseoyo.
If you quit eating fast food or if you exercise more, you can lower your cholesterol.

Speaking = Writing

A(이)라든가/는다든가/ㄴ다든가/   "A or B"   ★★
다든가 (i)radeunga/neundadeunga/
n-da-deunga/dadeunga B

You may recognize 라, 는다, ㄴ다, and 다 as indirect speech endings. In this case they aren't used to talk about something someone else said. However, they still attach to words the same way: (이)라든가 after nouns, 는/ㄴ다든가 after action verbs, and 다든가 after descriptive verbs. (See page 304 for more on indirect speech endings.)

라든가 and its companions mean "or" and are used to talk about two choices. In the case of (이)라든가, B is normally followed by an explanation of how exactly A and B are similar: "비빔밥이라든가 냉면이라든가 한국 음식 같은 **Bibimbapiradeunga naengmyeoniradeunga hanguk eumsig gateun**" ("Korean foods like bibimbap or naengmyeon") 는다든가, ㄴ다든가 and 다든가, on the other hand, are usually followed by 하다, which can then be conjugated however you'd like.

While (이)라든가 is normally used only after A, 는다든가/ㄴ다든가/다든가 follows both A and B.

비빔밥**이라든가** 불고기 같은 대표적인 한국 음식을 먹어 보세요.
Bibimbapiradeunga bulgogi gateun daepyojeogin hanguk eumsigeul meogeo boseyo.
Please try a representative (famous) Korean food like bibimbap or bulgogi.

커피**라든가** 차 같은 따뜻한 것을 마시고 싶어요.
Keopiradeunga cha gateun ttatteuthan geoseul masigo sipeoyo.
I want to drink something warm like coffee or tea.

스트레스가 쌓일 때 산책**이라든가** 수영**이라든가** 운동을 해요.
Seuteuleseuga ssahil ttae sanchaegiradeunga suyeongiradeunga undongeul haeyo.
When I'm stressed, I like to do some exercise like walking or swimming.

스트레스가 쌓일 때 산책을 **한다든가** 음악을 **듣는다든가** 해요.
Seuteuleseuga ssahil ttae sanchaegeul handadeunga eumageul deunneundadeunga haeyo.
When I'm stressed, I like to take a walk or listen to music.

방학 때 여행을 **간다든가** 친구와 **논다든가** 하고 싶어요.
Banghak ttae yeohaengeul gandadeunga chinguwa nondadeunga hago sipeoyo.
During vacation I want to travel or hang out with friends.

	Speaking = Writing
A건 geon B건 "Whether you do A or B..."	★

This is a shorter version of 거나, but it's used to mean "whether you do A or B." A and B should be opposites and 건 should follow each of them.

지하철을 타**건** 택시를 타**건** 늦을 거예요.
Jihacheoreul tageon taeksireul tageon neujeul geoyeyo.
Whether you take the subway or a taxi, you'll be late.

한국어를 잘 하**건** 못 하**건** 최선을 다 해야 돼요.
Hangukeoreul jal hageon mot hageon choeseoneul da haeya dwaeyo.
Whether you're good at Korean or not, you must do your best.

돈이 있<u>건</u> 없<u>건</u> 더 어려운 사람을 도와 주었으면 좋겠어요.
Doni itgeon eobsgeon deo eoryeoun sarameul dowa jueosseumyeon jokesseoyo.
Whether you have money or not, you should help those who need it.

Linking Sentences—Cause and Effect: The Big Three

There are three extremely common expressions that all essentially mean "so," and they are used in a few ways. The big three are ㄴ/는데, 아/어/여서 **n/neunde, a/eo/yeoseo**, and (으)니까 **(eu)nikka.** You'll see them used in three ways. One is in the middle of a sentence, one is at the end, and the other is roughly at the beginning tagging along with 그렇다 **geureota.** Let's start by talking about each expression and when to use it.

> **Speaking = Writing**
>
> A아/어/여서 B, A(이)라서 (i)raseo B   "A, so B"   ★★★★★

차가 막<u>혀서</u> 늦었어요. **Chaga makyeoseo neujeosseoyo.**
There was a lot of traffic, so I was late.

   This expression essentially means "so" and is extremely important. Not only is it used all the time, but it also forms the basis for many other expressions you'll want to learn.

HOW IT'S FORMED

아/어/여서 is an expression all on its own; (이)라서 is a combination of the indirect speech particle (이)라 and 아서.

HOW IT'S CONJUGATED

		All tenses
Action or descriptive verbs with 오 or 아	작다	작아서 jagaseo
Action or descriptive verbs with 어, 우, 으 or 이	먹다	먹어서 meogeoseo
하다	하다	해서 haeseo
Nouns ending in a vowel	남자	남자라서 namjaraseo
Nouns ending in a consonant	물	물이라서 muriraseo

TAKE NOTE

This can be used only in statements (no questions, suggestions, or commands). In other words, if your B clause is a question, suggestion or command, you should use a different expression. (으)니(까) is a good one; see page 67.

It's also used to replace 고 (see page 51) in expressions where 고 follows a verb that means "to come" or "to go" (오다, 가다, 들어오다, etc…) See the example below about shopping and Dongdaemun.

EXAMPLE SENTENCES

- 아/어/여서

    아침을 안 먹**어서** 지금 배고파요.
    Achimeul an meogeoseo jigeum baegopayo.
    I didn't eat breakfast, so I'm hungry.

    공부를 열심히 **해서** 시험에 100점을 받았어요.
    Gongbureul yeolsimhi haeseo siheome baekjeomeul badasseoyo.
    I studied hard, so I got 100 on the test.

    동대문에 가**서** 쇼핑을 할 거예요.
    Dongdaemune gaseo syopingeul hal geoyeyo.
    I'm going to Dongdaemun, so I can go shopping.

- (이)라서

    저는 외국인**이라서** 한국어를 잘 못 해요.
    Jeoneun oeguginiraseo hangukeoreul jal mot haeyo.
    I'm a foreigner, so I don't speak Korean well.

    오늘 생일**이라서** 케이크 먹을 거예요.
    Oneul saengiriraseo keikeu meogeul geoyeyo.
    Today's my birthday, so I'm going to eat cake.

    차가 람보르기니**라서** 아주 비싸요.
    Chaga Ramboreuginiraseo aju bissayo.
    The car is a Lamborghini, so it's very expensive.

A(으)니(까) (eu)ni(kka) B	"A, so B"	Speaking = Writing ★★★★★

차가 막혔**으니까** 늦었어요. Chaga makyeosseunikka neujeosseoyo.
Traffic was heavy, so I was late.

This is another common and versatile way to say "so."

HOW IT'S FORMED

You will see this expression written two ways: 니 and 니까. They mean exactly the same thing, but 니 is only used formally or in writing.

HOW IT'S CONJUGATED

		Past	Present	Future
Action verbs ending in a vowel	하다	했으니까 haesseunikka	하니까 hanikka	하니까 할 거니까 hal geonikka
Action verbs ending in a consonant	먹다	먹었으니까 meogeosseunikka	먹으니까 meogeunikka	먹으니까 먹을 거니까 meogeul geonikka
Descriptive verbs (adjectives) ending in a vowel	예쁘다	예뻤으니까 yeppeosseunikka	예쁘니까 yeppeunikka	예쁘니까 예쁠 거니까 yeppeul geonikka
Descriptive verbs (adjectives) ending in a consonant	작다	작았으니까 jagasseunikka	작으니까 jageunikka	작으니까 작을 거니까 jageul geonikka
Nouns ending in a vowel	남자	남자였으니까 namjayeosseunikka	남자이니까 namjainikka	남자이니까 남자일 거니까 namjail geonikka
Nouns ending in a consonant	물	물이었으니까 murieosseunikka	물이니까 mulinikka	물이니까 물 일거니까 mul ilgeonikka

TAKE NOTE

니(까) can be used in any kind of sentence and in any tense, though it isn't usually used when you're talking about yourself. If you feel narcissistic at the moment, you'd be better off using 어서.

Be aware that there is another expression, 니, which is used in 반말 at the end of questions: 점심을 먹었니? That's different. This 니 is in the middle of a sentence.

Also, 습니까 is not the same 니까 used here. 습니까 is the super-polite ending for a question (see page 15). That 니까 always goes after 습, while this one never does.

있다 and 없다 can be conjugated either as 있니(까) **inni(kka)** and 없니(까) **eobsni(kka)** or 있으니(까) **isseuni(kka)** and 없으니(까) **eobseuni(kka)**. Koreans do it both ways, so just use whichever you think sounds better.

EXAMPLE SENTENCES

어머니의 생신이**니까** 파티에 갈 수 없어요.
Eomeoniui saengsininikka patie gal su eobseoyo.
It's my mother's birthday, so I can't go to the party.

이 신발은 너무 작**으니까** 큰 것으로 바꿔 주세요.
I sinbareun neomu jageunikka keun geoseuro bakkwo juseyo.
These shoes are too small, so could you please change it to a bigger size?

> **Speaking > Writing**
> ★★★★★
>
> A(으)ㄴ/는데 (eu)n/neunde B   "A; B"

이 회의가 아주 중요**한데** 민수가 늦었어요.
I hoeuiga aju jungyohande Minsuga neujeosseoyo.
This meeting is very important, but Minsu was late.

(으)ㄴ/는데 functions much like an English semicolon. Clause A explains the background for clause B, which can be a statement, question, suggestion or command: this expression works with any kind of sentence. It can also be used to contrast two situations. It doesn't always mean "so," but it is often used that way and functions similarly to the expressions above, so I've put it in this section.

HOW IT'S CONJUGATED

ㄴ/은데 **n/eunde** is used after descriptive verbs and 는데 **neunde** after action verbs or past tense forms. If you want to use this expression after a noun, add 이 to the end of the noun and then conjugate it as if it were a descriptive verb.

		Past	Present	Future
Action verbs ending in a vowel	하다	했는데 haenneunde	하는데 haneunde	할 건데 hal geonde
Action verbs ending in a consonant	먹다	먹었는데 meogeonneunde	먹는데 meokneunde	먹을 건데 meogeul geonde
Descriptive verbs (adjectives) ending in a vowel	예쁘다	예뻤는데 yeppeonneunde	예쁜데 yeppeunde	예쁠 건데 yeppeul geonde
Descriptive verbs (adjectives) ending in a consonant	작다	작았는데 jaganneunde	작은데 jageunde	작을 건데 jageul geonde
Nouns ending in a vowel	남자	남자였는데 namjayeonneunde	남자인데 namjainde	남자일 건데 namjail geonde
Nouns ending in a consonant	물	물이었는데 murieonneunde	물인데 murinde	물일 건데 muril geonde

TAKE NOTE

There is another expression, (으)ㄴ/는 데, which is totally different and has to do with intentions. It's covered on page 170. You can tell it apart from (으)ㄴ/는데 by the space in the middle, but sometimes this space is omitted, so look for context.

EXAMPLE SENTENCES

어머니의 생신**인데** 무슨 선물이 좋을까요?
Eomeoniui saengsininde museun seonmuri joeulkkayo?
It's my mother's birthday; what kind of present would be good?

자고 있었**는데** 갑자기 전화가 왔어요.
Jago isseonneunde gapjagi jeonhwaga wasseoyo.
I was sleeping when the phone suddenly rang.

Ending sentences with 어서, and 니까 (and 거든!)   Speaking

These mean essentially the same thing when used at the end of a sentence. You can use them to explain the reason for an action. It's much like answering a question in English with "Because." They're more or less all interchangeable, but 서요 is quite uncommon while you'll hear the others all the time. 거든 is also usually used for commonplace situations about daily life, while the other two can be (but are not always) somewhat more formal.

거든 itself, in the middle of a sentence, has a slightly different meaning than 아/어/여 서 and 니까; see pages 66, 67 and 285. Here however, they are the same.

> A: 왜 비빔밥을 또 시켰어요? Wae bibimbapbeul tto sikyeosseoyo?
>   Why did you order bibimbap again?
>
> B: 맛있**으니까요**. Masisseunikkayo. Because it's delicious.

> A: 왜 비빔밥을 또 시켰어요? Why did you order bibimbap again?
>
> B: 맛있**거든요**. Masissgeodeunyo. Because it's delicious.

> A: 왜 비빔밥을 또 시켰어요? Why did you order bibimbap again?
>
> B: 맛있**어서요**. Masisseoseoyo. Because it's delicious.

새로운 코트를 샀어요. 요즘 날씨가 추워지**니까요**.
Saeloun koteureul sasseoyo. Yojeum nalssiga chuwojinikkayo.
I bought a new coat. It's because the weather is getting colder nowadays.

새로운 코트를 샀어요. 요즘 날씨가 추워지**거든요**.
Yojeum nalssiga chuwojigeodeunyo.
I bought a new coat. It's because the weather is getting colder nowadays.

새로운 코트를 샀어요. 요즘 날씨가 추워져**서요**.
Yojeum nalssiga chuwojyeoseoyo.
I bought a new coat. It's because the weather is getting colder nowadays.

오늘 피곤해요. 어젯밤에 일이 너무 많아서 별로 못 잤**으니까요**.
Oneul pigonhaeyo. Eojetbame iri neomu manaseo byeollo mot jasseunikkayo.
Today I'm tired. It's because last night I had too much work, so I hardly slept.

오늘 피곤해요. 어젯밤에 일이 너무 많아서 별로 못 잤**거든요**.
Oneul pigonhaeyo. Eojetbame iri neomu manaseo byeollo mot jatgeodeunyo.
Today I'm tired. It's because last night I had too much work, so I hardly slept.

Another important note about 거든: it has a second use which means "of course" and is used to explain something really obvious to people. When you use it in this way the intonation is different (and it's almost always in 반말). If you're using 거든 in the first way, to explain a reason, the intonation should go down at the end as if stating a fact. In the second way, it goes up and the emphasis tends to be on 거든 rather than on the rest of the sentence. It shouldn't be too hard to tell which 거든 Koreans are using: apart from the context, the intonation they use in the second is exactly how it sounds—someone who's been wrongly accused and is annoyed about it.

숙제를 했**거든**. Sukjereul haetgeodeun. Of course I did my homework!

아침을 먹었**거든**. Achimeul meogeotgeodeun. Of course I ate breakfast!

남자친구가 있**거든**. Namjachinguga itgeodeun. Of course I have a boyfriend!

Ending sentences with (으)ㄴ/는데요 (eu)n/neundeyo   **Speaking**

You can think of this ending as an ellipsis (…). It implies there's more to the story than what's just been said, as if you started a sentence that was going to have a second part, but then stopped before you got there. After (으)ㄴ/는데고 you can start a new sentence to explain yourself or if the second part of the story is mutually understood, just stop at 데요. I have heard (으)ㄴ/는데요 used as a more polite version of the second 거든 above.

Please also note that 는데, 는 데, and 는대 are all different. Isn't grammar fun?! I'll cover 는 데 on page 170 and 는대 along with the other indirect speech forms on page 304.

A: 소개팅 할래요? **Sogaeting hallaeyo?**
  Want to try 소개팅? (a kind of arranged dating)

B: 아니요. 나 남자친구 있**는데요**.
  Aniyo. Na namjachingu inneundeyo.
  No. I already have a boyfriend. (so I don't need another date)

A: 숙제 했어요? 보여 주세요. **Sukje haesseoyo? Boyeo juseyo.**
  Did you do your homework? Show me.

B: 숙제 했**는데요**… 집에 두고 왔어요.
  Sukje haenneundeyo…jibe dugo wasseoyo.
  I did it, but I left it at home.

A: 너, 오늘도 숙제 안 했지? **Neo, oneuldo sukje an haetji?**
  You, you also didn't do your homework today, right?

B: 오늘은 숙제 했**는데요**. **Oneuleun sukje haenneundeyo.**
  I did my homework today. (so why are you accusing me of not having done it?)

Starting sentences with 는데, 어서, and 니까 Speaking = Writing

You're in the middle of a lengthy explanation of the whys and hows of what happened. Naturally, sometimes you'll want to pause for breath (or to give your listeners a chance to catch their breath). So how can you do that while explaning things in Korean? 그렇다 **geureota** is here to help.

I'll discuss all the forms of 그렇다 further on page 377 along with other ways of putting an argument together, but let's put it in here also since it's used very commonly with the verb forms we're learning. In this section, we will finish one statement and then explain further with:

그래서	geuraeseo	and, so, then, thereupon
그러니까	geureonikka	so, therefore, for that reason
그런데	geureonde	now, by the way, but, and (depending on the context)

Let's see some examples.

아침을 안 먹었어요. **그래서** 배고파요.
Achimeul an meogeosseoyo. Geuraeseo baegopayo.
I didn't eat breakfast, so I'm hungry.

공부를 열심히 했어요. **그래서** 시험에 100점을 받았어요.
Gongbureul yeolsimhi haesseoyo. Geuraeseo siheome baekjeomeul badasseoyo.
I studied hard, so I got 100 on the test.

비가 오고 있어요. **그러니까** 우산을 가지고 오세요.
Biga ogo isseoyo. Geureonikka usaneul gajigo oseyo.
It's raining, so please bring an umbrella.

어머니 생신이에요. **그러니까** 파티에 갈 수 없어요.
Eomeoni saengsinieyo. Geureonikka patie gal su eobseoyo.
It's my mother's birthday, so I can't go to the party.

이 신발을 너무 작아요. **그러니까** 큰 것으로 바꾸어 주세요.
I sinbareul neomu jagayo. Geureonikka keun geoseuro bakkueo juseyo.
These shoes are too small, so could you change it to a bigger size?

친구가 많아요. **그런데** 슬퍼요. **Chinguga manayo. Geureonde seulpeoyo.**
I have many friends. But I'm sad.

피곤해요. **그런데** 파티에 가고 싶어요.
Pigonhaeyo. Geureonde patie gago sipeoyo.
I'm tired. But I want to go to the party.

그는 한국사람 이에요. **그런데** 한국음식을 못 먹어요.
Geuneun hanguksaram ieyo. Geureonde hangukeumsigeul mot meogeoyo.
He is a Korean. But he cannot eat Korean food.

Linking Sentences—Cause and Effect: More Ways to Say "So"

There are a couple of other useful expressions you can use to say that one thing resulted in another.

> **Speaking > Writing**
>
> A기에(는)/길래 gie(neun)/gillae B   "Since A, then B"   ★★★★

민수가 늦게 **오기에** 잠시 인터넷 하고 있어요.
Minsuga neutge ogie jamsi inteonet hago isseoyo.
Since Minsu is coming late, I'm using the internet for a while.

기에 and 길래 mean exactly the same thing, but 기에 is the written form of this expression and 길래 is the spoken or colloquial form. They mean "Since A, then B." A is a situation that you have observed. As a result of seeing and judging A, you have done, are doing, or are recommending B. You can also use this expression to ask the reason or background for a decision.

The second, similar meaning is a little more difficult to explain in English, but I think you can probably figure it out. It's pretty simple and is similar to 때문에 **ttaemune** ("because of"), which I'll cover on page 78.

When you add 는, the meaning of the expression changes a little. If you add the 는 for emphasis, your second clause should be something negative: something is B to A. If I were to translate "Too Legit to Quit" into Korean, it would be done using 기에는.

HOW IT'S CONJUGATED

		Past	Present	Future
Action verbs ending in a vowel	하다	했기에(는) haetgie(neun) 했길래 haetgillae	하기에(는) hagie(neun) 하길래 hagillae	하기에(는) 하길래
Action verbs ending in a consonant	먹다	먹었기에(는) meogeotgie(neun) 먹었길래 meogeotgillae	먹기에(는) meokgie(neun) 먹길래 meokgillae	먹기에(는) 먹길래
Descriptive verbs (adjectives) ending in a vowel	예쁘다	예뻤기에(는) yeppeotgie(neun) 예뻤길래 yeppeotgillae	예쁘기에(는) yeppeugie(neun) 예쁘길래 yeppeugillae	예쁘기에(는) 예쁘길래
Descriptive verbs (adjectives) ending in a consonant	작다	작았기에(는) jagatgie(neun) 작았길래 jagatgillae	작기에(는) jaggie(neun) 작길래 jaggillae	작기에(는) 작길래

		Past	Present	Future
Nouns ending in a vowel	남자	남자이었기에(는) namjaieotgie(neun) 남자이었길래 namjaieotgillae	남자기에(는) namjagie(neun) 남자길래 namjagillae	남자기에(는) 남자길래
Nouns ending in a consonant	물	물이었기에(는) murieotgie(neun) 물이었길래 murieotgillae	물이기에(는) murigie(neun) 물이길래 murigillae	물이기에(는) 물이길래

TAKE NOTE

기에 and 길래 can be used only with statements—not commands, questions, or suggestions. The subject of the first clause shouldn't be the speaker, and the subjects of both clauses should be different. Also, with 기에 and 길래 (but not 기에는), the first clause must be some new knowledge that was discovered by the speaker.

EXAMPLE SENTENCES

차가 많이 막히**길래**, 늦게 출발했어요.
Chaga mani makigillae, neutge chulbalhaesseoyo.

차가 많이 막히**기에**, 늦게 출발했어요.
Chaga mani makigie, neutge chulbalhaesseoyo.

Since traffic was heavy, I left late.

맛있**길래** 다시 시켰어요.　Masitgillae dasi sikyeosseoyo.

맛있**기에** 다시 시켰어요.　Masitgie dasi sikyeosseoyo.

Since it was delicious, I ordered it again.

청바지가 싸**길래** 샀어요.　Cheongbajiga ssagillae sasseoyo.

청바지가 싸**기에** 샀어요.　Cheongbajiga ssagie sasseoyo.

Since the jeans were cheap, I bought them.

Here are some examples with 기에는. Note that the B clause is always a negative thing.

이 책을 학생이 읽**기에는** 너무 어려워요.
I chaegeul haksaengi ilkgieneun neomu eoryeowoyo.
This book is too difficult for students to read.

라지 피자를 혼자 먹**기에는** 너무 많아요.
Lagi pijareul honja meokgieneun neomu manayo.
A large pizza is too much to eat alone.

그 차를 공무원이 사**기에는** 너무 비싸요.
Geu chareul gongmuwoni sagieneun neomu bissayo.
That car is too expensive for a public servant to buy.

		Speaking = Writing
A느라(고) neula(go) **B**	**"B, because of A" or "B, in order to A"**	★★★

열쇠를 찾<u>느라고</u> 집에서 늦게 출발했어요.
Yeolsoereul chatneulago jibeseo neutge chulbalhaesseoyo.
I left the house late because I was looking for my keys.

Be careful about using 느라고 **neurago** because there are rules about where and when it can be used. It is the prima donna of the Korean grammar world, and is extraordinarily picky about where it can be used properly. That said, if you learn how to use it, you can legitimately feel really cool and smart.

You can also use this expression to mean "in order to." In this case, you did clause B on purpose in order to bring about clause A. In this case B doesn't have to be negative (although it often is).

HOW IT'S FORMED

This expression is normally written and said as 느라고, but 느라 **neura** is also possible.

HOW IT'S CONJUGATED

		All tenses
Action verbs ending in a vowel	하다	하느라고 **haneurago**
Action verbs ending in a consonant	먹다	먹느라고 **meokneurago**

TAKE NOTE

This is somewhat tricky because it can be used only under very specific conditions. First of all, just like 고, the subjects of clause A and clause B must be identical. The first clause needs to end in an action verb: something is being done or has been done. It must be an action— not a condition like catching a cold, even though most of the time that 걸리다 **geollida** is considered to be an action verb—and it must have been done by an agent, not an inanimate object. That something takes or took a long time. As a result of this lengthy action in clause A, clause B unfortunately happened or became impossible. Clause A is stated in the present, not the past, and clause B must be something that has already happened or is happening now: this sentence structure can't be used to predict the future, however certain you may be about it.

To sum up:

A: An action, not a condition, done by an agent, taking place over a long time.
B: Same subject as A, something bad, not in the future.

Here are some examples:

EXAMPLE SENTENCES

■ "B because of A"

컴퓨터 게임을 하<u>느라고</u> 늦게 잤어요.
Keompyuteo geimeul haneurago neutge jasseoyo.
I didn't get to sleep until late because I was playing a computer game.

그 일을 하<u>느라고</u> 바빴어요. Geu ireul haneurago bappasseoyo.
I was busy because I was doing that work.

■ "B in order to A"

고향에 갔다 오<u>느라고</u> 돈을 많이 썼어요.
Gohyange gatda oneurago doneul mani sseosseoyo.
I spent a lot of money in order to visit my home.

부산에 가<u>느라고</u> 숙제를 안 했어요. Busane ganeurago sukjereul an haesseoyo.
I didn't do my homework because I went to Busan.

친구를 만나<u>느라고</u> 천안까지 갔어요.
Chingureul mannaneurago Cheonankkaji gasseoyo.
I went to Cheonan in order to meet my friend.

		Speaking < Writing
A(으)니만큼 (eu)nimankeum B	"B, since A"	★

늦었<u>으니만큼</u> 제값을 다 안 내도 돼요.
Neujeosseunimankeum jegabseul da an naedo dwaeyo.
Since you were late, you don't have to pay the full price.

This would translate easily as "inasmuch as" in formal English.

HOW IT'S FORMED

This is a combination of (으)니(까) ("so"; see page 67) and 만큼 ("as much as"; see page 126).

HOW IT'S CONJUGATED

		Past	Present	Future
Action verbs ending in a vowel	하다	했으니만큼 haesseunimankeum	하니만큼 hanimankeum	하겠으니만큼 hagesseunimankeum
Action verbs ending in a consonant	먹다	먹었으니만큼 meogeosseunimankeum	먹으니만큼 meogeunimankeum	먹겠으니만큼 yeppeugesseunimankeum

		Past	Present	Future
Descriptive verbs (adjectives) ending in a vowel	예쁘다	예뻤으니만큼 yeppeosseunimankeum	예쁘니만큼 yeppeunimankeum	예쁘겠으니만큼 yeppeugesseunimankeum
Descriptive verbs (adjectives) ending in a consonant	작다	작았으니만큼 jagasseunimankeum	작으니만큼 jageunimankeum	작겠으니만큼 jakgesseunimankeum
Nouns ending in a vowel	남자	남자였으니만큼 namjayeosseunimankeum	남자이니만큼 namjainimankeum	남자이겠으니만큼 namjaigesseunimankeum
Nouns ending in a consonant	물	물이었으니만큼 murieosseunimankeum	물이니만큼 murinimankeum	물이겠으니만큼 murigesseunimankeum

TAKE NOTE

만큼 all by itself is used for comparisons: it means "as much as"; (으)니만큼 isn't really the same expression.

The subject of the sentence normally isn't the speaker.

EXAMPLE SENTENCES

공부를 열심히 했으**니만큼** 시험을 잘 볼 거예요.
Gongbureul yeolsimhi haesseunimankeum siheomeul jal bol geoyeyo.
Since you studied hard, I'm sure you'll do well on the test.

오늘 휴일이**니만큼** 일 하지 마세요. Oneul hyuirinimankeum il haji maseyo.
Since today's a holiday, please don't work.

날씨가 추우**니만큼** 등산 가지 말아요.
Nalssiga chuunimankeum deungsan gaji marayo.
Since it's cold, let's not go hiking.

Linking Sentences–Cause and Effect: Through, Because Of, For the Sake Of

There are actually thirteen different grammar forms to cover here, and that's not even including 기에 which you can review on page 73 if you'd like. One of its uses also fits here, but because it's not too difficult and also fits in the previous section, there's no need to go over it again. The nice thing about all of these patterns is that you can use them any time—in the past, present or future—to talk about anyone or anything. There aren't many special rules about usage.

A(기) 때문에 (gi) ttaemune B   "B because of A"   **Speaking < Writing**
                                                            ★★★★★

교통 체증 **때문에** 늦게 왔어요. Gyotong chejeung ttaemune neutge wasseoyo.
I was late because of traffic.

This is probably the most common of all these patterns. It goes after a noun (or a verb, if you put 기 at the end of the verb) and means "Because of A, B." It can, but often doesn't, have negative connotations.

HOW IT'S CONJUGATED

		Past	Present	Future
Action verbs ending in a vowel	하다	했기 때문에 haetgi ttaemune	하기 때문에 hagi ttaemune	하기 때문에
Action verbs ending in a consonant	먹다	먹었기 때문에 meogeotgi ttaemune	먹기 때문에 meokgi ttaemune	먹기 때문에
Descriptive verbs (adjectives) ending in a vowel	예쁘다	예뻤기 때문에 yeppeotgi ttaemune	예쁘기 때문에 yeppeugi ttaemune	예쁘기 때문에
Descriptive verbs (adjectives) ending in a consonant	작다	작았기 때문에 jagatgi ttaemune	작기 때문에 jakgi ttaemune	작기 때문에
Nouns ending in a vowel	남자	남자 때문에 namja ttaemune	남자 때문에	남자 때문에
Nouns ending in a consonant	물	물 때문에 mul ttaemune	물 때문에	물 때문에

TAKE NOTE

A remark about the nouns above: 남자 때문에 means "because of the man," while "남자 이기 때문에" means "because he is a man." See the second example below.

If you're blaming someone, 때문에 is a good expression to use, but 는 바람에, 는 통에, **neun barame, neun tong e,** or (으)ㄴ/는 탓에 **(eu) n/neun tase** (see page 79) are even more negative. If you want to say that something good happened because of something else, you should use (으)ㄴ/는 덕분에 **(eu)n/neun deokbune** (see page 80).

EXAMPLE SENTENCES

담배 **때문에** 건강이 나빠졌어요. Dambae ttaemune geongangi nappajyeosseoyo.
My health has worsened because of cigarettes.

그는 장애인이**기 때문에** 잘 못 걸어요.
Geuneun jangaeinigi ttaemune jal mot georeoyo.
He can't walk well because he's handicapped.

(If I'd just said 장애인 때문에 **jangaein ttaemune**, it would mean "because of the handicapped person.")

A 는 바람에 neun barame B   **Speaking > Writing**
A 는 통에 neun tonge B   "B is A's fault"   ★ ★ ★
A (으) ㄴ / 는 탓에 (eu)n/neun tase B

차가 막히는 **통에** 늦게 왔어요.   Because of traffic, I was late.
Chaga makineun tonge neutge wasseoyo.

차가 막히는 **바람에** 늦게 왔어요.   Because of traffic, I was late.
Chaga makineun barame neutge wasseoyo.

차가 막히는 **탓에** 늦게 왔어요.   Because of traffic, I was late.
Chaga makineun tase neutge wasseoyo.

Again, "because of A, B," but these expressions can be used only when B is a negative result of A.

HOW IT'S FORMED

탓 **tat** literally means "fault" or "blame," while 통 **tong** just means "through."

HOW IT'S CONJUGATED

		Past	Present	Future
Action verbs ending in a vowel	하다	하는 바람에 haneun barame 하는 통에 haneun tonge 한 탓에 han tase	하는 바람에 하는 통에 하는 탓에 haneun tase	하는 바람에 하는 통에 하는 탓에
Action verbs ending in a consonant	먹다	먹는 바람에 meokneun barame 먹는 통에 meokneun tonge 먹은 탓에 meokeun tase	먹는 바람에 먹는 통에 먹는 탓에	먹는 바람에 먹는 통에 먹는 탓에
Descriptive verbs (adjectives) ending in a vowel	예쁘다	예뻤던 탓에 yeppeotdeon tase	예쁜 탓에 yeppeun tase	예쁜 탓에
Descriptive verbs (adjectives) ending in a consonant	작다	작었던 탓에 jageotdeon tase	작은 탓에 jageun tase	작은 탓에
Nouns ending in a vowel	남자	남자였던 탓에 namjayeotdeon tase	남자인 탓에 namjain tase	남자인 탓에
Nouns ending in a consonant	물	물이었던 탓에 murieotdeon tase	물인 탓에 murin tase	물인 탓에

TAKE NOTE

None of these expressions can be used with questions, suggestions, or commands; they all describe events that took place in the past, so you can use them only with statements that refer to something that's done. Only 탓에 can be used with descriptive verbs or nouns; the other two are for actions only.

There are some small differences among the three. 바람에 **barame** is used when the reason was unexpected and can be used for positive but unexpected results. 통에 **tonge** is used only when the event was something chaotic and drawn-out such as a war or a disaster.

Please be aware that 바람 by itself is a noun that means "wind"; I don't know if that has anything to do with the origin of this expression or not, but the 바람 in this sentence isn't "wind" and "wind" by itself isn't necessarily the kind of thing that warrants the use of 바람에. There's also 바랍니다 **barapnida**, which you will hear all the time on the subway and which is a form of 바라다 **barada** that means "to want." These are not what we're looking at here.

EXAMPLE SENTENCES

전쟁 **통에** 그녀가 고아가 되었어요.
Jeonjaeng tonge geunyeoga goaga doeeosseoyo.
Because of the war, she became an orphan.

너무 많이 걸은 **통에** 다리가 아파요. Neomu mani georeun tonge dariga apayo.
Because I walked too much, my leg hurts.

사고가 나는 **바람에** 그녀가 고아가 되었어요.
Aagoga naneun barame geunyeoga goaga doeeosseoyo.
Because of an accident, she was orphaned.

다리를 다치는 **바람에** 못 걸어요. Darireul dachineun barame mot georeoyo.
Because I hurt my leg, I can't walk.

전쟁 **탓에** 그녀가 고아가 되었어요.
Jeonjaeng tase geunyeoga goaga doeeosseoyo.
Because of the war, she became an orphan.

너무 많이 걸은 **탓에** 다리가 아파요. Neomu mani georeun tase dariga apayo.
Because I walked too much, my leg hurts.

Notice that I had to change my examples for 바람에 because the causes in the original examples were not unexpected, so I couldn't use 바람에 with them.

		Speaking = Writing
A(으)ㄴ/는 덕분에 (eu)n/neun deokbune B	"B, thanks to A"	★★★★

택시를 **탄 덕분에** 늦지 않았어요. Taeksireul tan deokbune neutji anasseoyo.
Because I took a taxi, I wasn't late.

Do you like Thanksgiving? Who doesn't? Unfortunately, I don't have any turkey for you, but I can show you how to give thanks in Korean. This expression means "Thanks to A, B." It's used only when A was a good thing with a positive result, B.

HOW IT'S CONJUGATED

		Past	Present
Action verbs ending in a vowel	하다	한 덕분에 han deokbune	하는 덕분에 haneun deokbune
Action verbs ending in a consonant	먹다	먹은 덕분에 meogeun deokbune	먹는 덕분에 meogneun deokbune
Nouns ending in a vowel	남자	남자 덕분에 namja deokbune	남자 덕분에
Nouns ending in a consonant	물	물 덕분에 mul deokbune	물 덕분에

TAKE NOTE

This is used only when you're thankful for something, so don't use it with negative expressions. Unless, of course, you enjoy misery.

EXAMPLE SENTENCES

열심히 일**한 덕분에** 성공하게 되었어요.
Yeolsimhi ilhan deokbune seonggonghage doeeosseoyo.
Thanks to your hard work, it was a success.

민수 **덕분에** 그 일을 일찍 끝냈어요. **Minsu deokbune geu ileul iljjik kkeutnaesseoyo.**
Thanks to Minsu, we finished the work early.

명절 **덕분에** 마침내 쉴 수 있어요.
Myeongjeol deokbune machimnae swil su isseoyo.
Thanks to the holiday, I can finally rest.

		Writing > Speaking
A에 의하여/의해(서) e uihayeo/uihae(seo) B	"B by A"	★★★

교사의 요청**에 의해서** 일찍 왔어요. **Gyosaui yocheonge uihaeseo iljjik wasseoyo.**
I came early by the teacher's request.

This expression can be used in a couple of different situations; one would be said as "by" in English (as in the example above) and the other is more like "according to." It means that something happened because of/in accordance with something else. This is useful if you want to say that something was done in accordance with a certain law or regulation or that something was decided by someone/something.

HOW IT'S FORMED

에 (ending preposition) plus 의하다 (roughly meaning "based on") plus (optionally) 여서.

HOW IT'S CONJUGATED

		All tenses
Nouns ending in a vowel	남자	남자에 의해(서) namjae uihae(seo)
Nouns ending in a consonant	물	물에 의해(서) mule uihae(seo)

TAKE NOTE

에 의하여 is exactly the same expression as 에 의해, but is more formal (as 하여 **hayeo** is normally used in more formal situations than 해 **hae**). 에 의해서 means exactly the same thing and can be used interchangeably with 에 의하여 or 에 의해. Despite the resemblance, this expression is not interchangeable with 에 의하면 **e uihamyeon**.

EXAMPLE SENTENCES

투표**에 의하여** 대통령이 재선되었어요.
Tupyoe uihayeo daetongryeongi jaeseondoe-eoss-eoyo.
The president was reelected by ballot.

필요**에 의해** 결정되었어요. **Pilyoe uihae gyeoljeongdoe-eoss-eoyo.**
The decision was made according to need.

습관**에 의해서** 그렇게 했어요. **Seupgwane uihaeseo geureoke haesseoyo.**
I did it from force of habit.

A(으)로써 (eu)rosseo B   "Through A, we can B"   **Speaking = Writing**
★ ★ ★

이**로써** 주문이 완료 됐어요. **Irosseo jumuni wallyo dwaesseoyo.**
With this, the order is complete.

This pattern means that A is a means to achieve B. It's the type of expression that would work really well on propaganda posters, although it's by no means limited to that kind of use; you can use it to talk about relieving stress (through whatever means you use) or about coercing someone into doing what you want. Also, there are a few common expressions which you can see in the "Take note" section below.

HOW IT'S CONJUGATED

		All tenses
Action verbs ending in a vowel	하다	함으로써 hameurosseo
Action verbs ending in a consonant	먹다	먹음으로써 meogeumeurosseo
Descriptive verbs (adjectives) ending in a vowel	예쁘다	예쁨으로서 yeppeumeuroseo
Descriptive verbs (adjectives) ending in a consonant	작다	작음으로써 jageumeurosseo

		All tenses
Nouns ending in a vowel	남자	남자로써 namjarosseo
Nouns ending in a consonant	힘 him*	힘으로써 himeurosseo

* Be aware that I changed my example for nouns ending in a consonant; this is because 물 and 로써 start with the same letter and so become 물로써. 힘 (strength) is a more accurate example of how 으로써 is normally used.

TAKE NOTE

Don't confuse (으)로서 (eu)roseo and (으)로써 (eu)rosseo. While they have a few things in common, ~(으)로서 means "as ~" rather than "through ~."

Here are some commonly used expressions that feature (으)로써···

이로써	irosseo	Through this/like this
예로써	yerosseo	By way of example (followed by the example)
사실로써	sasillosseo	Truthfully/with facts
권력으로써	gwollyeogeurosseo	Through power
노력으로써	noryeoguerosseo	Through effort

All are followed by what happened through or because of them, as you can see in the examples below.

EXAMPLE SENTENCES

한 예**로써** 작년에는 쌀값이 50%로 올랐어요.
Han yerosseo jagnyeoneneun ssalgabsi osippeosenteulo ollasseoyo.
For example, last year the price of rice rose by 50%.

노력**으로써** 어떤 일도 할 수 있어요. Noryeogeurosseo eotteon ildo hal su isseoyo.
Through effort, we can do anything.

운동을 **함으로써** 20킬로를 뺄 수 있었어요.
Undongeul hameurosseo ishipkilloreul ppael su isseosseoyo.
Through exercise I could lose 20 kilos.

A을/를 통해(서) eul/ leul tonghae(seo) B	"B through A"	Speaking = Writing ★★★

인터넷**을 통해서** 그 사실을 알았어요.
Inteoneseul tonghaeseo geu sasireul arasseoyo.
I learned it through the Internet.

This is just another way to say "through" a person or a thing. You can use it if you want to explain how you know something, how you learned something, how you decided on something, etc.

HOW IT'S FORMED

을/를 are the object marker endings and 통하다 is a verb which means "to go through." 서, from 여서 that means "so," is optional.

HOW IT'S CONJUGATED

		All tenses
Nouns ending in a vowel	남자	남자를 통해(서) namjareul tonghae(seo)
Nouns ending in a consonant	물	물을 통해(서) mureul tonghae(seo)

TAKE NOTE

는 통에 **neun tonge** is a different expression that means "because of" in negative situations—don't get it confused with the 을/를 통해 that we are studying here.

The expression is also used more literally in sentences like:

운하**를 통해서** 한강으로 갈 수 있어요.
Unhareul tonghaeseo Hangangeuro gal su isseoyo.
You can go to the Han River through the canal.

EXAMPLE SENTENCES

누구**를 통해** 그 사실을 아셨어요? **Nugureul tonghae geu sasireul asyeosseoyo?**
From whom did you find out that information?

민수**를 통해서** 그 사실을 알았어요. **Minsureul tonghaeseo geu sasireul arasseoyo.**
I learned it from Minsu.

	Speaking < Writing
A(으)로 인해 (eu)ro inhae B "B because of A"	★★

This means that B was caused by A.

HOW IT'S FORMED

It comes from the verb "인하다 **inhada**," which literally means "to be caused by" or "to arise from." The 로 part is our good friend which means "through" (see page 30).

HOW IT'S CONJUGATED

		All tenses
Nouns ending in a vowel	남자	남자로 인해 namjaro inhae
Nouns ending in a consonant	밥	밥으로 인해 babeuro inhae

EXAMPLE SENTENCES

교통 체증으로 인해 늦게 왔어요. **Gyotong chejeungeuro inhae neutge wasseoyo.**
I was late because of traffic.

담배로 인해 건강이 나빠졌어요. **Dambaero inhae geongangi nappajyeosseoyo.**
My health has worsened because of cigarettes.

그는 장애로 인해 잘 못 걸어요. **Geuneun jangaero inhae jal mot georeoyo.**
He can't walk well because he's handicapped.

	Speaking = Writing
A(으)ㄴ/는 까닭에 (eu)n/neun kkadalge B	"B because of A" ★★

차가 막힌 까닭에 늦었어요. **Chaga makhin kkadalge neujeosseoyo.**
He was late because traffic was heavy.

까닭 means reason, so this is another way to say that A is the reason for B: "Since A, then B." You can also use 까닭 by itself as a noun or with 으로 to give or ask a reason for something.

HOW IT'S CONJUGATED

		Past	Present
Action verbs ending in a vowel	하다	한 까닭에 han kkadalge	하는 까닭에 haneun kkadalge
Action verbs ending in a consonant	먹다	먹은 까닭에 meogeun kkadalge	먹는 까닭에 meokneun kkadalge
Descriptive verbs (adjectives) ending in a vowel	예쁘다	예쁜 까닭에 yeppeun kkadalge	예쁜 까닭에
Descriptive verbs (adjectives) ending in a consonant	작다	작은 까닭에 jageun kkadalge	작은 까닭에

TAKE NOTE

까닭 doesn't have any kind of emotion attached to it: it can be used with either positive or negative sentences. When it's used positively, you can use (으)ㄴ/는 덕분에 (see page 80). If it's used negatively, you can use the 바람에, 통에, or 탓에 expressions (see page 79). 기

때문에 (see page 78) is interchangeable with (으)ㄴ/는 까닭에, but much more common and can also be used with nouns.

까닭 is normally used to answer a question. For instance, in the soccer example below, your conversation partner might have asked, "왜 그렇게 기뻐요? **Wae geureoke gippeoyo?**" ("Why are you so happy?") Then you could answer using 까닭에. If the question isn't asked, pick a different expression: 때문에, 덕분에, 바람에, 탓에, or 통에 (see above).

EXAMPLE SENTENCES

Here are some examples of 까닭 used by itself to mean "reason."

무슨 **까닭**으로 왔어요? Museun kkadalgeuro wasseoyo?
For what reason (why) did you come here?

까닭 없이 왔어요. Kkadak eobsi wasseoyo. I just came for no reason.

And here it is as a linking expression.

우리 축구 팀이 이**긴 까닭에** 기뻤어요.
Uri chukgu timi igin kkadalge gippeosseoyo.
Since our soccer team won, we were very happy.

라면만 먹**은 까닭에** 건강이 나빠졌어요.
Ramyeonman meogeun kkadalge geongangi nappajyeosseoyo.
Since I ate only ramen, my health became worse.

맥주를 좋아하**는 까닭에** 맥주를 직접 만들어요.
Maekjureul johahaneun kkadalge maekjureul jikjeob mandeureoyo.
Because I like beer, I make it myself.

		Speaking > Writing
A([으]ㄴ 셈)**치고는** B ([eu]n sem)chigoneun B	"He's very B for an A"	★★

너는 스톰트루퍼**치고는** 좀 키가 작지 않은가요?
Neoneun seutomteurupeochigoneun jom kiga jakji aneungayo?
Aren't you a little short for a stormtrooper?

This pattern is used to talk about things that aren't normal for what they are such as sentences like "Aren't you a little short for a stormtrooper?" or "He's very mature for his age." It can also be used to say that all cases of a certain noun are the same: for example, "What Korean doesn't eat kimchi?"

HOW IT'S FORMED

셈 means "conjecture" and 치다 is its associated verb; together, they mean "to make a guess."

HOW IT'S CONJUGATED

Verbs take 셈치고는 preceded by the appropriate tense marker. Nouns just take 치고는.

		Past	Present	Future
Action verbs ending in a vowel	하다	한 셈치고는 han semchigoneun	하는 셈치고는 haneun semchigoneun	할 셈치고는 hal semchigoneun
Action verbs ending in a consonant	먹다	먹은 셈치고는 meogeun semchigoneun	먹는 셈치고는 meokneun semchigoneun	먹을 셈치고는 meogeul semchigoneun
Descriptive verbs (adjectives) ending in a vowel	예쁘다	예쁜 셈치고는 yeppeun semchigoneun	예쁜 셈치고는	예쁜 셈치고는
Descriptive verbs (adjectives) ending in a consonant	작다	작은 셈치고는 jageun semchigoneun	작은 셈치고는	작은 셈치고는
Nouns ending in a vowel	남자	남자치고는 namjachigoneun	남자치고(는)	남자치고(는)
Nouns ending in a consonant	물	물치고는 mulchigoneun	물치고(는)	물치고(는)

TAKE NOTE

A셈치고 B looks somewhat similar, but it isn't the same as 셈치고는; see page 292.

If 는 isn't enough for you and you really want to emphasize the oddness of what you're saying, you can use a double negative. See the last example below.

B has to be something you wouldn't expect from A such as a child is more mature than expected, a stormtrooper is short, or a Korean doesn't eat kimchi.

EXAMPLE SENTENCES

그는 아이**치고는** 아주 어른스러워요.
Geuneun aichigoneun aju eoreunseureowoyo.
He's very mature for a child.

한국 사람**치고는** 김치 안 먹는 사람이 없어요.
Hanguk saramchigoneun gimchi an meokneun sarami eobseoyo.
What Korean doesn't eat kimchi?

그 아이가 작은 **셈치고는** 농구를 잘 해요.
Geu aiga jageun semchigoneun nonggureul jal haeyo.
For a child so small, he plays basketball well.

공부를 그렇게 열심히 **한 셈치고는** 시험을 잘 못 봤어요.
Gongbureul geureoke yeolsimhi han semchigoneun siheomeul jal mot bwasseoyo.
He didn't do well on the test considering how hard he studied.

~에-달려 있다 e dallyeo itda   "depends on ~"

Speaking = Writing
★★

정시에 오는 것은 교통 상황에 달려 있어요.
Jeongsie oneun geoseun gyotong sanghwange dallyeo isseoyo.
Getting there on time depends on the traffic situation.

This expression is useful when things aren' t as straightforward and when you need to explain that something depends on something else. It can also mean "because of" when ~ was the main cause, the thing on which the first part of your sentence was dependent.

HOW IT'S FORMED

달리다 **dallida** means "to be hung" and is combined here with 어 있다 **eo itda** (to remain in a certain state), so this expression literally means that something has "been hung" on ~.

HOW IT'S CONJUGATED

		Past	Present	Future
Action verbs ending in a vowel	하다	한 것에 달려 있다 **han geose dallyeo itda** 하기에 달려 있다 **hagie dallyeo itda**	하는 것에 달려 있다 **haneun geose dallyeo itda** 하기에 달려 있다	할 것에 달려 있다 **hal geose dallyeo itda** 하기에 달려 있다
Action verbs ending in a consonant	먹다	먹은 것에 달려 있다 **meogeun geose dallyeo itda** 먹기에 달려 있다 **meokgie dallyeo itda**	먹는 것에 달려 있다 **meokneun geose dallyeo itda** 먹기에 달려 있다	먹을 것에 달려 있다 **meogeul geose dallyeo itda** 먹기에 달려 있다
Descriptive verbs (adjectives) ending in a vowel	예쁘다	예쁜 것에 달려 있다 **yeppeun geose dallyeo itda**	예쁜 것에 달려 있다	예쁜 것에 달려 있다
Descriptive verbs (adjectives) ending in a consonant	작다	작은 것에 달려 있다 **jageun geose dallyeo itda**	작은 것에 달려 있다	작은 것에 달려 있다
Nouns ending in a vowel	남자	남자에 달려 있다 **namjae dallyeo itda**	남자에 달려 있다	남자에 달려 있다
Nouns ending in a consonant	교육	교육에 달려 있다 **gyoyuge dallyeo itda**	교육에 달려 있다	교육에 달려 있다

TAKE NOTE

When following a question word (누구, 무엇, 어디, **nugu, mueos, eodi,** etc.), you should use the form (느)냐에 달려 있다. **(neu) nyae dallyeo itda.** (ㄴ)냐 is covered on page 304.

EXAMPLE SENTENCES

행복은 자기 자신이 어떻게 생각하느냐**에 달려 있어요**.
Haengbogeun jagi jasini eotteoke saenggakhaneunyae dallyeo isseoyo.
Happiness depends on how one thinks about oneself.

그 체인점의 인기가 음식이 싼 것**에 달려 있어요**.
Geu cheinjeomui ingiga eumsigi ssan geose dallyeo isseoyo.
That chain is popular because of its cheap food.

아인슈타인의 발견은 그의 지능**에 달려 있었어요**.
Ainsyutainui balgyeoneun geuui jineunge dallyeo isseosseoyo.
Einstein's discoveries were because of his intelligence.

	Speaking = Writing
A기로(는) giro(neun) B "When it comes to A…"	★

지각을 하**기로는** 민수가 최고이죠. **Jigageul hagironeun Minsuga choegoijyo.**
When it comes to being late, Minsu is later than anyone (Minsu is the best at being late).

This is a great way to give a compliment, whether straightforward or backhanded. It's used to talk about someone or something being the best or worst at something.

HOW IT'S FORMED

This is simply the 기 that you use to turn a verb into a noun, followed by the 로 which means "through." 는 is optional and can be added for emphasis.

HOW IT'S CONJUGATED

		All tenses
Action verbs ending in a vowel	하다	하기로(는) hagiro(neun)
Action verbs ending in a consonant	먹다	먹기로(는) meokgilo(neun)
Descriptive verbs (adjectives) ending in a vowel	예쁘다	예쁘기로(는) yeppeugiro(neun)
Descriptive verbs (adjectives) ending in a consonant	작다	작기로(는) jaggiro(neun)

TAKE NOTE

B should include a sentence indicating superiority. Here are a few examples:

최고이지요, 최고 아닐까요?, 최고예요
choegoijiyo, choego anilkkayo?, choegoyeyo

따를 _____ 없어요, 없죠 **ttaleul _____ eobseoyo, eobsjyo**

제일이에요, 제일이죠 **jeilieyo, jeilijyo**

기로 하다 **giro hada** is a different expression used to express determination; see page 225. There the 기로 is always followed by 하다 while here it will always be followed by a sentence explaining who or what is the best.

EXAMPLE SENTENCES

술을 마시**기로는** 제 아버지가 제일이에요.
Sureul masigironeun je abeojiga jeirieyo.
When it comes to drinking alcohol, my father can handle more than anyone (my father is the best at handling alcohol).

예쁘**기로는** 가영을 따를 사람이 없어요.
Yeppeugironeun Kayoungeul ttareul sarami eobseoyo.
When it comes to beauty, no one is more beautiful than Kayoung.

Cause and Effect: Origins

		Speaking < Writing
A이/가 i/ga B에서 비롯되다 eseo bilosdoeda A이/가 B에 뿌리(를) 두다 ye ppuli(reul) duda	"A came from B"	★

우리 숫자는 원래 아라비아**에서 비롯됐어요**.
Uri sutjaneun wonlae arabiaeseo birotdwaesseoyo.
우리 숫자는 원래 아라비아**에 뿌리를 두고 있어요**.
Uri sutjaneun wonlae arabiae ppurireul dugo isseoyo.
Our numerals originally came from Arabia.

Which came first: the chicken or the egg? That question may never be answered, but at least after reading this section you'll know how to discuss it along with where other things came from. These expressions are used used to say that A started from or came from B.

HOW IT'S FORMED

비롯되다 **birotdoeda** literally means "to originate from" and you ought to know 에서 by now. That's all there is to this one.

뿌리 **ppuri** means roots, like those of a tree. 두다 **duda** is a verb which means "to keep" and can be used to help many other verbs get their meanings across (see page 31). As for 에 well, you know 에, and if you don't, please refer back to the section on "Basic Particles" on page 30. Put it all together and you get "A has its roots in B."

HOW IT'S CONJUGATED

		Past	Present	Future
Nouns ending in a vowel	경제	경제에서 비롯됐다 gyeongje-e-seo birotdwaetda 경제에 뿌리를 두었다 gyeongje-e ppurireul dueotda	경제에서 비롯되다 gyeongje-e-seo birot deoda 경제에 뿌리를 두다 gyeongje-e ppurireul duda	경제에서 비롯되다 경제에 뿌리를 두다
Nouns ending in a consonant	교육	교육에서 비롯됐다 gyoyugeseo birotdwaetda 교육에 뿌리를 두었다 gyoyuge ppurireul dueotda	교육에서 비롯되다 gyoyugeseo birot doeda 교육에 뿌리를 두다 gyoyuge ppurireul duda	교육에서 비롯되다 교육에 뿌리를 두다

TAKE NOTE

뿌리를 두다 ppurireul duda should always be conjugated in the present progressive: for example, 뿌리를 두고 있어요 ppurireul dugo isseoyo.

EXAMPLE SENTENCES

아이의 행동은 부모의 행동**에서 비롯돼요**.
Aiui haengdongeun bumoui haengdongeseo birotdwaeyo.

아이의 행동은 부모의 행동**에 뿌리를 두고 있어요**.
Aiui haengdongeun bumoui haengdonge ppurireul dugo isseoyo.

A child's behavior originates from its parents' behavior.

그 전쟁은 욕심**에서 비롯되었어요**.
Geu jeonjaengeun yoksimeseo birotdoe-eoss-eoyo.

그 전쟁은 욕심**에 뿌리를 두고 있었어요**.
Geu jeonjaengeun yoksime ppurireul dugo isseosseoyo.

The war arose out of greed.

Cause and Effect, or Lack Thereof

Here's one for your nihilists out there. This section will teach you how to say that something is futile or had no effect. Another expression that's similar to the two below is A거나 말거나 B, which is covered in the section on 거나 on page 61.

Speaking = Writing

A(으)나 마나 (eu)na mana B   "Whether or not you A, B will happen"   ★★

택시를 타**나 마나** 늦을 거예요. Taeksireul tana mana neujeul geoyeyo.
Whether you take a taxi or not, you'll be late.

나 마나 means that whether you do A or not (A나 마나) the result, B, is the same.

HOW IT'S FORMED

There are a number of expressions in Korean using this particular 말, and you can explore them in more detail in the "Making decisions" section on page [123]. The 마 in this expression is that same 말 but abbreviated a little, and the 나 is (으)나, which normally means "but" (see page 60). A verb followed by an expression with 마 means "to ~ or not": for example, 할까 말까 **halkka malkka** or 가지 말지 **gaji malji**. With adjectives, you can use the opposite of your A verb instead of 마: for example, 좋나 싫나 **johna silhna** (whether you like it or not) or 크나 작으나 **keuna jageuna** (whether it's big or small).

HOW IT'S CONJUGATED

		Past	Present	Future
Action verbs ending in a vowel	하다	했으나 마나 haesseuna mana	하나 마나 hana mana	하나 마나
Action verbs ending in a consonant	먹다	먹었으나 마나 meogeosseuna mana	먹으나 마나 meogeuna mana	먹으나 마나
Descriptive verbs (adjectives) ending in a vowel	예쁘다	예뻤으나 못생겼으나 yeppeosseuna motsaenggyeosseuna	예쁘나 못 생기나 yeppeuna mot saenggina	예쁘나 못 생기나
Descriptive verbs (adjectives) ending in a consonant	작다	작았으나 컸으나 jagasseuna keosseuna	작으나 크나 jageuna keuna	작으나 크나

TAKE NOTE

This is quite similar to 아/어/여 봤자 **a/eo/yeo bwatja** (see the bottom of this page). The slight difference in meaning is that with 나 마나 the result is definitely fixed, whereas with 봤자/봐야, you won't get what you want regardless of whether or not you do A.

EXAMPLE SENTENCES

약을 먹**으나 마나** 감기가 떨어지지 않을 거예요.
Yageul meogeuna mana gamgiga tteoleojiji anheul geoyeyo.
Whether you take medicine or not, your cold won't go away.

그건 말하**나마**다. **Geugeon malhanamada.**
It goes without saying. (Something is a fact, whether or not it is mentioned in words.)

	Speaking = Writing
A아/어/여 봤자 Aa/eo/yeo bwatja B "There's no point	★★
A아/어/여봐야 a/eo/yeobwaya B in doing A"	★★

급하게 가 **봤자** 무슨 소용이겠어요? 벌써 늦어요.
Geubhage ga bwatja museun soyongigesseoyo? Beolsseo neujeoyo.
급하게 가 **봐야** 무슨 소용이겠어요? 벌써 늦어요.
Geubhage ga bwaya museun soyongigesseoyo? Beolsseo neujeoyo.
What's the point of hurrying? We're already late.

This is an expression you can use while wringing your hands and/or sitting on your bed dressed in black listening to The Cure. These two expressions mean that A is pointless or not worth doing.

HOW IT'S FORMED

The first expression combines 아/어/여 보다 ("to try to do something"), the past tense marker, and 자, which can mean "so," "and then," or quite a few other things and which we'll check out on page 273. Alternately, you can use 아/어/여 봐야, which means the same thing.

HOW IT'S CONJUGATED

		All tenses
Action verbs with 오 or 아	잡다 japda	잡아 봤자 jaba bwatja 잡아 봐야 jaba bwaya
Action verbs with 어, 우, 으 or 이	먹다	먹어 봤자 meogeo bwatja 먹어 봐야 meogeo bwaya
하다	하다	해 봤자 hae bwatja 해 봐야 hae bwaya

TAKE NOTE

For your B clause, you can choose an expression which means "useless." 소용 없어요 **soyong eobseoyo** is pretty common, but I'll show you a couple of others in the examples below. Just pick an expression from below, or if you're really advanced and/or a free thinker, invent your own. Either way, B can mean only one thing and that is "it's useless." If your B expression means anything else, this is not the grammar point you're looking for.

You can also skip the B clause altogether, end your sentence with 봤자예요 **bwatjayeyo**, and leave it to your listeners to deduce the futility of A based on the fact that you used 봤자. However, this doesn't work with 봐야.

Some expressions you can use for B are 아무 의미가 없어요 **amu uimiga eobseoyo** (there's no point), 시간낭비다 **si gannangbida** (it's a waste of time), 아무 소용 없을 것 같아요 **amu soyong eobseul geot gatayo** (it seems like it'll be useless), or 소용없는 짓이다 **soyongeobsneun jisida** (it tends to be useless).

This expression and (으)나 마나 are similar, but 봤자/봐야 means that whether you do A or not, you won't get the desired result, whereas 나 마나 means that whatever you do, the results won't change.

It's also possible, though less common, to use 았/었/였자 with verbs other than 보다. In this case it means "even if A, B."

> 열심히 공부**해 봤자** 시험에 떨어질 거예요.
> **Yeolsimhi gongbuhae bwatja siheome tteoleojil geoyeyo.**
> Even if I study hard, I will fail the test.

EXAMPLE SENTENCES

그에게 말을 **해 봤자** 소용 없어요. Geuege mareul hae bwatja soyong eobseoyo.

그에게 말을 **해 봐야** 소용 없어요. Geuege mareul hae bwaya soyong eobseoyo.

It's useless to try to talk to him.

이렇게 **해 봤자** 별 수 없어요. Ireoke hae bwatja byeol su eobseoyo.

이렇게 **해 봐야** 별 수 없어요. Ireoke hae bwaya byeol su eobseoyo.

There's no point in doing it like this.

Cause and Effect: Multiple Causes

		Speaking > Writing
A고 해서 go haeseo B	"A is one of B's causes"	★★

열쇄를 잃어버리**고 해서** 늦게 왔어요.
Yeolswaereul ilheobeorigo haeseo neutge wasseoyo.
I lost my keys (among other things), so I arrived late.

"But," you say, "things aren't always so simple. Sometimes life gets complicated." It sure does, and that's why you need this expression. It says that A is one cause among many for B, probably the most important cause or you'd hardly be singling it out, right? You can use this when all the other non-A causes aren't really that important or if you just want to emphasize A for some reason.

HOW IT'S FORMED

It's a combination of 고 하다 (see page 51) and 아/어/여서.

HOW IT'S CONJUGATED

		All tenses
Action verbs ending in a vowel	하다	하고 해서 hago haeseo
Action verbs ending in a consonant	먹다	먹고 해서 meokgo haeso

TAKE NOTE

고 can be used only with action verbs and only when the subjects of both clauses A and B are the same.

EXAMPLE SENTENCES

쇼핑을 하고 **해서** 동대문에 갔어요.
Syopingeul hago haeseo Dongdaemune gasseoyo.
I went to Dongdaemun to go shopping (among other things).

부모님한테 돈을 받고 **해서** 새로운 코트를 샀어요.
Bumonimhante doneul batgo haeseo saeroun koteureul sasseoyo.
I got some money from my parents (among other things), so I bought a new coat.

쇼핑도 하고 저녁도 먹고 **해서** 돈을 많이 썼어요.
Syopingdo hago jeonyeokdo meokgo haeseo doneul mani sseosseoyo.
I went shopping and ate dinner, so I spent a lot of money.

Speaking = Writing

A(으)ㄹ 겸 해서   "B in order to do A, etc."   ★★
(eu)l gyeom haeseo B

광고를 보지 않**을 겸 해서** 영화에 조금 늦게 왔어요.
Gwanggoreul boji anheul gyeom haeseo yeonghwae jogeum neutge wasseoyo.
I arrived a little late to the movies in order (to skip) the ads (among other things).

HOW IT'S FORMED

(으)ㄹ 겸 is basically a slash and allows you to say you did two or more things. You can brush up on this in the "and" section on page 49. 서 is from 아/어/여서 (see page 66) and means "so."

HOW IT'S CONJUGATED

		All tenses
Action verbs ending in a vowel	하다	할 겸 해서 hal gyeom haeseo
Action verbs ending in a consonant	먹다	먹을 겸 해서 meogeul gyeom haeseo

TAKE NOTE

You can use this with multiple examples in your A clause or just one. See the example sentences.

A should be the reason for B.

EXAMPLE SENTENCES

부모님한테 돈을 받**을 겸 해서** 부모님 집에 놀러 갔어요.
Bumonimhante doneul badeul gyeom haeseo bumonim jibe nolleo gasseoyo.
Since I got money from my parents, I went to hang out at their house.

쇼핑을 **할 겸 해서** 동대문에 갔어요.
Syopingeul hal gyeom haeseo Dongdaemune gasseoyo.
I went to Dongdaemun to go shopping (among other things).

쇼핑도 하고 저녁도 먹**을 겸 해서** 시장에 갔어요.
Syopingdo hago jeonyeokdo meogeul gyeom haeseo sijange gasseoyo.
I went to the market to go shopping and eat dinner.

Linking Sentences: Basic Comparisons

	Speaking = Writing
A이/가 i/ga B보다 boda C "A is more C than B"	★★★★★

민수가 가영이**보다** 더 늦었어요. Minsuga Kayoungiboda deo neujeosseoyo.
민수가 가영이**보다** 늦었어요. Minsuga Kayoungiboda neujeosseoyo.
Minsu was later than Kayoung.

This is the easiest and most basic form of comparison in Korean. All it means is that A is more C (bigger, faster, longer, shorter, easier, prettier, etc.) than B. So if you're all about keeping up with the Joneses and/or you like to one-up other people, you should learn this expression.

HOW IT'S CONJUGATED

보다 directly follows the noun that forms the basis for comparison: the lesser of the two nouns. A is the noun that is better than it. If A is implied, you can leave it out in the actual sentence: for example, 어제보다 기분이 좋아요 eojeboda gibuni joayo means "I feel better (now) than yesterday" and will be understood without you needing to mention that you feel better now and since you're speaking in the present tense, people can reasonably assume you mean now. After B, C should explain exactly what you're comparing. See the examples below for clarification:

		Past	Present	Future
Action verbs ending in a vowel	하다	한 것보다 han geotboda	하기보다 hagiboda 하는 것보다 haneun geotboda	할 것보다 hal geotboda
Action verbs ending in a consonant	먹다	먹은 것보다 meogeun geotboda	먹기보다 meokgiboda 먹는 것보다 meokneun geotboda	먹을 것보다 meokeul goetboda
Descriptive verbs (adjectives) ending in a vowel	예쁘다	예쁜 것보다 yeppeun geotboda	예쁜 것보다	예쁜 것보다

		Past	Present	Future
Descriptive verbs (adjectives) ending in a consonant	작다	작은 것보다 jageun geotboda	작은 것보다	작은 것보다
Nouns ending in a vowel	남자	남자보다 namjaboda	남자보다	남자보다
Nouns ending in a consonant	물	물보다 mulboda	물보다	물보다

RESTRICTIONS

Don't forget the subject marker after A. B often gets no marker: it can be directly followed by 보다.

This has nothing to do with the 보다 which means "to see." This 보다 is a particle which is always directly attached to a noun; the other 보다 is a verb which does all the things that verbs normally do in Korean.

You can put 는 after the 보다 if you want to add emphasis; see the last example below.

C often includes 더, which means "more."

EXAMPLE SENTENCES

공부하기가 쉬는 것**보다** 더 힘들어요.
Gongbuhagiga swineun geotboda deo himdeureoyo.

공부하기가 쉬는 것**보다** 힘들어요.
Gongbuhagiga swineun geotboda himdeureoyo.

Studying is more difficult than resting.

내가 너**보다** 더 똑똑해. Naega neoboda deo ttokttokhae.

내가 너**보다** 똑똑해. Naega neoboda ttokttokhae.

I'm smarter than you.

한국어가 불어**보다** 미국인에게 배우기 더 어려워요.
Hangukeoga bureoboda miguginege baeugi deo eoryeowoyo.

한국어가 불어**보다** 미국인에게 배우기 어려워요.
Hangukeoga bureoboda miguginege baeugi eoryeowoyo.

It's harder for Americans to learn Korean than to learn French.

나는 예쁜 여자**보다** 귀여운 여자를 더 좋아해요.
Naneun yeppeun yeojaboda gwiyeoun yeojareul deo johahaeyo.

I prefer cute women to beautiful women.

그녀는 예쁘기**보다**는 귀여워요.
Geunyeoneun yeppeugibodaneun gwiyeowoyo.

She is cute rather than pretty.

> **Speaking = Writing**
> ★ ★ ★
>
> A에 비해서 e bihaeseo B   "B, compared to A"
> A에 비하면 e bihamyeon B

가영**에 비하면** 민수가 더 늦었어요.
Kayounge bihamyeon Minsuga deo neujeosseoyo.

가영**에 비해서** 민수가 더 늦었어요.
Kayounge bihaeseo Minsuga deo neujeosseoyo.

Minsu was later than Kayoung.

These are other ways to make comparisons. They're a little more official than the other ways stated here, so you can make yourself sound smarter or more knowledgeable by using them. You'll often hear them on the news or read them in newspapers in sentences like "Unemployment is up this year compared to last year."

HOW IT'S FORMED

에 is the same particle you use to talk about going places, and here it simply indicates the basis for a comparison. In a way, with these expressions you are explaining the distance between A and B. 비하다 means "to compare" and can be combined here with 여서 (so) or 면 (if).

HOW IT'S CONJUGATED

		All tenses
Action verbs ending in a vowel	하다	하기에 비해서 hagie bihaeseo 하기에 비하면 hagie bihamyeon
Action verbs ending in a consonant	먹다	먹기에 비해서 meokgie bihaeseo 먹기에 비하면 meokgie bihamyeon
Descriptive verbs (adjectives) ending in a vowel	예쁘다	예쁘기에 비해서 yeppeugie bihaeseo 예쁘기에 비하면 yeppeugie bihamyeon
Descriptive verbs (adjectives) ending in a consonant	작다	작기에 비해서 jakgie bihaeseo 작기에 비하면 jakgie bihamyeon
Nouns ending in a vowel	남자	남자에 비해서 namjae bihaeseo 남자에 비하면 namjae bihamyeon
Nouns ending in a consonant	물	물에 비해서 mure bihaeseo 물에 비하면 mure bihamyeon

TAKE NOTE

These two expressions are not exactly identical, but about 90% of the time you can use either one without changing the meaning or ruining the sentence's grammar, and the rest of the time the differences are so small that you don't really need to worry about them. Because 비하면 is made with 면 (see page 283), it means "if you compare," whereas 비해서 means "when you compare."

While you can skip using 더 after 보다, you can't after 비하면/비해서. They are used for a wider variety of comparisons than 보다 which is always used to indicate that B is more of something than A. 비해서 and 비하면 are used merely to compare two situations: whether there's more, less, or the same amount, you can still use either one.

EXAMPLE SENTENCES

미국 경제**에 비하면** 중국 경제가 더 강해요.
Miguk gyeongjee bihamyeon jungguk gyeongjega deo ganghaeyo.

미국 경제**에 비해서** 중국 경제가 더 강해요.
Miguk gyeongjee bihaeseo jungguk gyeongjega deo ganghaeyo.

The Chinese economy is stronger than the American economy.

5년 전**에 비하면** 월급은 거의 오르지 않았어요.
O-nyeon jeone bihamyeon wolgeubeun geoui oreuji anasseoyo.

5년 전**에 비해서** 월급은 거의 오르지 않았어요.
O-nyeon jeone bihaeseo wolgeubeun geoui oreuji anasseoyo.

My salary has hardly increased in the past five years. (Compared to five years ago, these days my salary has hardly increased).

		Speaking = Writing
A만 해도 man haedo B	"Even if we just consider A... then B"	★★★

6개월 전**만 해도** 물가가 이렇게 비싸지 않았어요.
Yuk gaewol jeonman haedo mulgaga ireoke bissaji anasseoyo.
Just six months ago things weren't this expensive.

There are many big problems in this world: global warming, the economy, rising fuel prices, poverty, war, etc. Sometimes you want to talk to people about these problems, but they just don't get it, so instead of talking about the big picture you try to reduce it to something people can grasp by using an example that's small and/or close to home. This is where 만 해도 comes in. It means "if we consider A alone."

Similarly, it can be used to talk about the way things used to be. In this case, it's used with expressions like "10년 전만 해도 **sipnyeon jeonman haedo**" or "한달 전만 해도 **handal jeonman haedo**." The first translates to "just ten years ago," and the latter to "just a month ago." You can then talk about how things have changed: the area has gentrified, the price has risen drastically, your friend has slimmed down, and so on.

HOW IT'S FORMED

만, in this case, is a marker used with numbers to emphasize their meaning. Then 하다 ("to do") is combined with 여도 ("although"; see page 104) to get "even if we only do (consider) A."

HOW IT'S CONJUGATED

A is a noun indicating either the time period that you're considering or what you want to specifically look at.

		All tenses
Nouns ending in a vowel	남자	남자만 해도 namjaman haedo
Nouns ending in a consonant	물	물만 해도 mul mulman haedo

TAKE NOTE

You can't use this expression in the future tense.

It often follows an expression of time with 전 such as in the second example below to mean "just ~ ago." B is then a statement of what was true at that time (but presumably no longer is).

EXAMPLE SENTENCES

휘발유 값**만 해도** 500원이나 올랐어요.
Hwibalyu gabsman haedo obaekwonina ollasseoyo.
The price of gas alone has risen by 500 won.

요즘 취업이 아주 어려워요. 우리 가족**만 해도** 제 아버지와 제 삼촌이 실직 상태예요.
Yojeum chwieobi aju eoryeowoyo. Uri gajokman haedo je abeojiwa je samchoni siljik sangtaeyeyo.
These days it's really difficult to get a job. In my family alone my father and uncle are out of work.

요즘 취업이 아주 어려워요. 2년 전**만 해도** 지금보다 훨씬 좋았어요.
Yojeum chwieobi aju eoryeowoyo. Inyeon jeonman haedo jigeumboda hwolssin joasseoyo.
These days it's really difficult to get a job. Just two years ago, it was much better than now.

	Speaking = Writing
A(으)ㄴ/는가 하면 (eu) "There's A, but there's also B"	★★
n/neunga hamyeon B "Some people do A, but some people do B"	

제 수업에 정시에 오는 사람들은 있**는가 하면** 늦게 오는 사람들도 있어요.
Je sueobe jeongsie oneun saramdeureun inneunga hamyeon neutge oneun saramdeuldo isseoyo.
In my class, there are some people who come on time and some who are late.

If you live in Korea, you may often find yourself having to explain that stereotypes aren't true and that different people do different things. That's where you need this expression. It's used to explain that there are cases of both A and B.

HOW IT'S CONJUGATED

This expression is mainly used with two types of sentences. One is A가 있는가 하면 **ga inneunga hamyeon** B도 있다 **do itda** (There is A, but there is also B). The other is 어떤 **eotteon** (사람들은 **saramdeureun**, 때 **ttae**, 날 **nal**, ⋯) A(으)ㄴ가 하면 어떤 **(eu) n-ga hamyeon eotteon** (사람들은, 때, 날,⋯) B.

In the first type of sentence, A and B are nouns. B should be followed by 도 (too). In the second type of sentence, 는가 하면 **neunga hamyeon** can be used after action verbs while ㄴ가 하면 is used after descriptive verbs ending in vowels and 은가 하면 **eunga hamyeon** is used after descriptive verbs ending in consonants. You can put 이 after a noun and then conjugate it as a descriptive verb.

A is the first kind of case; B is the second. For example, A might be "students who study hard" while B is "students who don't study at all." You can then use (으)ㄴ/는가 하면 to explain that there are both students who study hard and students who don't study at all. Let's see an example of the first type of sentence:

> 공부를 열심히 하는 학생들이 있는가 하면 공부를 안 하는 학생들도 있어요.
> Gongbureul yeolsimhi haneun haksaengdeuri inneunga hamyeon gongbureul an haneun haksaengdeuldo isseoyo.

And an example of the second type:

> 어떤 학생들은 공부를 열심히 하는가 하면 어떤 학생들은 공부를 안 해요.
> Eotteon haksaengdeureun gongbureul yeolsimhi haneunga hamyeon eotteon haksaengdeureun gongbureul an haeyo.

This expression can be used in the past, present, or future tenses, but these tenses are expressed at the end of the sentence rather than with this expression.

		A이/가 있는가 하면 B도 있다	어떤⋯ A(으)ㄴ/는가 하면 어떤⋯ B⋯
Action verbs ending in a vowel	하다		하는가 하면 haneunga hamyeon
Action verbs ending in a consonant	먹다		먹는가 하면 meokneunga hamyeon
Descriptive verbs (adjectives) ending in a vowel	예쁘다		예쁜가 하면 yeppeunga hamyeon
Descriptive verbs (adjectives) ending in a consonant	작다		작은가 하면 jageunga hamyeon

		A이/가 있는가 하면 B도 있다	어떤… A(으)ㄴ/는가 하면 어떤… B…
Nouns ending in a vowel	남자	남자가 있는가 하면 namjaga inneunga hamyeon	
Nouns ending in a consonant	물	물이 있는가 하면 muri inneunga hamyeon	

TAKE NOTE

Be careful about which type of sentence you're using with this, and don't get tangled up in the grammar.

There are a few similar expressions. ~기도 하다 **gido hada** (see page 225) indicates that sometimes ~ also occurs. In this case, ~ is not as important as whatever usually occurs: it's just tagging along. ~(으)ㄹ 수도 있다 **(eu)r sudo itda** (see page 296) is another expression similar to 기도 하다. Again, it means that ~ can happen, but the other thing that happens is more important. (으)ㄴ/는가 하면, however, doesn't tell your listener what's more important or more common: it simply states that both cases A and B occur.

EXAMPLE SENTENCES

우리 학교에는 좋은 선생님들이 있**는가 하면 그냥 그런** 선생님들도 있어요.
Uri hakgyoeneun joeun seonsaengnimdeuri inneunga hamyeon geunyang geureon seonsaengnimdeuldo isseoyo.
At our school there are some really good teachers and some average teachers.

어떤 사람들은 똑똑**한가 하면 또 어떤** 사람들은 어리석어요.
Eotteon saramdeureun ttokttokanga hamyeon tto eotteon saramdeureun eoriseogeoyo.
Some people are smart while some people are foolish.

Speaking = Writing

오늘/그날**따라**   "(Unlike normal), today/that day B"   ★
oneul/geunalttara B

오늘 수업이 많은데, 오늘**따라** 회의가 있어서 정말 바빴어요.
Oneul sueobi manheunde, oneulttara hoeuiga isseoseo jeongmal bappasseoyo.
Today I had a lot of classes, and on top of that (unlike most days) I had a meeting, so I was really busy.

Have you ever had one of those days where everything goes wrong? When all the things that normally work suddenly don't? When your normally perfect hair refuses to settle down for the important date or you forgot your documents for the big meeting? 따라 is an expression you can use to talk about those days. It means that something happened on the day in question that was different from normal and is often used in expressions such as "Today it was freezing cold, and on top of that the heater at work suddenly broke."

HOW IT'S CONJUGATED

따라 is used directly after either 오늘 oneul or 그날 geunal: 오늘따라 oneulttala, 그날따라 geunalttala. It can be used in the past or present tense. B describes what was different on that day. If you're using it to say "and on top of that," then you can explain the first situation, conclude that with (으)ㄴ/는데 (eu) n/neunde, add 오늘/그날따라 oneul/geunalttala, and then say what was different about that day. See the examples below.

TAKE NOTE

There are a couple of 따라s in Korean. ~에 따라 e ttala means "according to ~" (see page 322), and ~를/을 따라 leul/eul ttala means "following ~." The 따라 in question here always follows only 오늘 or 그날 and is never preceded by 에 or 을/를 or any other word except 오늘 or 그날. ~에 따라 and ~을/를 따라 are made by conjugating the verb 따르다, which means "to follow" and isn't really applicable to 오늘따라 and 그날따라.

You can use 마침 machim instead of ~따라; it means the same thing, but can be used for sentences with times other than just this day or that day.

EXAMPLE SENTENCES

어제 많이 추웠는데, 그날 **따라** 히터가 고장나서 훨씬 더 추웠어요.
Eoje mani chuwonneunde, geunal ttala hiteoga gojangnaseo hwolssin deo chuwosseoyo.
어제 많이 추웠는데, **마침** 히터도 고장나서 훨씬 더 추웠어요.
Eoje mani chuwonneunde, machim hiteodo gojangnaseo hwolssin deo chuwosseoyo.
Yesterday was very cold, and on top of that (unlike most days) the heater broke, so I was even more cold.

올해 물가도 많이 올랐는데, **마침** 의료비도 많이 나와서 고생했어요.
Olhae mulgado mani ollanneunde, machim uiryobido mani nawaseo gosaenghaesseoyo.
This year prices have risen quite a lot also, and on top of that (unlike other years), I had to pay a lot for medical treatment, so it's been difficult for me. (따라 can't be used in this sentence.)

Linking Sentences–Contrast: Although/But

Another expression that can be used to mean "although" is 다가도 dagado. I felt it belonged in the temporal order section rather than here because it's used only while talking about a progression of events.

그녀는 급하게 서두르**다가도** 항상 다른 생각을 하다가 늦어요.
Geunyeoneun geuphage seodureudagado hangsang dareun saenggageul hadaga neujeoyo.
Even though she hurries, she always thinks about something else and ends up being late.

Likewise, 면서도 **myeonseodo** combines 면서 and 도 to mean "even while." Since it's about two simultaneous actions, I put it in the "while" section.

서둘렀<u>으면서도</u> 늦었어요. **Seodulleosseumyeonseodo neujeosseoyo.**
Even while I hurried, I was late.

다가도 **dagado** is on page 279 and 면서도 is on page 253 if you feel either of the two is the better fit for your sentence. Otherwise, here are some more applicable expressions to express contrast.

		Speaking = Writing
A아/어/여도 a/eo/yeodo B	"Although A, B"	★★★★★

택시를 타<u>도</u> 늦어요. **Taeksileul tado neujeoyo.** Even if I take a taxi, I'll be late.

When it comes to expressing contrast, the big player in Korean grammar is 도. It also has a few other uses, but with a little practice you'll find it easy enough to tell when it's used for contrast and when it's something else. With the former it will appear at the end of other expressions like the ones shown in this section: 아/어/여도, ㄴ/는데도, 면서도, 고도, 다 가도, etc. For now, let's look at the most basic form: 아/어/여도. It simply means "although."

HOW IT'S CONJUGATED

		Past	Present	Future
Action verbs ending in a vowel	하다	했어도 haesseodo	해도 haedo	해도
Action verbs ending in a consonant	먹다	먹었어도 meogeosseodo	먹어도 meogeodo	먹어도
Descriptive verbs (adjectives) ending in a vowel	예쁘다	예뻤어도 yeppeosseodo	예뻐도 yeppeodo	예뻐도
Descriptive verbs (adjectives) ending in a consonant	작다	작았어도 jagassado	작아도 jagado	작아도

TAKE NOTE

This expression is similar to 더라도, but it can be used more broadly. 더라도 can be used only hypothetically when the action in A hasn't yet occurred. 아/어/여도 can be used hypothetically in the past tense, like so:

택시를 탔<u>어도</u> 늦었어요. **Taeksireul tasseodo neujeosseoyo.**
Even if I had taken a taxi, I would have been late.

EXAMPLE SENTENCES

시간이 없<u>어도</u> 숙제를 해야 해요. **Sigani eobseodo sukjereul haeya haeyo.**
Even if you have no time, you must do your homework.

운동을 **해도** 살이 안 빠져요. Undongeul haedo sari an ppajyeoyo.
Even though I exercise, I'm not losing weight.

		Speaking = Writing
A지만 jiman B	"A, but B"	★ ★ ★ ★ ★

서둘렀**지만** 늦었어요. Seodulleotjiman neujeosseoyo. I hurried, but I was late.

This is by far the most commonly used of the "but" expressions and, along with the versatile 도, the only one you need to worry about if you're simply studying informally. In these sentences A and B have about the same weight: neither one is more important.

HOW IT'S CONJUGATED

		Past	Present	Future
Action verbs ending in a vowel	하다	했지만 haetjiman	하지만 hajiman	하지만
Action verbs ending in a consonant	먹다	먹었지만 meogeotjiman	먹지만 meogjiman	먹지만
Descriptive verbs (adjectives) ending in a vowel	예쁘다	예뻤지만 yeppeotjiman	예쁘지만 yeppeujiman	예쁘지만
Descriptive verbs (adjectives) ending in a consonant	작다	작았지만 jagatjiman	작지만 jagjiman	작지만
Nouns ending in a vowel	남자	남자였지만 namjayeotjiman	남자이지만 namjaijiman	남자이지만
Nouns ending in a consonant	물	물이었지만 murieotjiman	물이지만 murijiman	물이지만

TAKE NOTE

There is another, rather less common, expression "ㄴ지 만" (notice the space between 지 and 만) which is used to tell the period of time that has lapsed since an event. For example, "한국에 온지 만 5년 됐어요. **Hanguke onji man onyeon dwaesseoyo.**" (It's been five years since I came to Korea.) We'll cover this in the section on Progression and putting things in order on page 276. For now, just remember to watch for the space and the context.

EXAMPLE SENTENCES

그녀 예쁘**지만** 성격이 까다로워요.
Geunyeo yeppeujiman seonggyeogi kkadarowoyo.
She is beautiful but has a difficult personality.

운동을 했**지만** 살이 빠지지 않았어요.
Undongeul haetjiman sari ppajiji anasseoyo.
I exercised, but I didn't lose weight.

그 가수가 노래를 잘 하**지만** 기타를 칠 수 없어요.
Geu gasuga noraereul jal hajiman gitareul chil su eobseoyo.
That singer can sing well but can't play the guitar.

A더라도 deorado B	"Even though A, B"	Speaking = Writing ★★★

택시를 타**더라도** 늦을 거예요. Taeksireul tadeorado neujeul geoyeyo.
Even if I take a taxi, I'll be late.

This is much like 아/어/여도, but it's stronger." The result (B) in a 더라도 expression is even more contrary than that in an 아/어/여도 expression.

HOW IT'S FORMED

더라 is covered on page 185 and is normally used to indicate something you experienced personally; however, that doesn't really matter in this expression. 도 is a particle which means "although."

HOW IT'S CONJUGATED

		Past	Present	Future
Action verbs ending in a vowel	하다	했더라도 haetdeorado	하더라도 hadeorado	하더라도
Action verbs ending in a consonant	먹다	먹었더라도 meogeotdeorado	먹더라도 meokdeorado	먹더라도
Descriptive verbs (adjectives) ending in a vowel	예쁘다	예뻤더라도 yeppeotdeorado	예쁘더라도 yeppeudeorado	예쁘더라도
Descriptive verbs (adjectives) ending in a consonant	작다	작았더라도 jagatdeorado	작더라도 jagdeorado	작더라도
Nouns ending in a vowel	남자	남자였더라도 namjayeotdeorado	남자이더라도 namja-ideorado	남자이더라도
Nouns ending in a consonant	물	물이었더라도 murieotdeorado	물이더라도 murideorado	물이더라도

TAKE NOTE

This expression is much like 아/어/여도, but unlike 아/어/여도, it can be used only when the action in A hasn't yet taken place. It's stronger and more hypothetical than 아/어/여도.

EXAMPLE SENTENCES

시간이 없**더라도** 숙제를 해야 해요. Sigani eopdeorado sukjereul haeya haeyo.
Even if you have no time, you must do your homework.

운동을 열심히 하**더라도** 살이 빠지지 않을 거예요.
Undongeul yeolsimhi hadeorado sari ppajiji anheul geoyeyo.
Even if I exercise a lot, I won't lose weight.

더 일찍 왔**더라도** 그 사람이 죽었을 거예요.
Deo iljjig watdeolado geu sarami jugeosseul geoyeyo.
Even if you had arrived earlier, the man would still have died.

A(으)ㄴ/는데도
(eu)n/neundedo B | "Even though A, B" | **Speaking = Writing**
★★★

택시를 타**는데도** 늦을 거예요. Taeksileul taneundedo neujeul geoyeyo.
Even if I take a taxi, I'll be late.

Just like the above two expressions, this one means, "even though."

HOW IT'S FORMED

(으)ㄴ/는데 is used to give the background for a situation; see page 69. 도 is the particle used to indicate contrast.

HOW IT'S CONJUGATED

		Past	Present	Future
Action verbs ending in a vowel	하다	했는데도 haenneundedo	하는데도 haneundedo	하는데도
Action verbs ending in a consonant	먹다	먹었는데도 meogeonneundedo	먹는데도 meokneundedo	먹는데도
Descriptive verbs (adjectives) ending in a vowel	예쁘다	예뻤는데도 yeppeonneundedo	예쁜데도 yeppeundedo	예쁜데도
Descriptive verbs (adjectives) ending in a consonant	작다	작았는데도 jaganneundedo	작는데도 jakneundedo	작는데도
Nouns ending in a vowel	남자	남자였는데도 namjayeonneundedo	남자인데도 namjaindedo	남자인데도
Nouns ending in a consonant	물	물이었는데도 murieonneundedo	물인데도 murindedo	물인데도

TAKE NOTE

B can't include a suggestion, a proposition, or the future tense. It often begins with 불구하고 **bul guhago**, which is a word that often goes along with contrast expressions and emphasizes the contrast a little more.

EXAMPLE SENTENCES

시간이 없**는데도** 숙제를 해야 해요.
Sigani eobsneundedo sukjereul haeya haeyo.
Even if you have no time, you must do your homework.

운동을 했**는데도** 살이 빠지지 않았어요.
Undongeul haenneundedo sari ppajiji anasseoyo.
Even though I exercised, I didn't lose weight.

		Speaking = Writing
A고도 godo B	"Although A, B"	★★★

서두르**고도** 늦었어요.
Seodureugodo neujeosseoyo.
Although I hurried, I was late.

This translates as "although A, B." In other words, it has more to do with 도 (which sets up a contrast) than 고.

HOW IT'S FORMED

고 (and) plus 도 (indicating a contrast).

HOW IT'S CONJUGATED

		All tenses
Action verbs ending in a vowel	하다	하고도 hagodo
Action verbs ending in a consonant	먹다	먹고도 meokgodo

TAKE NOTE

고도 can be used only with action verbs and only when the subjects of both clause A and clause B are the same.

EXAMPLE SENTENCES

그 사람 돈을 잘 벌**고도** 자주 돈을 빌리고 싶어해요.
Geu saram doneul jal beolgodo jaju doneul billigo sipeohaeyo.
Although he makes a lot of money, he often wants to borrow more.

밥을 먹**고도** 배가 고파서 라면을 또 먹었어요.
Babeul meokgodo baega gopaseo ramyeoneul tto meogeosseoyo.
Although I ate a meal (or rice), I was hungry, so I ate ramen again.

	Speaking = Writing
A(으)ㄴ/는 반면(에) (eu) n/neun banmyeon(e) B	"A… but on the other hand, B" ★★★
A(으)ㄴ/는데 반해 (eu) n/neunde banhae B	★★

이 근처가 조용**한 반면에** 재미가 없어요.
I geuncheoga joyonghan banmyeone jaemiga eobseoyo.

이 근처가 조용**한데 반해** 재미가 없어요.
I geuncheoga joyonghande banhae jaemiga eobpseoyo.

This area is quiet but boring.

Here are two more expressions you can use to contrast A and B. They're just about exactly the same as the English expression "on the other hand."

HOW IT'S FORMED

반면 literally means "opposite side," and 에 is optional. I think it sounds more natural to use it, but you don't have to if you don't want to. 반하다 **banhada** means "to oppose" and is conjugated here after (으)ㄴ/는데.

HOW IT'S CONJUGATED

		All tenses
Action verbs ending in a vowel	하다	하는 반면(에) haneun banmyeon(e) 하는데 반해 haneunde banhae
Action verbs ending in a consonant	먹다	먹은 반면(에) meogeun banmyeon(e) 먹는데 반해 meokneunde banhae
Descriptive verbs (adjectives) ending in a vowel	예쁘다	예쁜 반면(에) yeppeun banmyeon(e) 예쁜데 반해 yeppeunde banhae
Descriptive verbs (adjectives) ending in a consonant	작다	작은 반면(에) jageun banmyeon(e) 작은데 반해 jageunde banhae

TAKE NOTE

The subjects of A and B should be the same.

This expression is quite similar to 지 (see page 112), 지만 **jiman** (see page 105) and A기는/긴 하는데/한데 **gineun/gin haneunde/hande** B (see page 113). Unlike the latter, 반면에 simply contrasts two facts and doesn't, on its own, imply anything about which of the two facts is more important. It has the same meaning as 지 or 지만 but sounds somewhat more official, so it's good for newspapers, reports, official discussions, and things of that nature.

You can use A(으)ㄴ/는데 반해 B interchangeably with A 반면에 B.

EXAMPLE SENTENCES

새로운 대통령이 인기가 <u>많은</u> **반면에** 정치 경험이 아직 많지 않아요.
Saeroun daetonglyeongi ingiga manheun banmyeone jeongchi gyeongheomi ajik manchi anayo.

새로운 대통령이 인기가 <u>많은데</u> **반해** 정치 경험이 아직 많지 않아요.
Saeroun daetonglyeongi ingiga manheunde banhae jeongchi gyeongheomi ajik manchi anayo.

The new president is very popular, but on the other hand, he has little political experience.

민수가 스포츠를 잘 하<u>는</u> **반면에** 음악을 못 해요.
Minsuga seupocheureul jal haneun banyeone eumageul mot haeyo.

민수가 스포츠를 잘 하<u>는데</u> **반해** 음악을 못 해요.
Minsuga seupocheureul jal haneunde banhae eumageul mot haeyo.

Minsu is good at sports, but on the other hand, he's not very good at music.

		Speaking ‹ Writing
A(으)나 (eu)na B	"A, but B"	★★

급히 왔<u>으나</u> 늦었어요. Geupi wasseuna neujeosseoyo. I hurried, but I was late.

For the writers among you, here's another way to say "but." This one has the same meaning as 지만 but is mainly used in writing.

HOW IT'S CONJUGATED

		Past	Present	Future
Action verbs ending in a vowel	하다	했으나 haesseuna	하나 hana	하나
Action verbs ending in a consonant	먹다	먹었으나 meogeosseuna	먹으나 meogeuna	먹으나
Descriptive verbs (adjectives) ending in a vowel	예쁘다	예뻤으나 yeppeosseuna	예쁘나 yeppeuna	예쁘나
Descriptive verbs (adjectives) ending in a consonant	작다	작았으나 jagasseuna	작으나 jageuna	작으나

TAKE NOTE

(으)나 is mostly used in writing; 지만 can be used anywhere. Otherwise they're interchangeable.

(이)나 **(i)na** means "or" and is used to link two nouns. (으)나 is used after verbs, so check whether the word before 나 is a noun or a verb. As always, it's also important to check the context in which the expression is used—(이)나 and (으)나 are not used in the same contexts.

나? can be a 반말 question particle. It's the 나 of 나요, which is on page 44. It will always appear at the end of a 반말 question. 나 of (으)나 will always be followed by a B clause.

(으)나 마나 is an expression which uses 나 but is worth investigating on its own; see page 91.

EXAMPLE SENTENCES

그녀는 예쁘**나** 성격이 까다로워요.
Geunyeoneun yeppeuna seonggyeogi kkadarowoyo.
She is beautiful but has a difficult personality.

그 가수가 노래를 잘 하**나** 기타를 칠 수 없어요.
Geu gasuga noraereul jal hana gitareul chil su eobseoyo.
That singer can sing well but can't play the guitar.

		Speaking < Writing
A에도 (불구하고) edo (bulguhago) B	"Even though A, B"	★★

교통**에도 불구하고** 늦지 않았어요. Gyotongedo bulguhago neutji anasseoyo.
In spite of traffic, I arrived on time.

This is the same expression as 아/어/여도 and means "in spite of/even though," but it is attached to nouns.

HOW IT'S FORMED

불구하다 is optional in this expression.

HOW IT'S CONJUGATED

Note that there are two expressions listed below for each noun. You can use this expression either with a noun alone (such as in the example above, "in spite of traffic"), or you can use it with 이 to mean "in spite of being": for instance, 남자임에도 불구하고 means "in spite of being a man."

		Past	Present	Future
Action verbs ending in a vowel	하다	했음에도 haesseumedo (불구하고)	함에도 hamedo (불구하고)	할 것임에도 hal geosimedo (불구하고)
Action verbs ending in a consonant	먹다	먹었음에도 meogeosseumedo (불구하고)	먹에도 meogedo (불구하고)	먹을 것임에도 meogeul geosimedo (불구하고)
Descriptive verbs (adjectives) ending in a vowel	예쁘다	예뻤음에도 yeppeosseumedo (불구하고)	예쁨에도 yeppeumedo (불구하고)	예쁠 것임에도 yeppeul geosimedo (불구하고)

		Past	Present	Future
Descriptive verbs (adjectives) ending in a consonant	작다	작았음에도 **jagasseumedo** (불구하고)	작음에도 **jageumedo** (불구하고)	작을 것임에도 **jageul geosimedo** (불구하고)
Nouns ending in a vowel	남자	남자에도 **namjaedo** (불구하고) 남자였음에도 **namjayeosseumedo** (불구하고)	남자에도 (불구하고) 남자임에도 **namjaimedo** (불구하고)	남자에도 (불구하고) 남자일 것임에도 **namjail geosimedo** (불구하고)
Nouns ending in a consonant	물	물에도 **muredo** (불구하고) 물이었음에도 **murieosseumedo** (불구하고)	물에도 (불구하고) 물임에도 **murimedo** (불구하고)	물에도 (불구하고) 물일 것임에도 **muril geosimedo** (불구하고)

TAKE NOTE

If you want to say "in spite of (verb or adjective)," you should use 아/어/여도 (see page 104) instead of 에도.

This expression is often used with verbs as well. In these cases you conjugate the verb with (으)ㅁ, like the second and third examples below.

This expression is more often used with major problems of the sort that appear on the news. For personal problems or other relatively minor issues, you can use (으)ㄴ/는데 and (으)ㄴ/는데도 불구하고 for more serious personal problems.

EXAMPLE SENTENCES

학교 폭력을 반대하는 캠패인을 함**에도 불구하고** 학교폭력 사건의 건 수 가 계속 증가하고 있어요.
Hakgyo poglyeogeul bandaehaneun kaempaeineul hamedo bulguhago haggyopoglyeog sageonui geon suga gyesog jeunggahago isseoyo.
In spite of the campaign against school violence, the number of incidences continues to rise.

물가가 높음**에도 불구하고** 사람들이 계속 새로운 물건을 사요.
Mulgaga nopeumedo bulguhago saramdeuri gyesok saeroun mulgeoneul sayo.
Although prices are high, people keep buying new things.

		Speaking = Writing
A지 ji B	"A, but B"	★★

서둘렀**지** 늦었어요. **Seodulleotji neujeosseoyo.** I hurried, but I was late.

This is really just a shortened version of 지만 (see page 105).

HOW IT'S CONJUGATED

		Past	Present	Future
Action verbs ending in a vowel	하다	했지 haetji	하지 haji	하지
Action verbs ending in a consonant	먹다	먹었지 meogeotji	먹지 meokji	먹지
Descriptive verbs (adjectives) ending in a vowel	예쁘다	예뻤지 yeppeotji	예쁘지 yeppeuji	예쁘지
Descriptive verbs (adjectives) ending in a consonant	작다	작았지 jagatji	작지 jakji	작지
Nouns ending in a vowel	남자	남자였지 namjayeotji	남자이지 namjaiji	남자이지
Nouns ending in a consonant	물	물이었지 murieotji	물이지 muriji	물이지

TAKE NOTE

There are many different 지s: ~지 않다 **ji anta** (isn't~), ~ㄴ 지 (since~), ~지 말다 **ji malda** (not~), etc. You can tell them apart from the context, but if you're confused, check the expression closely: 지 (since) always has ㄴ, 는 or ㄹ before it, and 지 않다 and 지 말다 are expressions all by themselves: you'll never see these 지s without some conjugation of 않다 or 말다 after them, nor will you see this 지 with any version of 않다 or 말다 right afterward.

EXAMPLE SENTENCES

그녀 예쁘**지** 성격이 까다로워요. **Geunyeo yeppeuji seonggyeogi kkadarowoyo.**
She is beautiful but has a difficult personality.

운동을 했**지** 살을 빠지 지 않았어요. **Undongeul haetji sareul ppajiji anasseoyo.**
I exercised, but I didn't lose weight.

그 가수가 노래를 잘 하**지** 기타를 칠 수 없어요.
Geu gasuga noraereul jal haji gitareul chil su eobseoyo.
That singer can sing well but can't play the guitar.

		Speaking = Writing
~기는 하다 gineun hada	"I really do ~"	★★

집에 일찍 출발하**기는 했**는데 교통이 막혀서 늦었어요.
Jibe iljjik chulbalhagineun haenneunde gyotongi maghyeoseo neujeosseoyo.
I *leave* my house early, but traffic was heavy, so I was late.

If you've read much of this book, you'll have noticed that I told you in a significant number of expressions that 는 was optional and added emphasis. Well, here it's decidedly not optional because the whole point of this expression is to emphasize ~. You can use this expression to say things like "I *did* my homework, but…" or "The food *was* good, but …" It's the part of the Korean language that replaces all these italicized words.

HOW IT'S FORMED

기 turns a verb into a noun and 는 adds emphasis.

HOW IT'S CONJUGATED

하다 normally ends with (으)ㄴ/는데 or 지만 and then a justification (the part of the sentence that comes after the "but"). Instead of using 하다, you can also just repeat the verb you used in A. Both ways are shown below. 기는/긴 하다 is used with descriptive verbs such as 예쁘다 or 똑똑하다, or with nouns with 이, while 하는데 is used with action verbs like 하다 or 가다. This is because of how (으)ㄴ/는데 works; see page 69.

		Past	Present	Future
Action verbs ending in a vowel	하다	하기는 했다 hagineun haetda	하기는 하다 hagineun hada	하기는 할 것이다 hagineun hal geosida
Action verbs ending in a consonant	먹다	먹기는 했다 meokgineun haetda 먹기는 먹었다 meokgineun meogeotda	먹기는 하다 meokgineun hada 먹기는 먹다 meokgineun meokda	먹기는 할 것이다 meokgineun hal geosida 먹기는 먹을 것이다 meokgineun meogeul geosida
Descriptive verbs (adjectives) ending in a vowel	예쁘다	예쁘기는 했다 yeppeugineun haetda 예쁘기는 예뻤다 yeppeugineun yeppeotda	예쁘기는 하다 yeppeugineun hada 예쁘기는 예쁘다 yeppeugineun yeppeuda	예쁘기는 할 것이다 yeppeugineun hal geosida 예쁘기는 예쁠 것이다 yeppeugineun yeppeul geosida
Descriptive verbs (adjectives) ending in a consonant	작다	작기는 했다 jakgineun haetda 작기는 작았다 jakgineun jagatda	작기는 하다 jakgineun hada 작기는 작다 jakgineun jakda	작기는 할 것이다 jakgineun hal geosida 작기는 작을 것이다 jakgineun jageul geosida

TAKE NOTE

기는 can also be shortened to 긴.

This expression is similar to 지만. The main difference is that with 지만 both parts of the sentence, A and B, have equal weight, while with 기는 or 긴 하는데 or 한데, B is more important. You present A to show that there's another side to the situation, but ultimately you find B more convincing.

EXAMPLE SENTENCES

그 여자가 예쁘**기는 예쁘**지만 성격이 나빠요.
Geu yeojaga yeppeugineun yeppeujiman seonggyeogi nappayo.
That woman is beautiful, but she doesn't have a good character.

먹**기는 먹**는데 이 음식 맛이 없어서 많이 먹기는 어려워요.
Meokgineun meokneunde i eumsig masi eobseoseo mani meokgineun eoryeowoyo.
I'm eating it, but the food doesn't taste good, so it's hard to eat a lot.

서두렀**긴 했**지만 늦었어요. Seodureotgin haetjiman neujeosseoyo.
Even though I hurried, I was late.

여행을 좋아하**긴 하**는데 돈이 없어서 자주 안 가요.
Yeohaengeul joahagin haneunde doni eobseoseo jaju an gayo.
I love traveling, but (more importantly) I have no money so I don't go often.

도시 생활이 편리하**기는 한**데 시끄러워요.
Dosi saenghwari pyeonlihagineun hande sikkeureowoyo.
Life in the city is convenient, but (more importantly) noisy.

A네 B네 해도 C	"Even if A and B, C"

Speaking > Writing ★

택시를 타**네** 급행열차를 타**네 해도 결국** 늦을 거예요.
Taeksireul tane geuphaengyeolchareul tane haedo gyeolguk neujeul geoyeyo.
Even if he takes a taxi or a fast train, he will be late.

In this expression, you are essentially saying that A and B don't matter and C is true regardless. For instance, if you just adore living in the country, you might say to someone who's not convinced, "Even if it's remote and there's nothing much to do, I still like living here." Or maybe you are that person who isn't convinced, in which case you could use this expression to tell your friend from the countryside, "Even if it's peaceful and the scenery is great, I still couldn't live here."

Another use of this expression translates more accurately as "whether or not A, C." In this case A and B are opposites, and C is true regardless of whether A or B is true in the case in question.

HOW IT'S CONJUGATED

		Past	Present	Future
Action verbs ending in a vowel	하다	했네 haenne	하네 hane	할 거네 hal geone
Action verbs ending in a consonant	먹다	먹었네 meogeonne	먹네 meokne	먹을 거네 meogeul geone
Descriptive verbs (adjectives) ending in a vowel	예쁘다	예뻤네 yeppeonne	예쁘네 yeppeune	예쁠 거네 yeppeul geone
Descriptive verbs (adjectives) ending in a consonant	작다	작았네 jaganne	작네 jakne	작을 거네 jageul geone
Nouns ending in a vowel	남자	남자였네 namjayeonne	남자네 namjane	남자일 거네 namjail geone
Nouns ending in a consonant	물	물이었네 murieonne	물이네 muline	물일 거네 muril geone

TAKE NOTE

This has nothing to do with the 네s that mean "yes" and "you."

A and B must be either direct opposites, or things that are either both positive or both negative. In the former case, C will be something that's true regardless of whether A is true or not; in the latter, C is true in spite of both A and B. See the examples below for clarification.

EXAMPLE SENTENCES

물가가 비싸**네** 사람이 많**네 해도** 도시에 살고 싶어요.
Mulgaga bissane sarami manne haedo dosie salgo sipeoyo.
Even if it's expensive and there are a lot of people, I want to live in the city.

돈이 많**네** 없**네 해도** 어려운 사람을 도와 줘야 돼요.
Doni manne eomne haedo eoryeoun sarameul dowa jwoya dwaeyo.
Whether you have a lot of money or not, you must help those who are having trouble.

보드카**네** 위스키**네 해도**, 역시 소주가 최고예요.
Bodeukane wiseukine haedo, yeoksi sojuga choegoyeyo.
Even if people are saying that vodka is good and whisky is good, soju is still the best.

		Speaking = Writing
A기로서니 giroseoni B	"Even though A, B is not all right"	★

아무리 바쁘**기로서니** 그렇게 늦게 와서야 되겠어요?
Amuri bappeugiroseoni geureoke neutge waseoya doegesseoyo?
Even though you were busy, do you really think it's all right to be that late?

This is for when your friend tells you something that leaves you aghast. You just can't believe he did such a thing.

HOW IT'S FORMED

기 turns verbs into nouns (see page 22), 로서 means "through" (see page 130) and 니 is short for 니까, which means "so" (see page 67).

HOW IT'S CONJUGATED

		Past	Present	Future
Action verbs ending in a vowel	하다	했기로서니 haetgiroseoni	하기로서니 hagiroseoni	하기로서니
Action verbs ending in a consonant	먹다	먹었기로서니 meogeotgiroseoni	먹기로서니 meokgiroseoni	먹기로서니
Descriptive verbs (adjectives) ending in a vowel	예쁘다	예뻤기로서니 yeppeotgiroseoni	예쁘기로서니 yeppeugiroseoni	예쁘기로서니
Descriptive verbs (adjectives) ending in a consonant	작다	작았기로서니 jagatgiroseoni	작기로서니 jakgiroseoni	작기로서니
Nouns ending in a vowel	남자	남자였기로서니 namjayeotgiroseoni	남자이기로서니 namja-i-giroseoni	남자이기로서니
Nouns ending in a consonant	물	물이었기로서니 murieotgiroseoni	물이기로서니 murigiroseoni	물이기로서니

TAKE NOTE

A should be in the second or third person; this expression is used to express shock at what someone else has done, not talk about what you've done. A often includes 아무리 **amuri** to express deeper shock.

   B should be a question or expression of disbelief. Here are some examples:

~(으)ㄴ/는단 말이야? (see page 318)   Are you saying…?
(eu)n/neundan mariya?

~(으)ㄹ 수(야) 없지요 (see page 294)   You know you can't…
~(eu)r su(ya) eopjiyo

~아/어/여서야 되겠냐? (see page 303)   Do you really think that's all right?
~a/eo/yeoseoya doegennya?

EXAMPLE SENTENCES

그 여자가 아무리 예쁜 여자이**기로서니** 그렇게 처다볼 수는 없지요.
Geu yeojaga amuri yeppeun yeoja-i-giroseoni geureoke cheodabol suneun eopjiyo.
No matter how beautiful a woman is, you can't stare at her like that.

당신이 아무리 일을 열심히 했**기로서니** 마음대로 회사에 안 나간단 말이에요?
dangsini amuri ireul lyeolsimhi haetgiroseoni maeumdaero hoesae an
nagandan mari eyo?
Even though you worked hard, you can't just skip work whenever you want to.

Linking Sentences—Contrast: Not A, But B

Do you enjoy telling people they're wrong? Here's how you can do that in Korean.

> **Speaking = Writing**
>
> A이/가 아니라 i/ga anira B,   "Not A, but B"   ★★★★
>   A이/가 아니고 i/ga anigo B

내가 **아니라** 민수 잘못 때문에 늦게 왔어요.
Naega anira Minsu jalmot ttaemune neutge waseoyo.

내가 **아니고** 민수 잘못 때문에 늦게 왔어요.
Naega anigo Minsu jalmot ttaemune neutge waseoyo.

It was not my fault, but Minsu's, that we were late.

These expressions are based on 아니다 (the dictionary form of good old 아니요) and are used to negate A and assert B: in other words, not A, but B.

HOW IT'S CONJUGATED

		Past	Present	Future
Action verbs ending in a vowel	하다	한 것이 아니라 han geosi anira 한 것이 아니고 han geosi anigo	하는 것이 아니라 haneun geosi anira 하는 것이 아니고 haneun geosi anigo	할 것이 아니라 hal geosi anira 할 것이 아니고 hal geosi anigo
Action verbs ending in a consonant	먹다	먹은 것이 아니라 meogeun geosi anira 먹은 것이 아니고 meogeun geosi anigo	먹는 것이 아니라 meongneun geosi anira 먹는 것이 아니고 meongneun geosi anigo	먹을 것이 아니라 meogeul geosi anira 먹을 것이 아니고 meogeul geosi anigo
Descriptive verbs (adjectives) ending in a vowel	예쁘다	예쁜 것이 아니라 yeppeun geosi anira 예쁜 것이 아니고 yeppeun geosi anigo	예쁜 것이 아니라 yeppeun geosi anira 예쁜 것이 아니고 yeppeun geosi anigo	예쁜 것이 아니라 yeppeun geosi anira 예쁜 것이 아니고 yeppeun geosi anigo
Descriptive verbs (adjectives) ending in a consonant	작다	작은 것이 아니라 jageun geosi anira 작은 것이 아니고 jageun geosi anigo	작은 것이 아니라 작은 것이 아니고	작은 것이 아니라 작은 것이 아니고
Nouns ending in a vowel	남자	남자(가) 아니라 namja(ga) anira 남자(가) 아니고 namja(ga) anigo	남자(가) 아니라 남자(가) 아니고	남자(가) 아니라 남자(가) 아니고
Nouns ending in a consonant	물	물(이) 아니라 mul(i) anira 물(이) 아니고 mul(i) anigo	물(이) 아니라 물(이) 아니고	물(이) 아니라 물(이) 아니고

TAKE NOTE

As you may recall (or can learn on page 51), 고 can be used only in sentences where both A and B have the same subject, and that's true of 아니고 as well. However, you probably don't need to worry about it too much since A and B usually have the same subject in these kinds of sentences anyway.

EXAMPLE SENTENCES

그는 의사**가 아니라** 변호사이에요. Geuneun uisaga anira byeonhosa-i-eyo.

그는 의사**가 아니고** 변호사이에요. Geuneun uisaga anigo byeonhosa-i-eyo.

He is not a doctor, but a lawyer.

비빔밥**이 아니라** 김밥을 주문했어요.
Bibimbapi anira gimbapeul jumunhaesseoyo.

비빔밥**이 아니고** 김밥을 주문했어요.
Bibimbapi anigo gimbapeul jumunhaesseoyo.

비빔밥을 주문한 것**이 아니라** 김밥을 주문했어요.
Bibimbapeul jumunhan geosi anira gimbapeul jumunhaesseoyo.

비빔밥을 주문한 것**이 아니고** 김밥을 주문했어요.
Bibimbapeul jumunhan geosi anigo gimbapeul jumunhaesseoyo.

비빔밥을 주문한 게 **아니라** 김밥을 주문했어요.
Bibimbapeul jumunhan ge anira gimbapeul jumunhaesseoyo.

비빔밥을 주문한 게 **아니고** 김밥을 주문했어요.
Bibimbapeul jumunhan ge anigo gimbapeul jumunhaesseoyo.

I didn't order bibimbap; I ordered kimbap.

(Yes, all six of these sentences mean the same thing. Keep in mind that 게, the abbreviated form of 것이, is conversational Korean while 것이 is a little more formal.)

		Speaking = Writing
A([으]ㄴ/는) 대신에 [eu]/neun) daesine B	"B rather than A"	★★★★

시간에 맞게 온 **대신에** 늦었어요. Sigane matge on daesine neujeosseoyo.
Instead of arriving on time, he was late.

This has two uses. The first one is to say "B instead of A," and the other is used is to make trades. In both cases, the same grammatical rules apply. Let's take a look:

HOW IT'S CONJUGATED

		Past	Present	Future
Action verbs ending in a vowel	하다	한 대신에 han daesine	하는 대신에 haneun daesine	하는 대신에
Action verbs ending in a consonant	먹다	먹은 대신에 meogeun daesine	먹는 대신에 meogneun daesine	먹는 대신에
Descriptive verbs (adjectives) ending in a vowel	예쁘다	예쁜 대신에 yeppeun daesine	예쁜 대신에	예쁜 대신에
Descriptive verbs (adjectives) ending in a consonant	작다	작은 대신에 jageun daesine	작은 대신에	작은 대신에
Nouns ending in a vowel	남자	남자(가) 대신에 namja(ga) daesine	남자(가) 대신에	남자(가) 대신에
Nouns ending in a consonant	물	물(이) 대신에 mul(i) daesine	물(이) 대신에	물(이) 대신에

EXAMPLE SENTENCES

Here's 대신에 used to mean "instead of":

비빔밥 **대신에** 김밥을 먹었어요.
Bibimbap daesine gimbapeul meogeosseoyo.
Instead of bibimbap, I ate kimbap.

기타 치는 **대신에** 노래를 부르겠어요.
Gita chineun daesine noraereul bureugesseoyo.
Instead of playing the guitar, I intend to sing a song.

And here are some examples of using 대신에 to make trades:

내가 친구 숙제를 도와주는 **대신에** 친구가 나한테 저녁을 살게요.
Naega chingu sukjereul dowajuneun daesine chinguga nahante jeonyeogeul salgeyo.
In exchange for helping my friend with his homework, he'll buy me dinner.

제가 친구 저녁을 사 주는 **대신에** 친구가 저에게 점심을 산다고 했어요.
Jega chingu jeonyeogeul sa juneun daesine chinguga jeoege jeomsimeul sandago haesseoyo.
In exchange for buying my friend dinner, he'll buy me lunch.

부모님이 민수에게 용돈을 주는 대신에 민수가 부모님 집청소를 해야 돼요.
Bumonimi Minsuege yongdoneul juneun daesine Minsuga bumonim jipcheongsoreul haeya dwaeyo.
In exchange for his allowance, Minsu must clean his parents' house.

		Speaking = Writing
A(이/가) 아니면 (i/ga) animyeon B	**"If not A, then B"**	★★★

늦을 거예요? **아니면** 시간에 맞출 거예요?
Neujeul geoyeyo? Animyeon sigane matchul geoyeyo?
Will you be late? Or will you arrive on time?

Either A or B is possible, but if it's not A then it's B. Think of English expressions like "Are you going to have steak, or are you trying something new today?" Since you obviously don't know if it's A or B (or you wouldn't be using this pattern), this expression is normally used for posing questions or making guesses.

HOW IT'S FORMED

Here's 아니다 (not) again. Add 면, which means "if" (see page 283), and you get "If not A, then B."

HOW IT'S CONJUGATED

Verbs can be used with 아니면 if they're first changed into nouns using 것이; however, this is not usually done, and Koreans will normally find another way around this kind of sentence. See, for example, the last two sentences below. It's awkward to say 늦는 것이 아니면 **neujneun geos i animyeon** and much simpler to divide one sentence into two.

		All tenses
Nouns ending in a vowel	남자	남자(가) 아니면 namja(ga) animyeon
Nouns ending in a consonant	물	물(이) 아니면 mul(i) animyeon

TAKE NOTE

The difference between 아니면 **animyeon** and 아니라/아니고 **anira/anigo** is that in the latter, you think A is definitely not true; in the former, you think it could be true, but if not, then B is definitely true instead. So in 아니라/아니고 you are clearly rejecting A, while in 아니면 you aren't.

Finally, you can use the expression 아니면 좋겠다 **animyeon joketda** to state "I hope." See page 178 for details on 좋겠다 **joketda**.

EXAMPLE SENTENCES

그는 의사일걸요? **아니면** 변호사일걸요?
Geuneun uisa-ilgeollyo? Animyeon byeonhosa-ilgeollyo?
Is he a doctor? (If not, then) a lawyer?

(ㄹ/을걸요 is an ending used mostly for making rough guesses; see page 149).

고기 먹었어요? **아니면** 회 먹었어요?
Gogi meogeosseoyo? Animyeon hoe meogeosseoyo?
Did you eat meat? or did you eat sashimi?

그는 의사가 **아니면** 변호사일걸요.
Geuneun uisaga animyeon byeonhosa-ilgeollyo.
He's a doctor or (if not, then) a lawyer.

스테이크가 **아니면** 다른 것을 먹을까요?
Seuteikeuga animyeon dareun geoseul meogeulkkayo?
Shall we eat steak, or something else?

늦게 올 거예요? **아니면** 시간에 맞춰 올 거예요?
Neutge ol geoyeyo? Animyeon sigane matchwo ol geoyeyo?
Will you be late, or will you arrive on time?

기타를 칠 거예요? **아니면** 노래를 부를 거예요?
Gitareul chil geoyeyo? Animyeon noraereul bureul geoyeyo?
Are you going to play the guitar? Or sing a song?

Speaking = Writing

A(이)라/(으)ㄴ/는다기보다(는)   "B rather than A"   ★★
(i)ra/(eu)n/neundagiboda(neun) B

그는 작가**라기보다** 사진사예요. **Geuneun jakgaragiboda sajinsayeyo.**
He's more of a photographer than a writer.

This means "more of B than of A" or "B is more true than A."

HOW IT'S FORMED

First, take an indirect speech particle and change it into a noun using 기. Then add 보다 (see page 96) which is used to compare two things. 는 is optional and can be added for emphasis if you'd like.

HOW IT'S CONJUGATED

		Past	Present
Action verbs ending in a vowel	하다	했다기보다(는) haetdagiboda(neun)	한다기보다(는) handagiboda(neun)
Action verbs ending in a consonant	먹다	먹었다기보다(는) meogeotdagiboda(neun)	먹는다기보다(는) meokneundagiboda(neun)
Descriptive verbs (adjectives) ending in a vowel	예쁘다	예뻤다기보다(는) yeppeotdagiboda(neun)	예쁘다기보다(는) yeppeudagiboda(neun)
Descriptive verbs (adjectives) ending in a consonant	작다	작았다기보다(는) jagatdagiboda(neun)	작다기보다(는) jakdagiboda(neun)

		Past	Present
Nouns ending in a vowel	남자	남자라기보다(는) namjaragiboda(neun)	남자라기보다(는)
Nouns ending in a consonant	물	물이라기보다(는) muriragiboda(neun)	물이라기보다(는)

EXAMPLE SENTENCES

떡볶이가 식사**라기보다** 간식이에요.
Ddeokbokkiga siksaragiboda gansigieyo.
Ddeokbokki is more of a snack than a meal.

김밥은 맛있**다기보다는** 싸기 때문에 자주 먹어요.
Kimbapeun masitdagibodaneun ssagi ttaemune jaju meogeoyo.
I often eat kimbap because it's cheap, not because I like it.

뛴**다기보다는** 빨리 걸어 가고 있어요.
Ttwindagibodaneun ppalli georeo gago isseoyo.
I'm not running; I'm walking quickly.

		Speaking = Writing
A느니 neuni B	"I'd rather B than A"	★★

늦게 오**느니** 그냥 오지 마세요. Neutge oneuni geunyang oji maseyo.
Rather than coming late, just don't come at all.

This expression is perfect for when you need to choose between two options but aren't terribly excited about either. Let's say you hate seafood, but are stuck overnight in a seaside town where the only open restaurant serves either 매운탕 **maeuntang** (spicy fish soup) or 회 **hoe** (raw fish). That's when you need 느니. A is the option you're rejecting and B is what you're choosing to do instead.

HOW IT'S CONJUGATED

		All tenses
Action verbs ending in a vowel	하다	하느니 haneuni
Action verbs ending in a consonant	먹다	먹느니 meogneuni

TAKE NOTE

차라리 **charari**, which means "rather," often follows 느니.
    B normally ends with a future tense: either (으)ㄹ 것이다 **(eu)r geosida** or 겠다 **getda**.

EXAMPLE SENTENCES

퇴직하<u>느니</u> 계속 일하겠어요. Toejikaneuni gyesog ilhagesseoyo.
I'd rather keep working than retire.

매운탕을 먹<u>느니</u> 회를 먹을 거예요.
Maeuntangeul meogneuni hoereul meogeul geoyeyo.
I'd rather eat raw fish than spicy fish soup.

	Speaking = Writing
A와/과(는) 달리 wa/gwa(neun) dalli B "B, unlike A"	★

어젯밤**과 달리**, 오늘 집에 일찍 돌아왔어요.
Eojetbamgwa dalli oneul jibe iljjik dolawasseoyo.
Unlike last night, today I got home early.

This comes from 다르다 **dareuda** or "to be different." It means "Unlike A, B." 달리 itself can be used in sentences as an adjective and is quite often used in sentences indicating that there is no alternative but A.

HOW IT'S FORMED

와/과 means "and"; see page 45. 는 is optional and can be used to add emphasis. 달리 comes from 다르다, which means "to be different."

HOW IT'S CONJUGATED

		All tenses
Nouns ending in a vowel	남자	남자와 달리 namjawa dalli
Nouns ending in a consonant	물	물과 달리 mulgwa dalli

TAKE NOTE

You can also use 달리 by itself to begin a sentence contrasting with the previous sentence or to contrast two clauses. The latter is a nice way to make you sound more fluent.

EXAMPLE SENTENCES

달리 친구가 없어요. Dalli chinguga eobseoyo. I don't have any other friends.

달리 할 방법이 없어요. Dalli hal bangbeobi eobseoyo.
There's no other way to do it.

어렸을 때는 지금**과는 달리** 축구를 자주 했어요.
Eoryeosseul ttaeneun jigeumgwaneun dalli chukgureul jaju haesseoyo.
When I was a child, I often played soccer, but not any more.

어렸을 때**와 달리** 이제 자주 안 해요. Eoryeosseul ttaewa dalli ije jaju an haeyo.
Unlike when I was a child, I rarely do it now.

도시**와는 달리**, 시골에는 차가 많지 않아요.
Dosiwaneun dalli, sigoreneun chaga manchi anayo.
Unlike in the city, there aren't many cars in the country.

어제**와는 달리** 오늘은 집에 일찍 들어왔어요.
Eojewaneun dalli oneureun jibe iljjik deureowasseoyo.
Unlike yesterday, I got home early.

Linking Sentences—Comparisons: As

| A([으]ㄴ/는 것)처럼 ([eu]n/ neun geot)cheoreom B | "B is like A" | Speaking = Writing ★★★★★ |

돈을 물**처럼** 썼어요. Doneul mulcheoreom sseosseoyo.
He spent money like water.

Very easy and very common, this expression simply means that B resembles A in some way. Grammatically, it turns a noun into an adverbial phrase. It can usually be replaced by 같이 if you prefer to do it that way. There are many common expressions with 처럼: like 좀처럼 jomcheoreom (like the first time), 전처럼 jeoncheoreom (like before) or 평소처럼 pyeongsocheoreom (as usual).

HOW IT'S CONJUGATED

		Past	Present	Future
Action verbs ending in a vowel	하다	한 것처럼 han geotcheoreom	하는 것처럼 haneun geotcheoreom	할 것처럼 hal geotcheoreom
Action verbs ending in a consonant	먹다	먹은 것처럼 meogeun geotcheoreom	먹는 것처럼 meogneun geotcheoreom	먹을 것처럼 meogeul geotcheoreom
Nouns ending in a vowel	남자	남자처럼 namjacheoreom	남자처럼	남자처럼
Nouns ending in a consonant	물	물처럼 mulcheoreom	물처럼	물처럼

TAKE NOTE

It's common to put 마치 machi before A. 마치 ~처럼 means "just like A."

EXAMPLE SENTENCES

그녀는 남자 **처럼** 행동해요. Geunyeoneun namja cheoreom haengdonghaeyo.
She acts like a man.

우리는 옛날 **처럼** 말을 탔어요. Urineun yennal cheoreom mareul tasseoyo.
We rode horses just like in the olden days.

그 열차가 너무 천천히 가서 마치 걷는 것 **처럼** 오래 걸려요. Geu yeolchaga
neomu cheoncheonhi gaseo machi geonneun geot cheoreom orae geollyeoyo.
That train is so slow that riding it takes as long as walking.

남자친구를 처음 만났을 때 마치 하늘을 날 것 **처럼** 기뻤어요. Namjachingureul
cheoeum mannaseul ttae machi haneureul nal geot cheoreom gippeoseoyo.
The first time I met my boyfriend, I was so happy I felt as if I were floating on air.

A([으]ㄴ/는/[으]ㄹ) 만큼   "B, as much as A"   **Speaking = Writing**
  ([eu]n/neun/[eu]l) mankeum B   ★★★★

민수씨는 가영씨**만큼** 늦었어요. Minsussineun Kayoungssimankeum neujeosseoyo.
Minsu was as late as Kayoung.

This is another good one for scientific types. It's used for comparing two things and declaring them to be about equal, and is generally used to express the degree of something.

HOW IT'S FORMED

만큼 is an expression by itself. You can add 도 after 만큼 to express an extreme degree of something.

HOW IT'S CONJUGATED

		Past	Present	Future
Action verbs ending in a vowel	하다	한 만큼 han mankeum	하는 만큼 haneun mankeum	할 만큼 hal mankeum
Action verbs ending in a consonant	먹다	먹은 만큼 meogeun mankeum	먹는 만큼 meogneun mankeum	먹을 만큼 meogeul mankeum
Descriptive verbs (adjectives) ending in a vowel	예쁘다	예쁜 만큼 yeppeun mankeum	예쁜 만큼	예쁜 만큼
Descriptive verbs (adjectives) ending in a consonant	작다	작은 만큼 jageun mankeum	작은 만큼	작은 만큼
Nouns ending in a vowel	남자	남자만큼 namjamankeum	남자만큼	남자만큼
Nouns ending in a consonant	물	물만큼 mulmankeum	물만큼	물만큼

TAKE NOTE

(으)니만큼 is a rarely used, related expression; see page 76. It means "inasmuch as" (in speech or in writing) or "since" (mostly in writing; not usually used in speech).

만큼 can follow immediately after a noun to say that something is as (adjective) as another (noun). When used with verbs, be sure to add the tense markers (으)ㄴ/는/(으)ㄹ.

만큼 can be interchangeable with 도록 **dorok** (see page 167) under certain rare circumstances in which 도록 is used to express a limit.

너를 죽**을 만큼** 사랑한다. Neoreul jugeul mankeum saranghanda.

너를 죽**도록** 사랑한다. Neoreul jugdorok saranghanda.

I'll love you until death.

날씨가 추우**니만큼** 등산에 가지 말래요.
Nalssiga chuunimankeum deungsane gaji mallaeyo.
Since it's cold, let's not go hiking.

EXAMPLE SENTENCES

그 엄마가 자기 아이**만큼** 작아요. Geu eommaga jagi aimankeum jagayo.
That mother is as small as her child.

그 엄마가 자기 아이**만큼도** 작아요. Geu eommaga jagi aimankeumdo jagayo.
That mother is as small as her child. (emphasizes how unusually tiny this mom's size is)

음식을 먹**을 만큼** 가지고 가세요. Eumsigeul meogeul mankeum gajigo gaseyo.
Take as much food as you're going to eat.

그 맥주가 물**만큼** 맛이 없어요. Geu maekjuga mulmankeum masi eobseoyo.
That beer is as tasteless as water.

		Speaking = Writing
A(으)ㄹ 정도(로) (eu)l jeongdo(ro)	"B, to the extent	★★★★
B, ~(으)ㄹ 정도이다 (eu)l jeongdo-ida	that A"	

차가 정말 막혔어요. 두 시간 동안 안 움직**일 정도였어요**.
Chaga jeongmal makhyeosseoyo. Du sigan dongan an umjigil jeongdoyeosseoyo.
Traffic was so congested that I was stopped for two hours.

Do you like to exaggerate? Do you want to make your stories sound more exciting than they really are? The expressions above all mean the same thing and are used to say "B, to the extent that A." They are used in Korean equivalents to English expressions like: "It's raining so hard I can't see. I'm so tired I can't even think."

HOW IT'S FORMED

정도 by itself is a noun that means "degree" and you'll see it used that way as well.

HOW IT'S CONJUGATED

		All tenses
Action verbs ending in a vowel	하다	할 정도 hal jeongdo
Action verbs ending in a consonant	먹다	먹을 정도 meogeul jeongdo
Descriptive verbs (adjectives) ending in a vowel	예쁘다	예쁠 정도 yeppeul jeongdo
Descriptive verbs (adjectives) ending in a consonant	작다	작을 정도 jageul jeongdo

TAKE NOTE

You can also talk about 이정도 (this much) or 그 정도 (that much) if you want.

> **그 정도** 돈을 쓰면 안 돼요. **Geu jeongdo doneul sseumyeon an dwaeyo.**
> You can't spend that much money.

EXAMPLE SENTENCES

아무 것도 안 보**일 정도로** 비가 많이 와요.
Amu geotdo an boil jeongdoro biga mani wayo.
It's raining so hard I can't see anything.

남자친구와 헤어져서 죽**을 정도로** 슬퍼요.
Namjachinguwa heeojyeoseo jugeul jeongdoro seulpeoyo.
Since I broke up with my boyfriend, I've been so sad I could die.

Speaking = Writing

A([으]ㄴ/는/[으]ㄹ) 듯이   "B is like A"   ★★★
([eu]n/neun/[eu]r) deunni B

늦었지만 정시에 **온 듯이** 행동했어요.
Neujeotjiman jeongsie on deusi haengdonghaesseoyo.
Although I came late, I acted as if I'd been there on time.

These expressions compare B to A and are often used in similes. If you feel like getting poetic and talking, for example, about "tears flowing like rain," you can use these expressions. They're very similar with just a few differences, so I've grouped them together.

HOW IT'S FORMED

This comes from the verb 듯하다, which means "to be like." You take away 하다 to form a noun, 듯, and then change the verb into an adverb using the 이 ending (covered on page 25), which turns A into an adverbial expression talking about how things are done. The 이 ending is optional.

HOW IT'S CONJUGATED

		Past	Present	Future
Action verbs ending in a vowel	하다	하듯(이) hadeus(i) 한 듯(이) han deus(i)	하듯(이) 하는 듯(이) haneun deus(i)	하듯(이) 할 듯(이) hal deus(i)
Action verbs ending in a consonant	먹다	먹듯(이) meokdeus(i) 먹은 듯(이) meogeun deus(i)	먹듯(이) 먹는 듯(이) meogneun deus(i)	먹듯(이) 먹을 듯(이) meogeul deus(i)
Descriptive verbs (adjectives) ending in a vowel	예쁘다	예쁘듯(이) yeppeudeus(i)	예쁘듯(이)	예쁘듯(이)
Descriptive verbs (adjectives) ending in a consonant	작다	작듯(이) jakdeus(i)	작듯(이)	작듯(이)

TAKE NOTE

When used to talk about events in the future, (으)ㄴ/는/(으)ㄹ 듯(이) can be used only with action verbs. 듯(이) all by itself can't be used after nouns; 인 듯(이) can, but almost never is, so you'd be better off using 처럼 (see page 125) if you want to compare something to a noun.

는 듯이 can also be added to the indirect speech particles (ㄴ/는)다/(이/으)라/자 (see page 304) to mean "as if to say" or "acting as if."

말싸움 후에 제가 아무 일도 없**다는 듯이** 했어요.
Mmalssaum hue jega amu ildo eobsdaneun deusi haesseoyo.
After the argument, I acted as if nothing had happened.

머리를 좋아**한다는 듯이** 여자친구의 머리 스타일이 예쁘다고 칭찬 했어요.
Meorireul joahandaneun deusi yeojachinguui meori seutairi yeppeudago chingchanhaesseoyo.
He praised his girlfriend's hairstyle as if he liked it. (The implication here being that he didn't.)

EXAMPLE SENTENCES

학생들이 쥐 죽**은 듯이** 조용했어요.
Haksaengdeuri jwi jugeun deusi joyonghaesseoyo.

학생들이 쥐 죽**을 듯이** 조용했어요.
Haksaengdeuri jwi jugeul deusi joyonghaesseoyo.
The students were (as) silent (as a dead mouse).

그는 그녀를 미**친 듯이** 사랑했어요.
Geuneun geunyeoreul michin deusi saranghaesseoyo.

그는 그녀를 미**칠 듯이** 사랑했어요.
Geuneun geunyeoreul michil deusi saranghaesseoyo.

He loved her like crazy. (He loved her as if he were crazy.)

A(으)로서 (eu)roseo B   "As A, B"   **Speaking < Writing**
                                                                      ★★★

선생님<u>으로서</u> 학생들에게 참 엄격해요.
Seonsaengnimeuroseo haksaengdeurege cham eomgyeokhaeyo.
As a teacher, he is very strict.

This one is for those who like to pull rank. (으)로서 means "as" or "in the capacity of." A is what the person or object in question is, and B is what results from them being A. It's another one that's easy to use but hard to explain. It's the expression used in the Korean equivalent of English sentences like: "As a doctor, I advise you to stop smoking. As an artist, he is a total failure."

HOW IT'S FORMED

(으)로 (eu)ro means "through" and 서 comes from 아/어/여서 (see page 66) and is followed by a result. In other words, through your capacity as A, you have the authority to say B.

HOW IT'S CONJUGATED

		All tenses
Nouns ending in a vowel	남자	남자로서 namjaroseo
Nouns ending in a consonant	선생님	선생님으로서 seonsaengnimeuroseo

TAKE NOTE

Don't confuse it with (으)로써 (eu)rosseo, which has a totally different meaning (see page 82).

EXAMPLE SENTENCES

대통령<u>으로서</u> 중요한 결정을 자주 해요.
Daetonglyeongeuroseo jungyohan gyeoljeongeul jaju haeyo.
As President, he often makes important decisions.

그 허브가 약<u>으로서</u> 효력이 없어요.
Geu heobeuga yageuroseo hyolyeogi eobseoyo.
That herb is ineffective as a medicine.

~다시피 하다 dasipi hada   "As if ~"   **Speaking = Writing**
                                                                   ★

늦을까 봐 경주하**다시피 해**서 빨리 갔어요.
Neujeulkka bwa gyeongjuhadasipi haeseo ppalli gasseoyo.
I was worried I'd be late, so I raced there (went quickly, as if I were racing).

Do you live a busy life full of endless work and Korean language studies? Are you heavily into dieting or physical fitness? Alternatively, do you enjoy exaggerating the extent of your suffering? This expression is used when doing something as if you were nearly doing something else such as "studying as if your life depended on it" or "eating nearly nothing."

HOW IT'S CONJUGATED

		Past	Present	Future
Action verbs ending in a vowel	하다	하다시피 했다 hadasipi haessda	하다시피 하다 hadasipi hada	하다시피 할 것이다 hadasipi hal geosida
Action verbs ending in a consonant	먹다	먹다시피 했다 meokdasipi haessda	먹다시피 하다 meokdasipi hada	먹다시피 할 것이다 meokdasipi hal geosida

TAKE NOTE

다시피 all by itself is a different expression which means "as you." Don't get them confused. 다시피 is covered on page 163. It's also far more common, so if you hear anyone talking about 다시피 anything, it's most likely that other 다시피.

EXAMPLE SENTENCES

민수가 우리 집에서 살**다시피 해**요. Minsuga uri jibeseo saldasipi haeyo.
Minsu practically lives at our house.

그는 싸움 후에 죽**다시피** 했어요. Geuneun ssaum hue jukdasipi haesseoyo.
After the fight, he was almost dead.

Linking Sentences–Comparisons: Equals (or Not)

> **Speaking = Writing**
>
> A이/가 i/ga B(이)나 다름없다   "A is just like B"   ★★
> (i)na dareumeobsda

그 컴퓨터가 여전히 빨라서 새것**이나 다름없어요**.
Geu keompyuteoga yeojeonhi ppallaseo saegeosina dareumeobseoyo.
That computer is still fast, so it's just like a new one.

This literally means "there is no difference between A and B" and can be used when you want to say that one thing is acting just like another one.

HOW IT'S FORMED

(이)나 means "or something" (see page 60) and 다름 comes from 다르다, "to be different." 없다 is, of course, "there isn't."

HOW IT'S CONJUGATED

		Past	Present	Future
Nouns ending in a vowel	남자	남자나 다름없었다 namjana dareumeobseossda	남자나 다름없다 namjana dareumeobsda	남자나 다름없을 것이아 namjana dareumeobseul geosia
Nouns ending in a consonant	물	물이나 다름없었다 murina dareumeobseossda	물이나 다름없다 murina dareumeobsda	물이나 다름없을 것이다 murina dareumeobseul geosida

TAKE NOTE

B is usually a general category and nothing specific. It would be ungrammatical to say "There is no difference between 민수 and 가영," but you can say "가영 is just like a sister to me."

> 민수가 가영이나 다름없어요. (ungrammatical)
> **Minsuga Kayoungina dareumeobseoyo.**
> There is no difference between Minsu and Kayoung.

> 가영이 예쁜 것은 언니나 다름없어요.
> **Kayoungi yeppeun geoseun eonnina dareumeobseoyo.**
> Kayoung's beauty is just like that of her elder sister.

EXAMPLE SENTENCES

> 이모가 나를 잘 챙겨줘서 어머니**나 다름없어요**.
> **Imoga nareul jal chaenggyeojwoseo eomeonina dareumeobseoyo.**
> My aunt took good care of me, so she was just like a mother to me.

> 그는 한국어를 잘 하고 매운 음식을 잘 먹고 절도 할 줄 알아서 한국 사람
> **이나 다름없어요**.
> **Geuneun hangukeoreul jal hago maeun eumsigeul jal meokgo jeoldo hal jul araseo hanguk sarami na dareumeobseoyo.**
> He speaks Korean well, eats spicy food and also bows, so he is just like a Korean.

Speaking = Writing

A가 ga B못지않게 motjianke   "A is about as good as B"   ★★

> 그 컴퓨터가 새로 산 것 **못지않게** 빨라요.
> **Geu keompyuteoga saero san geot motjianke ppallayo.**
> That computer is as good as a new one.

Remember how your teachers always told you not to use a double negative? In Korean, you can! You're finally free! This expression means that "A is roughly as good as B." It can also be used with question words like 무엇, 누구, or 어디, in which case it means "better than anything/anyone/anywhere."

HOW IT'S FORMED

못 is usually used to mean "can't." No doubt you're familiar with expressions such as "한국 말을 잘 못 해요 **hangukmareul jal mot haeyo.**" 지 않다 **ji anta** is another familiar expression that means "isn't." In this particular expression, the 지 and 않다 are usually put together with no space in between. Finally, 게 turns words into adverbs (쉽게 **swipge**, 빠르게 **ppaleuge**, etc.) The negatives basically cancel each other out and leave us an adverbial phrase that means "A is as good as B."

HOW IT'S CONJUGATED

		All tenses
Nouns ending in a vowel	남자	남자 못지않게 namja motjianke
Nouns ending in a consonant	물	물 못지않게 mul motjianke

TAKE NOTE

못지 않게 and 다름 없다 **dareum eobsda** are quite similar. 못지 않다 **motji anta** means "as good as" or "as (adjective) as."

> 한국 음식은 프랑스 음식 **못지않게** 맛있어요.
> Hanguk eumsigeun peuranseu eumsig motjianke masisseoyo.
> Korean food is as delicious as French food.

다름 없다 **dareum eobsda** means "There is no difference." So you can't say 한국 음식 은 프랑스 음식과 **다름없이** 맛있어요 **Hanguk eumsigeun peuranseu eumsikgwa dareumeobsi masisseoyo** because they are both delicious, but they are different. A better sentence would be:

> 경기도 음식과 서울 음식은 **다름없어요**.
> Gyeonggi-do eumsikgwa Seoul eumsigeun dareumeobseoyo.
> Gyeonggi-do food is not different from Seoul food.

In that case the two items being compared are quite similar, so it's appropriate to use 다 름없다. The sentence could also be written with 못지 않게.

You can either explain how A and B are similar in a clause after 못지않게 or just end the sentence right there (못지않아요) if you prefer to be cryptic.

EXAMPLE SENTENCES

> 이모가 어머니 **못지않게** 나를 잘 챙겼어요.
> Imoga eomeoni motjianke nareul jal chaenggyeosseoyo.
> My aunt took good care of me, so she was as good as a mother to me.

> 그는 한국어를 잘 하고 매운 음식을 잘 먹고 절도 해서 한국 사람 **못지않아요**.
> Geuneun Hangukeoreul jal hago maeun eumsigeul jal meokgo jeoldo haeseo hanguk saram motjianayo.
> He speaks Korean well, eats spicy food and also bows, so he is just like a Korean.

민수가 누구 **못지않게** 축구를 잘 해요.
Minsuga nugu motjianke chukgureul jal haeyo.
Minsu plays soccer better than anyone.

Speaking = Writing

A이/가 i/ga B만 못하다　　　"A isn't as good as B"　　　★★
　man mothada

일찍 오는 것이 늦게 오는 것**만 못해요**.
Iljjig oneun geosi neutge oneun geotman mothaeyo.
Being early is not as good as coming late.

Here's an expression for people who like to criticize. It means "A isn't as good as B."

HOW IT'S FORMED

만 means "only" and 못하다 means "can't." To translate very roughly, A can't keep up with B.

HOW IT'S CONJUGATED

만 못하다 is normally used in the present tense.

		Past	Present	Future
Action verbs ending in a vowel	하다	A하는 것이 haneun geosi B하는 것만 못했다 haneun geotman mothaetda	A하는 것이 B하는 것만 못하다	A하는 것이 B하는 것만 못하겠다
Action verbs ending in a consonant	먹다	A먹는 것이 meokneun geosi B먹는 것만 못했다 meokneun geotman mothaetda	A먹는 것이 B먹는 것만 못하다	A먹는 것이 B먹는 것만 못하겠다
Descriptive verbs (adjectives) ending in a vowel	예쁘다	A 예쁜 것이 yeppeun geosi B예쁜 것만 못했다 yeppeun geotman mothaetda	A 예쁜 것이 B예쁜 것만 못하다	A 예쁜 것이 B예쁜 것만 못할 것이다
Descriptive verbs (adjectives) ending in a consonant	작다	A 작은 것이 jageun geosi B 작은 것만 못했다 jageun geotman mothaetda	A 작은 것이 B 작은 것만 못하다	A 작은 것이 B 작은 것만 못할 것이다
Nouns ending in a vowel	남자	그 남자가 저 남자만 못했다 geu namjaga jeo namjaman mothaetda	그 남자가 저 남자만 못하다 geu namjaga jeo namjaman mothada	그 남자가 저 남자만 못하겠다 geu namjaga jeo namjaman mothagetda
Nouns ending in a consonant	물	그 물이 저 물만 못했다 geu muri jeo mulman mothaetda	그 물이 저 물만 못하다 geu muri jeo mulman motada	그 물이 저 물만 못하겠다 geu muri jeo mulman motagetda

TAKE NOTE

Keep an eye out for 못하다; A이/가 B만하다 (see farther down this page) means "A is the size of B."

EXAMPLE SENTENCES

쓰기는 민수가 가영**만 못해요**.
Sseugineun Minsuga Kayoungman motaeyo.
Kayoung is better than Minsu at writing.

90년대의 컴퓨터가 현대의 컴퓨터**만 못해요**.
Gusipnyeondae-ui keompyuteoga hyeondae-ui keompyuteoman motaeyo.
Computers in the nineties weren't as good as modern ones.

		Speaking = Writing
A이/가 i/ga B만하다 manhada	"A is the size of B"	★

제 고양이가 개**만해요**. Je goyangiga gaemanhaeyo. My cat is as big as a dog.

This is used to compare the size of two objects. It's used in many idiomatic expressions which you can use if you like to exaggerate.

HOW IT'S CONJUGATED

All you have to do here is to substitute the two nouns you're comparing for A and B, choose the appropriate subject marker, and then conjugate 하다 whichever way you want.

		Past	Present	Future
Nouns ending in a vowel	크기	크기만했다 keugimanhaetda	크기만하다 keugimanhada	크기만할 것이다 keugimanhal geosida
Nouns ending in a consonant	집	집만했다 jipmanhaetda	집만하다 jipmanhada	집만할 것이다 jipmanhal geosida

TAKE NOTE

There's another expression, (으)ㄹ 만하다 (see page 333) which is used to say that something is worth doing. That one goes after verbs. This one goes after nouns.

Yet another expression with 만 (it's a very common particle) is ~(기)만 하다 (see page 335), which means "to only do ~". First of all, it has a space between 만 and 하다, while the expression we're discussing here doesn't. Secondly, it follows verbs: the only time you'll see it after a noun is when that noun is usually followed by 하다. So that 만 하다 could follow 운동 (운동하다) undong (undonghada) or 공부 (공부하다) gongbu (gongbuhada), but not just any noun.

EXAMPLE SENTENCES

Because this is quite often used in idiomatic expressions, I'm going to focus on a few of these.

방이 손바닥**만해요**. Bangi sonbadak**manhaeyo**.
The room is tiny. (Literally: the size of the palm of one's hand)

방이 운동장**만해요**. Bangi undongjang**manhaeyo**.
The room is huge. (Literally: the size of a playing field)

월급이 쥐꼬리**만해요**. Wolgeubi jwikkori**manhaeyo**.
My salary is small. (Literally: the size of a mouse's tail)

눈이 단춧구멍**만해요**. Nuni danchutgumeong**manhaeyo**.
His eyes are tiny. (Literally: the size of buttons)

얼굴이 주먹**만해요**. Eolguri jumeok**manhaeyo**.
His face is tiny. (Literally: the size of a fist)

목소리가 모기 소리**만해요**. Moksoriga mogi sori**manhaeyo**.
His voice is tiny. (Literally: like the sound of a mosquito)

You can use it in your own expressions, too, if you want. Check the example at the beginning of this section.

Thinking: Making Guesses

One thing you may notice if you spend much time around Koreans is that they don't like to directly express their opinion. This is reflected in this section which, as you may have noticed, is the biggest in the entire book. Compare it to the Knowing section, which only has a few expressions. In other words, if you want to be able to speak without sounding like a know-it-all, this is a good section to study.

There are a few expressions which belong more appropriately in the "plans" section, but which can also be used for making guesses. All the expressions with 터이다 teo-ida (테다 teda, 테니까 tenikka, 텐데 tende, 테면 temyeon, 테고 tego and 테지만 tejiman) can be used for making guesses about someone's intentions when the subject of the sentence is in the third person. These expressions can be found from pages 218–225. 셈치고 semchigo (see page 291) is another expression that can be used to make plans or guesses. 셈치고 has to do with doing something based on another assumption (if we assume that A, then B) and so it's in the section on "if."

All the expressions below are used to guess or to say that something "looks like it may do something."

> **~(으)ㄴ/는 (으)ㄹ 것 같다**   "It seems like ~"   **Speaking = Writing**
> (eu)n/neun (eu)l geot gatda   ★★★★

민수가 늦을 **것 같아요**. Minsuga neujeul geot gatayo.
It seems like Minsu will be late.

This expression is very similar to 듯하다 **deutada** and functions in much the same way: to comment on a situation you are observing or have observed.

HOW IT'S FORMED

The tense markers (으)ㄴ/는/(으)ㄹ; plus 것, which transforms a verb into a noun; plus 같다, which means "to be the same as." Now, I realize it may not seem to make much sense to transform a noun into a verb and then back again as I've done below, but that's just how the expression goes. 남자 같다 **namja gatda** can also be used, but it's a little different and appears more often in the middle of a sentence like "남자 같은 여자들 **namja gateun yeojadeul**" ("women who are like men"). I discussed it on page 48. (으)ㄹ 것 같다 ends a clause and you can then end the sentence altogether or move on to the next clause.

HOW IT'S CONJUGATED

		Past	Present	Future
Action verbs ending in a vowel	하다	한 것 같다 han geot gatda	하는 것 같다 haneun geot gatda	할 것 같다 hal geot gatda
Action verbs ending in a consonant	먹다	먹은 것 같다 meogeun geot gatda	먹는 것 같다 meokneun geot gatda	먹을 것 같다 meogeul geot gatda
Descriptive verbs (adjectives) ending in a vowel	예쁘다	예쁜 것 같다 yeppeun geot gatda	예쁜 것 같다	예쁠 것 같다 yeppeul geot gatda
Descriptive verbs (adjectives) ending in a consonant	작다	작은 것 같다 jageun geot gatda	작은 것 같다	작을 것 같다 jageul geot gatda
Nouns ending in a vowel	남자	남자인 것 같다 namja-in geot gatda	남자인 것 같다	남자일 것 같다 namja-il geot gatda
Nouns ending in a consonant	물	물인 것 같다 murin geot gatda	물인 것 같다	물일 것 같다 muril geot gatda

TAKE NOTE

같다 has many uses outside this expression, but they all have similar meanings, so you shouldn't get too confused. 같이 means "together" while 같은, as discussed above and on page 48, can be used to either compare two items (usually nouns) or to list examples from a given category.

It can usually be replaced by 나 보다, (으)ㄴ/는/(으)ㄹ 듯하다 **deuthada** or 는 모양이 다 **neun moyangida** without any change in meaning.

While it can be conjugated with any tense marker, the expression, like most other guessing expressions, is most often used with the future tense marker (으)ㄹ.

EXAMPLE SENTENCES

그 여자가 한국사람**일 것 같아요**. Geu yeojaga hanguksaramil geot gatayo.
That woman seems like a Korean.

눈이 **올 것 같아요**. Nuni ol geot gatayo. It seems like it will snow.

Here are some examples of the other 같다s to help you see the differences in usage:

같이 갑시다. Gachi gapsida. Let's go together.

남자 친구와 **같이** 영화를 봤어요. Namja chinguwa gachi yeonghwareul bwasseoyo.
I saw a movie (together) with my boyfriend.

맥주 **같은** 주류를 너무 마시지 마세요.
Maekju gateun juryureul neomu masiji maseyo.
Don't drink too many alcoholic drinks like beer.

그 어른 **같은** 아이는 항상 심각한 표정을 하고 있어요.
Geu eoreun gateun a-i-neun hangsang simgakan pyojeongeul hago isseoyo.
That child who seems like an adult always has a very serious face.

		Speaking > Writing
~나/(으)ㄴ가 보다 na/(eu)n-ga boda	"It seems that ~"	★★★★
~(으)려나 보다 (eu)ryeona boda	"I think he's planning to ~"	★

민수가 늦**나 봐요**. Minsuga neunna bwayo. It looks like Minsu is late.

This is one of the most common of the expressions used for guessing, and you'll hear Koreans use it all the time. It's used for making assumptions about situations. When you add 려 in front of it, you're going even deeper: not only making an assumption based on what you see, but on what you think someone is planning. If you ever find yourself battling an evil Korean genius, you'll probably want to know this expression.

HOW IT'S FORMED

Remember our question forms 나 and (으)ㄴ가? If not, check page 44. They mean "Is it?" or "Does it?" They are used here again to begin this expression and are then followed by 보다 ("to see"). It means there is a little hesitation about what's being observed. (으)려 is short for (으)려고 하다 (see page 215), which has to do with plans.

HOW IT'S CONJUGATED

나 follows action verbs and past tense forms. (으)ㄴ가 follows adjectives in the present or future tense.

		Past	Present	Future
Action verbs ending in a vowel	하다	했나 보다 haenna boda	하나 보다 hana boda	하려나 보다 haryeona boda
Action verbs ending in a consonant	먹다	먹었나 보다 meogeotna boda	먹나 보다 meogna boda	먹으려나 보다 meogeuryeona boda
Descriptive verbs (adjectives) ending in a vowel	예쁘다	예뻤나 보다 yeppeotna boda	예쁜가 보다 yeppeunga boda	예쁜가 보다
Descriptive verbs (adjectives) ending in a consonant	작다	작았나 보다 jagatna boda	작은가 보다 jageunga boda	작은가 보다
Nouns ending in a vowel	남자	남자였나 보다 namjayeotna boda	남자인가 보다 namja-inga boda	남자인가 보다
Nouns ending in a consonant	물	물이었나 보다 murieotna boda	물인가 보다 muringa boda	물인가 보다

TAKE NOTE

It's interchangeable with (으)ㄴ/는/(으)ㄹ 것 같다 (eu)n/neun/(eu)r geot gatda, (으)ㄴ/는/(으)ㄹ모양이다 (eu)n/neun/(eu)r moyangida, and (으)ㄴ/는/(으)ㄹ듯하다 (eu)n/neun/(eu)r deuthada (see pages 137, 145 and 153). Like these, it is used to make a guess based on a situation that is being observed.

으려나 보다 euryeona boda is used to talk about other people's plans, not your own; you probably won't need to make guesses about your own plans. If your own plans are tentative, you can use (으)ㄹ까 보다/하다/싶다 (see page 226) to express that.

(으)려나 보다 is also used to talk specifically about plans, and not anything else. Thus, it indicates less certainty than either 나 보다 by itself or (으)ㄹ 것 같다.

(으)려나 all by itself at the end of a sentence is a 반말 way to wonder about something: for example, 나중에 비가 오려나? means "I wonder if it will rain later?"

You can add a 긴 before 나/(으)ㄴ가 보다 and then repeat the verb; this isn't very common, but you can do it to add emphasis. It works like this:

> 아이들이 숙제를 잘 못하는 걸 보니 이 단어를 아직 이해하기가 어렵긴 어려운 가 봐요.
> A-i-deuri sukjereul jal motaneun geol boni i daneoreul ajig ihaehagiga eoryeopgin eoryeo-unga bwayo.
> The children didn't do well on their homework, so it seems the vocabulary is still difficult for them.

> 마이크씨가 한국어 말하기 능력이 좋아지는 걸 보니 공부를 열심히 하**긴** 했**나 봐요**.
> Maikeussiga hangukeo malhagi neunglyeogi johajineun geol boni gongbureul yeolsimhi hagin haetna bwayo.
> Because Mike's Korean speaking ability has improved, I guess he's been studying hard.

This 긴 ~ 나/(으)ㄴ가 보다 expression usually comes after an observation followed by (으)ㄴ/는 걸 보니, which is an abbreviation of (으)ㄴ/는 것을 보니까. ([으]ㄴ/는 것 turns the verb into a noun, 보다 shows that you observed it, and 니까 means "so.")

EXAMPLE SENTENCES

그 여자가 한국사람**인가 봐요**. Geu yeojaga hanguksaraminga bwayo.
That woman seems like a Korean.

눈이 왔**나 봐요**. Nuni watna bwayo. It looks like it snowed.

민수 손이 작**은가 봐요**. Minsu soni jageunga bwayo. Minsu's hands look small.

민수가 다른 약속도 있어서 늦게 오**려나 봐요**.
Minsuga dareun yaksokdo isseoseo neutge oryeona bwayo.
Minsu has another engagement, so I think he's planning to come late.

가영이 자주 여행 웹사이트에 방문하는데 여행을 가**려나 봐요**.
Kayoungi jaju yeohaeng websaiteue bangmunhaneunde yeohaengeul
garyeona bwayo.
Kayoung often looks at travel websites. I think she's planning to go on a trip.

최근 여기에 공사가 많은데 새로운 가게를 내**려나 봐요**.
Choegeun yeogie gongsaga manheunde saeroun gagereul naeryeona bwayo.
There's a lot of construction here lately. Maybe they're planning to open a
new store.

		Speaking = Writing
~았/었/였을 것이다 ass/ eoss/yeosseul geosida	"will have ~"	★★★★

택시를 탔으면 늦지 않**았을 거예요**.
Taeksireul tasseumyeon neutji anasseul geoyeyo.

택시를 탔으면 늦지 않**았을 거야**.
Taeksireul tasseumyeon neutji anasseul geoya.

If you'd taken a taxi, you wouldn't have been late.

This expression is used when you're making a guess about something that's already been done, and it translates directly as "will have." For example: "She'll have arrived at the airport by now" or "You must have been famished!" It can also be used hypothetically, similar to English "would have" in sentences such as "If my father were still alive, he would have been happy to meet his grandson" or "If you had taken a taxi, you wouldn't have been late."

HOW IT'S FORMED

The past tense 았/었/였 is placed before the future tense 을 것이다. It's the other way around in English, but the meaning is the same: will have been, will have done, will have gone, etc.)

HOW IT'S CONJUGATED

		Past
Action verbs with 오 or 아	가다	갔을 거예요 gasseul geoyeyo 갔을 거야 gasseul geoya
Action verbs with 어, 우, 으 or 이	먹다	먹었을 거예요 meogeosseul geoyeyo 먹었을 거야 meogeosseul geoya
하다	하다	했을 거예요 haesseul geoyeyo 했을 거야 haesseul geoya
Descriptive verbs (adjectives) with 오 or 아	예쁘다	예뻤을 거예요 yeppeosseul geoyeyo 예뻤을 거야 yeppeosseul geoya
Descriptive verbs (adjectives) with 어, 우, 으 or 이	작다	작았을 거예요 jagasseul geoyeyo 작았을 거야 jagasseul geoya
Nouns ending in a vowel	남자	남자였을 거예요 namjayeosseul geoyeyo 남자였을 거야 namjayeosseul geoya
Nouns ending in a consonant	물	물이었을 거예요 murieosseul geoyeyo 물이었을 거야 murieosseul geoya

TAKE NOTE

This expression goes really well with 았/었/였다면 (see page 286).

Remember that 것이다 conjugates irregularly; in 존댓말 it becomes 거예요, and in 반말 it becomes 거야. Both forms are shown in the table above.

EXAMPLE SENTENCES

민수가 유명한 식당에서 저녁을 먹었어요. 진짜 맛있**었을 거예요**.
Minsuga yumyeonghan sikdangeseo jeonyeogeul meogeosseoyo.
Jinjja masisseosseul geoyeyo.

민수가 유명한 식당에서 저녁을 먹었어. 진짜 맛있**었을 거야**.
Minsuga yumyeonghan sikdangeseo jeonyeogeul meogeosseo.
Jinjja masisseosseul geoya.

Minsu ate dinner at a very famous restaurant. It must have been good.

백마 탄 왕자를 오래 기다리지 않았으면 벌써 결혼**했을 거예요**.
Baekma tan wangjareul orae gidariji anasseumyeon beolsseo
gyeolhonhaesseul geoyeyo.

백마 탄 왕자를 오래 기다리지 않았으면 벌써 결혼**했을 거야**.
Baekma tan wangjareul orae gidariji anasseumyeon beolsseo
gyeolhonhaesseul geoya.

If you hadn't waited so long for Prince Charming, you'd be married by now.

~어/아 보이다 eo/a bo-ida   "It looks ~"   **Speaking = Writing**
★ ★ ★ ★

그 치마 입을 때 가영이 정말 예**뻐 보여요**.
Geu chima ibeul ttae Kayoungi jeongmal yeppeo boyeoyo.
Kayoung looks really beautiful in (while wearing) that skirt.

This is a simple, common way to say that something looks a certain way.

HOW IT'S FORMED

보이다 means "to appear."

HOW IT'S CONJUGATED

		All tenses
Descriptive verbs (adjectives) with 어, 우, 이 or 으	넓다 neolpda	넓어 보이다 neolbeo bo-ida
Descriptive verbs (adjectives) with 오 or 아	작다	작아 보이다 jaga bo-ida

TAKE NOTE

Be sure to use 어/아 보이다; 아/어/여 보다 means "to try" (see page 185).

EXAMPLE SENTENCES

가구를 치우니 이 방이 넓**어 보였어요**. Gagureul chiuni i bangi neolbeo boyeosseoyo.
When we took out the furniture, this room looked really big.

그 책은 초등학생 읽기로는 너무 어려**워 보여요**.
Geu chaegeun chodeunghaksaeng ilkgironeun neomu eoryeowo boyeoyo.
This book looks too difficult for elementary school students.

A(으)ㄴ/는지 (eu)n/neunji B   "Maybe A, so B"   ★ ★ ★
A아/어/여서 그런지 a/eo/
  yeoseo geureonji B   "Maybe A, so B"   ★ ★ ★
~아/어/여서 그럴 것이다   "Maybe ~"   ★ ★ ★
  a/eo/yeoseo geureol geosida

Speaking = Writing

A: 민수가 왜 아직 안 와요? Minsuga wae ajig an wayo? Why isn't Minsu here yet?
B: 글쎄요. 교통이 막히**는지** 늦어요. Geulsseyo. Gyotongi makineunji neujeoyo.
   Who knows? Maybe traffic is heavy, so he's late.

This is a good expression for people who can't stand not knowing or who like to start
rumors. It's used to hypothesize that maybe A was the cause of B where B is a result that

you can see for yourself. 아/어/여서 그런지 is an extended form which is interchangeable with (으)ㄴ/는지 by itself. At the end of a sentence, you can use 아/어/여서 그를 것이다 instead.

HOW IT'S FORMED

아/어/여서 그런지 is 아/어/여서 plus 그렇다 ("to be like that") plus ㄴ지. The ㄴ지 part makes this expression into a guess: "maybe." Put it all together and you get "A, so maybe it's like that", where A is the reason for whatever question or statement your listener just made. In 그럴 것이다, you're adding the future tense ㄹ 것이다 to 그렇다.

HOW IT'S CONJUGATED

		Past	Present	Future
Action verbs ending in a vowel	하다	했는지 haetneunji 해서 그런지 haeseo geureonji 해서 그럴 거예요 haeseo geureol geoyeyo	하는지 haneunji 해서 그런지 해서 그럴 거예요	하는지 해서 그런지 해서 그럴 거예요
Action verbs ending in a consonant	먹다	먹었는지 meogeotneunji 먹어서 그런지 meogeoseo geureonji 먹어서 그럴 거예요 meogeoseo geureol geoyeyo	먹는지 meogneunji 먹어서 그런지 먹어서 그럴 거예요	먹는지 먹어서 그런지 먹어서 그럴 거예요
Descriptive verbs (adjectives) ending in a vowel	예쁘다	예뻤는지 yeppeotneunji 예뻐서 그런지 yeppeoseo geureonji 예뻐서 그럴 거예요 yeppeoseo geureol geoyeyo	예쁜지 yeppeunji 예뻐서 그런지 예뻐서 그럴 거예요	예쁜지 예뻐서 그런지 예뻐서 그럴 거예요
Descriptive verbs (adjectives) ending in a consonant	작다	작았는지 jagatneunji 작아서 그런지 jagaseo geureonji 작아서 그럴 거예요 jagaseo geureol geoyeyo	작는지 jakneunji 작아서 그런지 작아서 그럴 거예요	작는지 작아서 그런지 작아서 그럴 거예요
Nouns ending in a vowel	남자	남자였는지 namjayeotneunji 남자라서 그런지 namjaraseo geureonji 남자라서 그럴 거예요 namjaraseo geureol geoyeyo	남자인지 namjainji 남자라서 그런지 남자라서 그럴 거예요	남자인지 남자라서 그런지 남자라서 그럴 거예요
Nouns ending in a consonant	물	물이었는지 murieotneunji 물이라서 그런지 muriraseo geureonji 물이라서 그럴 거예요 muriraseo geureol geoyeyo	물인지 murinji 물이라서 그런지 물이라서 그럴 거예요	물인지 물이라서 그런지 물이라서 그럴 거예요

TAKE NOTE

아/어/여서 그런지 is normally used while speaking and can't be used for commands, suggestions, or questions.

EXAMPLE SENTENCES

A: 민수가 왜 아직 안 와요? Minsuga wae ajig an wayo?
Why isn't Minsu here yet?

B: 글쎄요. 교통이 막**혀서 그런지** 늦어요.
Geulsseyo. Gyotongi makyeoseo geureonji neujeoyo.
Who knows? Maybe traffic is heavy, so he's late.

_____

A: 민수가 왜 아직 안 와요? Minsuga wae ajig an wayo?
Why isn't Minsu here yet?

B: 글쎄요. 교통이 막**혀서 그럴 거예요**.
Geulsseyo. Gyotongi makyeoseo geureol geoyeyo.
Who knows? Maybe traffic is heavy.

_____

A: 오늘 지하철에서 사람들이 별로 없네요.
Oneul jihacheoreseo saramdeuri byeollo eobsneyo.

B: 오늘 명절이라서 사람들이 고향에 갔**는지** 지하철이 한산해요.
Oneul myeongjeoriraseo saramdeuri gohyange ganneunji jihacheori
hansanhaeyo.

A: 오늘 지하철에서 사람들이 별로 없네요.
Oneul jihacheoreseo saramdeuri byeollo eobsneyo.

B: 오늘 명절이라서 사람들이 고향에 가**서 그런지** 지하철이 한산해요.
Oneul myeongjeoriraseo saramdeuri gohyange gatneunji jihacheori
hansanhaeyo.

A: Today there's almost no one on the subway!

B: Since today's a national holiday, maybe everyone went home, so the subway
is quiet.

_____

A: 가영씨가 오늘 안 왔어요. 무슨 일 있어요?
Kayoungssiga oneul an wasseoyo. Museun il isseoyo?

B: 가영씨가 아**픈지** 집에서 쉬고 있어요.
Kayoungssiga apeunji jibeseo swigo isseo.

A: 가영씨가 오늘 안 왔어요. 무슨 일 있어요?
Kayoungssiga oneul an wasseoyo. Museun il isseoyo?

B: 가영씨가 아파**서 그런지** 집에서 쉬고 있어요.
Kayoungssiga apaseo geureonji jibeseo swigo isseoyo.

A: Kayoung didn't come today. Did something happen?

B: Maybe she's sick and stayed at home.

> ### ~(으)ㄴ/는/(으)ㄹ 모양이다
> (eu)n/neun/(eu)l moyangida
>
> "It seems that ~"
>
> **Speaking = Writing**
> ★★★

민수가 늦을 **모양이에요**. Minsuga neujeul moyang-i-eyo.
It seems like Minsu will be late.

This is another expression just like (으)ㄴ/는/(으)ㄹ 것 같다, 나 보다 and (으)ㄴ/는/(으)ㄹ 듯하다. It is used for making guesses about a situation you've observed.

HOW IT'S FORMED

Tense markers are followed by 모양, which is a noun that means "shape." So something is, was, or will be "in the shape of."

HOW IT'S CONJUGATED

		Past	Present	Future
Action verbs ending in a vowel	하다	한 모양이다 han moyangida	하는 모양이다 haneun moyangida	할 모양이다 hal moyangida
Action verbs ending in a consonant	먹다	먹은 모양이다 meogeun moyangida	먹는 모양이다 meokneun moyangida	먹을 모양이다 meogeul moyangida
Descriptive verbs (adjectives) ending in a vowel	예쁘다	예쁜 모양이다 yeppeun moyangida	예쁜 모양이다	예쁜 모양이다
Descriptive verbs (adjectives) ending in a consonant	작다	작은 모양이다 jageun moyangida	작은 모양이다	작은 모양이다
Nouns ending in a vowel	남자	남자인 모양이다 namjain moyangida	남자인 모양이다	남자인 모양이다
Nouns ending in a consonant	물	물인 모양이다 murin moyangida	물인 모양이다	물인 모양이다

TAKE NOTE

It's interchangeable with (으)ㄴ/는/(으)ㄹ 것 같다, 나/(으)ㄴ가/려나 보다 and (으)ㄴ/는/(으)ㄹ 듯하다 (see pages 137, 138 and 153 respectively). Like these, it is used to make a guess based on a situation that is being observed.

EXAMPLE SENTENCES

그 여자가 한국사람**인 모양이에요**. Geu yeojaga hanguksaramin moyang-i-eyo.
That woman seems Korean.

눈이 **올 모양이에요**. Nuni ol moyangieyo. It looks like it will snow.

아직 배 고파요? 점심을 적게 먹**은 모양이에요**.
Ajik bae gopayo? Jeomsimeul jeokge meogeun moyang-i-eyo.
Are you still hungry? It seemed that you ate only a little for lunch.

그 남자가 요트도 가지고 있어요? 돈이 많은 **모양이에요**.
Geu namjaga yoteudo gajigo isseoyo? Doni manheun moyangieyo.
Does he have a yacht? He seems rich.

		Speaking = Writing
A(으)ㄹ까 봐(서)	"B is done in fear that	★★★
(eu)l-kka bwa(seo) B	A might happen"	

늦을**까 봐** 집에 일찍 출발했어요. Neujeulkka bwa jibe iljjik chulbalhaesseoyo.
I was worried I'd be late, so I left the house early.

Are you a perpetually anxious person? Do you like to overprepare for everything so that you'll be ready for absolutely any situation that comes up? If so, this is an expression for you. This is used to say that you were worried about A, so you did B.

HOW IT'S FORMED

(으)ㄹ까 is an expression that means "shall" and is commonly used in (으)ㄹ까요 (see page 212) and (으)ㄹ까 말까 (see page 231). 보다 as used here means "to make a guess." 서 is optional and doesn't change the meaning of the expression.

HOW IT'S CONJUGATED

		Past	Present
Action verbs ending in a vowel	하다	했을까 봐(서) haesseulkka bwa(seo)	할까 봐(서) halkka bwa(seo)
Action verbs ending in a consonant	먹다	먹었을까 봐(서) meogeosseulkka bwa(seo)	먹을까 봐(서) meogeulkka bwa(seo)
Descriptive verbs (adjectives) ending in a vowel	예쁘다	예뻤을까 봐(서) yeppeosseulkka bwa(seo)	예쁠까 봐(서) yeppeulkka bwa(seo)
Descriptive verbs (adjectives) ending in a consonant	작다	작았을까 봐(서) jagasseulkka bwa(seo)	작을까 봐(서) jagaseulkka bwa(seo)
Nouns ending in a vowel	남자	남자였을까 봐(서) namjayeosseulkka bwa(seo)	남자일까 봐(서) namjailkka bwa(seo)
Nouns ending in a consonant	물	물이었을까 봐(서) murieosseulkka bwa(seo)	물일까 봐(서) murilkka bwa(seo)

TAKE NOTE

This expression can be used only when the action in B is something you're already doing or have done. You can't use this expression if you're talking about something you're only planning to do.

(으)ㄹ까 봐요 at the end of a sentence is not the same expression. It's used to talk about a plan that's not yet certain (see page 226).

(으)ㄹ까 봐 is interchangeable with (으)ㄹ까 싶어 and (으)ㄹ지도 몰라 (see page 160) although the latter is used only for things about which one is uncertain and not specifically for worries like (으)ㄹ까 봐.

EXAMPLE SENTENCES

비가 올**까 봐** 우산을 가지고 왔어요. Biga olkka bwa usaneul gajigo wasseoyo.
I was worried it would rain, so I brought an umbrella.

맛이 없**을까 봐서** 요리 할 때 음식 맛을 계속 봤어요.
Masi eobseulkka bwaseo yori hal ttae eumsik maseul gyesok bwasseoyo.
I was worried the food wouldn't taste good, so I kept tasting it while I was cooking.

~(이)라고/(ㄴ/는) 다고 보다/   **"In my opinion, ~"**   **Speaking = Writing**
생각하다/믿다 (i)rago/(n/neun)   **★★★**
dago boda/saenggakhada/mitda

교육에서는 가장 중요한 것이 부모님의 지지**라고 봐요**.
Gyoyugeseoneun gajang jungyohan geosi bumonimui jijirago bwayo.

교육에서는 가장 중요한 것은 부모님의 지지**라고 생각해요**.
Gyoyugeseoneun gajang jungyohan geosi bumonimui jijirago saenggakhaeyo.

교육에서는 가장 중요한 것은 부모님의 지지**라고 믿어요**.
Gyoyugeseoneun gajang jungyohan geosi bumonimui jijirago mideoyo.

I think the most important thing in education is the parents' support.

If you're ever debating in Korean and need to know how to express your opinion while sounding knowledgeable, here it is. Here are some ways to give your opinion about important topics like the economy, politics, global warming, or world peace.

HOW IT'S FORMED

Indirect speech particles 라고, 다고 and the rest (see page 304) are followed by 보다 (to see), 생각하다 (to think) or 믿다 (to believe), which means that "this is how you see or what you think of the situation."

HOW IT'S CONJUGATED

		Past	Present	Future
Action verbs ending in a vowel	하다	했다고 보다 haetdago boda 했다고 생각하다 haetdago saenggakhada 했다고 믿다 haetdago mitda	한다고 보다 handago boda 한다고 생각하다 handago saenggakhada 한다고 믿다 handago mitda	할 거라고 보다 hal georago boda 할 거라고 생각하다 hal georago saenggakhada 할 거라고 믿다 hal georago mitda

		Past	Present	Future
Action verbs ending in a consonant	먹다	먹었다고 보다 meogeotdago boda 먹었다고 생각하다 meogeotdago saenggakada 먹었다고 믿다 meogeotdago mitda	먹는다고 보다 meongneundago boda 먹는다고 생각하다 meongneundago saenggakada 먹는다고 믿다 meongneundago mitda	먹을 거라고 보다 meogeul georago boda 먹을 거라고 생각하다 meogeul georago saenggakada 먹을 거라고 믿다 meogeul georago mitda
Descriptive verbs (adjectives) ending in a vowel	예쁘다	예뻤다고 보다 yeppeotdago boda 예뻤다고 생각하다 yeppeotdago saenggakada 예뻤다고 믿다 yeppeotdago mitda	예쁘다고 보다 yeppeudago boda 예쁘다고 생각하다 yeppeudago saenggakada 예쁘다고 믿다 yeppeudago mitda	예쁠 거라고 보다 yeppeul georago boda 예쁠 거라고 생각하다 yeppeul georago saenggakada 예쁠 거라고 믿다 yeppeul georago mitda
Descriptive verbs (adjectives) ending in a consonant	작다	작았다고 보다 jagatdago boda 작았다고 생각하다 jagatdago saenggakada 작았다고 믿다 jagatdago mitda	작다고 보다 jakdago boda 작다고 생각하다 jakdago saenggakada 작다고 믿다 jakdago mitda	작을 거라고 보다 jageul georago boda 작을 거라고 생각하다 jageul georago saenggakada 작을 거라고 믿다 jageul georago mitda
Nouns ending in a vowel	남자	남자라고 보다 namjarago boda 남자라고 생각하다 namjarago saenggakada 남자라고 믿다 namjarago mitda	남자라고 보다 남자라고 생각하다 남자라고 믿다	남자라고 보다 남자라고 생각하다 남자라고 믿다
Nouns ending in a consonant	물	물이라고 보다 murirago boda 물이라고 생각하다 murirago saenggakada 물이라고 믿다 murirago mitda	물이라고 보다 물이라고 생각하다 물이라고 믿다	물이라고 보다 물이라고 생각하다 물이라고 믿다

TAKE NOTE

(이)라고/(ㄴ/는)다고 보다 is for important topics and used mainly in important discussions. Don't use it to talk about what you thought of that dress 혜진 **Hyejin** was wearing yesterday. (이)라고/(ㄴ/는)다고 생각하다 would be better for that.

These are all used to state your opinion rather than an objectively verifiable fact. For a fact, you can use a more decisive ending.

A word about 생각하다 and 믿다: the former can be used for both positive and negative things while 믿다 isn't normally used for negatives. So in the first example below, you can use either 생각하다 or 믿다, but you wouldn't say the opposite using 믿다.

EXAMPLE SENTENCES

올해는 경제가 좋아질 거<u>라고</u> **봐요**. Olhaeneun gyeongjega joajil georago bwayo

올해에 경제가 좋아질 거<u>라고</u> **생각해요**.
olhaee gyeongjega joajil georago saenggakaeyo.

올해에 경제가 좋아질 거<u>라고</u> **믿어요**. Olhaee gyeongjega joajil georago mideoyo.

I think the economy will improve next year.

올해는 경제가 나빠질 거<u>라고</u> **봐요**. Olhaeneun gyeongjega nappajil georago bwayo.

올해에 경제가 나빠질 거<u>라고</u> **생각해요**.
Olhaee gyeongjega nappajil georago saenggakaeyo.

I think the economy will improve next year.

(Here you shouldn't use 믿어요 since you're talking about a negative situation).

요즘 경제가 좋아<u>진다고</u> **봐요**. Yojeum gyeongjega joajindago bwayo.

요즘 경제가 좋아<u>진다고</u> **생각해요**. Yojeum gyeongjega joajindago saenggakaeyo.

요즘 경제가 좋아<u>진다고</u> **믿어요**. Yojeum gyeongjega joajindago mideoyo.

I think the economy is improving these days.

지난해에 경제가 좋아졌**다고** **봐요**. Jinanhaee gyeongjega joajyeotdago bwayo.

지난해에 경제가 좋아졌**다고** **생각해요**.
Jinanhaee gyeongjega joajyeotdago saenggakaeyo.

올해에 경제가 좋아질 거<u>라고</u> **믿어요**. Olhaee gyeongjega joajil georago mideoyo.

I think the economy improved last year.

나중에 커피를 마셨으면 좋겠**다고** **생각해요**.
Najunge keopireul masyeoseumyeon joketdago saenggakaeyo.
I think it would be nice to have some coffee later on.

(can be said with 생각하다, but not 보다 because it's hardly a major world issue)

		Speaking
~(으)ㄴ/는/(으)ㄹ걸(요)	"I think it might be ~"	★★★
(eu)n/neun/(eu)l-geol(yo)		

민수는 회의가 있어서 아마 늦**을걸요**.
Minsuneun hoeuiga iseoseo ama neujeulgeollyo.
Minsu has a meeting, so maybe he'll be late.

This is for those who hate committing themselves to anything, as well as those who like to speculate on what's happening, whether or not they really know anything about it. If you'd like to speculate and hate commitment, you can use this expression to make a guess about a situation, but it's specifically for guesses that you're not too confident about: something that you think might be true, but you're not really too sure of.

(으)ㄴ/는/(으)ㄹ걸(요) can also be used to deny things, like so:

> A: 오늘 늦었어요? **Oneul neujeoseoyo?** Were you late today?

> B: 늦지 않은걸요. 정시에 왔어요. **Neutji aneungeollyo. Jeongsie waseoyo.**
>   Late? Not at all. I was here on time.

This is used to gently contradict something someone else has said. It's another expression like 기는요 that comes across as being very modest when used to contradict praise or refuse a compliment that someone has given.

HOW IT'S CONJUGATED

In 반말, this expression is simply (으)ㄹ걸.

Note that you conjugate this expression differently when making guesses about the past than you do when denying things in the past. See below.

		Past (denial)	Past (guess)	Present (denial)	Present/future (guess)
Action verbs ending in a vowel	하다	했는걸요 haenneungeollyo	했을걸요 haeseulgeollyo	하는걸요 haneungeollyo	할걸요 halgeollyo
Action verbs ending in a consonant	먹다	먹었는걸요 meogeonneungeollyo	먹었을걸요 meogeoseulgeollyo	먹는걸요 meongneungeollyo	먹을걸요 meogeulgeollyo
Descriptive verbs (adjectives) ending in a vowel	예쁘다	예뻤는걸요 yeppeonneungeollyo	예뻤을걸요 yeppeoseulgeollyo	예쁜걸요 yeppeun-geollyo	예쁠걸요 yeppeulgeollyo
Descriptive verbs (adjectives) ending in a consonant	작다	작았는걸요 jaganneungeollyo	작았을걸요 jagaseulgeollyo	작은걸요 jageungeollyo	작을걸요 jageulgeollyo
Nouns ending in a vowel	남자	남자였는걸요 namjayeonneungeollyo	남자였을걸요 namjayeoseulgeollyo	남자인걸요 namjaingeollyo	남자일걸요 namjailgeollyo
Nouns ending in a consonant	물	물이었는걸요 murieonneungeollyo	물이었을걸요 murieoseulgeollyo	물인걸요 muringeollyo	물일걸요 murilgeollyo

TAKE NOTE

When using this expression to make guesses, always use it in the future tense with (으)ㄹ걸 (요). If you're denying something that happened in the past or present, you can use (으)ㄴ/는걸(요).

Even in 존댓말, this expression is not really used toward people higher in the hierarchy than you are, so be careful.

This is used only for rough guesses; you have some reason to assume whatever it is you're saying (for example, your assumption is based an something you've observed or something someone has told you), use ~(으)ㄴ/는/(으)ㄹ 것 같다 (see page 137), ~(으)ㄴ가/나 보다 (see page 138), ~(으)ㄴ/는/(으)ㄹ 모양이다 (see page 145), or ~(으)ㄴ/는/(으)ㄹ 듯하다 (see page 153).

기는요 (see page 40) and (으)ㄴ/는/(으)ㄹ걸요 are both used for similar purposes: they're both gentle ways to contradict people. The main difference between them is that when you use 기는요 you have to state what it is that you're contradicting, whereas with 걸요 you simply say the opposite of what was said. So if someone says you speak Korean well and you don't think you do, you can say 잘 하기는요 jal hagineunnyo or 잘 못하는걸요 jal motaneungeollyo.

Finally, another useful expression with (으)ㄹ 걸 is ~(으)ㄹ 걸 그랬어요; it's worthy of its own section on see page 173 because it's used only to express regret: "I should have gone" or "I shouldn't have eaten all that cake."

EXAMPLE SENTENCES

- Guesses

    민수가 회의도 있어서 아마 늦**을걸요**. Minsuga hoeuido iseoseo ama neujeulgeollyo. Minsu also has a meeting, so maybe he'll be late.

    (You have no solid reason to assume this; if, for example, Minsu called and told you he might be late, you'd say 늦을 것 같아요 neujeul geon gachiyo or 늦나 봐요 neunna bwayo.)

    A: 가영이 왜 안 왔어요? Kayoungi wae an waseoyo? Why didn't Kayoung come?

    B: 감기를 걸**렸을걸요**. Gamgireul geollyeoseulgeollyo.
    Maybe she caught a cold. (You don't know and are just speculating.)

    A: 지금 종로에서 교통이 어때요? Jigeum jongnoeseo gyotongi eottaeyo?
    How's traffic on Jongno right now?

    B: 복잡**할걸요**. Bokjaphalgeollyo.
    I'd guess it's congested. (You haven't been down Jongno lately or heard any traffic reports.)

- Denial

    A: 한국어를 아주 잘 하시네요! Hangukeoreul aju jal hasineyo!
    You speak Korean very well!

    B: 잘 못하**는걸요**. Jal motaneungeollyo. I really don't.

    A: 한국에서 10월이 더운가요? Hangukeseo shiwori deoungayo?
    Is Korea hot in October?

    B: 10월은 시원**할걸요**. Shiworeun siwonhalgeollyo. I think October is cool.

지금 10시인데 가영이 공항에 벌써 도착했**을걸요**
Jigeum yeolsiinde Kayoungi gonghange beolsseo dochakaeseulgeollyo.
It's ten o'clock now, so I think Kayoung will have already arrived at the airport.

	Speaking = Writing
~게요 geyo "Because ~"	★ ★ ★

무슨 일 있었어요? 회의에 늦**었게요**. Museun il iseoseoyo? hoeuie neujeotgeyo.
Did something happen? (I'm guessing so because) you're late to the meeting.

This is an ending you can use to make guesses. A sentence with 게요 normally follows a question. This question is your guess about your listener and the follow-up sentence with 게요 explains why you guessed that. For example: "Do you have a new boyfriend? Because you're sure smiling a lot today."

HOW IT'S CONJUGATED

		Past	Present	Future
Action verbs ending in a vowel	하다	했게요 haetgeyo	하게요 hageyo	하게요 hageyo
Action verbs ending in a consonant	먹다	먹었게요 meogeotgeyo	먹게요 meokgeyo	먹게요 meokgeyo
Descriptive verbs (adjectives) ending in a vowel	예쁘다	예뻤게요 yeppeotgeyo	예쁘게요 yeppeugeyo	예쁘게요
Descriptive verbs (adjectives) ending in a consonant	작다	작았게요 jagatgeyo	작게요 jakgeyo	작게요
Nouns ending in a vowel	남자	남자였게요 namjayeotgeyo	남자게요 namjageyo	남자게요
Nouns ending in a consonant	물	물이었게요 murieotgeyo	물이게요 murigeyo	물이게요

TAKE NOTE

This is a rarely used, informal expression used primarily in speaking. You'll likely never see it in writing or hear it in formal situations. You're also more likely to hear it in 반말 than in 존댓말.

It's not really the same as 게 in the middle of a sentence; see page 24.

EXAMPLE SENTENCES

밖에 추워? 손이 정말 차갑**게**. Bakke chuwo? Soni jeongmal chagapge.
Is it cold out? (I'm guessing so because) your hands are really cold.

새로운 남자친구 생겼어? 하루 종일 웃고 있었**게**.
Saeroun namjachingu saenggyeoseo? Haru jongil utgo iseotge.
Did you get a new boyfriend? (I'm guessingso because) you've been smiling all day.

~(으)ㄴ/는/(으)ㄹ 듯하다/듯싶다
(eu)n/neun/(eu)l deutada/deutsipda

"It seems ~"

Speaking = Writing
★★

민수가 늦을 <u>듯해요</u>. Minsuga neujeul deutaeyo. It looks like Minsu will be late.

This has two similar meanings. One is used to say that something "looks like" something else. The other is used as a prediction of sorts to say that something is "on the verge of" something. Use this expression to speculate on a situation you're observing.

HOW IT'S FORMED

듯하다 is a verb which means "to look like." When combined with the future marker (으)ㄹ, it means "looks like it's about to."

HOW IT'S CONJUGATED

		Past	Present	Future
Action verbs ending in a vowel	하다	한 듯하다 han deutada 한 듯싶다 han deutsipda	하는 듯하다 haneun deutada 하는 듯싶다 haneun deutsipda	할 듯하다 hal deutada 할 듯싶다 hal deutsipda
Action verbs ending in a consonant	먹다	먹은 듯하다 meogeun deutada 먹은 듯싶다 meogeun deutsipda	먹는 듯하다 meongneun deutada 먹는 듯싶다 meongneun deutsipda	먹을 듯하다 meogeul deutada 먹을 듯싶다 meogeul deutsipda
Descriptive verbs (adjectives) ending in a vowel	예쁘다	예쁜 듯하다 yeppeun deutada 예쁜 듯싶다 yeppeun deutsipda	예쁜 듯하다 yeppeun deutada 예쁜 듯싶다 yeppeun deutsipda	예쁠 듯하다 yeppeul deutada 예쁠 듯싶다 yeppeul deutsipda
Descriptive verbs (adjectives) ending in a consonant	작다	작은 듯하다 jageun deutada 작은 듯싶다 jageun deutsipda	작은 듯하다 jageun deutada 작은 듯싶다 jageun deutsipda	작을 듯하다 jageul deutada 작을 듯싶다 jageul deutsipda
Nouns ending in a vowel	남자	남자인 듯하다 namjain deutada 남자인 듯싶다 namjain deutsipda	남자인 듯하다 namjain deutada 남자인 듯싶다 namjain deutsipda	남자일 듯하다 namjail deutada 남자일 듯싶다 namjail deutsipda
Nouns ending in a consonant	물	물인 듯하다 murin deutada 물인 듯싶다 murin deutsipda	물인 듯하다 murin deutada 물인 듯싶다 murin deutsipda	물일 듯하다 muril deutada 물일 듯싶다 muril deutsipda

TAKE NOTE

It is interchangeable with 나 보다 (see page 138), (으)ㄴ/는/(으)ㄹ 것 같다 (see page 137), and (으)ㄴ/는/(으)ㄹ 모양이다 **(eu)n/neun/(eu)r moyangida** (see page 145). The only important thing to consider here is that 듯싶다 sentences can't be based on a snap judgement: they are the result of having observed a situation for some time and then making a guess about it.

듯하다 is interchangeable in meaning with 듯싶다 but is used only in writing.

EXAMPLE SENTENCES

그 여자가 한국인**인 듯해요**. Geu yeojaga hangukin**in deutaeyo**.
That woman seems Korean.

눈이 **올 듯해요**. Nuni **ol deutaeyo**. It looks like it will snow.

민수가 늦**을 듯싶어요**. Minsuga neujeul deutsipeoyo.
It looks like Minsu will be late.

그 여자가 한국사람**인 듯싶어요**. Geu yeojaga hanguksaramin deutsipeoyo.
That woman seems Korean.

눈이 **올 듯싶어요**. Nuni ol deutsipeoyo. It looks like it will snow.

Speaking = Writing

~(으)ㄴ/는/(으)ㄹ 셈이다   "Sort of/Kind of ~"   ★★
(eu)n/neun/(eu)l semida

아침을 아주 늦게 먹었어요. 아점을 먹**은 셈이에요**.
Achimeul aju neutge meogeoseoyo. Ajeomeul meogeun semieyo.
I ate a very late breakfast. It was sort of a brunch.

Not everything is black and white. If you're one who likes to see the world in shades of grey, this is a good expression for you. It means that something is "kind of but not exactly like something else," or is "almost the same as something else." When used with the future tense, (으)ㄹ 셈이다, it refers to a plan.

HOW IT'S FORMED

셈 is a noun that means "calculation" or "conjecture" by itself. In other words, in this expression, ~ is "calculated" or "conjectured" to be something.

HOW IT'S CONJUGATED

		Past	Present	Future
Action verbs ending in a vowel	하다	한 셈이다 han semida	하는 셈이다 haneun semida	할 셈이다 hal semida
Action verbs ending in a consonant	먹다	먹은 셈이다 meogeun semida	먹는 셈이다 meokneun semida	먹을 셈이다 meogeul semida

TAKE NOTE

Don't confuse 셈 with 셈치; they're two totally different expressions. 셈치 is about a hypothetical situation and is covered on page 291.

EXAMPLE SENTENCES

중고차를 사서 많이 고쳤어요. 그래서 돈을 많이 썼어요. 새차를 **산 셈이에요**.
Junggochareul saseo mani gochyeosseoyo. Geuraeseo doneul mani sseosseoyo.
Saechareul san semieyo.
I bought a used car and spent a lot of money for repairs. I sort of bought a new car.
(I spent the same amount of money as if I had bought a new car)

제가 갈비 양념을 준비했어요. 가영씨가 요리한 갈비는 제가 **만든 셈이에요**.
Jega galbi yangnyeomeul junbihaesseoyo. Kayoungssiga yorihan galbineun jega
mandeun semieyo.
I prepared the seasoning of the galbi. I made my galbi sort of like Kayoung's.

		Speaking = Writing
A(으)리라고/(으)리라는 (eu)rirago/(eu)riraneun B	"I believe/think/ can't believe A"	★

그가 자신의 생일 파티에도 늦**으리라고는** 상상도 못했어요.
Geuga jasinui saengil patiedo neujeuriragoneun sangsangdo motaesseoyo.
I never would have thought he'd even be late to his own birthday party.

This is a relatively uncommon expression used to talk about what you believe, think, or never would have thought of. This is a good for expressing outrage.

HOW IT'S FORMED

It's very similar to all the reported speech expressions, and indeed, you can just as well use 다고 생각하다 **dago saenggakada**, 라고 믿다 **rago mitda**, or any other verb that has to do with believing/thinking; 생각하다 **saenggakada** and 믿다 **mitda** are the most common, but if you have another favorite, feel free to use it instead. Bear in mind that 으리라고 **eurirago** and 으리라는 **euriraneun** are a little stronger than other reported speech expressions..

HOW IT'S CONJUGATED

		Past	Present	Future
Action verbs ending in a vowel	하다	했으리라고 haesseurirago 했으리라는 haesseuriraneun	하리라고 harirago 하리라는 hariraneun	하리라고 하리라는

		Past	Present	Future
Action verbs ending in a consonant	먹다	먹었으리라고 meogeosseurirago 먹었으리라는 meogeosseuriraneun	먹으리라고 meogeurirago 먹으리라는 meogeuriraneun	먹으리라고 먹으리라는
Descriptive verbs (adjectives) ending in a vowel	예쁘다	예뻤으리라고 yeppeosseurirago 예뻤으리라는 yeppeosseuriraneun	예쁘리라고 yeppeurirago 예쁘리라는 yeppeuriraneun	예쁘리라고 예쁘리라는
Descriptive verbs (adjectives) ending in a consonant	작다	작았으리라고 jagasseurirago 작았으리라는 jagasseuriraneun	작으리라고 jageurirago 작으리라는 jageuriraneun	작으리라고 작으리라는
Nouns ending in a vowel	남자	남자였으리라고 namjayeosseurirago 남자였으리라는 namjayeosseuriraneun	남자리라고 namjarirago 남자리라는 namjariraneun	남자리라고 남자리라는
Nouns ending in a consonant	물	물이었으리라고 murieosseurirago 물이었으리라는 murieosseuriraneun	물으리라고 mureurirago 물으리라는 mureuriraneun	물으리라고 물으리라는

TAKE NOTE

A is what you believe, think, or never would have expected, and B is a verb like 생각하다 or 믿다. You can also change B into a negative expression such as "상상도 못 했어요 sangsangdo mot haesseoyo" ("I never could have imagined") or "생각도 못했어요 saenggakdo motaesseoyo" ("I never would have thought"). In this case (으)리라고 is usually followed by 는 and the 고 can be dropped if you'd like. So you can use (으)리라고, (으)리라고는, or (으)리라는.

EXAMPLE SENTENCES

열심히 공부했으니까 시험을 잘 **보리라고** 생각해요.
Yeolsimhi gongbuhaesseunikka siheomeul jal borirago saenggakaeyo.
Since you studied so hard, I think you'll do well on the test.

열심히 공부했으니까 시험을 잘 **보리라는** 생각해요.
Yeolsimhi gongbuhaesseunikka siheomeul jal boriraneun saenggakaeyo.
Since you studied so hard, I think you'll do well on the test.

그녀가 그렇게 과속을 계속 하면 교통 사고가 **나리라고** 생각해요.
Geunyeoga geureoke gwasogeul gyesok hamyeon gyotong sagoga narirago saenggakaeyo.

그녀가 그렇게 과속을 계속 하면 교통 사고가 **나리라는** 생각해요.
Geunyeoga geureoke gwasogeul gyesok hamyeon gyotong sagoga nariraneun saenggakaeyo.

If she keeps driving that fast, I'm sure she'll have an accident.

늦<u>으리라고는</u> 상상도 못했어요.
Neujeuriragoneun sangsangdo motaesseoyo.
I never would have imagined he'd be late.

그녀가 그렇게 예쁘<u>리라고는</u> 생각도 못했어요.
Geunyeoga geureoke yeppeuriragoneun saenggakdo motaesseoyo.
I never would have thought she'd be this pretty.

그녀가 아직 살아있<u>으리라고는</u> 꿈도 못 꾸었어요.
Geunyeoga ajik sara-isseuriragoneun kkumdo mot kkueosseoyo.
I couldn't have dreamed she'd still be alive.

Thinking: Knowing

		Speaking > Writing
~잖아(요) jana(yo)	"As you (should) know, ~"	★★★★

어제 민수가 늦었**잖아요**. Eoje Minsuga neujeotjanayo.
As you know, Minsu was late yesterday.

Are you surrounded by incompetent people? Do you frequently need to remind people of things they either already know or really should know? English does this with tone of voice, but Koreans have a specific expression for it, and that expression is 잖아(요). It can be used to chide, but also to remind people of a fact. If you've ever wondered why Koreans often say "as you know" even when you clearly don't know whatever it is they're saying, it's because they're directly translating from a Korean sentence with 잖아요.

HOW IT'S CONJUGATED

		Past	Present	Future
Action verbs ending in a vowel	하다	했잖아요 haetjanayo	하잖아요 hajanayo	하잖아요
Action verbs ending in a consonant	먹다	먹었잖아요 meogeotjanayo	먹잖아요 meokjanayo	먹잖아요
Descriptive verbs (adjectives) ending in a vowel	예쁘다	예뻤잖아요 yeppeotjanayo	예쁘잖아요 yeppeujanayo	예쁘잖아요
Descriptive verbs (adjectives) ending in a consonant	작다	작았잖아요 jagatjanayo	작잖아요 jakjanayo	작잖아요
Nouns ending in a vowel	남자	남자였잖아요 namjayeotjanayo	남자잖아요 namjajanayo	남자잖아요
Nouns ending in a consonant	물	물이었잖아요 murieotjanayo	물이잖아요 murijanayo	물이잖아요

EXAMPLE SENTENCES

A: 가영은 오늘 왜 일 안 해요? Kayoungeun oneul wae il an haeyo?
Why isn't Kayoung working?

B: 가영이 머리가 아프**잖아요**. Kayoungi meoriga apeujanayo.
She has a headache, as you know.

얘들아! 교실에서 뛰면 안 되**잖아**. Yaedeura! Gyosireseo ttwimyeon an doejana.
Children! You know you're not allowed to run in the classroom.

		Speaking = Writing
~(으)ㄹ 줄 알다/모르다 (eu)l jul alda/moreuda	"To know/not know how to ~"	★★★★

요리를 **할 줄 알아요**. yorireul hal jul arayo. I know how to cook.

요리를 **할 줄 몰라요**. yorireul hal jul mollayo. I don't know how to cook.

This is used to talk about either knowing (알다) or not knowing (모르다) how to do something.

HOW IT'S CONJUGATED

		All tenses
Action verbs ending in a vowel	하다	할 줄 알다 hal jul alda 할 줄 모르다 hal jul moreuda
Action verbs ending in a consonant	먹다	먹을 줄 알다 meogeul jul alda 먹을 줄 모르다 meogeul jul moreuda

TAKE NOTE

If you use 알았다 instead of 알다, the meaning changes completely. (으)ㄴ/는/(으)ㄹ 줄 알았다 is an expression that means "you thought you knew something but later found out you were wrong." It's covered on the next page. Similarly, (으)ㄴ/는/(으)ㄹ 줄 몰랐다 (also on page 159) means you didn't know something that you know now.

EXAMPLE SENTENCES

한국어를 **쓸 줄 알아요**. Hangukeoreul sseul jul arayo. I know how to write Korean.

한국어를 **쓸 줄 몰라요**. Hangukeoreul sseul jul mollayo.
I don't know how to write Korean.

스키를 **탈 줄 알아요**. Seukireul tal jul arayo. I know how to ski.

스키를 **탈 줄 몰라요**. Seukireul tal jul mollayo. I don't know how to ski.

> ~(으)ㄴ/는/(으)ㄹ 줄
> 알았다/몰랐다 (eu)n/neun/
> (eu)l jul aratda/mollatda
>
> **Speaking = Writing**
> ★★★★
>
> "I thought I knew~,
> but was wrong"/"I didn't
> know ~, but now I know"

민수가 회의에 늦게 **온 줄 알았는데** 민수는 저보다 일찍 왔어요.
Minsuga hoeuie neutge on jul aranneunde Minsuneun jeoboda iljjig wasseoyo.
I thought Minsu was late to the meeting, but he came earlier than me.

Every so often, you need to admit your mistakes. Here's how to say you were wrong.

HOW IT'S FORMED

Unlike the other 줄 알다/모르다, this one is in the past tense. Bear this in mind; it's very important because it means the situation has since changed and you no longer know, or don't know what you thought you once knew or didn't know. In other words, either you found out you were wrong (줄 알았다) or you learned something you previously didn't know (줄 몰랐다).

HOW IT'S CONJUGATED

If you're talking about the future, you're talking about a guess you made that was wrong. (I thought it was going to rain / I didn't know it was going to rain).

		Past	Present	Future
Action verbs ending in a vowel	하다	한 줄 알았다 han jul aratda 한 줄 몰랐다 han jul mollatda	하는 줄 알았다 haneun jul aratda 하는 줄 몰랐다 haneun jul mollatda	할 줄 알았다 hal jul aratda 할 줄 몰랐다 hal jul mollatda
Action verbs ending in a consonant	먹다	먹은 줄 알았다 meogeun jul aratda 먹은 줄 몰랐다 meogeun jul mollatda	먹는 줄 알았다 meongneun jul aratda 먹는 줄 몰랐다 meongneun jul mollatda	먹을 줄 알았다 meogeul jul aratda 먹을 줄 몰랐다 meogeul jul mollatda
Descriptive verbs (adjectives) ending in a vowel	예쁘다	예쁜 줄 알았다 yeppeun jul aratda 예쁜 줄 몰랐다 yeppeun jul mollatda	예쁜 줄 알았다 yeppeun jul aratda 예쁜 줄 몰랐다 yeppeun jul mollatda	예쁠 줄 알았다 yeppeul jul aratda 예쁠 줄 몰랐다 yeppeul jul mollatda
Descriptive verbs (adjectives) ending in a consonant	작다	작은 줄 알았다 Jageun jul aratda 작은 줄 몰랐다 jageun jul mollatda	작은 줄 알았다 jageun jul aratda 작은 줄 몰랐다 jageun jul mollatda	작을 줄 알았다 jageul jul aratda 작을 줄 몰랐다 jageul jul mollatda
Nouns ending in a vowel	남자	남자인 줄 알았다 namjain jul aratda 남자인 줄 몰랐다 namjain jul mollatda	남자인 줄 알았다 namjain jul aratda 남자인 줄 몰랐다 namjain jul mollatda	남자일 줄 알았다 namjail jul aratda 남자일 줄 몰랐다 namjail jul mollatda

		Past	Present	Future
Nouns ending in a consonant	물	물인 줄 알았다 murin jul aratda 물인 줄 몰랐다 murin jul mollatda	물인 줄 알았다 murin jul aratda 물인 줄 몰랐다 murin jul mollatda	물일 줄 알았다 muril jul aratda 물일 줄 몰랐다 muril jul mollatda

TAKE NOTE

Make sure to put 알다 or 모르다 in the past tense; otherwise you'll be using a different expression, (으)ㄹ 줄 알다/모르다 (see page 158) and people do tend to get somewhat confused when you go around saying stuff like "I know how to fail a test!" (시험에 떨어질 줄 알아요 siheome tteoreojil jul arayo) rather than "I thought I had failed the test (but was wrong)" (시험에 떨어질 줄 알았어요 siheome tteoreojil jul arasseoyo). You can use these expressions without putting them in the past tense if you're later continuing your sentence in a way that makes it clear what you meant (see the last example below).

EXAMPLE SENTENCES

시험에 떨어**질 줄 알았**어요. Siheome tteoreojil jul allasseoyo
I thought I had failed the test (but I was wrong).

오늘이 휴일**인 줄 모르**고 학교에 그냥 갔어요.
Oneuri hyuirin jul moreugo hakgyoe geunyang gasseoyo.
I didn't know it was a holiday, so I went to school anyway.

> **Speaking > Writing**
>
> ~(으)ㄴ/는/(으)ㄹ지(도)   "I know/don't know~"   ★★★
> 알다/모르다 (eu)n/neun/
> (eu)l-ji (do) alda/moreuda

민수가 얼마나 늦**을지 아세요**? Minsuga eolmana neujeulji aseyo?
Do you know how late Minsu will be?

민수가 얼마나 늦**을지 알아요**. Minsuga eolmana neujeulji arayo.
I know how late Minsu will be.

민수가 늦**을지 몰라요**. Minsuga neujeulji mollayo. I think Minsu may be late.

No one likes to admit they don't know something, but sometimes you have to. On such an occasion (which, I'm sure, will be rare for you) here's how to say you're not sure about something.

HOW IT'S FORMED

(으)ㄴ/는/(으)ㄹ지 is part of a number of expressions having to do with something happening or not. 도, again, is just used as an intensifier here. It goes only with (으)ㄹ지 모르다 and in this case it is optional. 알다 and 모르다 are, of course, the verbs having to do with knowing: 알다 is "to know" and 모르다 is "to not know."

HOW IT'S CONJUGATED

		Past	Present	Future
Action verbs ending in a vowel	하다	했는지 알다 haenneunji alda 했는지 모르다 haenneunji moreuda 했을지(도) 모르다 haeseulji(do) moreuda	하는지 알다 haneunji alda 하는지 모르다 haneunji moreuda 할지(도) 모르다 halji(do) moreuda	할지 알다 halji alda 할지 모르다 halji moreuda 할지(도) 모르다 halji(do) moreuda
Action verbs ending in a consonant	먹다	먹었는지 알다 meogeonneunji alda 먹었는지 모르다 meogeonneunji moreuda 먹었을지(도) 모르다 meogeoseulji(do) moreuda	먹는지 알다 meongneunji alda 먹는지 모르다 meongneunji moreuda 먹을지(도) 모르다 meogeulji(do) moreuda	먹을지 알다 meogeulji alda 먹을지 모르다 meogeulji moreuda 먹을지(도) 모르다 meogeulji(do) moreuda
Descriptive verbs (adjectives) ending in a vowel	예쁘다	예뻤는지 알다 yeppeonneunji alda 예뻤는지 모르다 yeppeonneunji moreuda	예쁜지 알다 yeppeunji alda 예쁜지 모르다 yeppeunji moreuda	예쁜지 알다 yeppeunji alda 예쁜지 모르다 yeppeunji moreuda
Descriptive verbs (adjectives) ending in a consonant	작다	작았는지 알다 jaganneunji alda 작았는지 모르다 jaganneunji moreuda	작은지 알다 jageunji alda 작은지 모르다 jageunji moreuda	작은지 알다 jageunji alda 작은지 모르다 jageunji moreuda
Nouns ending in a vowel	남자	남자였는지 알다 namjayeonneunji alda 남자였는지 모르다 namjayeonneunji moreuda 남자였을지(도) 모르다 namjayeoseulji(do) moreuda	남자인지 알다 namjainji alda 남자인지 모르다 namjainji moreuda 남자일지(도) 모르다 namjailji(do) moreuda	남자인지 알다 남자인지 모르다 남자일지(도) 모르다
Nouns ending in a consonant	물	물이었는지 알다 murieonneunji alda 물이었는지 모르다 murieonneunji moreuda 물이었을지(도) 모르다 murieoseulji(do) moreuda	물인지 알다 murinji alda 물인지 모르다 murinji moreuda 물일지(도) 모르다 murilji(do) moreuda	물인지 알다 물인지 모르다 물일지(도) 모르다

TAKE NOTE

I've actually combined two different but similar grammar patterns here. (으)ㄹ지(도) 모르다 is used to make guesses. As such, even if you want to make a guess about something that's already finished, you should keep the (으)ㄹ and just put 았/었/였 before it. ㄹ지(도) 모르다 means "I don't know if" and is more of a guess that means "you think ~ might be true," but aren't really sure.

With ㄴ/는/ㄹ지 알다/모르다, use the tense markers ㄴ/는/ㄹ as usual to form sentences like "I don't know if it (past tense verb)," "I don't know if it's (present tense verb)," or "I don't know if it'll be (verb)."

Because both uses of ㄹ지 모르다 are about a future you can't possibly know yet, there ends up being very little difference between the two ㄹ지 모르다s. With the former you actually have no idea, whereas with the latter you're making a very tentative guess. See the last examples below (about tomorrow's snow and Minsu's tardiness) for more clarification.

EXAMPLE SENTENCES

약국은 어디 있**는지 아세요**? Yakgugeun eodi inneunji aseyo?
Do you know where the pharmacy is?

약국은 어디 있**는지 알아요**. Yakgugeun eodi inneunji arayo.
I know where the pharmacy is.

약국은 어디 있**는지 몰라요**. Yakgugeun eodi inneunji mollayo.
I don't know where the pharmacy is.

가영이 이 책을 벌써 읽었**는지 아세요**?
Kayoungi i chaegeul beolsseo ilgeonneunji aseyo?
Do you know if Kayoung has already read this book?

가영이 이 책을 벌써 읽었**는지 알아요**.
Kayoungi i chaegeul beolsseo ilgeonneunji arayo.
I know if Kayoung has already read this book.

가영이 이 책을 벌써 읽었**는지 몰라요**.
Kayoungi i chaegeul beolsseo ilgeonneunji mollayo.
I don't know if Kayoung has read this book yet.

(And yes, the middle sentences above are just as strange in Korean as they are in English. Presumably you're going on to explain whether or not Minsu will be late, where the pharmacy is, or if Kayoung has read the book in question. However, that would be an entirely different grammatical point, so I'm not going to pursue this here.)

우체국은 일요일에 문을 **여는지 안 여는지 몰라요**.
Uchegugeun ilyoire muneul yeoneunji an yeoneunji mollayo.
I don't know if the post office is open or not on Sunday.

내일 눈이 **올지도 몰라요**. Naeil nuni oljido mollayo.
I don't know if it'll snow tomorrow. (I think it might.)

내일 눈이 **올지 안 올지 몰라요**. Naeil nuni olji an olji mollayo.
I don't know if it'll snow tomorrow. (I have no idea.)

민수가 늦을지 안 늦을지 몰라요. Minsuga neujeulji an neujeulji mollayo.
I don't know if Minsu will be late. (I have no idea.)

민수가 늦을지도 몰라요. Minsuga neujeuljido mollayo.
I don't know if Minsu will be late. (I think he might be.)

~다시피 dasipi	"As you ~"	Speaking = Writing ★★★

보**다시피** 민수가 또 늦어요.
Bodasipi Minsuga tto neujeoyo.
As you can see, Minsu is late again.

Here's an easy one that you can use for presentations, if you have to do presentations in Korean. It means "as you" and can be attached only to a few verbs, all of which have to do with gaining information.

HOW IT'S CONJUGATED

다시피 is often seen with 보다, 알다, 듣다, and 배우다. Thus we get the following constructions:

알다시피, 아시다시피 aldasipi, asidasipi as you know

보다시피, 보시다시피 bodasipi, bosidasipi as you can see

들다시피, 들으시다시피 deuldasipi, deureusidasipi as you heard

배웠다시피 baewotdasipi as you learned

TAKE NOTE

This expression can be used only with verbs having to do with knowing or learning, similar to the ones above.

Remember that when speaking to people higher in rank or status, you need to add 시 to your verbs in order to be polite and respectful. That's why you so often hear verbs ending with "시다시피."

다시피 하다 dasipi hada is a different expression and is covered on page 130.

EXAMPLE SENTENCES

아시**다시피** 회의를 다음 월요일에 할 예정이에요.
Asidasipi hoeuireul daeum wollyoire hal yejeongieyo.
As you know, the meeting will be held next Monday.

오늘 배웠**다시피** 한국어 동사는 다 규칙적으로 활용시킬 수 없어요.
Oneul baewotdasipi hangukeo dongsaneun da gyuchikjeogeuro hwallyongsikil su eopseoyo.
As you learned today, Korean verbs can't all be conjugated regularly.

~(으)ㄴ/는/(으)ㄹ 게/것이
틀림없다 (eu)n/neun/(eu)l
ge/geosi teullimeopda

"I'm almost
certain that ~"

Speaking = Writing
★★

민수는 항상 늦어요. 오늘도 늦을 **게 틀림없어요**.
Minsuneun hangsang neujeoyo oneuldo neujeulge teullimeobseoyo.
Minsu is always late. I'm quite sure he'll be late today as well.

This expression straddles the border between thinking and knowing. It's used to make a guess about something which you feel to be very certain.

HOW IT'S FORMED

Tense markers (으)ㄴ/는/(으)ㄹ plus 것이 (which can be shortened to 게). 틀리다 means "to be wrong" and is a word which you'll probably hear all too often in the course of your Korean studies. Such is education. 틀림 is the noun form of that verb. 없다, of course, means "there isn't." In other words, you really think that your guess (followed by the appropriate tense marker and nounified by 것이) isn't wrong. Put it all together and you've got "There's no doubt that ~" or "I'm almost certain that ~."

HOW IT'S CONJUGATED

		Past	Present	Future
Action verbs ending in a vowel	하다	한 것이 틀림없다 han geosi teullimeobsda 한 게 틀림없다 han ge teullimeobsda	하는 것이 틀림없다 haneun geosi teullimeobsda 하는 게 틀림없다 haneun ge teullimeobsda	할 것이 틀림없다 hal geosi teullimeobsda 할 게 틀림없다 hal ge teullimeobsda
Action verbs ending in a consonant	먹다	먹은 것이 틀림없다 meogeun geosi teullimeobsda 먹은 게 틀림없다 meogeun ge teullimeobsda	먹는 것이 틀림없다 meogneun geosi teullimeobsda 먹는 게 틀림없다 meogneun ge teullimeobsda	먹을 것이 틀림없다 meogeul geosi teullimeobsda 먹을 게 틀림없다 meogeul ge teullimeobsda
Descriptive verbs (adjectives) ending in a vowel	예쁘다	예쁜 것이 틀림없다 yeppeun geosi teullimeobsda 예쁜 게 틀림없다 yeppeun ge teullimeobsda	예쁜 것이 틀림없다 예쁜 게 틀림없다	예쁜 것이 틀림없다 예쁜 게 틀림없다
Descriptive verbs (adjectives) ending in a consonant	작다	작은 것이 틀림없다 jageun geosi teullimeobsda 작은 게 틀림없다 jageun ge teullimeobsda	작은 것이 틀림없다 작은 게 틀림없다	작은 것이 틀림없다 작은 게 틀림없다

		Past	Present	Future
Nouns ending in a vowel	남자	남자인 것이 틀림없다 namjain geosi teullimeobsda 남자인 게 틀림 없다 namjain ge teullim eobsda	남자인 것이 틀림없다 남자인 게 틀림 없다	남자인 것이 틀림없다 남자인 게 틀림 없다
Nouns ending in a consonant	물	물인 것이 틀림없다 murin geosi teullimeobsda 물인 게 틀림없다 murin ge teullimeobsda	물인 것이 틀림없다 물인 게 틀림없다	물인 것이 틀림없다 물인 게 틀림없다

TAKE NOTE

If you're not all that certain about making your guess, there are plenty of expressions in the "Guess" section to help you out. ~(으)ㄴ가/나 보다 (see page 138) or (으)ㄹ 것 같다 (see page 137) would be good places to start.

EXAMPLE SENTENCES

그 남자는 약을 먹었어요. 아픈 **게 틀림없어요**.
Geu namjaneun yageul meogeosseoyo. Apeun ge teullimeobseoyo.
I saw him take some medicine. I'm pretty sure he's sick.

민수가 가영을 항상 쳐다봐요. 사랑하**는 것이 틀림없어요**.
Minsuga Kayoungeul hangsang chyeodabwayo. Saranghaneun geosi teullimeobseoyo.
Minsu is always staring at Kayoung. I'm certain he's in love.

Thinking: Making Decisions

		Speaking = Writing
A게 ge B	"B so that A"	★★★★
A게끔 gekkeum B		★
A게시리 gesiri B		★

늦지 않**게** 일찍 준비했어요. Neutji anke iljjik junbihaesseoyo.
I got ready early so as not to be late.

What is life without purpose? Here's how you can express a purpose or intention in Korean. This expression means you do B so that A can happen.

HOW IT'S FORMED

게 by itself is the particle used to make adverbs, which in this case transforms A into an adverbial clause (purpose clause). 게끔 and 게시리 mean the same but are more emphatic, and 게시리 is more literary in style.

HOW IT'S CONJUGATED

		All tenses
Action verbs ending in a vowel	하다	하게 hage 하게끔 hagekkeum 하게시리 hagesiri
Action verbs ending in a consonant	먹다	먹게 meokge 먹게끔 meokgekkeum 먹게시리 meokgesiri
Descriptive verbs (adjectives) ending in a vowel	예쁘다	예쁘게 yeppeuge 예쁘게끔 yeppeugekkeum 예쁘게시리 yeppeugesiri
Descriptive verbs (adjectives) ending in a consonant	작다	작게 jakge 작게끔 jakgekkeum 작게시리 jakgesiri

TAKE NOTE

It's also possible to end your sentence with 게 (followed, of course, by the appropriate level of politeness) if the action taken doesn't really need to be stated. Likewise, you can use 게 하다 to mean "to make something a certain way." Again, the action taken to get the thing that way is implied and/or not important enough to the sentence to be mentioned.

This 게 and the 게 which is added to adjectives to turn them into adverbs are the same, but they are used differently. You can tell them apart from context, in most cases, though sometimes the meanings end up being very nearly the same anyway – for example, the teacher speaking loudly in the second example. In other cases, such as 조용하게 침실에 갔어요 ("I went quietly to the bedroom"), it's clear that you didn't go to the bedroom for the purpose of being quiet.

There is another 게, which is an abbreviation of 것이 (see page 23). This may seem confusing at first. The easiest way to tell them apart is to remember that the 게 in question here, which makes words into adverbs,, is always added directly to the end of a verb stem with no space in between while the abbreviation of 것이 is always on its own with a space between it and the word before it. Aside from that, you can tell by context and by what parts of speech are around the two 게s. 는 게, (으)ㄴ 게 or (으)ㄹ 게 will always equal 는 것이, (으)ㄴ 것이, and (으)ㄹ 것이, and will never be the adverbial 게 we're discussing here.

게 and 도록 (see next page) can be used interchangeably as long as you're using 게 to turn a phrase into an adverbial phrase. If it's just changing a single word into an adverb, it can't be changed to 도록.

EXAMPLE SENTENCES

늦지 않**게끔** 일찍 준비했어요. Neutji ankekkeum iljjik junbihaesseoyo.

늦지 않**게시리** 일찍 준비했어요. Neutji ankesiri iljjik junbihaesseoyo.

I got ready early so as not to be late. (more emphatic than 게 alone)

학생들이 잘 들을 수 있**게** 큰 목소리로 말할 거예요.
Haksaengdeuri jal deureul su itge keun moksoriro malhal geoyeyo.
I'll speak loudly so the students can hear.

후회하지 않**게** 최선을 다하세요. **Huhoehaji anke choeseoneul dahaseyo.**
Please do your best, so you won't have regrets later.

후회하지 않**게끔** 최선을 다하세요. **Huhoehaji ankekkeum choeseoneul dahaseyo.**
후회하지 않**게시리** 최선을 다하세요. **Huhoehaji ankesiri choeseoneul dahaseyo.**

Please do your best, so you won't have regrets later. (more emphatic)

A도록 dorok B	"B so that A"	**Speaking = Writing** ★★★★

늦지 않**도록** 일찍 출발하세요. **Neutji antorok iljjik chulbalhaseyo.**
Please leave early so as not to be late.

도록 is another very common expression used to express a purpose. It means to do B so that A can happen.

Read the paragraph below if you want to find out more about the grammatical explanation behind this; otherwise, go to the next section.

Remember how 게 turns verbs into adverbs? Well, 도록 does the same thing, although its uses are limited to phrases. Its primary meaning is to turn phrases into adverbial phrases indicating purpose, but it also has a secondary meaning, which is to state a limit to some kind of action. This limit can be based on time, degree, or manner. This simply means turning phrases into different kinds of adverbial phrases.

If you're still confused, take a look at the example sentences below to see how 도록 can be used to turn phrases into adverbial phrases indicating manner, time, degree, or purpose.

HOW IT'S FORMED

도록 is an expression that stands by itself, but you can also use ~도록 하다 which translates to "be sure to~" or "do your best to ~."

HOW IT'S CONJUGATED

		All tenses
Action verbs ending in a vowel	하다	하도록 hadorok
Action verbs ending in a consonant	먹다	먹도록 meokdorok
Descriptive verbs (adjectives) ending in a vowel	예쁘다	예쁘도록 yeppeudorok
Descriptive verbs (adjectives) ending in a consonant	작다	작도록 jakdorok

TAKE NOTE

도록 and 게 (see page 166) can be used interchangeably most of the time. The difference is that 게 has a definite goal, whereas 도록 is concerned with the conditions around that goal.

늦지 않**게** 일찍 준비했어요. **Neutji anke iljjik junbihaesseoyo.**

늦지 않**도록** 일찍 준비했어요. **Neutji antoroj iljjik junbihaesseoyo.**

Both expressions mean "I got ready early so as not to be late," but in the first example with 게, the point is to not be late. In the second, the point is your own actions – the way you arrange the situation (maybe getting up early, getting your outfit ready the night before, or whatever actions you have done) such that you're not late. It's a very slight difference that you will almost never need to worry about.

도록 can also be used interchangeably with 기 위해(서) (see next page) as long as the subjects of clause A and clause B are the same.

When used to give a limit, 도록 is interchangeable with 만큼 (see page 126). Also, there are a number of idiomatic expressions that go with 도록.

눈이 빠지도록 기다리다
nuni ppajidorok gidarida

to wait until your eyes fall out

눈이 퉁퉁 붓도록 울다
nuni tungtung butdorok ulda

to cry until your eyes are swollen

죽도록 사랑하다
jukdorok saranghada

to love until death

귀가 닳도록 듣다
gwiga daltorok deutda

to listen until your ears are worn out

입이 닳도록 말하다
ibi daltorok malhada

to talk until your mouth is worn out

손이 발이 되도록 빌다
soni bari doedork bilda

to beg until your hands become (as tough as) feet

코가 삐뚤어지도록 술을 마시다
koga ppittureojidorok sureul masida

to drink until your nose is crooked

EXAMPLE SENTENCES

감기에 걸리지 않**도록** 조심하세요. **Gamgie geolliji antorok josimhaseyo.**
Be careful not to catch a cold. (Be careful so that you don't catch a cold.)

운전 할 때 사고가 나지 않**도록** 하세요. **Unjeon hal ttae sagoga naji antorok haseyo.**
Be sure not to have an accident while driving.

월급을 받을 수 있**도록** 계약을 맺으세요.
Wolgeubeul badeul su itdorok gyeyageul maejeuseyo.
Sign the contract in order to get your salary.

A(기)(을/를) 위해(서)   "B for A"   **Speaking > Writing**
(gi)(eul/reul) wihae(seo) B   ★★★★

늦지 않**기 위해서** 일찍 준비했어요. Neutji anki wihaeseo iljjik junbihaesseoyo.
I got ready early so as not to be late.

If you go out drinking with Koreans, you'll be familiar with this one, whether you real-ize it or not. It's the same expression as the "위하여! wihayeo!" Koreans use when making a toast. 위해(서) means "for." When we toast in English, we say, for example, "To Chris!" or "To a Happy New Year!" In Korean, they just say "To!" following whatever the speaker proposed a toast to. This is that 위하여.

HOW IT'S FORMED

위하다 **wihada** actually means "to take care of" and is conjugated like a 하다 verb; hence the addition of 여 in 위하여 and the shorter 위해. 서 comes from 아/어/여서 and is optional. This verb can also be conjugated as 위한 **wihan** if you want to use it as an adjective (see the examples below). As 위하여, 위해, or 위해서 it changes a phrase into an adverbial phrase.

HOW IT'S CONJUGATED

		All tenses
Action verbs ending in a vowel	하다	하기 위해(서) hagi wihae(seo)
Action verbs ending in a consonant	먹다	먹기 위해(서) meokgi wihae(seo)
Nouns ending in a vowel	남자	남자를 위해(서) namjareul wihae(seo)
Nouns ending in a consonant	물	물을 위해(서) mureul wihae(seo)

TAKE NOTE

위해(서) can be used only when the subjects of A and B are the same. It is interchangeable with 도록 except that 도록 can be used a little more broadly (see page 167).

위하여 is the exact same expression as 위해 or 위해서, but it is more commonly used in formal situations or in writing.

When 위해(서) is added to nouns, the nouns get the object markers 을/를.

EXAMPLE SENTENCES

■ Examples with (기) 위해(서)

용돈을 받**기 위해서** 부모님을 도와줬어요.
Yongdoneul batgi wihaeseo bumonimeul dowajwosseoyo.
I helped my parents in order to get an allowance.

여자 친구**를 위해서** 꽃을 샀어요. Yeoja chingureul wihaeseo kkocheul sasseoyo.
I bought flowers for my girlfriend.

■ Examples with 위한

여자친구를 **위한** 꽃이에요.　Yeojachingureul wihan kkochieyo.
They are flowers for my girlfriend.

초보를 **위한** 문법책을 샀어요.　Choboreul wihan munbeopchaegeul sasseoyo.
I bought a grammar book for beginners.

A(으)ㄴ/는 데 (eu)n/neun de B	"For A, B"	**Speaking = Writing** ★★	

정시에 도착하**는 데** 정시에 출발하는 것이 필수적이에요.
Jeongsie dochakaneun de jeongsie chulbalhaneun geosi pilsujeogieyo.
In order to arrive on time, you need to leave on time.

Do you like to give advice whether you're asked for it or not? This expression is used to make a statement about something being good or being bad for something else. The entire sentence ends up to mean "B is good or bad (effective or ineffective) for A."

HOW IT'S FORMED

데 can stand by itself but is more properly followed by 에, and you can add 는 for more emphasis.

HOW IT'S CONJUGATED

		Past	Present
Action verbs ending in a vowel	하다	한 데(에)(는) han de(e)(neun)	하는 데(에)(는) haneun de(e)(neun)
Action verbs ending in a consonant	먹다	먹은 데(에)(는) meogeun de(e)(neun)	먹는 데(에)(는) meongneun de(e)(neun)

TAKE NOTE

The expression is similar to 기 위해(서), although somewhat more limited in use because it can only be finished in certain ways. The whole expression needs to end with a phrase that indicates good or bad: 좋다/나쁘다 jota/nappeuda, 도움이 되다/안 되다 doumi doeda/an doeda, 중요하다/중요하지 않다 jongyohada/jungyohaji anda, and 필요하다/필요 없다 pillyohada/pillyo eopda are all possible. Statements indicating effectiveness (효과적이다, 효과가 있다 hyogwa jeogida, hyogwaga itda) are often used.

　A(으)ㄴ/는 데 B is another expression which is used to talk about the place where an activity is done or an event takes place. Check for context: this 는 데 will always be followed by a sentence indicating effectiveness or quality, or lack thereof, while the other one will always have to do with places.

EXAMPLE SENTENCES

다이어트를 하<u>는 데</u> 건강하게 먹는 것이 효과적이에요.
Daieoteureul haneun de geonganghage meokneun geosi hyogwajeogieyo.
Eating healthy is important for dieting.

아이들이 학교에 가<u>는 데</u> 큰 차가 있으면 좋아요.
Aideuri hakgyoe ganeun de keun chaga isseumyeon joayo.
It is good to have a big car for children to ride to school.

Emotions: Surprise

The most commonly used expression to indicate surprise in Korean is ~네요. I've included 군요 below because, although it isn't always used to express surprise, it does serve that function quite often. You can use 라/다/(으)ㄴ다/는다니요 to express surprise at something that someone said. This expression is covered on page 319 because I felt it more appropriately fits in the section on responding to what other people said.

		Speaking > Writing
~네요 neyo	"~!"	★★★★★

진짜 늦었<u>네요</u>! You're really late!

There are many things you'll find surprising while living in Korea. Even if you're not living in Korea, there are many aspects you'll find surprising about the Korean language. How can you express this in Korean? 네요 is here and can be thought of as an exclamation point.

HOW IT'S CONJUGATED

		Past	Present	Future
Action verbs ending in a vowel	하다	했네요 haenneyo	하네요 haneyo	하겠네요 hagenneyo
Action verbs ending in a consonant	먹다	먹었네요 meogeonneyo	먹네요 meokneyo	먹겠네요 meokgenneyo
Descriptive verbs (adjectives) ending in a vowel	예쁘다	예뻤네요 yeppeonneyo	예쁘네요 yeppeuneyo	예쁘겠네요 yeppeugenneyo
Descriptive verbs (adjectives) ending in a consonant	작다	작았네요 jaganneyo	작네요 jakneyo	작겠네요 jakgenneyo
Nouns ending in a vowel	남자	남자였네요 namjayeonneyo	남자이네요 namja-i-neyo	남자이겠네요 namja-i-genneyo
Nouns ending in a consonant	물	물이었네요 murieonneyo	물이네요 murineyo	물이겠네요 murigenneyo

TAKE NOTE

Sentences ending in 네요 are usually quite short. There's no rule about this; it's just how the expression is commonly used. 네요 always goes at the end of a sentence.

Sentences ending in 네(요) are also very commonly used as responses to someone talking. You'll notice in talking with Koreans that they'll keep talking over you with these kinds of responses; this is considered polite because it shows they're actively listening to you.

EXAMPLE SENTENCES

한국어를 잘 하시**네요**! Hangukeoreul jal hasineyo! You speak Korean really well!

맛있**네요**! Masinneyo! It's really delicious!

		Speaking > Writing
~(는)**군요**/(는)**구나** (neun) gunyo/(neun)guna	"I see that ~, ~!"	★★★★★

진짜 늦었**군요**. Jinjja neujeotgunyo. (I've just discovered that) you're late.

진짜 늦었**구나**. Jinjja neujeotguna.

Hopefully, with this book and your other Korean studies, you're learning many new things. Sometimes you'll probably want to talk about something new and interesting that you've just discovered. So how can we do that? 군요 and 구나 are verb endings used at the end of a sentence where you talk about something you've just realized or just learned. They often, but not always, convey a feeling of surprise; you can tell by someone's intonation whether they're surprised or simply stating a fact.

HOW IT'S CONJUGATED

		Past	Present
Action verbs ending in a vowel	하다	했군요 haetgunyo 했구나 haetguna	하는군요 haneungunyo 하는구나 haneunguna
Action verbs ending in a consonant	먹다	먹었군요 meogeotgunyo 먹었구나 meogeotguna	먹는군요 meokneungunyo 먹는구나 meokneunguna
Descriptive verbs (adjectives) ending in a vowel	예쁘다	예뻤군요 yeppeotgunyo 예뻤구나 yeppeotguna	예쁘군요 yeppeugunyo 예쁘구나 yeppeuguna
Descriptive verbs (adjectives) ending in a consonant	작다	작았군요 jagatgunyo 작았구나 jagatguna	작군요 jakgunyo 작구나 jakguna
Nouns ending in a vowel	남자	남자였군요 namjayeotgunyo 남자였구나 namjayeotguna	남자이군요 namja-i-gunyo 남자이구나 namja-i-guna
Nouns ending in a consonant	물	물이었군요 murieotgunyo 물이었구나 murieotguna	물이군요 murigunyo 물이구나 muriguna

TAKE NOTE

This is one of the rare cases where you can't make the 반말 simply by dropping 요. It's 구나, not 군.

The difference between this and 네요 is that while 네요 indicates only surprise (regardless of when you learned whatever you just stated), 군요/구나 sometimes indicates surprise and sometimes merely indicates that you learned something new.

구나 and 군요 always go at the end of a sentence.

EXAMPLE SENTENCES

한국어를 잘 하시**는군요**. Hangukeoreul jal hasineungunyo.
(I've just noticed that) you speak Korean really well.

한국어를 잘 하시**는구나**. Hangukeoreul jal hasineunguna.

맛있**군요**! Masitgunyo! (I've just realized that) it's really delicious!
맛있**구나**! Masitguna!

그렇**군요**! Geureokunyo! Oh, I see!*
그렇**구나**! Geureokuna!

*I highly recommend that you learn this one here and now. It's very useful and even if you never plan to use this expression yourself, you will hear it all the time, so it's important that you know what it means.

Emotions: Regret

> **Speaking > Writing**
>
> ~(으)ㄹ걸 (그랬어요)   "I should/shouldn't have~"   ★★★
>   (eu)l-geol (geuraesseoyo)

또 늦었어요. 택시를 **탈걸 그랬어요**.
Tto neujeosseoyo. Taeksireul talgeol geuraesseoyo.

또 늦었어. 택시를 **탈걸**. Tto neujeoseo. Taeksireul talgeol.

I'm late again. I should have taken a taxi.

Life doesn't always go exactly the way you want it to. Sometimes you make mistakes. Sometimes you realize you should have done things differently. Here's one for all you forlorn lovers out there. (으)ㄹ걸 그랬다 means "I should/shouldn't have" and implies regret.

HOW IT'S CONJUGATED

The table below shows 존댓말 and 반말 forms for (으)ㄹ 걸 그랬다 (I should have), 안 ~(으)ㄹ걸 그랬다 (I shouldn't have) and 지 말걸 그랬다 (I shouldn't have).

		Past
Action verbs ending in a vowel	하다	할걸 그랬다 halgeol geuraetda 할걸 halgeol 안 할걸 그랬다 an halgeol geuraetda 안 할걸 an halgeol 하지 말걸 그랬다 haji malgeol geuraetda 하지 말걸 haji malgeol
Action verbs ending in a consonant	먹다	먹을걸 그랬다 meogeulgeol geuraetda 먹을걸 meogeulgeol 안 먹을걸 그랬다 an meogeulgeol geuraetda 안 먹을걸 an meogeulgeol 먹지 말걸 그랬다 meokji malgeol geuraetda 먹지 말걸 meokji malgeol

TAKE NOTE

There is another expression, (으)ㄹ걸(요), which is used to make a guess (see page 149). This second (으)ㄹ걸 is used only in informal speech and has a different intonation: rising instead of falling. When using 존댓말 you'll have no trouble telling them apart because this one ends in 그랬어요 and that one ends with 요 right after 걸; however, listen carefully for the difference in 반말.

This expression can be used only in the past tense and it's only for your own regrets: if you want to say someone else should have done something, you can use 았/었/였으면 좋겠다/좋았을 텐데요.

(으)ㄹ걸 그랬다 is similar to 았/었/였어야 했는데 (see next page). 었어야 했는데 is used to express regret for something that was not done or not accomplished while with (으)ㄹ걸 그랬다 you believe you should have (or shouldn't have) done something differently. This is not a very big difference, so don't worry about it too much.

EXAMPLE SENTENCES

The first sentence in each example is formal; the second is the very informal 반말.

시험에 떨어졌어요. 더 열심히 공부**할걸 그랬어요**.
Siheome tteoreojyeosseoyo. Deo yeolsimhi gongbuhalgeol geuraesseoyo.

시험에 떨어졌어. 더 열심히 공부**할걸**.
Siheome tteoreojyeosseo. Deo yeolsimhi gongbuhalgeol.

I failed the test. I should have studied harder.

배가 아파요. 그렇게 많이 먹**지 말걸 그랬어요**.
Baega apayo. Geureoke mani meokji malgeol geuraesseoyo.

배가 아파요. 그렇게 많이 안 먹**을걸 그랬어요**.
Baega apayo. Geureoke mani an meogeulgeol geuraesseoyo.

배가 아파. 그렇게 많이 먹**지 말걸**. Baega apa. Geureoke mani meokji malgeol.

My stomach hurts. I shouldn't have eaten so much.

| A았/었/였어야 했는데 at/eot/ yeosseoya haenneunde B | "I regret that I did/ didn't A" | Speaking > Writing ★★ |

또 늦었어요. 택시를 **탔어야 했는데**.
Tto neujeosseoyo. Taeksireul tasseoya haenneunde.
I'm late again. I should have taken a taxi.

This is another way to express regret. It's quite similar to (으)ㄹ걸 그랬다.

HOW IT'S FORMED

았/었/였 past tense marker plus 어야, which implies an obligation or required condition. Then 하다 is put into the past tense and combined with 는데, which uses A as a background for B (see page 69). Put it all together and you get "I should have…, so…"

HOW IT'S CONJUGATED

		Past
Action verbs ending in a vowel	하다	했어야 했는데 haesseoya haenneunde
Action verbs ending in a consonant	먹다	먹었어야 했는데 meogeosseoya haenneunde
Descriptive verbs (adjectives) ending in a vowel	예쁘다	예뻤어야 했는데 yeppeosseoya haenneunde
Descriptive verbs (adjectives) ending in a consonant	작다	작았어야 했는데 jagasseoya haenneunde
Nouns ending in a vowel	남자	남자였어야 했는데 namjayeosseoya haenneunde
Nouns ending in a consonant	물	물이었어야 했는데 murieosseoya haenneunde

TAKE NOTE

This expression can be used only in the first person to express regret for something you yourself have done.

B is either a statement of regret (후회가 돼요 huhwega dwaeyo, 죄송해요 joesonghaeyo, …) or a statement of what you did instead of A. You can also just trail off after 했는데 just as you can after any other 는데. Because the expression is used to show regret, it works only in the past tense.

It's very similar to (으)ㄹ걸 그랬다, but the difference is that 었어야 했는데 is used to express regret for something that was not done or not accomplished, while with (으)ㄹ걸 그랬다 you believe you should have (or shouldn't have) done something differently. It's not a big difference, as you can see if you compare the sentences below with those on the previous page; I didn't even have to change any of the examples to make both expressions work.

EXAMPLE SENTENCES

시험에 떨어졌어요. 더 열심히 공부**했어야 했는데** 후회가 돼요.
Siheome tteoreojyeosseoyo. Deo yeolsimi gongbuhaesseoya haenneunde huhwega dwaeyo.
I failed the test. I should have studied harder.

배가 아파요. 그렇게 많이 먹지 않<u>**았어야 했는데**</u> 음식이 맛있어서 계속 먹었어요.
Baega apayo. Geureoke mani meokji anasseoya haenneunde eumsigi masisseoseo gyesok meogeosseoyo.
My stomach hurts. I shouldn't have eaten so much, but the food was so delicious that I kept on eating.

Emotions: Thanks

A very common way to say "thanks to ~" in Korean is ~덕분에 **deokbune**, which was covered on page 80 in the section on cause and effect (through/because of). 망정 **mangjeong** can also be used in a couple of different ways to express gratitude.

		Speaking > Writing
~기에 망정이다 gie mangjeongida	"Thanks to ~"	★★
~(으)니(까) 망정이다 (eu)ni(kka) mangjeongida		★★

일찍 출발했<u>**기에 망정이지**</u> 안 그랬으면 늦을 뻔했어요.
Iljjik chulbalhaeggie mangjeongiji an geuraesseumyeon neujeul ppeonhaeseoyo.

일찍 출발했<u>**으니까 망정이지**</u> 안 그랬으면 늦을 뻔했어요.
Iljjik chulbalhaesseunikka mangjeongiji an geuraesseumyeon neujeul ppeonhaeseoyo.

We're lucky we left early or we would have been late.

Just as you sometimes wish things had turned out differently, other times you're grateful they worked out the way they did. ~기에 or (으)니(까) plus 망정이다 means "thanks to ~." The two are interchangeable.

HOW IT'S FORMED

기에 roughly means "since" (see page 73). 망정 by itself is a noun which can mean thanks to (as seen here) or "I'd rather..." (as seen in the expression (으)ㄹ 망정 on page 182). Think of it as a way of expressing a preference: in 기에 망정이다 you prefer what actually happened to what could have happened, and in A(으)ㄹ 망정 B you prefer A to B, which is what could have happened.
 (으)니(까) means "so" and is covered on page 67. The 까 is optional.

HOW IT'S CONJUGATED

They are conjugated the same way as 기에 and (으)니(까) by themselves, so if you remember how to do these, then you're set. If not, check the table below.

		Past
Action verbs ending in a vowel	하다	했기에 망정이다 haetgie mangjeongida 했으니(까) 망정이다 haesseuni(kka) mangjeongida
Action verbs ending in a consonant	먹다	먹었기에 망정이다 meogeotgie mangjeongida 먹었으니(까) 망정이다 meogeosseuni(kka) mangjeongida
Descriptive verbs (adjectives) ending in a vowel	예쁘다	예뻤기에 망정이다 yeppeotgie mangjeongida 예뻤으니(까) 망정이다 yeppeosseuni(kka) mangjeongida
Descriptive verbs (adjectives) ending in a consonant	작다	작았기에 망정이다 jagatgie mangjeongida 작았으니(까) 망정이다 Jagasseuni(kka) mangjeongida
Nouns ending in a vowel	남자	남자였기에 망정이다 namjayeotgie mangjeongida 남자였으니(까) 망정이다 namjayeosseuni(kka) mangjeongida
Nouns ending in a consonant	물	물이었기에 망정이다 murieotgie mangjeongida 물이었으니(까) 망정이다 murieosseuni(kka) mangjeongida

TAKE NOTE

These expressions are always used for replying to someone else's or question don't just toss them out of nowhere into a conversation.

These expressions and (으)ㄹ 망정 are somewhat similar, but not quite the same. This one means it was fortunate that ~ happened while the other one expresses a preference. You can tell them apart by looking at what comes before 망정: in this case it will always be 기에 or 으니(까), while with the other expression the verb before 망정 will always end in ㄹ.

망정이다 is often changed to 망정이지 and then followed by a B clause including a phrase like 안 그랬으면 or 아니면 ("If it hadn't been that way, then ..."). The B clause often finishes with (으)ㄹ 뻔했다 ("I almost"), which you can find on page 261. 았/었/였을 것이다 (see page 140) can also be used.

EXAMPLE SENTENCES

돈이 있었**기에 망정이지** 안 그랬으면 먹을 수 없을 뻔했어요.
Doni isseotgie mangjeongiji an geuraesseumyeon meogeul su eopsseul ppeonhaesseoyo.

돈이 있었**으니 망정이지** 안 그랬으면 먹을 수 없을 뻔했어요.
Doni isseosseuni mangjeongiji an geuraesseumyeon meogeul su eopsseul ppeonhaesseoyo.

Fortunately, I had money or I wouldn't have been able to eat.

돈이 있었**기에 망정이지요**. Doni isseotgie mangjeongijiyo.
Fortunately, I had money.

Emotions: Desires

> **~고 싶다** go sipda   "I want to ~"   **Speaking = Writing**
> ★★★★★

지금 가<u>고 싶어요</u>. Jigeum gago sipeoyo. I want to go now.

This is the most common and basic way to talk about what you want or to ask what other people want.

HOW IT'S CONJUGATED

If you want to use this expression with an adjective such as "I want to be beautiful," then you have to turn the adjective into a verb using 아/어/여지다. For nouns, you can use 되다: for example, 남자가 되고 싶어요 Namjaga doego sipeoyo.

		Past	Present
Action verbs ending in a vowel	하다	하고 싶었다 hago sipeotda	하고 싶다 hago sipda
Action verbs ending in a consonant	먹다	먹고 싶었다 meokgo sipeotda	먹고 싶다 meokgo sipda

TAKE NOTE

If you want to talk about what someone else wants, use 고 싶어하다 instead of 고 싶다.

가<u>고 싶어요</u>. Gago sipeoyo. I want to go.

민수는 가<u>고 싶어해요</u>. Minsuneun gago sipeohaeyo. Minsu wants to go.

EXAMPLE SENTENCES

저녁을 먹<u>고 싶어요</u>? Jeonyeogeul meokgo sipeoyo? Do you want to eat dinner?

어제 자<u>고 싶었어요</u>. Eoje jago sipeosseoyo. Yesterday I wanted to sleep.

> **Speaking = Writing**
> **~았/었/였으면 좋겠다/싶다/**   "It would be nice if ~"   ★★★★
> **하다** at/eot/yeosseumyeon
> joketda/sipda/hada

정시에 <u>왔으면 좋겠어요</u>. Jeongsie wasseumyeon jokesseoyo.
정시에 <u>왔으면 해요</u>. Jeongsie wasseumyeon haeyo.
정시에 <u>왔으면 싶어요</u>. Jeongsie wasseumyeon sipeoyo.
It would have been better if you'd arrived on time.

These are good expressions for daydreamers or people trying to give not-so-subtle hints. The three expressions above all mean exactly the same thing. 았/었/였으면 좋겠다 is by far the most common and is, in fact, probably one of the first expressions you learned while studying beginning Korean. If you didn't, now's your chance!

HOW IT'S FORMED

The past tense marker 았/었/였 is followed by 으면, which means "if." The second part of the expression is 좋다 (to be good) in the future tense with 겠. In other words, "if it had been that way, it would be good." 하다 is plain old 하다 and there's no special reason why it should serve the function it does in this expression, but it does. 싶다 is most commonly seen in 고 싶다 (see the previous page) and expresses a desire. It serves the same function here with 었으면.

HOW IT'S CONJUGATED

		Past
Action verbs ending in a vowel	하다	했으면 좋겠다 haesseumyeon joketda 했으면 하다 haesseumyeon hada 했으면 싶다 haesseumyeon sipda
Action verbs ending in a consonant	먹다	먹었으면 좋겠다 meogeosseumyeon joketda 먹었으면 하다 meogeosseumyeon hada 먹었으면 싶다 meogeosseumyeon sipda
Descriptive verbs (adjectives) ending in a vowel	예쁘다	예뻤으면 좋겠다 yeppeosseumyeon joketda 예뻤으면 하다 yeppeosseumyeon hada 예뻤으면 싶다 yeppeosseumyeon sipda
Descriptive verbs (adjectives) ending in a consonant	작다	작았으면 좋겠다 jagasseumyeon joketda 작았으면 하다 jagasseumyeon hada 작았으면 싶다 jagasseumyeon sipda
Nouns ending in a vowel	남자	남자였으면 좋겠다 namjayeosseumyeon joketda 남자였으면 하다 namjayeosseumyeon hada 남자였으면 싶다 namjayeosseumyeon sipda
Nouns ending in a consonant	물	물이었으면 좋겠다 murieosseumyeon joketda 물이었으면 하다 murieosseumyeon hada 물이었으면 싶다 murieosseumyeon sipda

TAKE NOTE

좋겠다 is, again, the most common way to end this expression, and 았/었/였으면 is by far the most common way to start it; however, if you'd like some variety, you can also use 는 다면 좋겠다 or 으면 좋겠다. They all mean the same. 는다면 or 으면 are covered on pages 286 and 283 respectively.)

These expressions are normally used at the ends of sentences, though they don't have to be.

EXAMPLE SENTENCES

값이 더 쌌으면 **좋겠어요**. Gapsi deo ssasseumyeon jokesseoyo.

값이 더 쌌으면 **해요**. Gapsi deo ssasseumyeon haeyo.

값이 더 쌌으면 **싶어요**. Gapsi deo ssasseumyeon sipeoyo.

I wish the price were lower.

이 물이 와인이**었으면 좋겠어요**. I muri wainieosseumyeon jokesseoyo.

이 물이 와인이**었으면 해요**. I muri wainieosseumyeon haeyo.

이 물이 와인이**었으면 싶어요**. I muri wainieosseumyeon sipeoyo.

I wish this water were wine.

		Speaking = Writing
~기 바라다 ~gi barada	"We'd like you to ~"	★★★★

최선을 다해 주시**기 바랍니다**. Choeseoneul dahae jusigi baramnida.
Please do your best.

If you ever take the subway in Korea, you'll hear this all the time. It's an extremely formal way to express a desire and is usually used in sentences such as "We hope you'll have a pleasant journey."

HOW IT'S FORMED

기 makes a verb into a noun. 바라다 means "to want."

HOW IT'S CONJUGATED

Most importantly, because it's very formal, it's almost always conjugated as ~기 바랍니다 and the respectful 시 is usually added to the verb before it. It doesn't have to be, but that's how you'll almost always hear it used. It can also be conjugated as 바랄게요 if you don't need to be quite that formal.

		Present
Action verbs ending in a vowel	하다	하기 바라다 hagi barada
Action verbs ending in a consonant	먹다	먹기 바라다 meokgi barada

EXAMPLE SENTENCES

이해해 주시**기 바랍니다**. Ihaehae jusigi baramnida. Please understand.

안전한 여행이 되시**기 바랍니다**. Anjeonhan yeohaengi doesigi baramnida.

안전한 여행이 되**기 바랄게요**. Anjeonhan yeohaengi doegi baralggeyo. (less formal)
We wish you a safe journey.

		Speaking = Writing
A(으)ㄹ 바에야 (eu)r baeya B	"I'd rather B	★★
A(으)ㄹ 바에는 (eu)r baeneun B	than have to A"	★★

늦게 **갈 바에야** 차라리 가지 않겠어요.
Neutge gal baeya charari gaji ankesseoyo.

늦게 **갈 바에는** 차라리 가지 않겠어요.
Neutge gal baeneun charari gaji ankesseoyo.

I'd rather not go at all than be late.

Not all things are created equal, and often you're going to have to make a choice between two (or more) things. Here's how to do that. A(으)ㄹ 바에야 B and A(으)ㄹ 바에는 B are used to express a preference for B over A: B may or may not necessarily be your first choice, but it's better than the alternative A.

HOW IT'S FORMED

(으)ㄹ is the future tense marker, which in this case is used to indicate that the continuation of A is hypothetical; it hasn't happened yet. 바 is a noun that can mean a few things, but in this case it means "situation" or "circumstances." See page 324 for more on 바. 에 is used grammatically to set up A as something to which something else is being compared. 야 is from 아/어/여야 and 는 and is used for emphasis.

HOW IT'S CONJUGATED

		Present/Future
Action verbs ending in a vowel	하다	할 바에야 hal baeya 할 바에는 hal baeneun
Action verbs ending in a consonant	먹다	먹을 바에야 meogeul baeya 먹을 바에는 meogeul baeneun

TAKE NOTE

B often begins with 차라리 **charari** ("rather") or a similar expression and can end with the present tense or with 겠다. It doesn't have any past tense ever.

You can replace (으)ㄹ 바에야/바에는 with 기 대신에 **gi daesine**, which means "instead of," but doesn't, by itself, indicate a preference; see page 119. It's also interchangeable with 느니, which is covered on page 123.

EXAMPLE SENTENCES

포기**할 바에야** 차라리 죽겠어요. Pogihal baeya charari jukgesseoyo.

포기**할 바에는** 차라리 죽겠어요. Pogihal baeneun charari jukgesseoyo.

I'd rather die than give up.

구걸**할 바에야** 그냥 굶어 죽을 거예요.
Gugeolhal baeya geunyang gulmeo jugeul ggeoyeyo.

구걸**할 바에는** 그냥 굶어 죽을 거예요.
Gugeolhal baeneun geunyang gulmeo jugeul ggeoyeyo.

I'd rather starve than have to beg.

Speaking = Writing

A(으)ㄹ 망정 (eu)r mangjeong B   "I'd rather A than B"   ★★

가지 않**을 망정** 늦게 가지 않겠어요.
Gaji aneul mangjeong neutge gaji ankesseoyo.
I'd rather not go at all than be late. (I won't be late. I'd rather not go.)

Remember (으)ㄹ 바에야 and 바에는? If not, see the previous page. This is a similar expression, only this time instead of preferring B, you prefer A.

HOW IT'S FORMED

(으)ㄹ is the future tense marker used here because A is something that may happen in the future or may continue happening. 망정 is a noun which doesn't really have a clear English equivalent. It's used to talk about preferences here in (으)ㄹ 망정 or also in 기에 망정이다.

HOW IT'S CONJUGATED

		Future
Action verbs ending in a vowel	하다	할 망정 hal mangjeong
Action verbs ending in a consonant	먹다	먹을 망정 meogeul mangjeong

TAKE NOTE

Don't confuse this expression with 기에 망정이지, which means that something was lucky (see page 176). In the expression in question here, the verb is always conjugated with (으)ㄹ.

B always ends with the future tense—either 겠다 or (으)ㄹ 것이다—and explains what you will do. See the examples below.

You can replace (으)ㄹ 망정 with (으)ㄴ/는 대신에, which means "instead of," but doesn't, by itself, indicate a preference; see page 119. In this case you have to change the order of A and B.

포기하는 **대신에** 죽었을 거예요. Pogihaneun daesine jugeosseul geoyeyo.
I'd die rather than give up.

EXAMPLE SENTENCES

죽을 **망정** 포기하지 않을 거예요. Jugeul mangjeong pogihaji aneul geoyeyo.
I'll die rather than give up.

굶을 **망정** 구걸하지 않겠어요. Gulmeul mangjeong gugeolhaji ankesseoyo.
I'll starve rather than have to beg.

		Speaking = Writing
A**같아선** gataseon B	"If it were up to me/if it were like that time…"	★

마음 **같아선** 정시에 오고 싶어요. Maeum gataseon jeongsie ogo sipeoyo.
If it were up to me, I'd be on time (but I can't).

같아선 has three different meanings, which can make it rather confusing. Fortunately, it works only with a relatively small number of words in the A clause, so all you have to do is look at A to understand which of the meanings the sentence refers to.

First, it can follow 마음, 생각, 성질, 욕심, **maeum, saenggak, seongji, yoksim,** or 기분 **gibun.** You may recognize these as words having to do with what's on your mind. Any of them can be followed by 같아선 to mean "if it were up to me" B must include 고 싶다. An expression with 같아선 implies that what you want to do is impossible.

마음 **같아선** 그 남자에게 선물을 사주고 싶어요.
Maeum gataseon geu namjaege seonmureul sajugo sipeoyo.
I want to buy that man a present (but I can't).

생각 **같아선** 회사를 그만두고 싶지만 할 수 없어요.
Saenggak gataseon hoesareul geumandugo sipjiman hal su eopsseoyo.
I want to quit my job (but I can't).

성질 **같아선** 예의 없는 아줌마에게 화를 내고 싶어요.
Seongjil gataseon ye-ui eobsneun ajummaege hwareul naego sipeoyo.
If it were up to me, I'd scold that rude ajumma.

The second meaning goes with expressions of time like 요즘 **yojeum,** 옛날 **yennal,** or 예전 **yejeon,** and it simply means "If it were like that time." So 옛날 같아선 **yennal gataseon** means "if it were like old times." This is often used when talking about things that are now possible but used to be impossible.

옛날 **같아선** 선생님께 말대꾸하는 건 생각조차 못했어요.
Yennal gataseon seonsaengnimkke maldaekkuhaneun geon saenggakjocha motaesseoyo.
In the old days, you wouldn't even dream of arguing with your teacher.

요즘 **같아선** 살 맛이 없어요. Yojeum gataseon sal masi eopsseoyo.
These days I don't even feel like living.

The third meaning works only with two expressions: 올 겨울 **ol gyeoul** (this winter) and 올 여름 **ol yeoreum** (this summer). The only sentence it's used in is this:

올 겨울 **같아선** 정말 못 살겠어요.
Ol gyeoul gataseon jeongmal mot salgesseoyo.
This winter is unbearable.

The implication is that it's unbearable because of the cold (or heat, if you want to talk about 올 여름).

HOW IT'S FORMED

같다 means "to be similar"; here it's conjugated with the 아서 verb ending, which means "so." 는 is added to this for emphasis and then 같아서는 **gataseoneun** is contracted to 같아선.

HOW IT'S CONJUGATED

There's no need for a conjugation table here. 같아선 follows only nouns and doesn't change regardless of the noun.

TAKE NOTE

마음 and 생각; 마음 is normally used for good things and 생각 for bad. So if you want to punch someone, use 생각 같아선; if you want to hug them, use 마음 같아선.

Emotions: Personal Experiences

Focus – 더 deo

Korean has a special particle that is used when talking about things that you personally observed; 더 is that particle. It's not the same as the 더 that means "more"; that 더 always appears as a word all by itself, while the particle 더 appears as part of a grammatical expression. There are a number of these expressions which are all covered in their own individual sections, but for the purpose of easy comparison, I've also listed them all here.

Now for the rules in using 더. First of all, it's easy to conjugate; it doesn't ask you to do anything more with your verbs than to stick it at the end of verbs, and it prefers not to be paired with 았/었/였 or 겠 except in a small number of very specific situations.

Secondly, the only time you can use 더 with first-person expressions is when you're talking about how you felt. You can't use it to talk about what you did yourself except with 았/었/였더니 (see page 185). You can always use 더 to talk about what other people did (second or third person), but you can't use it to talk about how they felt; this is something you can't consider yourself to have personally witnessed in Korean unless maybe you're in some kind of strange sci-fi universe where you can live inside another person's head.

Now let's compare some 더 expressions:

Expression	Page	Explanation	Example
A던데 deonde B	188	"I noticed that A, so/but/and B."	민수가 어제 늦었던데 아마 오늘도 늦을걸요. Minsuga eoje neujeotdeonde ama oneuldo neujeulgeoryo. (I noticed that) Minsu was late yesterday, so maybe he'll be late today as well.
~던데(요) ~deonde(yo)	188	"I noticed that ~."	민수가 어제 늦었던데요. Minsuga eoje neujeotdeondeyo. (I noticed that) Minsu was late yesterday.
A더니(만) B deoni(man) B	190	"I noticed that A, so/but/and B."	어제는 민수가 늦더니 오늘은 정시에 왔어요. Eojeneun minsuga neutdeoni oneureun jeongsie wasseoyo. Yesterday Minsu was late, but today he arrived on time.
A았/었/였이더니 B A at/eot/ yeotdeoni B	190	"I noticed that A, so/but/and B."	집에서 늦게 출발했더니 늦게 도착했어요. Jibeseo neutge chulbalhaetdeoni neutge dochakhaesseoyo. I left the house late, so I arrived late.
A더라 deora B	192	"I noticed that ~!"	민수가 어제 정말 늦었더라. Minsuga eoje jeongmal neujeotdeora. (I saw that) Minsu was really late yesterday!
~더라고(요) ~deorago(yo)	195	"I noticed that ~."	민수가 어제 정말 늦었더라고요. Minsuga eoje jeongmal neujeotdeoragoyo. (I saw that) Minsu was really late yesterday.
~더구나/더군요 ~deoguna/ deogunnyo	196	"I noticed that ~!"	민수가 어제 정말 늦었더구나. Minsuga eoje jeongmal neujeotdeoguna. (I saw that) Minsu was really late yesterday
~던가요 ~deongayo	195	"Did you ~?"	회의에 늦었던가요? Hoe-ui-e neujeotdeongayo? Were you late to the meeting?

You'll notice that most of them are quite similar in meaning. Pay attention to the exclamation point at the end of some translations: it indicates surprise or wonder whereas the others are just straightforward statements about things you noticed. 던데 and 더니 are 더 combined with ㄴ데 and then 니, so if you know how to use ㄴ데 and 니, you can probably figure out how to use 던데 and 더니. They're used to make a statement about something you saw and then followed up with whatever you think follows from that first statement. They're expressions that are flexible to use.

There are a few other expressions which use 더, but with none of its implications: it's just a part of the expression and can be used whether or not you're talking about something you personally saw. These expressions are 던, 더라도, and 았/었/였더라면. They don't belong here and will not be covered in this section, but you can look them up on pages 237, 106, and 289, respectively.

	Speaking > Writing
~아/어/여 보다 ~a/eo/yeo boda "Try ~"	★★★★★

빨리 **와 보**세요. **Ppalli wa boseyo.** Please try to come quickly.

Are you into experiments? If not, there's always 아/어/여 보지 않아요 **a/eo/yeo boji anayo**. Otherwise 아/어/여 보다 means "to try."

HOW IT'S FORMED

아/어/여 is the verb ending which means that the verb carries over to the next verb, and 보다 means "to see." In other words, "to do and see" or "to try."

HOW IT'S CONJUGATED

If you want to use a noun with this, you'll have to add a verb after it. For example, "try some kimchi" would be 김치를 먹어 보세요 **Kimchireul meogeo boseyo**.

		Past	Present	Future
Action verbs ending in 아 or 오	잡다	잡아 봤다 jaba bwatda	잡아 보다 jaba boda	잡아 볼 것이다 jaba bol geosida
Action verbs ending in 어, 우, 으 or 이	먹다	먹어 봤다 meogeo bwatda	먹어 보다 meogeo boda	먹어 볼 것이다 meogeo bol geosida
하다	하다	해 봤다 hae bwatda	해 보다 hae boda	해 볼 것이다 hae bol geosida

TAKE NOTE

The meaning of this expression changes a little depending on tense: in the past tense you're talking about a previous experience, and 아/어/여 보다 has a similar meaning to (으)ㄴ 적이 있다 **(eu)n jeogi itda** (see page 187). In the present it's usually a recommendation, like "try some kimchi" above. In the future you can use it to talk about something you plan to do.

There are many words which already have 아/어/여 보다 built into them. Some examples:

물어보다 **mureoboda** to ask
알아보다 **araboda**   to recognize

One useful conjugation of 아/어/여 보다 is 아/어/여 보니. It's a combination of 아/어/여 보다 and 니(까) (see page 67), and it means "to try and then discover…"

그는 만**나 보니** 아주 친절한 사람이에요.
Geuneun manna boni aju chinjeolhan saramieyo.
When I met him, I discovered that he was really kind.

김치를 먹**어 보니** 맛이 없었어요. **Kimchireul meogeo boni masi eopseosseoyo.**
When I tried kimchi, I found it wasn't very tasty.

It's similar to 고 보니 (see page 282) and 다 보니 (see page 353), but the difference is in timing. A고 보니 B means you did something, finished doing it, and then discovered B. A 아/어/여 보니 B means that you tried it: whether you finished or not, or how many times you tried doesn't really enter into the expression. A 다 보니 B means you did something repeatedly and then noticed B.

김치를 먹**어 보니** 맛이 없었어요. Kimchireul meogeo boni masi eopseosseoyo.
When I tried kimchi, it wasn't tasty.

김치를 먹**고 보니** 배가 아팠어요. Kimchireul meokgo boni baega apasseoyo.
After I ate kimchi, my stomach hurt.

김치를 먹**다 보니** 맛있어요. Kimchireul meokda boni masisseoyo.
After repeatedly eating kimchi, I started to find it tasty.

EXAMPLE SENTENCES

김치를 먹**어 봤**어요? Kimchireul meogeo bwasseoyo? Have you tried kimchi?

김치를 먹**어 볼** 거예요. Kimchireul meogeo bol geoyeyo. I'm going to try kimchi.

스키는 재미있으니까 한번 **해 보세요**.
Seukineun jaemi-isseunikka hanbeon hae boseyo.
Skiing is fun. You should try it!

Speaking = Writing

~(으)ㄴ 적(이)/일(이) 있다/   "I have/have never ~"   ★★★★
없다 (eu)n jeok(i)/il(i) itda/eopda

수업에 늦**은 적이 없어요**. Sueobe neujeun jeogi eopsseoyo.
I've never been late to class.

Here's an expression that's perfect for braggarts or drinking games. You can use it to talk about what you have or have never done.

HOW IT'S FORMED

First, add the past tense marker (으)ㄴ to your verb. 적 (or, alternatively, 일) means "experience" and can take the subject marker 이. Finally, 있다/없다 (there is/there isn't). Before all this it's also very common to add 아/어/여 보다 ("try"; see page 185), so then the entire expression becomes 아/어/여 본 적(이) 있다/없다.

HOW IT'S CONJUGATED

		Past
Action verbs ending in a vowel with 오 or 아	가다 gada	간 적(이) 있다 gan jeok(i) itda 간 적(이) 없다 gan jeok(i) eopda 가 본 적(이) 있다 ga bon jeok(i) itda 가 본 적(이) 없다 ga bon jeok(i) eopda

		Past
Action verbs ending in a consonant with 오 or 아	잡다 japda	잡은 적(이) 있다 jabeun jeok(i) itda 잡은 적(이) 없다 jabeun jeok(i) eopda 잡아 본 적(이) 있다 jaba bon jeok(i) itda 잡아 본 적(이) 없다 jaba bon jeok(i) eopda
Action verbs ending in a vowel with 어, 우, 으 or 이	서다 seoda	선 적(이) 있다 seon jeok(i) itda 선 적(이) 없다 seon jeok(i) eopda 서 본 적(이) 있다 seo bon jeok(i) itda 서 본 적(이) 없다 seo bon jeok(i) eopda
Action verbs ending in a consonant with 어, 우, 으 or 이	먹다 meokda	먹은 적(이) 있다 meogeun jeok(i) itda 먹은 적(이) 없다 meogeun jeok(i) eopda 먹어 본 적(이) 있다 meogeo bon jeok(i) itda 먹어 본 적(이) 없다 meogeo bon jeok(i) eopda
하다	하다 hada	한 적(이) 있다 han jeok(i) itda 한 적(이) 없다 han jeok(i) eopda 해 본 적(이) 있다 hae bon jeok(i) itda 해 본 적(이) 없다 hae bon jeok(i) eopda

TAKE NOTE

This expression is quite often used to talk about where you've been. See the examples.

EXAMPLE SENTENCES

수업에 늦은 적이 있어요. Sueobe neujeun jeogi isseoyo. I've been late to class.
수업에 늦어 본 적이 있어요. Sueobe neujeo bon jeogi isseoyo.

미국에 간 적이 없어요. Miguge gan jeogi eopsseoyo. I've never been to the US.
미국에 가 본 적이 없어요. Miguge ga bon jeogi eopsseoyo.

미국에 간 적이 있어요. Miguge gan jeogi isseoyo. I've been to the US.
미국에 가 본 적이 있어요. Miguge ga bon jeogi isseoyo.

스키를 탄 적 있어요. Seukireul tan jeok isseoyo. I've been skiing.
스키를 타 본 적 있어요. Seukireul ta bon jeok isseoyo.

스키를 탄 적 없어요. Seukireul tan jeok eopsseoyo. I've never been skiing.
스키를 타 본 적 없어요. Seukireul ta bon jeok eopsseoyo.

Speaking > Writing

A던데 deonde B, ~던데
(요) deonde(yo)   "I noticed that A, so/but B"   ★★★

민수가 어제 늦었**던데** 아마 오늘도 늦을걸요.
Minsuga eoje neujeotdeonde ama oneuldo neujeulgeolyo.
(I noticed that) Minsu was late yesterday, so maybe he'll be late today too.

Who doesn't love a good story? And who doesn't love telling stories about what they've seen? Here's an expression you can use to do that in Korean. 던데 and 던데요 are expressions used to talk about what the speaker has personally seen or experienced.

HOW IT'S FORMED

The particle 더 is used to indicate that you're talking about something you personally saw or experienced (but not something you yourself did). It's pretty common in Korean , and there's a whole section on it on page 184 if you'd like to know more about how to use it. In this case, it's combined with ㄴ데(요), which is covered on page 69 and has a wide variety of meanings: most often "so" or "but." Put them together and you've got "I noticed that A, so/but B."

HOW IT'S CONJUGATED

더 is very kind to you when it comes to conjugation; it will happily follow any letter without needing any special consideration. A is what you saw and B is what you're saying based on that. You can also just use 던데요 at the end of a sentence to simply mention something you noticed.

As 더 implies recollection, you don't need to put A in the past tense most of the time. If, however, the event you saw is completely finished, you can use 았/었/였이던데 to indicate that. For example, you wouldn't use 었던데 to talk about seeing someone beautiful (unless she has since turned ugly), but you would use it to talk about how it rained earlier (and has since stopped). Although I've put 예뻤던데, 작았던데, 남자였던데 and 물이었던데 in the table below so you can see how to form, they are not the expressions you'll normally use when talking about seeing something that was beautiful or small, or seeing a man or water: 작던데, 예쁘던데, 남자이던데 and 물이던데 will usually be the forms you want. 예뻤던데, 작았던데, 남자였던데 and 물이었던데 would be used if you were talking about someone who was beautiful but isn't any longer, something that was small but has grown, someone who was once a man but now is not, and something that was once water but is now something else.

그녀는 예쁘던데요. **Geunyeoneun yeppeudeondeyo.**
I saw her, and she was very pretty.

비가 왔던데 지금은 맑아요. **Biga watdeonde jigeumeun malgayo.**
It was raining earlier, but it has since cleared up.

겠던데 **getdeonde** is also a viable expression, though not commonly used. It's used to make a guess about what's going to happen based on what you have observed. In the example below, maybe you saw that the sky was getting cloudy.

비가 오겠던데 우산을 가지고 오세요. **Biga ogetdeonde usaneul gajigo oseyo.**
I think it's going to rain, so bring your umbrella.

		Past	Present	Future
Action verbs ending in a vowel	하다	했던데 haetdeonde	하던데 hadeonde	하겠던데 hagetdeonde
Action verbs ending in a consonant	먹다	먹었던데 meogeotdeonde	먹던데 meokdeonde	먹겠던데 meokgetdeonde
Descriptive verbs (adjectives) ending in a vowel	예쁘다	예뻤던데 yeppeotdeonde	예쁘던데 yeppeudeonde	예쁘겠던데 yeppeugetdeonde
Descriptive verbs (adjectives) ending in a consonant	작다	작았던데 jagatdeonde	작던데 jakdeonde	작겠던데 jakgetdeonde
Nouns ending in a vowel	남자	남자였던데 namjayeotdeonde	남자이던데 namja-i-deonde	남자이겠던데 namja-i-getdeonde
Nouns ending in a consonant	물	물이었던데 murieotdeonde	물이던데 murideonde	물이겠던데 murigetdeonde

TAKE NOTE

Be careful about past and future tense markers: see the conjugation section for an explanation.

던데 can't be used when talking about something you personally did—only something you saw. The only exception to this is if you're talking about how you felt, in which case it's fine to use 던데(요).

The difference between 던데 and 더니 is the same as the difference between ㄴ데 and 니: see page 69 for more on ㄴ데 and page 67 for more on 니(까).

EXAMPLE SENTENCES

가영의 남자친구가 정말 멋있**던데요**.
Kayoungui namjachinguga jeongmal meositdeondeyo.
(I noticed that) Kayoung's boyfriend is really cool.

민수가 어제 정말 늦었던데요. Minsuga eoje jeongmal neujeotdeondeyo.
(I noticed that) Minsu was really late yesterday.

이틀동안 비가 오**던데** 내일도 비가 올지 모르겠어요.
Iteul dongan biga odeonde naeildo biga olji moreugesseoyo.
(I see that) It's been raining for two days, so I think it might rain tomorrow as well.

		Speaking = Writing
A더니(만) deoni(man) B, A았/ 었/였니 at/eot/yeotdeoni B	"I noticed that A, so/but B"	★★★★

어제는 민수가 늦**더니** 오늘은 정시에 왔어요.
Eojeneun Minsuga neutdeoni oneureun jeongsie wasseoyo.
Yesterday Minsu was late, but today he arrived on time.

Just like 던데, these are expressions in which you use 더 to talk about something you noticed and its result, or how it has since changed. 더니 and 었더니 are not exactly the same expression, but they're very similar in meaning, so I've put them together here.

HOW IT'S FORMED

더 is a particle added to verbs to indicate that the situation in question is something you personally observed; see page184 for more on 더 and all its uses. 니 is the short form of 니까; they are exactly the same, but 니까 is never used in its full form in either of the 더니 expressions.

HOW IT'S CONJUGATED

		Past	Present/Future
Action verbs ending in a vowel	하다	했더니 haetdeoni 하더니 hadeoni	하더니
Action verbs ending in a consonant	먹다	먹었더니 meogeotdeoni 먹더니 meokdeoni	먹더니
Descriptive verbs (adjectives) ending in a vowel	예쁘다	예쁘더니 yeppeudeoni	예쁘더니
Descriptive verbs (adjectives) ending in a consonant	작다	작더니 jakdeoni	작더니
Nouns ending in a vowel	남자	남자이더니 namja-i-deoni	남자이더니
Nouns ending in a consonant	물	물이더니 murideoni	물이더니

TAKE NOTE

The difference between 더니 and 았/었/였더니 is that 더니, like the rest of the 더 expressions, is normally used only to talk about things you saw—not things you did yourself. That means it can be used only when the subject of the sentence is someone else. 았/었/였더니 is the expression you can use if you want to talk about things you yourself did.

With both expressions, the subjects of A and B must be the same.

There is another expression, 다니, which sounds somewhat similar but has a totally different meaning. It's used to express surprise at something you heard and is covered on page 319.

The difference between 던데 and 더니 is essentially the same as the difference between (으)ㄴ/는데 (see page 69) and (으)니(까) (see page 67).

EXAMPLE SENTENCES

■ 았/었/였더니 at/eot/yeotdeoni

집에서 늦게 출발**했더니** 늦게 도착했어요.
Jibeseo neutge chulbalhaetdeoni neutge dochakhaesseoyo.
I left the house late, so I arrived late.

한국어 소설을 읽**었더니** 머리가 아팠어요.
Hangugeo soseoreul ilgeotdeoni meoriga apasseoyo.
I read a Korean novel, but it gave me a headache.

말다툼을 했던 사람한테 전화**했더니** 그녀가 전화를 안 받았어요.
Maldatumeul haetdeon saramhante jeonhwahaetdeoni geunyeoga jeonhwareul an badasseoyo.
I tried to call the person I'd argued with, but she didn't answer.

■ **더니** deoni

가영씨, 열심히 공부하**더니** 시험을 잘 봤어요?
Kayoungssi, yeolssimhi gongbuhadeoni siheomeul jal bwasseoyo?
Kayoung, I know (I saw that) you studied hard. Did you do well on the test?

민수씨가 날마다 담배를 피우**더니** 건강이 나빠졌어요.
Minsussiga nalmada dambaereul piudeoni geongangi nappajyeosseoyo.
(I've noticed that) Minsu smokes every day, so his health has worsened.

		Speaking > Writing
~더라 ~deora	"I noticed that ~!"	★★★★

민수가 어제 정말 늦었**더라**. Minsuga eoje jeongmal neujeotdeora. (I saw that) Minsu was really late yesterday!

더라 is another way of making a statement about something you noticed. It's used only in 반말 and is used for talking about things you noticed which surprised you.

HOW IT'S CONJUGATED

더라 goes at the very end of a sentence.

		Past	Present
Action verbs ending in a vowel	하다	했더라 haetdeora	하더라 hadeora
Action verbs ending in a consonant	먹다	먹었더라 meogeotdeora	먹더라 meokdeora
Descriptive verbs (adjectives) ending in a vowel	예쁘다	예뻤더라 yeppeotdeora	예쁘더라 yeppeudeora
Descriptive verbs (adjectives) ending in a consonant	작다	작았더라 jagatdeora	작더라 jakdeora
Nouns ending in a vowel	남자	남자였더라 namjayeotdeora	남자더라 namjadeora
Nouns ending in a consonant	물	물이었더라 murieotdeora	물이더라 murideora

TAKE NOTE

This expression can't be used for sentences about the speaker himself—only sentences with second- or third-person subjects. The only exception to this is when it's used to talk about the speaker's emotions, in which case you can use 더라. You can't use it to talk about other people's emotions. You also can't use it in the future tense.

It can also be used to talk only about things you just learned.

더라고요 deoragoyo, covered a bit further down this page, is a very similar expression. 더라 is used only in 반말: there is no 더라요 or 더랍니다. If you want to use a similar expression in 존댓말, you should use 던데요 deondeyo (see page 188).

Another very slight difference is that using 더라 will make you sound more excited than 더라고요. 더라고요 also emphasizes things a little more than 더라 does, although this is, again, not a big difference. Another similar expression is 더군(요) deogun(yo) (see page 196), which is equivalent to 더라 but can be used in 반말 or 존댓말.

EXAMPLE SENTENCES

그는 아직 학생이<u>더라</u>. Geuneun ajik haksaengideora.
(I saw that) he is still a student!

가영이 벌써 집에 가<u>더라</u>. Gayeongi beolsseo jibe gadeora.
(I saw that) Kayoung already went home!

		Speaking > Writing
~더라고요 ~deoragoyo	"I noticed that ~"	★★★★

민수가 어제 정말 늦었<u>더라고요</u>. Minsuga eoje jeongmal neujeotdeoragoyo.
(I saw that) Minsu was really late yesterday.

This is almost the same expression as 더라 (covered on the previous page), but it sounds a little calmer and more objective: less like, "! Minsu was really late!" and more like "So I see Minsu was quite late..."

HOW IT'S CONJUGATED

If you're talking about something that's already completely finished, you can use 았/었/였 to indicate that.

오늘 아침에 비가 오더라고요. Oneul achime biga odeoragoyo.
This morning it rained. (The rain may or may not have stopped by now.)

오늘 아침에 비가 왔더라고요. Oneul achime biga watdeoragoyo.
This morning it rained. (It's no longer raining.)

		Past	Present
Action verbs ending in a vowel	하다	했더라고요 haetdeoragoyo	하더라고요 hadeoragoyo
Action verbs ending in a consonant	먹다	먹었더라고요 meogeotdeoragoyo	먹더라고요 meokdeoragoyo
Descriptive verbs (adjectives) ending in a vowel	예쁘다	예뻤더라고요 yeppeotdeoragoyo	예쁘더라고요 yeppeudeoragoyo
Descriptive verbs (adjectives) ending in a consonant	작다	작았더라고요 jagatdeoragoyo	작더라고요 jakdeoragoyo

		Past	Present
Nouns ending in a vowel	남자	남자였더라고요 namjayeotdeoragoyo	남자더라고요 namjadeoragoyo
Nouns ending in a consonant	물	물이었더라고요 murieotdeoragoyo	물이더라고요 murideoragoyo

TAKE NOTE

Since this is almost exactly the same expression as 더라, it has all the same restrictions. Here they are again for your edification.

This expression can't be used for sentences about the speaker himself: only sentences with second- or third-person subjects. The only exception to this is when it's used to talk about the speaker's emotions, in which case you can use 더라고요. You can't use it to talk about other people's emotions.

It can also be used to talk only about things you just learned, and not things you personally saw. So in the examples above about rain, you didn't actually see it rain, but maybe you noticed the ground was wet when you went outside.

더라, covered on page 192, is a very similar expression, but is used only in 반말. 더라고 요 can be used in either 반말 or 존댓말 just like most other grammar points; simply add or drop the 요.

Another very slight difference is that 더라 will make you sound more excited than 더라 고요. 더라고요 also emphasizes things a little more than 더라 does, although this is, again, not a big difference. Another similar expression is 더군 (요) (see page 196), which is equivalent to 더라 but can be used in 반말 or 존댓말.

EXAMPLE SENTENCES

그는 아직 학생이**더라고요**. Geuneun ajik haksaengideoragoyo.
(I saw that) he is still a student.

가영이 벌써 집에 갔**더라고요**. Kayoungi beolsseo jibe gatdeoragoyo.
(I saw that) Kayoung already went home.

		Speaking = Writing
~았/었/였던 것 같다 at/ eot/yeotdeon geot gatda	"It seems like ~ used to be true"	★★

대학교 때 민수가 보통 늦**었던 것 같아요**.
Daehakgyo ttae Minsuga botong neujeotdeon geot gatayo.
I think I remember that in our university days, Minsu was usually late.

This expression is perfect for people with poor long-term memories. It's used when you think of something that used to be a certain way, but aren't a hundred percent sure. Alternatively, you can use it to make educated guesses about the past.

HOW IT'S FORMED

First, take the past-tense marker 았/었/였 and then add yet another past-tense marker 던 (see page 237) to talk about things that happened in the past, often things that you experienced yourself. Then 것 turns the entire phrase into a noun. Finally, add 같다, which means "to be like."

HOW IT'S CONJUGATED

		Past
Action verbs with 아 or 오	잡다	잡았던 것 같다 Jabatdeon geot gatda
Action verbs with 어, 우, 으 or 이	먹다	먹었던 것 같다 meogeotdeon geot gatda
Action verbs ending in a vowel	하다	했던 것 같다 haetdeon geot gatda
Descriptive verbs (adjectives) ending in a vowel	예쁘다	예뻤던 것 같다 yeppeotdeon geot gatda
Descriptive verbs (adjectives) ending in a consonant	작다	작았던 것 같다 jagatdeon geot gatda
Nouns ending in a vowel	남자	남자였던 것 같다 namjayeotdeon geot gatda
Nouns ending in a consonant	물	물이었던 것 같다 murieotdeon geot gatda

EXAMPLE SENTENCES

옛날에는 사람들이 말을 **탔던 것 같아요**.
Yennareneun saramdeuri mareul tatdeon geot gatayo.
It seems like people rode horses in the old days.

어렸을 때 축구를 자주 **했던 것 같아요**.
Eoryeosseul ttae chukgureul jaju haetdeon geot gatayo.
I think I used to play soccer a lot when I was a child.

		Speaking > Writing
~던가요? ~deongayo?	"Did you ~?"	★★

회의에 늦었**던가요**? Hoe-ui-e neujeotdeongayo? Were you late to the meeting?

You may remember the question form ~(으)ㄴ가요? from the section on questions. If not, go to page 44. This is essentially that same question form, but here it's added to 더, so you're asking your listener to reminisce about their own personal experience.

HOW IT'S FORMED

더, the personal experience particle (see page 184) plus ㄴ가요?, which is used to ask questions.

HOW IT'S CONJUGATED

		Past	Present	Future
Action verbs ending in a vowel	하다	했던가요? haetdeongayo?	하던가요? hadeongayo?	하겠던가요? hagetdeongayo?
Action verbs ending in a consonant	먹다	먹었던가요? meogeotdeongayo?	먹던가요? meokdeongayo?	먹겠던가요? meokgetdeongayo?
Descriptive verbs (adjectives) ending in a vowel	예쁘다	예뻤던가요? yeppeotdeongayo?	예쁘던가요? yeppeudeongayo?	예쁘겠던가요? yeppeugetdeongayo?
Descriptive verbs (adjectives) ending in a consonant	작다	작았던가요? jagatdeongayo?	작던가요? jakdeongayo?	작겠던가요? jakgetdeongayo?
Nouns ending in a vowel	남자	남자였던가요? namjayeotdeongayo?	남자이던가요? namja-i-deongayo?	남자이던가요? namja-i-deongayo?
Nouns ending in a consonant	물	물이었던가요? murieotdeongayo?	물이던가요? murideongayo?	물이던가요? murideongayo?

TAKE NOTE

You can, and Koreans generally do, simply use the regular question forms or a statement form with rising intonation. They just don't have quite the same nuances as 던가요.

회의에 늦었**어요**? Hoe-ui-e neujeosseoyo?
회의에 늦었**나요**? Hoe-ui-e neujeonnayo?
Were you late to the meeting?

EXAMPLE SENTENCES

민수의 새로운 여자 친구가 예쁘**던가요**?
Minsu-ui saeroun yeoja chinguga yeppeudeongayo?
Is Minsu's new girlfriend beautiful?

파티 준비가 다 되었**던가요**? Pati junbiga da doe-eotdeongayo?
Do you think everything was ready for the party?

파티 준비가 다 되겠**던가요**? Pati junbiga da doegetdeongayo?
Do you think everything will be ready for the party?

(Note: In all cases above, the speaker expects that the listener knows the answer: the listener has met Minsu's new girlfriend and is involved in planning the party.)

Speaking > Writing

~더군요/더구나   "I noticed that ~"   ★
~deogunnyo/deoguna

민수가 어제 정말 늦었**더구나**. Minsuga eoje jeongmal neujeotdeoguna.
(I saw that) Minsu was really late yesterday

This is just another, but much less common, way to say 더라 (which is commonly used by Koreans, grammar guides, AND the TOPIK. This is covered in depth on page 192).

HOW IT'S FORMED

The "personal observation" particle 더 plus 군, which is used to comment on things you learned for the first time. See page 172 for more on 군.

HOW IT'S CONJUGATED

Like 군요 itself, the 반말 form isn't conjugated in the regular manner--in this case it's 더구나.

		Past	Present
Action verbs ending in a vowel	하다	했더군요 haetdeogunnyo 했더구나 haetdeoguna	하더군요 hadeogunnyo 하더구나 hadeoguna
Action verbs ending in a consonant	먹다	먹었더군요 meogeotdeogunnyo 먹었더구나 meogeotdeoguna	먹더군요 meokdeogunnyo 먹더구나 meokdeoguna
Descriptive verbs (adjectives) ending in a vowel	예쁘다	예뻤더군요 yeppeotdeogunnyo 예뻤더구나 yeppeotdeoguna	예쁘더군요 yeppeudeogunnyo 예쁘더구나 yeppeudeoguna
Descriptive verbs (adjectives) ending in a consonant	작다	작았더군요 jagatdeogunnyo 작았더구나 jagatdeoguna	작더군요 jakdeogunnyo 작더구나 jakdeoguna
Nouns ending in a vowel	남자	남자였더군요 namjayeotdeogunnyo 남자였더구나 namjayeotdeoguna	남자더군요 namjadeogunnyo 남자더구나 namjadeoguna
Nouns ending in a consonant	물	물이었더군요 murieotdeogunnyo 물이었더구나 murieotdeoguna	물이더군요 murideogunnyo 물이더구나 murideoguna

TAKE NOTE

더군요 and 더라 are identical in meaning.

The usual rules about dealing with 더 apply (see page 184): No first-person sentences unless you're talking about your emotions, and only second- or third-person sentences unless you're talking about other people's emotions; sentences about other people's emotions are not allowed. Also, the event must be something that you personally observed.

더군요 can be used only to talk about things you just learned.

EXAMPLE SENTENCES

민수가 어제 정말 늦었**더군요**. (존댓말) Minsuga eoje jeongmal neujeotdeogunnyo.
민수가 어제 정말 늦었**더구나**. (반말) Minsuga eoje jeongmal neujeotdeoguna.
(I saw that) Minsu was really late yesterday.

그는 아직 학생이**더군요**. Geuneun ajik haksaengideogunnyo.
(I saw that) he is still a student.

가영이 벌써 집에 갔**더군요**. Kayoungi beolsseo jibe gatdeogunnyo.
(I saw that) Kayoung already went home.

Obligations, Orders and Permission

In addition to the grammar points covered here, you can also use 지(요) to offer to do something or to suggest that someone else do it. This is covered along with the rest of 지요's meanings on page 315.

> **Speaking = Writing**
>
> **~아/어/여야 하다** a/eo/yeoya hada,   "One has to ~"   ★★★★★
> **~아/어/여야 되다** a/eo/yeoya doeda

늦지 않으려면 집에서 일찍 출발**해야 해요**.
Neutji aneuryeomyeon jibeseo iljjik chulbalhaeya haeyo.

늦지 않으려면 집에서 일찍 출발**해야 돼요**.
Neutji aneuryeomyeon jibeseo iljjik chulbalhaeya dwaeyo.

You'd better leave the house early so as not to be late.

아/어/여야 하다 and 되다 are by far the most common ways to express obligation in Korean. 아/어/여야 되다 is a little more colloquial while 아/어/여야 하다 is used slightly more often in writing, but you can use either expression whenever you want to without sounding strange. Personally, I prefer 해야 되다 because 해야 해요 just sounds awkward to me, but that's a matter of opinion; Koreans use both.

HOW IT'S FORMED

아/어/여야 is used to express obligation or necessity (see page 202). 하다 and 되다 are, well, 하다 and 되다. Normally they are different words, but in this expression they both mean exactly the same thing.

HOW IT'S CONJUGATED

These expressions work only with action verbs, so if you want to say something such as "You must be beautiful," you'll need to turn 예쁘다 into an action verb by adding 아/어/여지다 to the end of it; see page 25.

		Past	Present	Future
Action verbs ending in a vowel	하다	해야 했다 haeya haetda 해야 됐다 haeya dwaetda	해야 하다 haeya hada 해야 되다 haeya doeda	해야 하겠다 haeya hagetda 해야 되겠다 haeya doegetda
Action verbs ending in a consonant	먹다	먹어야 했다 meogeoya haetda 먹어야 됐다 meogeoya dwaetda	먹어야 하다 meogeoya hada 먹어야 되다 meogeoya doeda	먹어야 하겠다 meogeoya hagetda 먹어야 되겠다 meogeoya doegetda

TAKE NOTE

The difference between these expressions and 아/어/여야지요 is that the latter has somewhat more of a chiding tone to it and is used to remind someone they have to do something they should already know about. 아/어/여 하다/되다 doesn't have this connotation.

To express prohibition, it's far more natural to use ~(으)면 안 되다 **~(eu)myeon an doeda** (see page 200) rather than ~지 않아야 해요 **~ji anaya haeyo**, although the latter is not ungrammatical.

EXAMPLE SENTENCES

숙제를 **해야 해요**. Sukjereul haeya haeyo.

숙제를 **해야 돼요**. Sukjereul haeya dwaeyo.

You must do your homework.

내일 제가 일본에 가**야 해요**. Naeil jega Ilbone gaya haeyo.

내일 제가 일본에 가**야 돼요**. Naeil jega Ilbone gaya dwaeyo.

Tomorrow I must go to Japan.

| ~지 말다 ~ji malda, A
지 말고 ji malgo B | "Don't ~" | **Speaking = Writing**
★★★★★ |

늦**지 마세요**. Neutji maseyo. Don't be late.

If you work in the Korean school system, you'll already be very familiar with these two expressions. They're ways to tell people not to do something. If you often find yourself needing to say things such as "Don't run!" or "Don't shout!" or "Don't eat your glue!"—, you'll want to know this expression.

HOW IT'S FORMED

지 plus 말다, which is a verb that means "to stop." You can add 고 if you want to continue the sentence by telling the other person what they should do instead of A; if you're not already familiar with 고 and how it works, it basically means "and" and is explained in detail on page 51.

HOW IT'S CONJUGATED

You can then conjugate 말다 **malda** (마 in 반말, 마세요 **maseyo** in informal polite or 마십시오 **masipsio** in super-polite language) to end the sentence, or you can use 지 말고 **ji malgo** and then continue the sentence, in which case, A is what the person shouldn't do and B is what they should do instead.

		Present
Action verbs ending in a vowel	하다	하지 마 haji ma 하지 마세요 haji maseyo 하지 맙시다 haji mapsida 하지 말고 haji malgo
Action verbs ending in a consonant	먹다	먹지 마 meokji ma 먹지 마세요 meokji maseyo 먹지 맙시다 meokji mapsida 먹지 말고 meokji malgo

TAKE NOTE

No past or future tenses are used with this expression. When you use 지 말고, the subjects of A and B must be the same. 지 말고 can also be used to end a sentence in 반말; just end with 지 말고 instead of 지 마. This may or may not be technically correct, but it's often done.

EXAMPLE SENTENCES

사탕을 너무 많이 먹**지 마세요**. Satangeul neomu mani meokji maseyo.
Don't eat too much candy.

싸우**지 마십시오**. Ssauji masipsio. (존댓말)
싸우**지 마**. Ssauji ma. (반말)
싸우**지 말고**. Ssauji malgo. (반말)
Don't fight.

And here are a few for you teachers out there.

뛰지 마. **Ttwiji ma.** Don't run.
떠들지 마. **Tteodeulji ma.** Don't be noisy.
싸우지 마. **Ssauji ma.** Don't fight.
놀지 마. **Nolji ma.** Don't play.
밀지 마. **Milji ma.** Don't push.
한국어로 말하지 마. **Hangugeoro malhaji ma.** Don't speak Korean.
연필을 잡지 마. **Yeonpireul japji ma.** Don't hold your pencil.
먹지 마. **Meokji ma.** Don't eat.
만지지 마. **Manjiji ma.** Don't touch.

		Speaking = Writing
~(으)면 되다 (eu)myeon doeda	"~ is okay/	★★★★★
~아/어/여도 되다 a/eo/yeodo doeda	not okay"	★★★★★
~(으)면 안 되다 (eu)myeon an doeda		★★★★★

늦으**면 안 돼요**. **Neujeumyeon an dwaeyo.** It's not okay to be late.

Here's another good expression for teachers. (으)면 되다 and 아/어/여도 되다 are ways to say that it's okay to do something. (으)면 되다 normally means that it's okay to do something for some purpose: for example, it's okay to eat that yogurt even though it's slightly after the best-before date. ~아/어/여도 되다 means that you're allowed to do ~. (으)면 안 되다 means it's not okay.

HOW IT'S FORMED

(으)면 means "if" (see page 283). 아/어/여도 means "even if" and is covered on page 104. 되다 is a versatile verb with many meanings, one of which is "is okay." In other words, "if/even if you do ~, it's okay." If you throw in 안 (not) then you get "if you do ~, it's not okay."

HOW IT'S CONJUGATED

		Present
Action verbs ending in a vowel	하다	하면 (안) 되다 hamyeon (an) doeda 해도 되다 haedo doeda
Action verbs ending in a consonant	먹다	먹으면 (안) 되다 meogeumyeon (an) doeda 먹어도 되다 meogeodo doeda

TAKE NOTE

(으)면 되다 and 아/어/여도 되다 are equivalent expressions.

~지 말다 and ~(으)면 안 되다 are similar in meaning, but 지 말다 is used to directly tell a person not to do something while (으)면 안 되다 is a general statement about what's okay or not okay. So if you want to tell a running child not to do so, you can say 뛰지 마! If you want to say it's not okay to run somewhere, regardless of whether or not anyone is actually running at that moment, you can say 뛰면 안 돼. Of course, if someone is already running and you say 뛰면 안 돼, you may as well be saying 뛰지 마.

Likewise, ~(으)면 되다 and ~아/어/여도 되다 mean that it's okay to do something, regardless of whether or not anyone should do it or wants to do it. It can be used to give someone permission to do something, like in the examples below. If you want to say someone should do something, you can use 아/어/여야지 A/eo/yeoyaji (see the next page) or simply 지 (see page 315).

EXAMPLE SENTENCES

여기에서 놀**면 안 돼요**. Yeogieseo nol**myeon an dwaeyo**.
You're not allowed to play here.

이 방에서 뛰**어도 돼요**. I bangeseo ttwi**eodo dwaeyo**.
It's okay to run in this room.

지금 집에 가**도 돼요**. Jigeum jibe ga**do dwaeyo**.
지금 집에 가**면 돼요**. Jigeum jibe ga**myeon dwaeyo**.
It's okay to go home now.

머리가 아파요? Meoriga apayo?

이 약을 먹<u>으면 돼요</u>. I yageul meogeumyeon dwaeyo.

Do you have headache? If you take this medicine, you'll be okay.

이 약을 먹<u>어도 돼요</u>. I yageul meogeodo dwaeyo.

You're allowed to take this medicine.

이 약을 먹<u>으면 안 돼요</u>. I yageul meogeumyeon an dwaeyo.

You're not allowed to take this medicine.

		Speaking = Writing
A아/어/여야(지/만) a/eo/yeoya(ji/man) B	"One must A in order to B"	★★★★
A(이)라야 (i)raya B		★
~아/어/여야지(요) a/eo/yeoyaji(yo)		★★★

일찍 집에서 출발해야 늦지 않을 거예요.

Iljjik jibeseo chulbalhaeya neutji aneul geoyeyo.

You must leave the house early in order not to be late.

These expressions are for anyone who likes obeying rules, or better yet, making them. It's used to say that A is necessary for B to happen and is a good translation of sentences like "You must study hard in order to do well on the test ," or "You must have a student card in order to use the library."

HOW IT'S FORMED

아/어/여야 stands on its own. You can add 지 or 만 to add emphasis, but neither one is necessary. 지 can be added during informal speech while 만 is more commonly used in formal speech or in writing.

(이)라 is a particle commonly used after nouns when you plan to do something else with these nouns. For example, A(이)라는 is something that is called A. A라고 하다 means that A is said. Add 아야 to 라 and you get 라야. Again, 만 can be added to emphasize that you really, really must be A in order to B.

HOW IT'S CONJUGATED

(이)라야(만) means exactly the same thing as 아/어/여야(만), but it only follows nouns.

If you want to tell someone they must A in order to B, then you can use 지 않아야 with descriptive verbs, 지 말아야 with action verbs, or 이/가 아니어야 with nouns.

		Past	Present	Future
Action verbs ending in a vowel	하다	했어야 haesseoya 했어야지 haesseoyaji 했어야만 haesseoyaman 하지 말았어야 haji marasseoya 하지 말았어야지 haji marasseoyaji 하지 말았어야만 haji marasseoyaman	해야 haeya 해야지 haeyaji 해야만 haeyaman 하지 말아야 haji maraya 하지 말아야지 haji marayaji 하지 말아야만 haji marayaman	해야 해야지 해야만 하지 말어야 하지 말아야지 하지 말아야만
Action verbs ending in a consonant	먹다	먹었어야 meogeosseoya 먹었어야지 meogeosseoyaji 먹었어야만 meogeosseoyaman 먹지 말았어야 meokji marasseoya 먹지 말았어야지 meokji marasseoyaji 먹지 말았어야만 meokji marasseoyaman	먹어야 meogeoya 먹어야지 meogeoyaji 먹어야만 meogeoyaman 먹지 말아야 meokji maraya 먹지 말아야지 meokji marayaji 먹지 말아야만 meokji marayaman	먹어야 먹어야지 먹어야만 먹지 말아야 먹지 말아야지 먹지 말아야만
Descriptive verbs (adjectives) ending in a vowel	예쁘다	예뻐야 예뻐야지 예뻐야만 예쁘지 않아야 예쁘지 않아야지 예쁘지 않아야만 yeppeuji anayaman	예뻐야 yeppeoya 예뻐야지 yeppeoyaji 예뻐야만 yeppeoyaman 예쁘지 않아야 yeppeuji anaya 예쁘지 않아야지 yeppeuji anayaji 예쁘지 않아야 yeppeuji anayaman	예뻐야 예뻐야지 예뻐야만 예쁘지 않아야 예쁘지 않아야지 예쁘지 않아야
Descriptive verbs (adjectives) ending in a consonant	작다	작아야 jagaya 작아야지 jagayaji 작아야만 jagayaman 작지 않아야 jakji anaya 작지 않아야지 jakji anayaji 작지 않아야만 jakji anayaman	작아야 작아야지 작아야만 작지 않아야 작지 말아야지 작지 말아야만	작아야 작아야지 작아야만 하지 말아야 하지 말아야지 작지 말아야만
Nouns ending in a vowel	남자	남자여야 남자여야지 남자여야만 남자가 아니어야 남자가 아니어야지 남자가 아니어야만 남자이라야 남자이라야만	남자여야 namjayeoya 남자여야지 namjayeoyaji 남자여야만 namjayeoyaman 남자가 아니어야 namjaga anieoya 남자가 아니어야지 namjaga anieoyaji 남자가 아니어야만 namjaga anieoyaman 남자이라야 namjairaya 남자이라야만 namjairayaman	남자여야 남자여야지 남자여야만 남자가 아니어야 남자가 아니어야지 남자가 아니어야만 남자이라야 남자이라야만

		Past	Present	Future
Nouns ending in a consonant	물	물이어야 물이어야지 물이어야만 물이 아니어야 물이 아니어야지 물이 아니어야만 물이라야 물이라야만	물이어야 murieoya 물이어야지 murieoyaji 물이어야만 murieoyaman 물이 아니어야 muri anieoya 물이 아니어야지 muri anieoyaji 물이 아니어야만 muri anieoyaman 물이라야 muriraya 물이라야만 murirayaman	물이어야 물이어야지 물이어야만 물이 아니어야 물이 　아니어야지 물이 　아니어야만 물이라야 물이라야만

TAKE NOTE

B often ends with expressions like (으)ㄹ 수 있다 (see page 294) or (으)ㄹ 거예요 (see page 239). B must also be a statement rather than a question, suggestion, or command.

If you end a sentence with 아/어/여야지(요), it means you're either telling someone what to do or reminding yourself that you must do something. In the latter case, just use 아/어/여지; it's not common to talk about yourself using 존댓말. The 지 here is an ending that means "isn't it?" and it has a similar connotation in 아/어/여야지(요): when you use this expression, you're normally reminding someone of something they should already know rather than telling them anything new. 아/어/여야겠다 (see page 207) is interchangeable with 아/어/여야지 when talking to yourself.

아/어/여야(지) in the middle of a sentence and 아/어/여야지(요) are grouped together here because they're almost the same expression, but remember that at the end of a sentence this expression is used to tell someone they must do something or to remind yourself that you must do something. In the middle, it refers to a necessary condition in order to do B: it doesn't mean the other person is obligated to do A, but they must do A if they want to do B. If they don't want to do B, they won't really care about your 아/어/여야 sentence in the first place.

EXAMPLE SENTENCES

■ A아/어/여야 a/eo/yeoya B

75프로를 넘**어야** 시험에 합격할 수 있어요.
Chilsibo-peuroreul neomeoya siheome hapgyeokhal su isseoyo.
You have to get more than 75% in order to pass the test.

신발을 벗**어야** 집에 들어올 수 있어요
Sinbareul beoseoya jibe deureool su isseoyo.
You have to take off your shoes in order to go in the house.

■ A(이)라야 (i)raya B

남자**라야** 이 찜질방에 갈 수 있어요. **Namjaraya i jjimjilbange gal su isseoyo.**
You must be a man in order to go into this jjimjilbang (sauna).

제일 좋은 학생이**라야** 그 장학금을 받을 수 있어요.
Jeil joeun haksaengiraya geu janghakgeumeul badeul su isseoyo.
You must be the best student in order to get that scholarship.

■ ~아/어/여야지(요) ~a/eo/yeoyaji(yo)

늦지 않으려면 일찍 집에서 출발**해야지요**.
Neutji aneuryeomyeon iljjik jibeseo chulbalhaeyajiyo.
You know you'd better leave the house early so as not to be late.

12시 이후에는 먹지 말**아야지요**. **Yeoldusi ihueneun meokji marayajiyo.**
You know you can't eat after 12:00.

~게 하다 ~ge hada	"make someone do ~"	Speaking = Writing ★★★★

남자친구가 나를 행복하**게 했어요**.
Namjachinguga nareul haengbokhage haesseoyo.
My boyfriend made me very happy.

You can't always do what you want. Sometimes people are going to make you do certain things, and you're going to have to explain those things: that's where this expression comes in. It means "to make someone ~," or "to let someone ~," depending on the situation, so it can be used to say either "My teacher made me stay after school" or "My teacher let me go home early." People will understand your meaning from the context.

HOW IT'S FORMED

게 is the particle that changes verbs into adverbs. In this case it changes ~ into an adverbial phrase. 하다, of course, just means "to do." In this case it implies intent: that someone made that adverbial phrase be that way.

HOW IT'S CONJUGATED

Here's where things get a little complicated. First of all, this can be used with action verbs or descriptive verbs. Descriptive verbs are the easy part, so we'll do them first.

Let's say Y and Z are the two people involved in the situation. Y is the person who makes Z a certain way. So your sentence describing this will look like Y 이/가 Z를/을 ~게 하다. See below for examples.

Now, with action verbs, you have to construct your sentence differently depending on whether your verb is transitive or intransitive. If you already know what that's all about, feel free to skip the next paragraph.

Intransitive verbs are verbs that don't take a direct object. Some common examples are *go*, *sleep*, *arrive* and *die*. Transitive verbs, on the other hand, do take a direct object. Some examples are "eat the pizza," "play the guitar," and "carry a book." The direct objects are the things affected by the verb: the pizza, guitar, and book. You'll recognize them as the parts of the sentence that take the 를/을 suffix. These objects can't follow intransitive verbs: you don't "go the house" or "sleep the bed."

Now, when you use 게 하다 with an intransitive verb, the sentence looks the same as it does when you use a descriptive verb: Y이/가 Z를/을 ~게 하다.

With a transitive verb, you need to use 를/을 for the direct object of the verb and thus you can't use it for the person you're making do the action). So in this case, the person gets the suffix 에게 and the direct object keeps 를/을. The sentence structure then becomes Y 이/가 Z에게 ~게 하다. Here's an example sentence that may help you understand:

엄마가 민수에게 자주 TV를 보**게 해요**.
Eommaga Minsuege jaju tibireul boge haeyo.
Minsu's mom often lets him watch TV.

As you can see, the direct object of the verb (TV) gets the 를 ending while Minsu (who would have had that 를 ending for himself if the TV hadn't been in the sentence) gets 에게 instead to show him as the person who is being made (or, in this case, *allowed*) to do the action (watch TV).

As for tenses, you conjugate 하다 to put the sentence in the past or the future tense. You can use 못 ~게 하다 to express prohibition.

		Past	Present	Future
Action verbs ending in a vowel	하다	하게 했다 hage haetda 못 하게 했다 mot hage haetda	하게 하다 hage hada 못 하게 하다 mot hage hada	하게 하겠다 hage hagetda 못 하게 하겠다 mot hage hagetda
Action verbs ending in a consonant	먹다	먹게 했다 meokge haetda 못 먹게 했다 mot meokge haetda	먹게 하다 meokge hada 못 먹게 하다 mot meokge hada	먹게 하겠다 meokge hagetda 못 먹게 하겠다 mot meokge hagetda
Descriptive verbs (adjectives) ending in a vowel	예쁘다	예쁘게 했다 yeppeuge haetda	예쁘게 하다 yeppeuge hada	예쁘게 하겠다 yeppeuge hagetda
Descriptive verbs (adjectives) ending in a consonant	작다	작게 했다 jakge haetda	작게 하다 jakge hada	작게 하겠다 jakge hagetda

TAKE NOTE

Be careful about constructing your sentences correctly with all the different types of verbs: see above on how to do that.

The difference between 게 하다 and 게 되다 is that 하다 (to do) is an active verb whereas 되다 (to become) is passive. Thus, 게 하다 means to make something a certain way (active) whereas 게 되다 means to become a certain way (passive). 게 되다 says nothing about how the thing became that way. You can learn more about it, along with other passive verbs, on page 33.

게 하다 and 도록 하다 **dorok hada** are interchangeable in certain situations: 게 하다 can always be changed into 도록 하다, but the reverse isn't true; see page 167. 게 만들다 **ge mandeulda** is another similar, although much less common, expression.

게 하다 is a causative expression. Causative verbs are covered in more detail on page 34. The difference between 게 하다 and causative verbs made with 이, 히, etc., is that causative verbs using 이, 히 and so on imply a physical connection similar to a mother dressing her child (입히다) **ipida**. 게 하다 doesn't imply any such connection: in this case the mother told her child to put on his clothes (입게 하다) **ipge hada**.

EXAMPLE SENTENCES

- Descriptive verbs

  명상이 제 마음을 깨끗하**게 했어요**.
  Myeongsangi je maeumeul kkaekkeutage haesseoyo.
  Meditation cleansed my spirit. (made my spirit clean)

- Intransitive action verbs

  선생님이 우리를 공부하**게 하셨어요**.
  Seonsaengnimi urireul gongbuhage hasyeosseoyo. The teacher made us study.

  의사가 나를 못 뛰**게 하셨어요**. **Uisaga nareul mot ttwige ha-syeoss-eoyo.**
  The doctor told me not to run.

- Transitive action verbs

  엄마가 민수에게 사탕을 못 먹**게 해요**.
  Eommaga Minsuege satangeul mot meokge haeyo.
  Minsu's mom won't let him eat candy.

  엄마가 민수에게 자주 TV를 보**게 해요**.
  Eommaga Minsuege jaju tibireul boge haeyo.
  Minsu's mom often lets him watch TV.

	Speaking = Writing
~아/어/여야겠다 a/eo/yeoyagetda "I'll have to ~"	★★★

회의에 정시에 도착하기 위해서 집에서 일찍 출발**해야겠다**.
Hoe-ui-e jeongsie dochakhagi wihaeseo jibeseo iljjik chulbalhaeyagetda.
In order to get to the meeting on time, I'll have to leave my house early.

Here's an expression for busy, forgetful, or busy and forgetful people. 아/어/여야겠다 is used to remind yourself about something you have to do.

HOW IT'S FORMED

아/어/여야 is used to express obligation; see page 202. 겠 is the future tense marker and is covered on page 239.

HOW IT'S CONJUGATED

Because this expression is used only when talking to oneself, it's always at the end of a sentence and always in 반말, just as it appears above: 아/어/여야겠다.

		Future
Action verbs with 오 or 아	잡다	잡아야겠다 jabayagetda
Action verbs with 어, 우, 으 or 이	먹다	먹어야겠다 meogeoyagetda
Action verbs ending in a vowel	하다	해야겠다 haeyagetda

TAKE NOTE

This expression and 아/어/여야지 can be used interchangeably when talking about something you need to do.

EXAMPLE SENTENCES

가영의 파티에 꼭 가**야겠다**. Kayoungui patie kkok gayagetda.
I'll definitely have to go to Kayoung's party.

오늘 더운데 물을 더 마**셔야겠다**. Oneul deo-un-de mureul deo masyeoyagetda.
It's hot today. I'll have to drink more water.

Speaking > Writing

~(으)렴/려무나 (eu)ryeom/ryeomuna   "Please ~"   ★

민수야, 학교에 빨리 가**렴**! 늦을 거야.
Minsuya, hakgyoe ppalli garyeom! Neujeul geoya.
민수야, 학교에 빨리 가**려무나**! 늦을 거야.
Minsuya, hakgyoe ppalli garyeomuna! Neujeul geoya.

Minsu, please hurry up! You're going to be late for school.

This is a way to kindly grant a favor or suggest someone do something, most often used by mothers talking to their children. Please note that it is 반말 and isn't used outside of 반말. So use it toward a child, but not toward someone older unless you want to be rude.

HOW IT'S CONJUGATED

It always goes at the end of a sentence.

		Present
Action verbs ending in a vowel	하다	하렴 haryeom 하려무나 haryeomuna
Action verbs ending in a consonant	먹다	먹으렴 meogeuryeom 먹으려무나 meogeuryeomuna

TAKE NOTE

This has a similar meaning to 아/어/여라 a/eo/yeora, the simplest way of telling someone to do something in one form of 반말 (see page 17). Again, it's only 반말; 아/어/여 주세요 a/eo/yeo juseyo (see page 32) is a good way to politely request a favor from someone who is older than you or whom you don't know.

EXAMPLE SENTENCES

그렇게 싸우지 마렴. Geureoke ssauji maryeom.
그렇게 싸우지 마려무나. Geureoke ssauji maryeomuna.
Please don't fight like that.

그래. 네 마음대로 하렴. Geurae. Ne maeumdaero haryeom.
그래. 네 마음대로 하려무나. Geurae. Ne maeumdaero haryeomuna.
Fine. Go ahead and do what you want.

Warnings

	Speaking = Writing
A다(가) 보면B A da(ga) bomyeon B	"If you do A for a long time, ★★★ B will happen"

계속 이야기 하다 보면 늦을 거예요. Gyesok iyagi hada bomyeon neujeul geoyeyo.
If you keep talking, you'll be late.

Remember when your mom used to tell you, "If you keep on making that face, your face will stay that way!" or "If you don't eat your vegetables, you won't get tall!" Yeah, me too. I'm still short. For all you moms and teachers out there, this expression's for you. It's either a threat or a promise depending on the content and is used only to talk about the future because it wouldn't be conditional otherwise.

HOW IT'S FORMED

다가 plus 보다 (to watch/try) plus 면 (if). The 가 part of 다가 is optional. Just like the rest of the 다가 expressions, this describes an action that lasts for some time. Just like everything else with 면, it's conditional.

HOW IT'S CONJUGATED

		Future
Action verbs ending in a vowel	하다	하다가 보면 hadaga bomyeon
Action verbs ending in a consonant	먹다	먹다가 보면 meokdaga bomyeon

TAKE NOTE

Like the other 다가 expressions, make sure the subjects of both clauses are the same and that you use the expression only with action verbs. Again, it's used only in the future. (으)ㄹ 거예요, 겠 and (으)ㄹ 수 있다 are all common endings for the B clause.

살다 보면 (with or without the space) is a commonly used expression meaning "as you live" or "in life."

> **살다 보면** 좋은 일도 생기고 나쁜 일도 생기지요.
> Salda bomyeon joeun ildo saenggigo nappeun ildo saenggijiyo.
>
> **살다보면** 좋은 일도 나쁜 일도 생기지요.
> Saldabomyeon joeun ildo nappeun ildo saenggijiyo.
>
> Good things and bad things happen in life.

EXAMPLE SENTENCES

> 계속 공부하**다가 보면** 유창해질 거예요.
> Gyesok gongbuhadaga bomyeon yuchanghaejil geoyeyo.
> If you keep studying, you'll become fluent.
>
> 돈을 그렇게 많이 쓰**다 보면** 돈이 다 없어질 거예요.
> Doneul geureoke mani sseuda bomyeon doni da eopsseojil geoyeyo.
> If you keep spending that much money, you won't have any left.

Speaking = Writing

A다가는 daganeun B   "Unfortunately, if you do A,   ★★
B might happen"

> 이렇게 천천히 준비하**다가는** 늦을 거예요.
> Ireoke cheoncheonhi junbihadaganeun neujeul geoyeyo.
> If you take your time getting ready, you'll be late.

While 다가 by itself is the little child who won't let you get anything done, 다가는 is the kind of verb moms love. It's used to foretell a bad result (B) if someone does a specific action (A).

HOW IT'S FORMED

다가 plus 는. There is no special interaction between the two.

HOW IT'S CONJUGATED

		Future
Action verbs ending in a vowel	하다	하다가는 hadaganeun
Action verbs ending in a consonant	먹다	먹다가는 meokdaganeun
Descriptive verbs (adjectives) ending in a vowel	예쁘다	예쁘다가는 yeppeudaganeun
Descriptive verbs (adjectives) ending in a consonant	작다	작다가는 jakdaganeun

TAKE NOTE

Because this is used to predict negative results, it cannot be used in a positive sentence. And because it's a type of sentence that predicts, it can be used only in the future. It is usually combined with expressions that indicate guesses, so you should end your B clause with something like ~(으)ㄹ 거예요 **(eu)r geoyeyo**, ~(으)ㄹ 텐데요 **(eu)r tendeyo**, or 겠어요 **gesseoyo**. You can also use A 았/었/였다가는 B for hypothetical sentences. It means "If A were to happen, B would happen."

EXAMPLE SENTENCES

날씨가 이렇게 너무 덥**다가는** 큰일 날 텐데요.
Nalssiga ireoke neomu deopdaganeun keunil nal tendeyo.
If the weather is too hot like this there'll be many problems.

지금 태풍이 왔**다가는** 많은 사람들이 죽을 거예요.
Jigeum taepungi watdaganeun maneun saramdeuri jugeul geoyeyo.
If there were to be a typhoon now, many people would die.

Plans

If you've ever lived in Korea, you'll know that plans tend to be less like "plans" and more like "vague ideas." They change at any time up to, including, and after the event in question has already started, and you're wise not to take them too seriously. However, you'll probably still want to discuss them, and so here are some ways to do that.

First of all, two ways that aren't covered in this section are 아/어/여야지 **a/eo/yeoyaji** and 아/어/여야겠다 **a/eo/yeoyagetda**. These expressions fit better under "obligations." They're both used to remind yourself about something you have to do. If you need to do that, you can find these expressions on pages 202 and 207, respectively. Another expression that's useful for planning is ~(으)ㄹ 셈이다 **(eu)r semida**, which simply means that you plan to ~. Because it has a few more uses having to do with guesses, it more properly belongs in the *Guess* section.

You can also simply use the future expressions (으)ㄹ 것이다 or 겠다. These are covered in the Making Guesses section on past and future tenses on page 239.

~(으)ㄹ까요 (eu)lkkayo?	"Shall we ~?"	Speaking > Writing ★★★★★

늦을까 걱정이에요. 지금 출발**할까요**?
Neujeulkka geokjeongieyo. Jigeum chulbalhalkkayo?
I'm worried we'll be late. Shall we leave now?

This can be most easily translated as "shall" or "let's." If you propose something using this ending, you're giving the other person much say in the final result. Further uses include asking what other people think about something and making guesses about an event in the future. You can also use it to ask yourself questions, in which case you should probably leave off the 요 unless you want to get strange looks.

HOW IT'S CONJUGATED

		Present	Future
Action verbs ending in a vowel	하다	할까요? halkkayo?	할까요?
Action verbs ending in a consonant	먹다	먹을까요? meogeulkkayo?	먹을까요?

TAKE NOTE

(으)ㄹ까요 is one of the gentlest ways to suggest something. (으)ㄹ래요 (eu)llaeyo is another mild one which means "let's." It's the next expression on this page. If you'd like to be a little more forceful, you can use (으)ㄹ게요 (eu)lgeyo (see page 214), which means you're going to do something if it's okay with the other person. To be even more resolute, try (으)ㄹ 거 예요 (eu)l geoyeyo or 겠다 getda (see page 239), and if you're really determined to do ~ no matter what, ~기로 하다 gi ro hada conveys that determination; see page 225.

EXAMPLE SENTENCES

비빔밥을 먹**을까요**? Bibimbapeul meogeulkkayo? Shall we eat some bibimbap?

내일 쇼핑을 **할까요**? Naeil syopingeul halkkayo? Let's go shopping tomorrow.

지하철을 **탈까요**? Jihacheoreul talkkayo? Shall we take the subway?

~(으)ㄹ래요 (eu)llaeyo?	"Let's ~"	Speaking > Writing ★★★★

늦을 것 같아요. 지금 출발**할래요**? Neujeul geot gatayo. Jigeum chulbalhallaeyo?
I think we are going to be late. Shall we leave now?

This is somewhat similar to ㄹ까요. You can use it to propose something or to express your own intentions.

HOW IT'S CONJUGATED

		Present	Future
Action verbs ending in a vowel	하다	할래요 hallaeyo	할래요
Action verbs ending in a consonant	먹다	먹을래요 meogeullaeyo	먹을래요

TAKE NOTE

It can be used only in the first person (singular or plural).

(으)ㄹ래요 can be used to mean "let's" or to tell someone your own intentions. In the latter case, it's not at all forceful but more like (으)ㄹ게요, which suggests that the other person has the ability to veto or change your plans. (으)ㄹ게요 can also be used to answer a question asked with (으)ㄹ래요, like so:

A: 밥 먹**을래요**? Bap meogeullaeyo? Shall we eat?

B: 그럴**게요**. Geureolgeyo. Yeah, sure.

(으)ㄹ까요 (see the previous page) is one of the gentlest ways to suggest something. For the rest of this paragraph see Take Note on page 212. (으)ㄹ래요 is another gentle one which means "let's." If you'd like to be a little more forceful, you can use (으)ㄹ게요, which means you're going to do something if it's all right with the other person. To be even more resolute, try (으)ㄹ 거예요 or 겠다, and if you're really determined to do ~ no matter what, ~기로 하다 conveys that determination.

EXAMPLE SENTENCES

비빔밥을 먹**을래요**? Bibimbapeul meogeullaeyo? Let's eat some bibimbap.

내일 쇼핑을 **할래요**? Naeil syopingeul hallaeyo? Let's go shopping tomorrow.

지하철을 **탈래요**? Jihacheoreul tallaeyo? Let's take the subway.

비빔밥을 먹**을래요**. Bibimbapeul meogeullaeyo. I'm going to eat some bibimbap.

내일 쇼핑을 **할래요**. Naeil syopingeul hallaeyo. I'm going shopping tomorrow.

지하철을 **탈래요**. Jihacheoreul tallaeyo. I'm going to take the subway.

Whether a sentence with (으)ㄹ래요 is a statement or a question depends on your intonation, as above. You can also add pronouns if you want to further clarify your meaning.

저는 비빔밥을 먹**을래요**. Jeoneun bibimbapeul meogeullaeyo.
I'm going to eat bibimbap.

우리 비빔밥을 먹**을래요**? Uri bibimbapeul meogeullaeyo?
Let's eat some bibimbap.

~(으)ㄹ게요 (eu)lgeyo   "I'm going to ~"   **Speaking > Writing**
                                                                            ★★★★

늦을 것 같아요. 지금 출발**할게요**.
Neujeul geot gatayo. Jigeum chulbalhalgeyo.
I think I am going to be late. I'm going to leave now.

This is very similar to ㄹ 거예요, but it carries the connotation of "Is it all right with you if I?" It's used in spoken Korean and can also be used when you're changing your plans as a result of something someone else said.

HOW IT'S CONJUGATED

		Future
Action verbs ending in a vowel	하다	할게요 halgeyo
Action verbs ending in a consonant	먹다	먹을게요 meogeulgeyo

TAKE NOTE

You should be aware that ㄹ 거예요 (see page 239) and ㄹ게요, while sounding and acting similarly, do have different connotations and you don't want to use ㄹ 거예요 when you mean ㄹ게요 because it's rather more forceful. If you really do mean to say "I'm going to eat bibimbap whether you like it or not!" then yes, by all means, go for ㄹ 거예요. Otherwise you might want to be gentle and use ㄹ게요.

(으)ㄹ까요 (see page 212) is one of the gentlest ways to suggest something. (For the rest, see Take Note on page 212.) (으)ㄹ래요 is another mild one which means "let's." If you'd like to be a little more forceful, you can use (으)ㄹ게요, which means you're going to do something if it's all right with the other person. To be even more resolute, try (으)ㄹ 거예요 or 겠다, and if you're really determined to do ~ no matter what, ~기로 하다 conveys that determination.

EXAMPLE SENTENCES

비빔밥 먹**을게요**. Bibimbap meogeulgeyo.
I'm going to eat some bibimbap (if it's all right with you).

내일 쇼핑을 **할게요**. Naeil syopingeul halgeyo.
I'm going shopping tomorrow (if it's all right with you).

지하철을 **탈게요**. Jihacheoreul talgeyo.
I'm going to take the subway (if it's all right with you).

| ~려고 하다 ~ryeogo hada | "I'm planning to ~" | Speaking = Writing
★★★★ |

늦지 않기 위해서 집에서 일찍 출발하**려고 해요**.
Neutji anki wihaeseo jibeseo iljjik chulbalharyeogo haeyo.
I plan to leave the house early so as not to be late.

This is the most common and basic way to talk about plans.

HOW IT'S FORMED

려 in a grammatical expression almost always indicates that a person is talking about plans. In this case it's combined with 고, which means "and." Finally, 하다 means "to do;" in this case it implies an intention.

HOW IT'S CONJUGATED

If you want to use this expression with adjectives, you need to first change them into verbs; for example, if you plan to become pretty, you can't say 예쁘려고 해요 **yeppeuryeogo haeyo**. 예뻐지려고 해요 **yeppeojiryeogo haeyo** is the correct expression. See page 25 to learn how to change adjectives (descriptive verbs) into action verbs.

		Past	Present	Future
Action verbs ending in a vowel	하다	하려고 했다 haryeogo haetda	하려고 하다 haryeogo hada	하려고 하다
Action verbs ending in a consonant	먹다	먹으려고 했다 meogeuryeogo haetda	먹으려고 하다 meogeuryeogo hada	먹으려고 하다

TAKE NOTE

You can use 들다 instead of 하다, though this is rather less common. It implies a little more stubbornness and a little less uncertainty; in these cases the 려 usually refers to a plan that's already been carried out.

친구가 제말을 안 들**으려고 드니** 화가 났어요.
Chinguga jemareul an deureuryeogo deuni hwaga nasseoyo.
My friend didn't listen to what I was saying, so I got angry.

(으)ㄹ까 하다 is a similar expression to (으)려고 하다, but if you use (으)려고 하다 you're talking about a plan that's more certain than the one stated using (으)ㄹ까 하다. If you want to talk about a plan that's absolutely definite, use one of the future tense forms: (으)ㄹ 것이다 or 겠다.

(으)ㄹ 테 and (으)려고 하다 (see page 218) have the same meaning and are interchangeable when talking about the future or your own plans, like so:

비가 **올 테**니까 우산을 준비하세요. Biga ol tenikka usaneul junbihaseyo.
비가 **오려고 하**니까 우산을 준비하세요. Biga oryeogo hanikka usaneul junbihaseyo.
It's going to rain, so take an umbrella.

저는 공부**할 테**니까 엄마는 주무세요.
Jeoneun gongbuhal tenikka eommaneun jumuseyo.
저는 공부하**려고 하**니까 엄마는 주무세요.
Jeoneun gongbuharyeogo hanikka eommaneun jumuseyo.
I'm going to study; go to sleep, mom.

However, (으)려고 하다 can't be used when making a guess about someone else's plans.

피곤**할 테**니까 잠깐 쉬세요. Pigonhal tenikka jamkkan swiseyo.
You must be tired; rest for a while.

피곤 하**려고 하**니까 잠깐 쉬세요. Pigon haryeogo hanikka jamkkan swiseyo.
(ungrammatical)

EXAMPLE SENTENCES

우리는 먼저 영화를 보고 나중에 식사를 하**려고 해요**.
Urineun meonjeo yeonghwareul bogo najunge siksareul haryeogo haeyo.
First we plan to see a movie and then we plan to have dinner.

한국어를 열심히 공부하**려고 해요**. Hangugeoreul yeolsimhi gongbuharyeogo haeyo.
I plan to study Korean hard.

There are any number of possible combinations of 려 (by itself or with 고 하다) and other expressions. Basically, any time you see 려 used in an expression, you can safely assume that expression has to do with guessing or the future (remember, they're not that far apart in meaning in Korean). Here's a table showing some possible combinations:

Expression	Meaning
~(으)려고 하다 ~(eu)ryeogo hada	Plan to ~
A(으)려고 해도 B A (eu)ryeogo haedo B	Even though I want to A, B
A (으)려고 해서 B A (eu)ryeogo haeseo B	I plan to A, so B
A(으)려면 B A (eu)ryeomyeon B	If you plan to A, then B
A(으)려거든 B A (eu)ryeogeodeun B	If you plan to A, then B
~(으)려나 보다 ~(eu)ryeona boda	I think he's planning to ~
A(으)려다가 B A (eu)ryeodaga B	I planned to A, but was interrupted by B
~(으)려던 참이다 ~(eu)ryeodeon chamida	Just about to ~

Combine (으)려고 하다 with 여도 **yeodo** and you get A(으)려고 해도 B, which means "Even though I want to A, B."

숙제를 하**려고 해도** 잘 몰라서 못 해요.
Sukjereul haryeogo haedo jal mollaseo mot taeyo.
Even though I want to do my homework, I don't know how, so I can't.

(으)려고 하다 plus 여서 equals A(으)려고 해서 B, which means "I plan to A, so B."

케이크를 만들**려고 해서** 밀가루를 샀어요.
Keikeureul mandeullyeogo haeseo milgarureul sasseoyo.
I planned to make a cake, so I bought flour.

Next up is (으)려면. Here you're combining 려 (the planning particle) with 면 (if; see page 283) to get "If you plan to A, then B." This one is somewhat more common than the other 려 expressions.

B often ends with an expression indicating obligation: some variant of 아/어/여야 (see page 202). 아/어/여 하다 or 되다 (see page 198) are very commonly used. You can also use a suggestion or command form (see page 17 for some examples).

늦지 않**으려면** 택시를 타야 돼요. Neutji aneuryeomyeon taeksireul taya dwaeyo.
If you don't want to be late, you'd better take a taxi.

그 연극을 보**려면** 표를 빨리 사야 해요.
Geu yeongeugeul boryeomyeon pyoreul ppalli saya haeyo.
If you want to see that performance, you should buy tickets quickly.

사장님을 만나**려면** 먼저 비서한테 이메일을 보내 주세요.
Sajangnimeul mannaryeomyeon meonjeo biseohante imeireul bonae juseyo.
If you want to meet the director, please email his secretary first.

If you combine (으)려고 하다 with 다가 and shorten it, you get (으)려다가. 다가 (see page 269) in its original form implies an interruption, and that's how it works here as well: you were planning to A, but then you got interrupted by B.

등산을 하**려다가** 비가 와서 집에 있었어요.
Deungsaneul haryeodaga biga waseo jibe isseosseoyo.
I planned to go hiking, but then it rained, so I stayed home.

(으)려고 하다 plus 거든 equals (으)려고 하거든 which is then shortened to (으)려거든. 거든 is similar in meaning to 면 (if); see page 285. A(으)려거든 B, likewise, is equivalent to (으)려면. It means "If you're planning to A, then B."

늦지 않**으려거든** 택시를 타야 돼요.
Neutji aneuryeogeodeun taeksireul taya dwaeyo.
If you don't want to be late, you'd better take a taxi.

Finally, ~(으)려던 참이다 is worthy of its own section and is examined in more detail on page 262; briefly, it's a way of saying you were just about to do something.

전 가려턴 참이었어요. Jeon garyeodeon chamieosseoyo. I was just about to go.

~(으)려나 보다 ~(eu)ryeona boda is really more of a variation on ~나 보다, so it's in that section, which you can find on page 138.

Speaking = Writing

~(으)려 가다/오다/다니다   "go/come in order to ~"   ★★★★
(eu)reo gada/oda/danida

비빔밥을 먹<u>으려</u> 식당에 **갔어요**. Bibimbapeul meogeureo sikdange gasseoyo.
I went to the restaurant to eat bibimbap.

This expression is used when you're planning to go or come somewhere to do something.

HOW IT'S CONJUGATED

You can use 가다 or 오다 depending on whether you're coming or going; make sure you use the verb going in the right direction. 다니다, another motion verb, can also be used with this expression.

TAKE NOTE

(으)려 can be followed only by 가다, 다니다, or 오다. If you want to plan something using any other verb, you should use 려고 하다 (see page 215). Variants of 가다 or 오다 (들어가다, 나가다, 들어오다, etc.) can be used with (으)려.

EXAMPLE SENTENCES

비빔밥을 먹<u>으려</u> 식당에 **왔어요**. Bibimbapeul meogeureo sikdange wasseoyo.
I came to the restaurant to eat bibimbap.

공부를 하<u>려</u> **왔어요**. Gongbureul hareo wasseoyo. I came to study.

공부를 하<u>려</u> **갑시다.** Gongbureul hareo gapsida. Let's go study.

Speaking > Writing

~(으)ㄹ 터이다/테다 (eu)r teoida/teda   "plan to ~"   ★★★★

벌써 8시인데 정시에 **올 테야**? Beolsseo yeodeolsi-inde jeongsie ol teya?
It's already eight. Are you planning to come on time?

This is the easiest, simplest way to tell someone you're planning to do something. It's a good one for you evil geniuses out there. It also forms the basis of a few other very useful expressions: (으)ㄹ 테니까(요), (으)ㄹ 텐데(요), (으)ㄹ 테면, (으)ㄹ 테고, and (으)ㄹ 테지만. In other words, even if you're not an evil genius, this is a good expression to learn. It means "I plan to ~" or "Do you plan to ~?" Alternatively, it can be used to make guesses about what other people are planning. These guesses are made with confidence: if you use this expression to make a guess, you really think you're right. (으)ㄹ 테니까 and (으)ㄹ 텐데(요) are by far the most common expressions with 테다: all the others are not used often, but they're easy enough to learn if you want to know them. Here's a summary of the expressions that begin with (으)ㄹ 테다:

Expression	Page	Meaning	Example sentence
(으)ㄹ 터이다/테다 (eu)r teoida/teda	–	Plan to ~	나중에 파티에 **갈 테야**. Najunge patie gal teya. Later I'm planning to go to the party.
A(으)ㄹ 테니까 B A (eu)r tenikka B	221	I plan to A, so B	민수가 늦을 테니까 지금 시작합시다. Minsuga neujeul tenikka jigeum sijakhapsida. I think Minsu is going to be late, so let's start.
A(으)ㄹ 텐데 B A (eu)r tende B	222	I plan to A; B	민수가 늦을 텐데 지금 시작합시다. Minsuga neujeul tende jigeum sijakhapsida. I think Minsu is going to be late. Let's start.
A(으)ㄹ 테면 B A (eu)r temyeon B	223	If you plan to A, then B	어떤 얘기든 할 테면 그냥 하세요. Eotteon yaegideun hal temyeon geunyang haseyo. Whatever you want to say, just say it.
A(으)ㄹ 테고 B A (eu)r tego B	223	I plan to A, and then B	버스로 가면 시간이 걸릴 테고 힘들 거예요. Beoseuro gamyeon sigani geollil tego himdeul geoyeyo. If we go by bus, it'll take time and it might be difficult.
A(으)ㄹ 테지만 B A (eu)r tejiman B	224	I plan to A, but B	잘 할 수 있을 거라고 생각해서 공부를 별로 하지 않았을 테지만 시험에 떨어졌어요. Jal hal su isseul georago saenggakaeseo gongbureul byeollo haji anasseul tejiman siheome tteoreojyeosseoyo. I thought I would do well, so I barely studied, but I failed the test.

HOW IT'S FORMED

터 is actually a noun, though it's never used outside of this expression. It refers to either a plan or a guess. (으)ㄹ is the future tense marker; you can, in theory, use the other tense markers (으)ㄴ/는, but only when you're talking about a plan in the past. You will most often see and hear this expression used with (으)ㄹ.

HOW IT'S CONJUGATED

	Past	Present	Future
Action verbs ending in a vowel	하다	한 터이다 han teoida 한 테다 han teda	할 터이다 hal teoida 할 테다 hal teda	할 터이다 할 테다
Action verbs ending in a consonant	먹다	먹은 터이다 meogeun teoida 먹은 테다 meogeun teda	먹을 터이다 meogeul teoida 먹을 테다 meogeul teda	먹을 터이다 먹을 테다

TAKE NOTE

(으)ㄹ 테다 by itself is colloquial and is used only in 반말. It can be used in first-person sentences to explain your own plans or in second-person sentences to ask about another person's plans, but it cannot be used in third-person sentences. In this case you should use 겠다 or (으)ㄹ 것이다 (see page 239).

(으)ㄹ 텐데 and (으)ㄹ 테니까 are very similar expressions. The difference between the two is the same as the difference between ㄴ데 and 니까, both covered in the Cause and Effect section on page 66 if you'd like to review. They're quite often, but not always, interchangeable, although the nuances are different; ㄴ데 is used to explain the background for a situation (in this case, a request or command) and 니까 is used to give a reason. Also, (으)ㄹ 테니까 refers to a slightly firmer plan or expectation.

피곤**할 텐데** 잠깐 쉬세요. Pigonhal tende jamkkan swiseyo.
You may be tired. Please rest.

피곤**할 테니까** 잠깐 쉬세요. Pigonhal tenikka jamkkan swiseyo.
You must be tired, so please rest.

(으)ㄹ 테 and (으)려고 하다 (see page 215) have the same meaning and are interchangeable when talking about the future or your own plans, like so:

비가 **올 테**니까 우산을 준비하세요.
Biga ol tenikka usaneul junbihaseyo.

비가 **오려고 하**니까 우산을 준비하세요.
Biga oryeogo hanikka usaneul junbihaseyo.

It's going to rain, so take an umbrella.

저는 공부**할 테**니까 엄마는 주무세요.
Jeoneun gongbuhal tenikka eommaneun jumuseyo.

저는 공부하**려고 하**니까 엄마는 주무세요.
Jeoneun gongbuharyeogo hanikka eommaneun jumuseyo.

I'm going to study; go to sleep, mom.

However, (으)려고 하다 can't be used when making a guess about someone else's plans.

피곤**할 테니까** 잠깐 쉬세요. Pigonhal tenikka jamkkan swiseyo.
You must be tired; rest for a while.

피곤 하**려고 하**니까 잠깐 쉬세요. Pigon haryeogo hanikka jamkkan swiseyo.
(ungrammatical)

Here are a few example sentences with (으)ㄹ 테다:

나중에 파티에 **갈 테야**. Najunge patie gal teya.
Later I'm planning to go to the party.

어떤 영화를 **볼 테야**? Eotteon yeonghwareul bol teya?
What movie are you planning to see?

And here are a few more expressions based on (으)ㄹ 테다.

A(으)ㄹ 테니까 (eu)l tenikka B, ~(으)ㄹ 테니까요 (eu)l tenikkayo

What's more fun than bossing other people around? Here's an expression you can use to make suggestions or give commands based on your thoughts and plans. It means "I think or plan to A, so you should B."

HOW IT'S FORMED

(으)ㄹ 테다 is combined here with 니까(요) which means "so"; see page 67 for more. 니까 can be abbreviated to 니, but that's not usually done with this expression.

		Past	Present	Future
Action verbs ending in a vowel	하다	했을 테니까(요) haesseul tenikka(yo)	할 테니까(요) hal tenikka(yo)	할 테니까 (요)
Action verbs ending in a consonant	먹다	먹었을 테니까(요) meogeosseul tenikka(yo)	먹을 테니까(요) meogeul tenikka(yo)	먹을 테니까 (요)
Descriptive verbs (adjectives) ending in a vowel	예쁘다	예뻤을 테니까(요) yeppeosseul tenikka(yo)	예쁠 테니까(요) yeppeul tenikka(yo)	예쁠 테니까 (요)
Descriptive verbs (adjectives) ending in a consonant	작다	작았을 테니까(요) jagasseul tenikka(yo)	작을 테니까(요) jageul tenikka(yo)	작을 테니까 (요)
Nouns ending in a vowel	남자	남자였을 테니까(요) namjayeosseul tenikka(yo)	남자일 테니까(요) namjail tenikka(yo)	남자일 테니까(요)
Nouns ending in a consonant	물	물이었을 테니까(요) murieosseul tenikka(yo)	물일 테니까(요) muril tenikka(yo)	물일 테니까 (요)

If you're talking about a plan, A can only be about yourself. If you're talking about what you expect to happen, it can be about a second or third person.

EXAMPLE SENTENCES

나중에 프레젠테이션을 **할 테니까** 회의실을 좀 준비해 주세요.
Najunge peu-re-jen-te-isyeoneul hal tenikka hoe-ui-sireul jom junbihae juseyo.
I'm doing a presentation later, so please get the meeting room ready.

걱정하지 마세요. 준비를 금방 끝**낼 테니까요**.
Geokjeonghaji maseyo. Junbireul geumbang kkeunnael tenikkayo.
Don't worry. I plan to finish the preparations soon.

가영의 항공이 벌써 도착했**을 테니까** 빨리 공항에 갑시다.
Kayoungui hanggongi beolsseo dochakhaesseul tenikka ppalli gonghange gapsida.
I think Kayoung's flight will have already arrived, so let's go to the airport quickly.

민수가 늦을 **테니까** 지금 시작합시다.
Minsuga neujeul tenikka jigeum sijakhapsida.
I think Minsu is going to be late, so let's start.

A(으)ㄹ 텐데 (eu)r tende B, ~(으)ㄹ 텐데요 (eu)r tendeyo

This expression is a combination of (으)ㄹ 테다 and ㄴ데 (see page 69) which is used to explain the background for something. It means "I plan or expect to A; B."

HOW IT'S CONJUGATED

You can reverse the sentence structure and make the suggestion or give the command first and then follow it with the background explanation; in this case you can end your sentence with (으)ㄹ 텐데요.

		Past	Present	Future
Action verbs ending in a vowel	하다	했을 텐데 haesseul tende	할 텐데 hal tende	할 텐데
Action verbs ending in a consonant	먹다	먹었을 텐데 meogeosseul tende	먹을 텐데 meogeul tende	먹을 텐데
Descriptive verbs (adjectives) ending in a vowel	예쁘다	예뻤을 텐데 yeppeosseul tende	예쁠 텐데 yeppeul tende	예쁠 텐데
Descriptive verbs (adjectives) ending in a consonant	작다	작았을 텐데 jagasseul tende	작을 텐데 jageul tende	작을 텐데
Nouns ending in a vowel	남자	남자였을 텐데 namjayeosseul tende	남자일 텐데 namja-il tende	남자일 텐데
Nouns ending in a consonant	물	물이었을 텐데 murieosseul tende	물일 텐데 muril tende	물일 텐데

Like the other expressions with 테다, this one can be used with sentences in the first person to talk about plans or with sentences which make guesses about a second or third person.

EXAMPLE SENTENCES

나중에 프레젠테이션을 **할 텐데** 회의실을 좀 준비해 주세요.
Najunge peu-re-jen-te-i-syeoneul hal tende hoe-ui-sireul jom junbihae juseyo.
I'm doing a presentation later. Please get the meeting room ready.

가영의 항공이 벌써 도착했을 **텐데** 빨리 공항에 갑시다.
Kayoungui hanggongi beolsseo dochakhaesseul tende ppalli gonghange gapsida.
빨리 공항에 갑시다. 가영의 항공이 벌써 도착했을 **텐데요.**
Ppalli gonghange gapsida. Kayoungui hanggongi beolsseo dochakhaesseul tendeyo.
I think Kayoung's flight will have already arrived. Let's go to the airport quickly.

민수가 늦을 **텐데** 지금 시작합시다. **Minsuga neujeul tende jigeum sijakhapsida.**
I think Minsu is going to be late. Let's start.

A(으)ㄹ 테면 (eu)l temyeon B

(으)ㄹ 테다 is combined with 면, which means "if" and is on page 283.

HOW IT'S CONJUGATED

		All tenses
Action verbs ending in a vowel	하다	할 테면 hal temyeon
Action verbs ending in a consonant	먹다	먹을 테면 meogeul temyeon

TAKE NOTE

A can only be a second-person expression. B can only be a command. The verb in B should be the same as the verb in A; see the examples below.

Other expressions with 테다 are (으)ㄹ 텐데 and (으)ㄹ 테니까. They are different from (으)ㄹ 테면 in that they are used to talk about things the speaker is planning or expecting while (으)ㄹ 테면 is only about the listener's plans. Also, 니까 means "so" and ㄴ데 is used to provide background information for whatever comes after it, while 면 means "if."

EXAMPLE SENTENCES

어떤 얘기든 **할 테면** 그냥 하세요.
Eotteon yaegideun hal temyeon geunyang haseyo.
Whatever you want to say, just say it.

떠날 **테면** 후회없이 떠나세요. Tteonal temyeon hu-hoe-eopssi tteonaseyo.
If you want to leave, then leave without regrets.

늦게 **올 테면** 저녁을 먹고 오세요.
Neutge ol temyeon jeonyeogeul meokgo oseyo.
If you plan to come late, please come after you eat dinner.

A(으)ㄹ 테고 (eu)l tego B

Combine (으)ㄹ 테다 with 고 ("and"; page 51) to get this expression, which means "I plan or expect to do A, and then B."

		Past	Present	Future
Action verbs ending in a vowel	하다	했을 테고 haesseul tego	할 테고 hal tego	할 테고
Action verbs ending in a consonant	먹다	먹었을 테고 meogeosseul tego	먹을 테고 meogeul tego	먹을 테고
Descriptive verbs (adjectives) ending in a vowel	예쁘다	예뻤을 테고 yeppeosseul tego	예쁠 테고 yeppeul tego	예쁠 테고
Descriptive verbs (adjectives) ending in a consonant	작다	작았을 테고 jagasseul tego	작을 테고 jageul tego	작을 테고

		Past	Present	Future
Nouns ending in a vowel	남자	남자였을 테고 namjayeosseul tego	남자일 테고 namjail tego	남자일 테고
Nouns ending in a consonant	물	물이었을 테고 murieosseul tego	물일 테고 muril tego	물일 테고

버스로 가면 시간이 걸**릴 테고** 힘들 거예요.
Beoseuro gamyeon sigani geollil tego himdeul geoyeyo.
If we go by bus, it'll take time and it might be difficult.

10시까지 직장에 도착할 테고 그러면 12시까지 식당에 도착할 수 있을 거예요.
Yeolsi-kkaji jikjange dochakhal tego geureomyeon yeoldusikkaji sikdange
dochakhal su isseul geoyeyo.
I plan to arrive at work by 10:00, and if so, I should be able to get to the
restaurant by 12:00.

A(으)ㄹ 테지만 (eu)l tejiman

Finally, you can combine (으)ㄹ 테다 with 지만 to get this expression, which means "I plan/
expect to do A, but B" (see page 105).

		Past	Present	Future
Action verbs ending in a vowel	하다	했을 테지만 Haesseul tejiman	할 테지만 hal tejiman	할 테지만
Action verbs ending in a consonant	먹다	먹었을 테지만 meogeosseul tejiman	먹을 테지만 meogeul tejiman	먹을 테지만
Descriptive verbs (adjectives) ending in a vowel	예쁘다	예뻤을 테지만 yeppeosseul tejiman	예쁠 테지만 yeppeul tejiman	예쁠 테지만
Descriptive verbs (adjectives) ending in a consonant	작다	작았을 테지만 jagasseul tejiman	작을 테지만 jageul tejiman	작을 테지만
Nouns ending in a vowel	남자	남자였을 테지만 namjayeosseul tejiman	남자일 테지만 namjail tejiman	남자일 테지만
Nouns ending in a consonant	물	물이었을 테지만 murieosseul tejiman	물일 테지만 muril tejiman	물일 테지만

잘할 수 있을거라고 생각해서 공부를 별로 하지 않았을 테지만 시험에 떨어졌
어요.
Jalhal su isseulgeorago saenggakhaeseo gongbureul byeollo haji anasseul tejiman
siheome tteoreojyeosseoyo.
I thought I could do well, so I barely studied, but I failed the test.

정시에 올 수 있을 거라고 생각해서 서두르지 않았**을 테지만** 늦게 왔어요.
Jeongsie ol su isseul georago saenggakhaeseo seodureuji anasseul tejiman
neutge wasseoyo.
I thought I could get there on time, so I didn't hurry, but I was late.

Speaking = Writing

~(으)ㄹ 예정이다 (eu)l yejeongida   "I plan to ~"   ★★★★

오늘 회의가 있어서 파티에 늦게 **갈 예정인**데요.
Oneul hoe-ui-ga isseoseo patie neutge gal yejeongindeyo.
Today there's a meeting, so I plan to go late to the party.

Here's a simple, useful way to talk about your future plans.

HOW IT'S FORMED

(으)ㄹ is the future tense marker. 예정 is a noun that literally means "schedule."

HOW IT'S CONJUGATED

		Future
Action verbs ending in a vowel	하다	할 예정이다 hal yejeongida
Action verbs ending in a consonant	먹다	먹을 예정이다 meogeul yejeongida

TAKE NOTE

This is basically interchangeable with (으)ㄹ 거예요 (eu)l geoyeyo or the (으)ㄹ 테 (eu)l te expressions; it's just another way to talk about plans.

EXAMPLE SENTENCES

오늘 회의가 있을 **예정이어서** 파티에 늦게 갈 거예요.
Oneul hoe-ui-ga isseul yejeongieoseo patie neutge gal geoyeyo.
Today we plan to have a meeting, so I'll be late to the party.

내일 새로운 식당에서**먹을 예정인**데 같이 먹을래요?
Naeil saeroun sikdangeseo meogeul yejeonginde gachi meogeullaeyo?
Tomorrow we're planning to eat at the new restaurant; want to join us (eat together)?

Speaking = Writing

~기로 하다 giro hada   "I've decided to ~"   ★★★★

내일 일찍 일어나**기로 했어요**. Naeil iljjik ireonagiro haesseoyo.
I decided to get up early tomorrow.

This expression is quite strong and implies determination and decision. Often it's like a vow you've made or the result of a lengthy decision-making process.

HOW IT'S FORMED

기 (the particle that turns verbs into nouns) plus 로 ("through") plus 하다. However, these are only sort of applicable to this expression, and don't really provide much insight.

HOW IT'S CONJUGATED

		Past	Present	Future
Action verbs ending in a vowel	하다	하기로 했다 hagiro haetda	하기로 하다 hagiro hada	하기로 하겠다 hagiro hagetda
Action verbs ending in a consonant	먹다	먹기로 했다 meokgiro haetda	먹기로 하다 meokgiro hada	먹기로 하겠다 meokgiro hagetda

TAKE NOTE

This is used only for expressing your own decisions, so it can be used only in the first person. It is normally used in the past tense to talk about a decision you've already made.

Instead of 하다 at the end, you can also use 기로 계획이다 **giro gyehoegida** ("It's my plan to"), 기로 약속하다 **giro yaksokhada** ("I promise to") or 기로 결심하다 **giro gyeolsimhada** ("It's my decision to").

(으)ㄹ까요 (see page 212) is one of the gentlest ways to suggest something. (으)ㄹ래요 is another mild one which means "let's." It's on page 212. If you'd like to be a little more forceful, you can use (으)ㄹ게요 (see page 214), which means you're going to do something if it's all right with the other person. To be even more resolute, try (으)ㄹ 거예요 or 겠다 (see page 239), and if you're really determined to do ~ no matter what, ~기로 하다 conveys that determination (see page 225).

EXAMPLE SENTENCES

살을 빼고 싶어서 다이어트를 하**기로 했어요**.
Sareul ppaego sipeoseo da-i-eo-teureul hagiro haesseoyo.
I wanted to lose weight, so I decided to go on a diet.

돈이 없어서 직업을 찾**기로 했어요**. Doni eopsseoseo jigeobeul chatgiro haesseoyo.
I had no money, so I decided to get a job.

Speaking > Writing

~(으)ㄹ까 하다/보다/싶다　　"I think I might ~"　　★★★
(eu)lkka hada/boda/sipda

다른 약속도 있어서 가영의 파티에 조금 늦게 **갈까 해요**.
Dareun yaksokdo isseoseo Kayoungui patie jogeum neutge galkka haeyo.
다른 약속도 있어서 가영의 파티에 조금 늦게 **갈까 봐요**.
Dareun yaksokdo isseoseo Kayoungui patie jogeum neutge galkka bwayo.
다른 약속도 있어서 가영의 파티에 조금 늦게 **갈까 싶어요**.
Dareun yaksokdo isseoseo Kayoungui patie jogeum neutge galkka sipeoyo.

I have another engagement, so I might come a little late to Kayoung's party.

The three expressions above are all equivalent. (으)ㄹ까 하다 is probably the most common, but the others can also be used. They are all ways to express a tentative plan.

HOW IT'S FORMED

(으)ㄹ까 means "shall" (see page 212) and can be followed here by 하다 (to do), 보다 (to try) or 싶다 (which doesn't really have an English translation, but has to do with wanting and planning).

HOW IT'S CONJUGATED

If you want to talk about what you're planning not to do, you can use 안 ~(으)ㄹ까 하다/보다/싶다 or ~지 말까 하다/보다/싶다.

		Past	Present/Future
Action verbs ending in a vowel	하다	할까 했다 halkka haetda 할까 봤다 halkka bwatda 할까 싶었다 halkka sipeotda	할까 하다 halkka hada 할까 보다 halkka boda 할까 싶다 halkka sipda
		안 할까 했다 an halkka haetda 안 할까 봤다 an halkka bwatda 안 할까 싶었다 an halkka sipeotda	안 할까 하다 an halkka hada 안 할까 보다 an halkka boda 안 할까 싶다 an halkka sipda
		하지 말까 했다 haji malkka haetda 하지 말까 봤다 haji malkka bwatda 하지 말까 싶었다 haji malkka sipeotda	하지 말까 하다 haji malkka hada 하지 말까 보다 haji malkka boda 하지 말까 싶다 haji malkka sipda
Action verbs ending in a consonant	먹다	먹을까 했다 meogeulkka haetda 먹을까 봤다 meogeulkka bwatda 먹을까 싶었다 meogeulkka sipeotda	먹을까 하다 meogeulkka hada 먹을까 보다 meogeulkka boda 먹을까 싶다 meogeulkka sipda
		안 먹을까 했다 an meogeulkka haetda 안 먹을까 봤다 an meogeulkka bwatda 안 먹을까 싶었다 an meogeulkka sipeotda	안 먹을까 하다 an meogeulkka hada 안 먹을까 보다 an meogeulkka boda 안 먹을까 싶다 an meogeulkka sipda
		먹지 말까 했다 meokji malkka haetda 먹지 말까 봤다 meokji malkka bwatda 먹지 말까 싶었다 meokji malkka sipeotda	먹지 말까 하다 meokji malkka hada 먹지 말까 보다 meokji malkka boda 먹지 말까 싶다 meokji malkka sipda

TAKE NOTE

These expressions can be used only with statements—not commands, questions, or propositions. If you'd like to ask a question, give a command or propose something based on what you're planning, you can conjugate 하다/보다/싶다 accordingly with 는데 or 니까 and then continue with whatever you wanted to ask, propose, or command. See example 3.

No future tenses allowed, and no adjectives or nouns either. This is a very picky expression. 보다 in is exceptionally picky and also cannot be used in the past tense or in the middle of a sentence.

(으)ㄹ까 하다/보다/싶다 describes a tentative plan. A more certain plan can be described with (으)려고 하다 (see page 215) or any of its associated expressions, and a very certain plan can be described using (으)ㄹ 것이다 or 겠다 (page 239).

You can also use (으)ㄹ까 말까 to talk about something that you can't decide whether to do or not; see page 231 for more on this.

A(으)ㄹ까 봐(서) B and A(으)ㄹ까 싶(어서) B go in the middle of a sentence, but they are not the same expressions as the ones we're discussing here. A(으)ㄹ까 봐(서) B and A (으)ㄹ까 싶(어서) B are used when you're worried about something happening (see page 146).

EXAMPLE SENTENCES

작년에 일본에서 여행을 **할까 했어요**.
Jangnyeone ilboneseo yeohaengeul halkka haesseoyo.

작년에 일본에서 여행을 **할까 싶었어요**.
Jangnyeone ilboneseo yeohaengeul halkka sipeosseoyo.

Last year I was thinking of traveling around Japan (but I didn't).

(Note: (으)ㄹ까 보다 sounds strange in the past tense, so choose one of the other two expressions instead.)

내일 새로운 식당에서 저녁을 먹**을까 하**는데 같이 갈까요?
Naeil saeroun sikdangeseo jeonyeogeul meogeulkka haneunde gachi galkkayo?

내일 새로운 식당에서 저녁을 먹**을까 싶**은데 같이 갈까요?
Naeil saeroun sikdangeseo jeonyeogeul meogeulkka sipeunde gachi galkkayo?

내일 새로운 식당에서 저녁을 먹**을까 봐요**. 같이 갈까요?
Naeil saeroun sikdangeseo jeonyeogeul meogeulkka bwayo. Gachi galkkayo?

I'm thinking about eating dinner at that new restaurant tomorrow. Do you want to go together?

Again, (으)ㄹ까 보다 is picky and shouldn't be used in the middle of a sentence.

Speaking > Writing

~(으)ㄹ 건가요 (eu)l geongayo   "What's the plan?"   ★★

오늘 파티에 늦게 **올 건가요**? Oneul patie neutge ol geongayo?
Are you planning to come late to today's party?

This is a question form used to talk about plans. I would suggest using it often in Korea because plans there do change often: be sure to reconfirm, reconfirm, reconfirm.

HOW IT'S FORMED

This is really two different grammar points combined: (으)ㄹ 것이다 (the future tense, as seen on page 239) and (으)ㄴ가요 (a question form covered on page 44). Add them together, shorten it a little and you get (으)ㄹ 건가요?

HOW IT'S CONJUGATED

(으)ㄹ 건가요 is always used at the end of a sentence and never follows any other tense markers.

		Future
Action verbs ending in a vowel	하다	할 건가요 hal geongayo
Action verbs ending in a consonant	먹다	먹을 건가요 meogeul geongayo

TAKE NOTE

This is used only to confirm plans or to ask others' opinions.

EXAMPLE SENTENCES

누가 이 일을 **할 건가요**? Nuga i ireul hal geongayo? Who's going to do this job?

언제 시험을 **볼 건가요**? Eonje siheomeul bol geongayo?
When are we going to take the test?

A고자 goja B	"B in order to A"	Speaking < Writing ★★

늦지 않게 **오고자** 집에서 일찍 출발했어요.
Neutji anke ogoja jibeseo iljjik chulbalhaesseoyo.
I left the house early so as not to be late.

If you ever have to do a job interview in Korean, this is a good one to know. It's a relatively formal expression used for describing plans or intentions, similar to a more official (으)려고. It could be translated as "in order to," "since," or "to."

HOW IT'S CONJUGATED

		All tenses
Action verbs ending in a vowel	하다	하고자 hagoja
Action verbs ending in a consonant	먹다	먹고자 meokgoja

TAKE NOTE

고 can be used only with action verbs and only when the subjects of both clause A and clause B are the same.

It can also be used at the end of a sentence describing your plans (see the third example below), in which case it is followed by 하다. When used this way, it can't be used with negative particles like 안 or 못.

As stated in the intro, 고자 has the same meaning as (으)려고 but is more formal. It can also be replaced with 기 위해(서) (see page 169).

EXAMPLE SENTENCES

영어를 가르치**고자** 한국에 왔어요.
Yeongeoreul gareuchigoja hanguge wasseoyo.
I came to Korea to teach English.

그 회사에 취직하**고자** 이력서를 냈어요.
Geu hoesae chwijikhagoja iryeokseoreul naesseoyo.
I sent my resume to that company to get a job.

		Speaking > Writing
A(느)ㄴ다 (neu)nda A(느)ㄴ다 하는 게 (neu)nda haneun ge B	"I tried and tried to do A, but failed"	★★

운동을 **한다 한다 하는 게** 게으름을 피우다가 안 했어요.
Undongeul handa handa haneun ge geeureumeul piudaga an haesseoyo.
I tried and tried to exercise, but I kept on being lazy and never did it.

We've covered many expressions involving plans and determination. That's all well and good, but plans don't always succeed. Sometimes, no matter how much you want to do something, other things keep getting in the way. This is an expression you can use when that happens.

HOW IT'S FORMED

게 **ge** is an abbreviation of 것이 **geosi** and not the adverb form 게.

HOW IT'S CONJUGATED

		Past	Present	Future
Action verbs ending in a vowel	하다	한다 한다 했는 게 Handa handa haenneun ge	한다 한다 하는 게 handa handa haneun ge	한다 한다 하는 게
Action verbs ending in a consonant	먹다	먹는다 먹는다 했는 게 meokneunda meokneunda haenneun ge	먹는다 먹는다 하는 게 meokneunda meokneunda haneun ge	먹는다 먹는다 하는 게

TAKE NOTE

Be sure to repeat A twice.

If A is a verb with a direct object, like 운동을 하다 **undongeul hada**, you need to repeat only the verb, not the whole expression, the second time, like so: 운동을 한다 한다 하는 게 **undongeul handa handa haneun ge**.

EXAMPLE SENTENCES

그 공연에 **간다 간다 했는 게** 계속 잊어버려서 결국 못 갔어요.

Geu gongyeone **ganda ganda haenneun ge** gyesok ijeobeoryeoseo gyeolguk
mot gasseoyo.

I really meant to go to that show, but I kept forgetting, so in the end I wasn't
able to go.

순대를 **먹는다 먹는다 했는 게** 너무 역겨워서 못 먹었어요.

Sundaereul **meokneunda meokneunda haenneun ge** neomu yeokgyeowoseo
mot meogeosseoyo.

I tried and tried to eat *soondae*, but it was too disgusting, so I couldn't eat it.

		Speaking > Writing
~(으)ㄹ까 말까 하다 (eu)lkka malkka hada	"I can't decide whether to ~ or not"	★★

운동을 **할까 말까 해요**. Undongeul **halkka malkka haeyo**.

I can't decide whether to exercise or not.

If you're indecisive, here's an expression for you. This is used to say that you still haven't
decided "whether to ~ or not."

HOW IT'S FORMED

(으)ㄹ까 means "shall"; see page 212. 말다 contradicts the verb before it, and 하다 is 하다,
as always.

HOW IT'S CONJUGATED

		Past	Present	Future
Action verbs ending in a vowel	하다	할까 말까 했다 halkka malkka haetda	할까 말까 하다 halkka malkka hada	할까 말까 할 것이다 halkka malkka hal geosida
Action verbs ending in a consonant	먹다	먹을까 말까 했다 meogeulkka malkka haetda	먹을까 말까 하다 meogeulkka malkka hada	먹을까 말까 할 것이다 meogeulkka malkka hal geosida

TAKE NOTE

(으)ㄹ까 말까 하다 is normally used at the end of short sentences saying nothing but that
you couldn't decide whether to ~ or not.

(으)ㄹ락 말락 하다 (eu)rrak mallak hada has a similar form, but while (으)ㄹ까 말까
implies indecision, (으)ㄹ락 말락 means that something was about to (but didn't) do
something: that it was on the verge of raining (but didn't) or that someone was about to
fall over (but didn't).

When using (으)ㄹ까 말까 to answer a question, it's fairly common to begin with 글쎄
which roughly means "Hmm" or, "I don't know."

You don't have to use 하다 after ㄹ까 말까. The example sentence above could also be written like this:

운동을 **할까 말까** 결정 못했어요.
Undongeul halkka malkka gyeoljeong motaesseoyo.
I couldn't decide whether or not to exercise.

In this case, (으)ㄹ까 말까 is interchangeable with (으)ㄹ지 말지 **(eu)lji malji.**

운동을 **할지 말지** 결정 못했어요.
Undongeul halji malji gyeoljeong motaesseoyo.
I couldn't decide whether or not to exercise.

EXAMPLE SENTENCES

A: 파티에 갈 거예요? **Patie gal geoyeyo?** Are you going to the party?

B: 글쎄요. **갈까 말까 해요**. Geulsseyo. Galkka malkka haeyo.
   I don't know. I can't decide whether to go or not.

오늘 배가 아파서 점심을 먹**을까 말까 해요**.
Oneul baega apaseo jeomsimeul meogeulkka malkka haeyo.
My stomach hurts today, so I can't decide whether to eat lunch or not.

		Speaking > Writing
~고 말겠다 go malgetda/A고 **말 테니까** go mal tenikka B	"I'm definitely going to ~"	★

이번에는 꼭 정시에 **오고 말겠어요**.
Ibeoneneun kkok jeongsie ogo malgesseoyo.
This time I'm definitely going to come on time.

This expression is for those who are determined. 고 말았다 means something happened by accident, but in contrast, 고 말겠다 or 고 말 테니까 means something is very firmly planned.

HOW IT'S FORMED

고 말다 plus 겠다. 겠다 is the future tense marker (see page 239) and 고 말다 is normally used to talk about something unplanned and unfortunate; in this case, with 겠, it takes the opposite meaning. (으)ㄹ 테니까 (an expression used to talk about plans and covered in detail on page 221) can also follow 고 말다 and together they have the same meaning as 고 말겠다.

HOW IT'S CONJUGATED

		Future
Action verbs ending in a vowel	하다	하고 말겠다 hago malgetda 하고 말 테니까 hago mal tenikka
Action verbs ending in a consonant	먹다	먹고 말겠다 meokgo malgetda 먹고 말 테니까 meokgo mal tenikka

TAKE NOTE

There are three expressions with 고 말다, and they're all quite different, so it's important to be careful which one you use. 고 말고(요) is used at the end of very short sentences to agree strongly with something another person has said. It's covered on page 37. 고 말았다, at the bottom of this page, means that something happened by accident. It will always be in the past tense. 고 말겠다 and 고 말 테니까 are always seen in these forms, so if the 고 말다 expression you see or hear has any conjugation of 겠다 or 테니까, it means someone is determined to do something.

If you're not all that determined, you can use (으)려고 하다 (see page 215) and if you're really not determined at all but just have a notion, (으)ㄹ까 하다/보다/싶다 (see page 226) is what you'll want to use. Meanwhile, if what you're planning is absolutely guaranteed to happen, use a future tense expression: 겠다 or (으)ㄹ 것이다 (see page 239).

Words like 꼭 kkok or 반드시 bandeusi are often used with 고 말겠다 or 고 말 테니까.

EXAMPLE SENTENCES

이 면접을 꼭 잘 보**고 말겠어요**.
I myeonjeobeul kkok jal bogo malgesseoyo.
I'm determined to do well in this interview.

내일 그 일을 반드시 끝내**고 말 테니까** 당신이 맡은 부분도 좀 끝내 주세요.
Naeil geu ireul bandeusi kkeunnaego mal tenikka dangsini mateun bubundo jom kkeunnae juseyo.
Tomorrow I'm definitely going to finish that job, so please finish your part as well.

Accidents

	Speaking = Writing
~고 말았다 go maratda "Unfortunately, ~ happened"	★★★

정시에 온다는 것이 결국 늦게 오**고 말았어요**.
Jeongsie ondaneun geosi gyeolguk neutge ogo marasseoyo.
I meant to come on time, but (unfortunately) I ended up being late.

One thing you'll notice if you have lived in Korea for a while is that plans are nice and all, but things quite often don't happen according to plans. Naturally, there's an expression for that. 고 말았다 means that something happened accidentally and unfortunately, and conveys feelings of regret.

HOW IT'S FORMED

Our old friend 고 plus 말다 in the past tense, though neither particularly relates to this expression.If you're really sorry for the way things turned out, you can add 아/어/여 버리다 (which literally means "something is thrown away") in front of the expression to get 아/어/여 버리고 말았다. This strengthens the expression by implying that not only did ~ happen and is now over with, but it's "thrown away"—it can't even be recovered, and there is no way to go back.

HOW IT'S CONJUGATED

		Past
Action verbs ending in a vowel	하다	하고 말았다 hago maratda
Action verbs ending in a consonant	먹다	먹고 말았다 meokgo maratda

TAKE NOTE

The other 고 말다 expressions are 고 말고(요) and 고 말겠다. The former means "of course" and is on page 37, and the latter means "I'm determined to ~" and is on page 232. Pay attention to the tense of any 고 말다 expression: the one in question here is only ever seen in the past tense[말았다], while the others are used only in the present (고 말고[요]) and future (고 말겠다) tenses.

A good expression to use before 고 말았다 is (느)ㄴ다는 것이 (see the next expression), which means that you meant to do A but B ended up happening.

EXAMPLE SENTENCES

잠깐 쉰다는 것이 6시간 동안 자**고 말았어요**.
Jamkkan swindaneun geosi yeoseotsigan dongan jago marasseoyo.
I planned to rest for just a little while, but then I ended up falling asleep for six hours.

요리를 하고 싶었지만, 가스가 없어서 배달을 시키**고 말았어요**.
Yorireul hago sipeotjiman, gaseuga eopsseoseo baedareul sikigo marasseoyo.
I wanted to cook, but I didn't have gas and ended up ordering delivery food.

		Speaking > Writing
Aㄴ/는다는 것이 (게) n/ neundaneun geosi (ge) B	"I meant to A, but ended up B"	★★

정시에 **온다는 것이** 결국 늦게 오고 말았어요.
Jeongsie ondaneun geosi gyeolguk neutge ogo marasseoyo.
I meant to come on time, but (unfortunately) I ended up being late.

This expression and 고 말았다 (see page 232) go hand in hand; 고 말았다 deals with things that happened accidentally, and A(느)ㄴ다는 것이 B means you meant to A but B ended up happening by accident. If you're prone to making mistakes, you'll want to know this expression well.

HOW IT'S FORMED

(느)ㄴ다 is the indirect speech particle that follows action verbs. It's often used in Korean grammar even when no indirect speech is actually involved, as is the case here. It's conjugated with 는 것이, which turns the verb in A into a noun. 것이 can be shortened to 게.

HOW IT'S CONJUGATED

		Past
Action verbs ending in a vowel	하다	한다는 것이 handaneun geosi 한다는 게 handaneun ge
Action verbs ending in a consonant	먹다	먹는다는 것이 meokneundaneun geosi 먹는다는 게 meokneundaneun ge

TAKE NOTE

게 is the short form of 것이, not the 게 that turns verbs into adjectives. 게 and 것이 are completely interchangeable.

For your B clause, you should use an expression indicating regret. 아/어/여 버리다 (see page 31) and 고 말았다 (see page 232) are commonly used.

EXAMPLE SENTENCES

잠깐 **쉰다는 것이** 6시간 동안 자 버렸어요.
Jamkkan swindaneun geosi yeoseotsigan dongan ja beoryeosseoyo.
I planned to rest for just a little while, but then I ended up falling asleep for six hours.

요리를 **한다는 게** 음식을 잊어버려서 타 버리고 말았어요.
Yorireul handaneun ge eumsigeul ijeobeoryeoseo ta beorigo marasseoyo.
I wanted to cook, but I forgot about the food and it ended up burned.

Progression: Review of Past and Future Tenses

Past (았/었/였다 at/eot/yeotda)

To change a present-tense Korean verb into a past-tense Korean verb, add 았/었/였 to the end. 았 is added to verbs with 오 or 아 as their last vowel:

잡다 japda catch   잡**았**다 jabatda caught
놀다 nolda play   놀**았**다 noratda played
오다 oda come   **왔**다 watda came

And 었다 is added to verbs with any other vowel (어, 우, 이, 으) **eo, u, i, eu** as their last vowel.

먹다 **meokda** eat   먹**었**다 **meogeotda** ate
예쁘다 **yeppeuda** to be beautiful   예**뻤**다 **yeppeotda** was beautiful
숨다 **sumda** hide   숨**었**다 **sumeotda** hid
잡히다 **japida** to be caught   잡**혔**다 **japyeotda** was caught

였다 is only added to 하다

하다 **hada** do   했다 did

았다 is also added to verbs ending in 아, but it is shortened to 갔다 to save those few seconds. Likewise, 사다 becomes 샀다. Verbs ending in 오 like 오다 get 았다 added right to that last syllable, so it becomes 왔다. 쏘다 (to shoot) becomes 쐈다. In cases like this where it's awkward to try to say 쐈다, you can just use 쏘았다. However, 왔다 is never 오았다.

가다 **gada** go   갔다 **gotda** went
사다 **sada** buy   샀다 **satda** bought
오다 **oda** come   왔다 **watda** came
쏘다 **ssoda** shoot   쐈다 **sswatda** or 쏘았다 **ssoatda** shot

Similar rules apply for verbs ending in 어, 우 or 이. 어 absorbs the 어 in 었다, 우 becomes 웠다, and 이 becomes 였다.

서다 **seoda** stand   섰다 **seotda** stood
피우다 **piuda** to smoke   피웠다 **piwotda** smoked
두다 **duda** keep   뒀다 **dwotda** or 두었다 **dueotda** kept
피다 **pida** to bloom   폈다 **pyeotda** bloomed

Verbs ending in 으 normally lose the 으 because it's a weak vowel sound and easily pushed around by stronger vowel sounds. If the 으 is the only vowel, then you get rid of it and use 었다.

쓰다 **sseuda** to use   썼다 **sseotda** used

There are a very small number of cases where 으 is the ending of the second syllable in a multi-syllable word. In these cases, it disappears and you use 았다 or 었다 depending on the vowel in the first syllable.

모으다 **moeuda** to collect   모았다 **moatda** collected

Past past (았/었/였었다 at/eot/yeosseotda)

So the past tense tells us that something is finished, but if you really want to emphasize just how finished an event is, you can double the past tense. 았/었/였었다 can be added to a verb to show that it was true in the past, but that it's long over and completely done with now. See page 235 for basic rules on conjugating the past tense; all this expression does is add one more 었.

작년에 부산에 **갔었어요**. Jangnyeone Busane gasseoseoyo.
I went to Busan last year. (but came back)

어렸을 때 미국에서 살**았었어요**. Eoryeosseul ttae migugeseo sarasseosseoyo.
When I was a child, I lived in the US. (but I no longer do)

이 회사에 취직하기 전에 다른 회사에 면접을 **봤었어요**.
I hoesae chwijikhagi jeone dareun hoesae myeonjeobeul bwasseosseoyo.
I had an interview with another company before I got a job at this company.

나는 영어를 잠깐 배**웠었어요**. Naneun yeongeoreul jamkkan baewosseosseoyo.
I learned English for a short time. (but I no longer do)

You can also, as a joke, just keep on repeating 었었었었 as long as you'd like during your sentence; this further emphasizes the fact that whatever you're talking about is really, definitely, absolutely, positively no longer true.

Past – adjectives ([으]ㄴ, 던, 았/었/였던 [eu]n, deon, at/eot/yeotdeon)

던 is used when you want to turn a verb into an adjective describing something that was done in the past. For example, 하던 일 means "the work that was done," or 보던 사람 means "the person I saw." It is used only for things that happened repeatedly in the past. These can be things that are still done or things that are no longer done. If you'd like to indicate for certain that something is no longer done, you can use (으)ㄴ. If you'd like to talk about something that was done only once in the past, you can use 았/었/였이던 or (으)ㄴ.

항상 늦**던** 사람이 계속 미안하다고 했어요.
Hangsang neutdeon sarami gyesok mianhadago haesseoyo.
That man who always used to be always late kept on apologizing.

늦**었던** 사람이 계속 미안하다고 했어요.
Neujeotdeon sarami gyesok mianhadago haesseoyo.
That man who was late (that one time) kept on apologizing.

늦**은** 사람이 계속 미안하다고 했어요.
Neujeun sarami gyesok mianhadago haesseoyo.
That man who was late kept on apologizing.

내가 마시**던** 커피가 맛있었어요. Naega masideon keopiga masisseosseoyo.
That coffee that I used to drink was delicious.

내가 마**셨던** 커피가 맛있었어요. **Naega masyeotdeon keopiga masisseosseoyo.**
That coffee I drank (that one time) was delicious.

내가 마**신** 커피가 맛있었어요. **Naega masin keopiga masisseosseoyo.**
That coffee I drank (but am no longer drinking) was delicious.

더 by itself is a particle having to do with personal recollections (see page 184). Thus, 던 and 았/었/였이던 should be used only when talking about things you've personally experienced. Normally 더 isn't used to talk about things you've done yourself, but 던 is often used that way. While 던 is like 더 with the past tense particle ㄴ on the end, it doesn't play by the same rules as 더.

4급에서 공부하**던** 문법이 참 어려웠어요.
Sageubeseo gongbuhadeon munbeobi cham eoryeowosseoyo
The grammar we studied in level four was really difficult.

지난주 먹**었던** 케이크가 맛있었어요.
Jinanju meogeotdeon keikeuga masisseosseoyo.
The cake I ate last week was delicious.

어렸을 때 자주 가던 식당이 요즘 없어졌어요.
Eoryeosseul ttae jaju gadeon sikdangi yojeum eopsseojyeosseoyo.
The restaurant I often used to go to a a child is now gone.

Past, present and future − (으)ㄴ, 는, (으)ㄹ (eu)n, neun, (eu)r

은 is the past tense marker for verbs ending in consonants, ㄴ is the past tense marker for verbs ending in vowels, 는 is the present tense marker for anything, 을 is the future tense marker for verbs ending in consonants, and ㄹ is the future tense marker for verbs ending in vowels. Adjectives (descriptive verbs) are almost always conjugated using (으)ㄴ.

These markers are a short, convenient way of turning verbs into adjectives.

온 사람	on saram	the person who came
오는 사람	oneun saram	the person who is coming
올 사람	ol saram	the person who will come
먹**은** 음식	meogeun eumsik	the food that was eaten
먹**는** 음식	meokneun eumsik	the food that is being eaten
먹**을** 음식	meogeul eumsik	the food that will be eaten
예**쁜** 여자	yeppeun yeoja	beautiful woman
작**은** 남자	jageun namja	small man

In addition to being used that way, the above markers are also part of many grammatical expressions. In this book and every other Korean textbook I've seen, they are considered part of the expression and you will learn them along with the rest of the expression. Some expressions ([으]ㄹ 수 있다/없다, [으]ㄹ 것이다, many of the expressions used to make guesses or plans, etc.) can be used only in certain tenses while others ([으]ㄴ/는/[으]ㄹ 듯이, [으]ㄴ/는/[으]ㄹ 때, etc.) can be used in any tense. You'll have to choose your tense marker according to what you're trying to convey.

One big difference between (으)ㄴ and 던 is that with (으)ㄴ, the action is always completely finished and over with. (This is not true of descriptive verbs: a 예쁜 여자 is still 예쁜 at the time the sentence was formed.) You could say 제가 하던 일 **jega hadeon il** if you were talking about something you were working on earlier (which may or may not have been finished), but you can't call it 한 일 **han il** unless it's all done.

It is extremely easy to get confused, particularly with ㄴ and ㄹ, as to whether the ㄴ or ㄹ you see is a past or future tense marker, or just the end of a word. This is particularly true with words like 한 of 한 일 above, where 한 has many other meanings besides 하다 plus ㄴ. There's really no easy way to distinguish the words in this case; it's really just a matter of practice and familiarity.

Note as well that the past, present, or future tense marker with (으)ㄴ/는/(으)ㄹ compares the time of that action to what's happening in the rest of your sentence. So if clause A happened before clause B, use (으)ㄴ regardless of what tense your sentence is in relative to the present.

늦게 **온** 사람이 계속 미안**하다고 했어요**.
Neutge on sarami gyesok mianhadago haesseoyo.
That man who was late kept on apologizing.

늦게 **온** 사람이 계속 미안**하다고 해요**.
Neutge on sarami gyesok mianhadago haeyo.
That man who was late keeps on apologizing.

If A and B happen at the same time, use 는 regardless of B's tense.

늦게 **오는** 사람이 계속 미안**하다고 했어요**.
Neutge oneun sarami gyesok mianhadago haesseoyo.
That man who was late kept on apologizing.

늦**은** 사람이 계속 미안**하다고 해요**. Neujeun sarami gyesok mianhadago haeyo.
That man who was late keeps on apologizing.

The future – (으)ㄹ 것이다, 겠다 (eu)l geosida, getda

There are two expressions most commonly used to talk about the future in Korean. 겠다 is simple to use but a bit more limited, while (으)ㄹ 것이다 is a willing, cheerful participant in almost any phrase. Let's look at (으)ㄹ 것이다 first.

(으)ㄹ 것이다 can be used for just about any statement about the future, no matter who's doing it or why. You can add it to any kind of verb. 을 것이다 is added to verbs ending in consonants and ㄹ 것이다 is added to verbs ending in vowels. For nouns, it's better to use 되다 (to become) and then conjugate that with ㄹ 것이다. See the third example sentence below.

This is conjugated as (으)ㄹ 거예요 in 존댓말 and (으)ㄹ 거야 in 반말. If you need to be super-polite, just conjugate (으)ㄹ 것이다 correctly: (으)ㄹ 것입니다. However, this is somewhat less common. The table below shows the basic form of (으)ㄹ 것이다 plus the polite and 반말 forms.

		Future
Action verbs ending in a vowel	하다	할 것이다 hal geosida 할 거예요 hal geoyeyo 할 거야 hal geoya
Action verbs ending in a consonant	먹다	먹을 것이다 meogeul geosida 먹을 거예요 meogeul geoyeyo 먹을 거야 meogeul geoya
Descriptive verbs (adjectives) ending in a vowel	예쁘다	예쁠 것이다 yeppeul geosida 예쁠 거예요 yeppeul geoyeyo 예쁠 거야 yeppeul geoya
Descriptive verbs (adjectives) ending in a consonant	작다	작을 것이다 jageul geosida 작을 거예요 jageul geoyeyo 작을 거야 jageul geoya
Nouns ending in a vowel	남자	남자일 것이다 namjail geosida 남자일 거예요 namjail geoyeyo 남자일 거야 namjail geoya
Nouns ending in a consonant	물	물일 것이다 muril geosida 물일 거예요 muril geoyeyo 물일 거야 muril geoya

And here are some examples:

파티에 늦게 **올 거예요**. Patie neutge ol geoyeyo.
파티에 늦게 **올 거야**. Patie neutge ol geoya.
I'll come to the party late.

그 치마를 입으면 **예쁠 거예요**. Geu chimareul ibeumyeon yeppeul geoyeyo.
그 치마를 입으면 **예쁠 거야**. Geu chimareul ibeumyeon yeppeul geoya.
If you wear that skirt, you'll be beautiful.

가영이는 의사가 **될 거예요**. Kayoung-i-neun uisaga doel geoyeyo.
가영이는 의사가 **될 거야**. Kayoung-i-neun uisaga doel geoya.
Kayoung is going to be a doctor.

(으)ㄹ 거예요 and (으)ㄹ게요 (see page 214) are very similar, and it's easy to confuse one for the other. The difference is that (으)ㄹ게요 depends more on your listener. With (으)ㄹ 거예요 you're simply stating what you think will happen in the future, whereas (으)ㄹ게요 has more of a connotation of "I'm going to do ~ (if it's okay with you)." (으)ㄹ게요 can also be used when you're making/changing your plans as a result of what the other person has said. Either way, it always has something to do with that other person's reaction. (으)ㄹ 거예요, on the other hand, has nothing at all to do with what the other person says.

As for 겠다, it's more commonly used with very formal Korean (습니다, 입니다, etc.) You can use it to talk about your own or someone else's intentions for the future, especially if you or they are quite determined to carry out these intentions. You can't normally use it with sentences about the future that are not describing someone's intentions; in these cases you should use (으)ㄹ 것이다.

Additionally, 겠다 is often used to make guesses, much like 나/(으)ㄴ가 보다 (see page 138) or (으)ㄹ 것 같다 (see page 137). You'll often hear Koreans say things like "맛있겠다!" upon seeing a plate of food or "아프겠다! **Apeugetda**" upon seeing a friend wearing a cast on their arm. This doesn't mean they're anticipating future pain for the person; it's just a way of making a guess. 맛있겠다 **masitgetda** means "Looks good!" and 아프겠다 means "Looks painful!"

Finally, there are a few idiomatic expressions with 겠다. The most common are 모르겠다 **moreugetda** and 알겠다 **algetda** ("I don't know" and "I know," or more accurately, "I understand"). This has nothing to do with the future or with guessing; it's just it's said.

As for conjugation, simply add 겠 to any action or descriptive verb regardless of its ending. Just like (으)ㄹ 것이다, nouns are normally followed by 되다 and then 겠다 (so, 되겠다).

		Future
Action verbs ending in a vowel	하다	하겠다 hagetda
Action verbs ending in a consonant	먹다	먹겠다 meokgetda
Descriptive verbs (adjectives) ending in a vowel	예쁘다	예쁘겠다 yeppeugetda
Descriptive verbs (adjectives) ending in a consonant	작다	작겠다 jakgetda

Here are some examples.

늦**겠어요**. **Neutgesseoyo.** You're going to be late.

어디로 가시**겠어요**? **Eodiro gasigesseoyo?** Where would you like to go?

괜찮**겠어요**? **Gwaen-chan-kesseoyo?** Will you be okay?

Progression: While

A동안(에) dong-an(e) B	"B while A"	Speaking = Writing ★★★★★

숙제 하**는 동안에** 음악을 들었어요.
Sukje haneun dong-ane eumageul deureosseoyo.
While I was doing my homework, I listened to music.

동안에 is another expression that means "while." It is used only while talking about time.

HOW IT'S FORMED

동안 means "while" and can be used on its own. 에 is a preposition of location which, in this case, serves to emphasize 동안. (으)ㄴ and 는 are tense markers which go between verbs and 동안(에).

HOW IT'S CONJUGATED

동안에 can follow either an action verb or a noun indicating a period of time (일 년 il nyeon, 한 달 han dal, 아침 achim, etc) or an action or activity, like a class (수업 sueop) or lunch (점심 jeomsim) that takes a period of time. If it follows a verb, put 는 before that verb regardless of which tense it's in. The assumption is that A was in the present tense at the time B happened. If your verb has to do with coming and going (가다 gada, 오다 oda, 떠나다 tteonada, etc.) and it happened in the past, then you can use (으)ㄴ 동안에. B is something that happened while A was ongoing.

		All tenses
Action verbs ending in a vowel	하다	하는 동안(에) haneun dongan(e)
Action verbs ending in a consonant	먹다	먹는 동안(에) meokneun dongan(e)
가다, 오다, 떠나다 and other verbs describing coming and going	가다	가는 동안(에) ganeun dongan(e)
Nouns ending in a vowel	휴가	휴가 동안(에) hyuga dongan(e)
Nouns ending in a consonant	아침	아침 동안(에) achim dongan(e)

TAKE NOTE

사이에 is a similar expression which can be used to talk about other things besides just time; see page 251 for other ways to use 사이에. The difference between the two is that 동안에 can be used whether or not the subjects of A and B are the same, while 사이에 can be used only if the subjects are different.

(으)ㄴ/는 동안(에) is completely interchangeable with (으)ㄹ 때; see the next page for more on (으)ㄹ 때.

(도)중에 (page 244) has a similar meaning but can be used only with action verbs.

EXAMPLE SENTENCES

민수가 공부하**는 동안에** 가영이 TV를 보고 있어요.
Minsuga gongbuhaneun dongane Kayoungi tibireul bogo isseoyo
While Minsu studies, Kayoung is watching TV.

영국에 **가 있는 동안에** 어머니가 죽었어요.
Yeonguke ga inneun dong-ane eomeoniga jugeosseoyo.
While I was in England, my mother died.

A(으)ㄹ 때(에는) (eu)r ttae(e-neun) B   "B while A"

Speaking = Writing
★★★★★

대학교 **때** 민수가 자주 늦었어요. Daehakgyo ttae Minsuga jaju neujeosseoyo.
During university Minsu was often late.

때 is an important word to know if you ever want to talk about time in Korean. It's used in many expressions that mean "while," "during," "when," "at times," and the like.

HOW IT'S FORMED

(으)ㄹ, though it appears to be the future tense marker, doesn't really mean anything like that in this expression and the expression remains (으)ㄹ 때(에는) no matter what time you're talking about. 때 is a noun which simply means "time." 에 is a preposition of location that is quite frequently seen in expressions involving time; it roughly means "at," as in "at that time." 는 is the topic marker (see page 30) and serves to emphasize the period of time. Both 에 and 는 are optional, so you can use either or both.

HOW IT'S CONJUGATED

A must be a period of time or something that you were doing for a period of time: note that the nouns below had to be changed to things that take some time.

		Past	Present	Future
Action verbs ending in a vowel	하다	했을 때 haesseul ttae	할 때 hal ttae	할 때
Action verbs ending in a consonant	먹다	먹었을 때 meogeosseul ttae	먹을 때 meogeul ttae	먹을 때
Descriptive verbs (adjectives) ending in a vowel	예쁘다	예뻤을 때 yeppeosseul ttae	예쁠 때 yeppeul ttae	예쁠 때
Descriptive verbs (adjectives) ending in a consonant	작다	작았을 때 jagasseul ttae	작을 때 jageul ttae	작을 때
Nouns ending in a vowel	휴가	휴가 때 hyuga ttae	휴가 때	휴가 때
Nouns ending in a consonant	아침	아침 때 achim ttae	아침 때	아침 때

TAKE NOTE

(으)ㄴ/는 동안(에) is completely interchangeable with (으)ㄹ 때; see page 241 for more on (으)ㄴ/는 동안(에). Similar expressions are 사이에 **saie** and (도)중에 **(do)junge** (see pages 251 and 244, respectively), but these follow action verbs rather than nouns indicating periods of time. 사이에 can be used to talk about locations, while 동안에 and 중에 cannot. It can also be used for expressions like "among friends" and for actions occurring at the same time. 사이에 is covered on page 251. (으)ㄹ 때, like 동안에, is used to talk only about time.

Some commonly used expressions with 때 include:

어렸을 때/어릴 때 eoryeosseul ttae/eoril ttae during childhood

한창 때 hanchang ttae in one's prime

아무 때 amu ttae at any time

어느 때/어떤 때/어떨 때 eoneu ttae/eotteon ttae/eotteol ttae sometimes

그 때 geu ttae at that time

이 때 i ttae at this time

그맘때 geumamttae around that time

날 때부터 nal ttaebuteo from birth

EXAMPLE SENTENCES

A: 언제 그 일을 끝내야 돼요? Eonje geu ireul kkeunnaeya dwaeyo?
When do I have to finish this job?

B: 아무 때나 끝내도 돼요. Amu ttaena kkeunnaedo dwaeyo.
You can finish it whenever you like.

여기를 걸을 때 조심하세요. Yeogireul georeul ttae josimhaseyo.
Be careful while walking here.

Speaking = Writing

A(는) (도)중에(서)　　　　　"B while A"　　　　★★★★★
(neun) (do)junge(seo) B

숙제 하는 중에 음악을 들어요. Sukje haneun jung-e eumageul deureoyo.
While doing my homework, I listen to music.

중에 and all its variations have two meanings. You can use it to talk about two actions that happen at the same time, or you can use it to present alternatives: Among all the boys in the class, which one(s) would you want to date? Or, between Korean and Western food, which one do you feel like eating for lunch today?

HOW IT'S FORMED

중 jung by itself means "middle" and is very commonly used in words like 중학교 junghak-gyo (middle school) and 집중 jipjung ("concentration"; literally "collect at the center"). 에 e and 에서 eseo are prepositions of location which, in this case, emphasize 중. 에 is used in any sentence involving 중 while 에서 is used only when talking about choices; 남자 중 에서 namjajungeseo is fine, but 가는 중에서 isn't. 도 is optional and only be added only when 중 means "on the way"; 가는 중에 ganeun junge can become 가는 도중에 ganeun dojunge, but 남자 중에 can't become 남자 도중에.

HOW IT'S CONJUGATED

는 (도)중에 can be used only with action verbs. When used with action verbs, it means "while." 중에 by itself can also follow nouns indicating some period of time: 일 년, 한 달, 수업, 아침, etc.

		All tenses
Action verbs ending in a vowel	하다	하는 중에 haneun junge 하는 도중에 haneun dojunge
Action verbs ending in a consonant	먹다	먹는 중에 meokneun junge 먹는 도중에 meokneun dojunge
Nouns ending in a vowel	휴가	휴가 중에 hyuga junge
Nouns ending in a consonant	학생	학생 중에 haksaeng junge

중에서 can be used only with nouns and in this case it means "between" or "among," and the next part of the sentence offers a choice.

		Present
Nouns ending in a vowel	남자	남자 중에 namja junge 남자 중에서 namja jungeseo
Nouns ending in a consonant	책	책 중에 chaek junge 책 중에서 chaek jungeseo

TAKE NOTE

Be careful about all these forms of 중에. Check the tables above to see which one is appropriate when.

The subjects of both clauses should be the same.

Similar expressions are ([으]ㄴ/는) 동안에, ([으]ㄴ/는) 사이에, and (으)ㄹ 때. 동안에 (see page 241) is used only to talk about time and co-occurring actions. 사이에 can be used to talk about locations, while 동안에 and 중에 cannot. It can also be used for expressions like "among friends" and for co-occurring actions. 사이에 is covered on page 251. (으)ㄹ 때 (see page 243), like 동안에, is used only to talk about time. Thus, when talking about two actions that occur at the same time, 중에, 도중에, 동안에, 사이에 and (으)ㄹ 때 are all interchangeable; when talking about making a choice, they are not.

다가 (see page 269) describes an interruption in action and is quite often interchangeable with 중에: for example, "My friend called while I was in the shower."

You can also use 는 중이다 at the end of a sentence to describe being in the middle of something. Now, when the aforementioned friend calls you, you'll know how to explain that you were in the middle of taking a shower when he called. 중에 있다 can be used here as well.

EXAMPLE SENTENCES

학교에 **가는 중에** 사고를 봤어요. Hakgyoe ganeun junge sagoreul bwasseoyo.
While I was going to school, I saw an accident.

수업 **중에** 핸드폰을 쓰면 안 돼요.
Sueop junge haendeuponeul sseumyeon an dwaeyo.
During class you can't use your cell phone.

지금 샤워 하**는 중이에요**. Jigeum syawo haneun jungieyo
I'm in the middle of taking a shower right now.

지금 샤워 하**는 중에 있어요**. Jigeum syawo haneun junge isseoyo.
I'm in the middle of taking a shower right now.

저 남자들 **중에서** 어떤 남자가 제일 잘 생겼다고 생각하세요?
Jeo namjadeul jungeseo eotteon namjaga je-il jal saenggyeotdago saenggakaseyo?
Which of those men do you think is the most handsome?

책 **중에서** 하나만 골라 읽어 보세요. Chaek jungeseo hanaman golla ilgeo boseyo.
Please choose and read just one of the books.

		Speaking = Writing
A(으)면서 (eu)myeonseo B	"B while A"	★★★★★

늦을까 봐 운전하**면서** 계속 시계를 봤어요.
Neujeulkka bwa unjeonhamyeonseo gyesok sigyereul bwasseoyo.
I was afraid I'd be late, so I kept checking my watch as I drove.

This is a very basic way to talk about A and B happening at the same time.

HOW IT'S FORMED

It's an expression on its own and has nothing to do with (으)면 or 아/어/여서.

HOW IT'S CONJUGATED

		All tenses
Action verbs ending in a vowel	하다	하면서 hamyeonseo
Action verbs ending in a consonant	먹다	먹으면서 meogeumyeonseo
Descriptive verbs (adjectives) ending in a vowel	예쁘다	예쁘면서 yeppeumyeonseo
Descriptive verbs (adjectives) ending in a consonant	작다	작으면서 jageumyeonseo
Nouns ending in a vowel	남자	남자이면서 namjaimyeonseo
Nouns ending in a consonant	물	물이면서 murimyeonseo

TAKE NOTE

Again, this is completely different from 면; see page 283 for more on 면.

Since A and B happen at the same time, there's no need to conjugate the verb before (으)면서: the verb at the end of the B clause expresses the tense of both clauses. So a verb with (으)면서 is always conjugated as if it were in the present tense.

(으)면서도 (see page 253) is a similar expression, but can be used only when A and B contrast: when B isn't something that would normally be expected to co-occur with A. 면서 can be used instead of 면서도 in all cases, but the reverse is not true.

EXAMPLE SENTENCES

빨래를 하**면서** 음악을 들어요. Ppallaereul ha**myeonseo** eumageul deureoyo.
I listen to music while doing laundry.

아이가 먹**으면서** TV를 보고 있어요.
Aiga meog**eumyeonseo** tibireul bogo isseoyo.
The child is watching TV while eating.

밥을 먹**으면서** 맥주도 마셨어요.
Babeul meog**eumyeonseo** maekjudo masyeosseoyo.
While I was eating, I also drank beer.

Speaking = Writing

A(으)면 A(으)ㄹ수록 (eu)　"The more A, the more B"　★★★
 myeon A (eu)l-surok B

멀리 가**면** 갈수록 피곤해졌어요. Meolli ga**myeon** galsurok pigonhaejyeosseoyo.
멀리 **갈수록** 피곤해졌어요. Meolli **galsurok** pigonhaejyeosseoyo.
The farther I went, the more tired I became.

This expression simply means that the more A happens, the more B happens, or as A progresses, B progresses as well.

HOW IT'S FORMED

You can use (으)ㄹ수록 on its own or you can repeat the verb in A and follow the first A with (으)면 and the second with (으)ㄹ수록. It's really up to you. The meaning is the same either way.

HOW IT'S CONJUGATED

		All tenses
Action verbs ending in a vowel	하다	(하면) 할수록 (hamyeon) halsurok
Action verbs ending in a consonant	먹다	(먹으면) 먹을수록 (meogeumyeon) meogeulsurok

	All tenses
Descriptive verbs (adjectives) ending in a vowel	예쁘다	(예쁘면) 예쁠수록 (yeppeumyeon) yeppeulsurok
Descriptive verbs (adjectives) ending in a consonant	작다	(작으면) 작을수록 (jageumyeon) jageulsurok
Nouns ending in a vowel	남자	(남자면) 남자일수록 (namjamyeon) namjailsurok
Nouns ending in a consonant	물	(물이면) 물일수록 (murimyeon) murilsurok

TAKE NOTE

B is a sentence describing what happens the more A, so it often ends with an expression meaning "to become": 아/어/여지다 or 게 되다 (see page 251). However, this is not strictly necessary; people will understand from your use of (으)ㄹ수록 **(eu)l-surok** that the situation is changing.

수록하다/되다 **surokada/doeda** is a verb having to do with containment; it has nothing to do with this 수록, which always follows a verb stem ending in ㄹ.

갈수록 **galsurok** is an expression which can literally mean "as you go," but can also mean "as time passes."

EXAMPLE SENTENCES

좋**으면** 좋**을수록** 잘 써져요. Joeumyeon joeulsurok jal sseojyeoyo.
좋**을수록** 잘 써져요. Joeulsurok jal sseojyeoyo.
The better it is, the more it's used.

공부하**면** 공부**할수록** 듣기 능력이 더 좋아져요.
Gongbuhamyeon gongbuhalsurok deutgi neung-nyeog-i deo joa-jyeo-yo.
공부**할수록** 듣기 능력이 더 좋아져요.
Gongbuhalsurok deutgi neung-nyeog-i deo joa-jyeo-yo.
The more I study, the better my listening ability gets.

		Speaking = Writing
A는 길에 neun gire B	"B happened while I was doing A"	★★★

학교에 가**는 길에** 친구를 만나서 늦었어요.
Hakgyoe ganeun gire chingureul mannaseo neujeosseoyo.
While on the way to school, I met a friend, so I was late.

This is another expression like (도)중에, which means that "something happened while you were in the middle of something else." However, 는 길에 is more particular to use than 도중에.

HOW IT'S FORMED

는 is the present tense marker. 길 literally means "road" and 에 is a preposition meaning "to" or "on." This expression literally means "while on the road."

HOW IT'S CONJUGATED

는 길에 is rarely used with any verbs in A other than those indicating movement. Here are a few examples of verbs with which you can use 는 길에:

가다 **gada** to go
오다 **oda** to come
돌아가다, 들어오다 **doragada, deureooda**, etc. to return, to come in, etc.
떠나다 **tteonada** to leave
다니다 **danida** to go around
퇴근하다/출근하다 **toegeunhada/chulgeunhada** to leave/go to work

Take your A verb and add 는 길에. Although 는 is the present tense marker, it is used with 길에 regardless of when the incident happened: A was still in the present tense when B happened, so it gets the present tense marker.

I can't find any directional verbs that end in a consonant, but if you should need to conjugate any, they're conjugated the same way: just add 는 길에.

		Past	Present
Directional verbs	가다	가는 길에 **ganeun gire**	가는 길에

TAKE NOTE

Be careful to use this expression only with verbs of direction.

Two other similar expressions are (으)ㄴ/는 김에 **(eu)n/neun gime** (on page 250) and 는 (도)중에 (on page 244). The difference between 는 길에 and 는 김에 is that the former can be used for things that happened by accident, while 는 김에 is used only for events or activities that were planned. 는 도중에 can be used with any verb, whether it has to do with coming and going, or not. So if you wanted to talk about what happened while you were working, you could say 일하는 중에 **ilhaneun junge** or 일하는 도중에 **ilhaneun dojunge**, but not 일하는 길에 **ilhaneun gire**. But if something terribly interesting happened while you were out going somewhere and you wanted to tell someone all about it, you could say 가는 중에 **ganeun junge**, 가는 도중에 **ganeun dojunge**, or 가는 길에 **ganeun gire**.

Finally, in certain sentences, 다가 and 는 길에 are interchangeable. A다가 B (see page 269) means that B happened during an action and interrupted A. Sentences in which the verb in A is a directional verb can use either 다가 or 는 길에.

You can use 는 길이다 to end a sentence saying "you are or were on your way somewhere."

EXAMPLE SENTENCES

집에 오**는 길에** 슈퍼에 갔어요. **Jibe oneun gire syupeoe gasseoyo.**
While coming home, I went to the supermarket.

홍콩으로 여행을 떠나**는 길에** 이 선물을 홍콩에 있는 제 친구에게 전해주세요.
Hongkong-euro yeo-haeng-eul tteonaneun gire i seonmureul Hongkonge inneun je chinguege jeon-hae-juseyo
While you are on your trip to Hong Kong, please give this present to my friend in Hong Kong.

미국에서 돌아오**는 길에** 공항 면세점에서 기념품을 사 주세요.
Migugeseo dor-a-o-neun gire gonghang myeonsejeomeseo gin-yeom-pum-eul sa juseyo.
While you are coming back from USA, please buy a souvenir at the airport duty-free shop.

A: 어디 가**는 길이에요**? **Eodi ganeun girieyo?** Where are you going?

B: 은행에 가**는 길이에요**. **Eunhaenge ganeun girieyo.** I'm on my way to the bank.

A(으)ㄴ/는 김에 (eu)n/neun gime B	"While you're A, would you mind B as well?"	**Speaking > Writing** ★★★

온 김에 같이 저녁 먹을래요. **On gime gachi jeonyeok meogeullaeyo.**
Since you're here, let's have dinner together.

This expression is good for people who are lazy and/or good planners. It's used to talk about doing B incidentally or on your way to or from A. You can use it to make requests of people, as in the title of this section, or to talk about errands you combined: "While you're A, would you mind B as well?" or "While on my way to A, I also took care of B" are the kind of sentences you'd translate into (으)ㄴ/는 김에.

HOW IT'S FORMED

The past and present tense markers (으)ㄴ/는 are combined with 김에, which doesn't mean anything by itself.

HOW IT'S CONJUGATED

		Past	Present	Future
Action verbs ending in a vowel	하다	한 김에 **han gime**	하는 김에 **haneun gime**	하는 김에
Action verbs ending in a consonant	먹다	먹은 김에 **meogeun gime**	먹는 김에 **meokneun gime**	먹는 김에

TAKE NOTE

A is the main objective, the thing you originally set out to do, and B is what you're doing incidentally or asking someone to do.

A somewhat similar expression is (으)ㄴ/는 길에 (see page 248). The difference between the two is that while in both cases A is the main objective, with (으)ㄴ/는 김에 B is always something planned, while with (으)ㄴ/는 길에 B can also have happened accidentally. So you'd use 김에 to talk about stopping by the grocery store on your way to the bank while 길에 is what you'd use to describe accidentally running into your friend on the street on the way to the grocery store or the bank. Also, 길에 can be used only with verbs indicating direction (like 오다 or 가다) while 김에 can be used with any action verb.

은행에 가**는 김에** 슈퍼에 들렀어요.
Eunhaenge ganeun gime syupeoe deulleosseoyo.
While on my way to the bank, I stopped by the supermarket.

은행에 가**는 길에** 친구를 만났어요.
Eunhaenge ganeun gire chingureul mannasseoyo.
While on my way to the bank, I (accidentally) ran into my friend.

EXAMPLE SENTENCES

파티에 가**는 김에** 멋있는 옷도 준비했어요.
Patie ganeun gime meosinneun otdo junbihaesseoyo.
Because I was going to the party, I prepared some stylish clothes.

우체국에 가**는 김에** 그 옆에 있는 은행도 들렀어요.
Ucheguge ganeun gime geu yeope inneun eunhaengdo deulleosseoyo.
On my way to the post office, I dropped by the bank.

여자친구 선물을 사**는 김에** 어머니 선물도 같이 샀어요.
Yeoja-chin-gu seonmureul saneun gime eomeoni seonmuldo gachi sasseoyo.
While buying a gift for my girlfriend, I also bought a gift for my mother.

A commonly used expression with 김에 is 말(이) 나온 김에 **mal(i) naon gime** ~, which means "While we're on the subject of ~."

A: 다음 회의에 그 문제에 대해서 이야기를 더 해야 돼요.
  Daeum hoe-ui-e geu mun-je-e daehaeseo iyagireul deo haeya dwaeyo.
  We need to talk about that problem more at our next meeting.

B: **말이 나온 김에** 다음 회의 날짜를 정할까요?
  Mari naon gime daeum hoe-ui naljjareul jeonghalkkayo?
  While we're on the subject, shall we set the date for our next meeting?

		Speaking = Writing
A사이에 saie B	"B while A"	★★★

저녁을 먹**는 사이에** 친구가 들렸어요.
Jeonyeogeul meokneun saie chinguga deul-lyeosseoyo.
While I was eating dinner, my friend dropped by.

You can use 사이에 to talk about people, places, or activities. It can mean either "while" (when talking about activities) or "between" (when talking about people or places).

HOW IT'S FORMED

사이 means between and 에 is the preposition of location. When 사이에 is used to talk about activities: either the past tense marker (으)ㄴ or the present tense marker 는 can be used.

HOW IT'S CONJUGATED

Since we're essentially talking about two different meanings that happen to share an expression, let's divide this into two parts. (으)ㄴ/는 사이에 (the top table, shown below) can be used only with action verbs; it means "while." A and B are two simultaneous activities. Almost all verbs with 사이에 take the present tense marker 는 no matter when they happened. The only exceptions are verbs having to do with coming and going: 가다, 오다, 떠나다, etc. When used in past tense sentences, these verbs take the past tense marker (으)ㄴ.

		Past	Present	Future
Action verbs ending in a vowel	하다	하는 사이에 haneun saie	하는 사이에	하는 사이에
Action verbs ending in a consonant	먹다	먹는 사이에 meokneun saie	먹는 사이에	먹는 사이에
가다, 오다, 떠나다, and other verbs indicating going or coming	가다	간 사이에 gan saie	가는 사이에	가는 사이에

Plain old 사이에 (below) follows nouns. When talking about places, it means "between" (between the post office and the bank, between the hospital and the school, etc.) and goes after the two places it links.

When talking about people it means "between" or "among" (between friends, among ourselves, etc.) and goes after the people it links. This can be two people (너와 나 사이에서 neowa na saieseo) or a group of people (친구 사이에서 chingu saieseo).

		All tenses
Nouns ending in a vowel	남자	남자 사이에 namja saie
Nouns ending in a consonant	물	물 사이에 mul saie

TAKE NOTE

When using 사이에 to talk about activities (B while A), the subjects of clause A and clause B must be different. If the subjects are the same, you should use 동안에, which is covered on page 241.

사이에서 means a metaphorical space between people while 사이에 means a physical one such as the space between two buildings. See the examples.

Similar expressions are ([으]ㄴ/는) 동안에, ([으]ㄴ/는) (는) (도)중에 (see page 244), and (으)ㄹ 때 (see page 243). 동안에 is used to talk only about time and co-occurring actions. (으)ㄹ 때, like 동안에, is used to talk only about time. Thus, when talking about two actions that occur at the same time, 중에, 도중에, 동안에, 사이에 and (으)ㄹ 때 are all interchangeable; when talking about making a choice, they are not.

EXAMPLE SENTENCES

민수가 공부하는 **사이에** 가영이 TV를 보고 있어요.
Minsuga gongbuhaneun saie Kayoungi tibireul bogo isseoyo.
While Minsu studies, Kayoung is watching TV.

영국에 **간 사이에** 어머니가 죽었어요.
Yeong-gug-e gan saie eomeoniga jugeosseoyo.
While I was in England, my mother died.

우리 **사이에** 비밀이 어디 있어? Uri saie bimiri eodi isseo?
There are no secrets between us.

외국인들 **사이에서** 그 식당이 인기 있어요.
Oe-gug-in-deul sa-i-eseo geu sikdangi ingi isseoyo.
That restaurant is popular among foreigners.

지하철 역이 학교와 공원 **사이에** 있어요.
Jihacheol yeogi hakgyowa gongwon saie isseoyo.
The subway stop is between the school and the park.

		Speaking = Writing
A(으)**면서도** (eu)myeonseodo B	"B, even while A"	★★

서둘렀**으면서도** 늦었어요. Seo-dul-leoss-eu-myeon-seo-do neujeosseoyo.
Even though I hurried, I was late.

Here's another way to say "while," but this one adds an element of contrast: you wouldn't expect B to happen while A is happening, but somehow it is.

HOW IT'S FORMED

(으)면서 means "while" (see page 246). 도 is a particle used to indicate contrast and is covered in detail on page 104.

HOW IT'S CONJUGATED

You can use (으)ㄹ 거면서도 for hypothetical events or events in the future.

		Past	Present	Future
Action verbs end-ing in a vowel	하다	했으면서도 haesseumyeonseodo	하면서도 hamyeonseodo	할 거면서도 hal geomyeonseodo
Action verbs end-ing in a consonant	먹다	먹었으면서도 meogeosseumyeonseodo	먹으면서도 meogeumyeonseodo	먹을 거면서도 meogeul geomyeonseodo
Descriptive verbs (adjectives) end-ing in a vowel	예쁘다	예뻤으면서도 yeppeosseumyeonseodo	예쁘면서도 yeppeumyeonseodo	예쁠 거면서도 yeppeul geomyeonseodo

		Past	Present	Future
Descriptive verbs (adjectives) ending in a consonant	작다	작았으면서도 jagasseumyeonseodo	작으면서도 jageumyeonseodo	작을 거면서도 jageul geomyeonseodo
Nouns ending in a vowel	남자	남자였으면서도 namjayeosseumyeonseodo	남자이면서도 namjaimyeonseodo	남자일 거면서도 namjail geomyeonseo
Nouns ending in a consonant	물	물이었으면서도 murieosseumyeonseodo	물이면서도 murimyeonseodo	물일 거면서도 muril geomyeonseodo

TAKE NOTE

This expression can be changed to (으)면서, but (으)면서 can't always be changed to (으)면서도. (으)면서도 can also be replaced by 지만 (see page 105) although it loses some of the nuance. You can't use (으)면서도 in the past tense if the subject is the first person ("I" or "we").

서둘렀**으면서도** 늦었어요. Seodulleosseumyeonseodo neujeosseoyo.
Even though I hurried, I was late.

서둘렀**지만** 늦었어요. Seodulleotjiman neujeosseoyo. I hurried, but I was late.

EXAMPLE SENTENCES

남자친구에게 화가 나**면서도** 그를 사랑해요.
Namjachinguege hwaga namyeonseodo geureul saranghaeyo.
Even when I'm angry at my boyfriend, I still love him.

이 옷은 예쁘**면서도** 잘 안 팔려요. I oseun yeppeumyeonseodo jal an pallyeoyo.
Even though these clothes are beautiful, they don't sell well.

> **Speaking = Writing**
>
> A아/어/여 가면서 a/eo/ "to A intermittently while B"   ★★
> yeo gamyeonseo B

늦을까 봐 시계를 **봐 가면서** 운전했어요.
Neujeulkka bwa sigyereul bwa gamyeonseo unjeonhaesseoyo.
I was worried I'd be late, so I kept looking at my watch while driving.

Like (으)면서, this expression is used to talk about doing two things at the same time. However, in this case B is the main thing you're doing and A is what you're doing occasionally while focusing on B.

HOW IT'S FORMED

아/어/여 가다 means to do something while going. 면서 means "while" and is covered on page 246.

HOW IT'S CONJUGATED

		All tenses
Action verbs ending in a vowel	하다	해 가면서 hae gamyeonseo
Action verbs ending in a consonant	먹다	먹어 가면서 meogeo gamyeonseo

TAKE NOTE

Remember that B is the main thing; you're saying "I drank coffee while studying" (커피를 마셔 가면서 공부했어요 **Keopireul masyeo gamyeonseo gongbuhaesseoyo**) rather than "I studied while drinking coffee" (공부해 가면서 커피를 마셨어요 **Gongbuhae gamyeonseo keopireul masyeosseoyo**), assuming you mean you raised a mug to your lips once in a while in between studying rather than steadily downing pot after pot.

EXAMPLE SENTENCES

담배를 피**워 가면서** 경치를 봤어요.
Dambaereul piwo gamyeonseo gyeongchireul bwasseoyo.
I looked at the scenery while smoking a cigarette.

이 책을 **봐 가면서** 새로운 사실을 알게 되었어요.
I chaegeul bwa gamyeonseo saeroun sa-si-reul alge doe-eosseoyo.
While reading this book, I learned many new facts.

Progression: Continuing States

~고 있다 go itda,   "~ing, being ~"   **Speaking = Writing**
~어/아 있다 eo/a itda   ★★★★★

제가 새로운 한국어 단어를 공책에 쓰**고 있었어요**.
Jega saeroun hangugeo dan-eo-reul gongchaege sseugo isseosseoyo.
I was writing the new Korean vocabulary in my notebook.

새로운 한국어 단어가 공책에 **써 있었어요**.
Saeroun hangugeo dan-eo-ga gongchaege sseo isseosseoyo.
The new Korean vocabulary was written in my notebook.

고 and 아/어/여 있다 are the Korean present progressive. I've put them together because they're really two sides of the same coin: one is used for continued actions while one is used for continued states.

HOW IT'S FORMED

First, take either 고 (see page 51) or 아/어. Both have a variety of uses, most of which aren't really relevant to understanding the expressions above. One thing to remember about 아/어 is that it normally is used for either continued states or verbs that have some relevance to the next clause. See the section on helping verbs (page 31) for more on this. Finally, 있다 means "there is," which implies continuity; if "there is" a chair in the classroom, the chair has usually been there for some time, whether that time is long or short. That's how 있다 is used in 고 있다 and 아/어 있다: it means that the action or state of ~ exists for some time.

HOW IT'S CONJUGATED

고 있다 is simply added to the end of an action verb. This verb should specifically describe an action that is happening at the time rather than a state that is continued: e. g., 먹다 **meokda**, 운동하다 **undonghada**, 피아노를 치다 **pianoreul chida**, 놀다 **nolda**. 아/어/여 있다 is added to the end of an action verb, but an action verb describing a state that continues uninterrupted for some time: examples are 서다 **seoda** (to stand), 앉다 **anda** (to sit), 넣다 **neota** (to put), or 눕다 **nupda** (to lie down). 아 있다 follows verbs with 오 or 아 as their last vowel and 어 있다 follows verbs with 어, 우, 으 or 이 as their last vowel. You can conjugate 있다 in either the past or future.

		Past	Present	Future
Verbs describing an action and ending in a vowel	하다	하고 있었다 hago isseotda	하고 있다 hago itda	하고 있을 것이다 hago isseul geosida
Verbs describing an action and ending in a consonant	먹다	먹고 있었다 meokgo isseotda	먹고 있다 meokgo itda	먹고 있을 것이다 meokgo isseul geosida
Verbs describing a state and with their last vowel as 오 or 아	앉다	앉아 있었다 anja isseotda	앉아 있다 anja itda	앉아 있을 것이다 anja isseul geosida
Verbs describing a state and with their last vowel as 으, 이, 어 or 우	넣다	넣어 있었다 neoeo isseotda	넣어 있다 neoeo itda	넣어 있을 것이다 neoeo isseul geosida

TAKE NOTE

The present progressive is less commonly used in Korean than it is in English. Where we would say "He's swimming," Koreans are more likely to say "그는 수영해요 **Geuneun suyeonghaeyo**" rather than "그는 수영하고 있어요 **Geuneun suyeonghago isseoyo**," even though both are correct.

Remember that if the action still isn't finished at the time, you should use 고 있다 whereas if there is no ongoing action but rather a continued state, go with 어/아 있다.

EXAMPLE SENTENCES

아이들이 **서 있어요**. Aideuri **seo isseoyo**. The children are standing.

아이들이 일어서**고 있어요**. Aideuri ireoseo**go isseoyo**.
The children are (in the middle of) standing (up).

가영이 몸이 아파서 지금 누<u>워 있어요</u>.
Kayoungi momi apaseo jigeum nuwo isseoyo.
Kayoung's in pain, so she's lying down right now.

책상에서 꽃이 놓<u>여 있었어요</u>. Chaeksange kkochi noyeo isseosseoyo.
The flower was put on the desk.

민수가 책을 읽<u>고 있어요</u>. Minsuga chaegeul ilgo isseoyo.
Minsu is reading a book.

그 아이가 놀<u>고 있어요</u>. Geu aiga nolgo isseoyo. The child is playing.

		Speaking = Writing
~아/어/여 두다/놓다 a/eo/yeo duda/nota	"To ~ and keep the result"	★★★

어머니가 미트 로프를 만들<u>어 두었어요</u>.
Eomeoniga miteu ropeureul mandeureo dueosseoyo.
My mother made (and saved) a meatloaf.

어머니가 미트 로프를 만들<u>어 놓았어요</u>.
Eomeoniga miteu ropeureul mandeureo noasseoyo.
My mother made (and put aside) a meatloaf.

There are some things you just don't want to get rid of. Here's an expression you can use to talk about that meatloaf that's been in your fridge forever.

HOW IT'S FORMED

아/어/여 is a verb ending which usually implies that the result of ~ carries over somehow to the next word. 두다 is a verb which literally means to "put," "keep," "leave behind," "set down," various other similar connotations. 놓다 is a similar verb which means "to put."

책상에 꽃을 **두었어요**. Chaeksange kkocheul dueosseoyo.
Someone left a flower on the desk.

책상에 꽃을 **놓았어요**. Chaeksange kkocheul noasseoyo.
Someone put a flower on the desk.

HOW IT'S CONJUGATED

This expression doesn't go with adjectives or nouns; if you want to "stay beautiful" you would use an expression like 아름답게 지내다 Areumdapge jinaeda, and if you want to keep that aforementioned meatloaf, you need a verb to go along with it and stay with 두다 duda: 미트 로프를 만들어 두다 Miteu ropeureul mandeureo duda would work.

		Past	Present	Future
Action verbs with 아 or 오	잡다	잡아 두었다 jaba dueotda 잡아 놓았다 jaba noatda	잡아 두다 jaba duda 잡아 놓다 jaba nota	잡아 둘 것이다 jaba dul geosida 잡아 놓을 것이다 jaba noeul geosida
Action verbs with 어, 우, 으 or 이	먹다	먹어 두었다 meogeo dueotda 먹어 놓았다 meogeo noatda	먹어 두다 meogeo duda 먹어 놓다 meogeo nota	먹어 둘 것이다 meogeo dul geosida 먹어 놓을 것이다 meogeo noeul geosida
하다	하다	해 두었다 hae dueotda 해 놓았다 hae noatda	해 두다 hae duda 해 놓다 hae nota	해 둘 것이다 hae dul geosida 해 놓을 것이다 hae noeul geosida

TAKE NOTE

While 아/어 있다 and 고 있다 have some similarities to 아/어/여 두다/놓다, 두다 specifically implies that you are saving or keeping something, and 놓다 means you are putting it somewhere. 아/어 있다 and 고 있다 by themselves don't imply anything about what's going to happen after the sentence is finished.

아/어/여 놓다 and 아/어/여 두다 are normally interchangeable: use the one that better fits whatever you mean to say. 두다 is refers to "keeping" and 놓다 refers to putting somewhere.

두다 **duda** has many meanings beyond this expression; it's beyond the scope of this book to go into that in detail, but they're worth learning. For example, 두다 is the verb used to play board games like chess or 바둑 **baduk**: you can say 바둑을 두다 **badugeul duda** (to play 바둑) or 바둑 한 판 둘래요? **baduk han pan dullaeyo** (Would you like to play a game of 바둑?)

EXAMPLE SENTENCES

창문을 열**어 두세요**. Changmuneul yeoreo duseyo.
Please open the window (and keep it open).

창문을 열**어 놓으세요**. Changmuneul yeoreo noeuseyo.
Please open the window).

새로운 단어를 공책에 **써 두었어요**.
Saeroun daneoreul gongchaege sseo du-eosseoyo.
I wrote the new vocabulary words down in my notebook (and kept it).

새로운 단어를 공책에 **써 놓았어요**.
Saeroun daneoreul gongchaege sseo noasseoyo.
I wrote the new vocabulary words down in my notebook.

	Speaking = Writing
A(으)ㄴ 채(로) "B is done while in the state of A"	★★
(eu)n chae(ro) B	

늦을까 봐 양복을 입<u>은 채</u> 민수의 생일 파티에 갔어요.

Neujeulkka bwa yangbogeul ibeun chae Minsuui saengil patie gasseoyo.

I was worried I'd be late, so I went to Minsu's party while still wearing my suit.

채(로) is a good expression if you ever need to talk about people who are drunk, lazy, or both. It means to do one thing while in the state of A such as falling asleep with your clothes on, or the door unlocked, or the TV on.

HOW IT'S FORMED

The (으)ㄴ in this expression is the past tense marker; whatever A was happens before B, so the past tense marker must be used regardless of which tense your sentence is actually in. 채 by itself doesn't mean anything other than to remain in a certain state. 로 (through) is optional and adds a little emphasis to the fact that the situation was maintained.

HOW IT'S CONJUGATED

		All tenses
Action verbs ending in a vowel	하다	한 채(로) han chae(ro)
Action verbs ending in a consonant	먹다	먹은 채(로) meogeun chae(ro)

TAKE NOTE

A and B should always have the same subject.

가다 and 오다 are never used before (으)ㄴ 채로. You can use 아서 (see page 66) instead.

A고서는 B (see page 301) is similar to (으)ㄴ 채로, but 고서는 is used only in cases where being in the state of A is a necessary condition for doing B. 채로 has no such implications. So 고서는 could be replaced by 채로, but not always vice versa. And while the sentences below are interchangeable:

신발을 신<u>고서는</u> 방을 들어올 수 없어요.

Sinbareul singoseoneun bangeul deureool su eopsseoyo.

신발을 신<u>은 채</u> 방을 들어올 수 없어요.

Sinbareul sineun chae bangeul deureool su eopsseoyo.

A sentence like 창문을 연 채 피아노를 쳤어요 Changmuneul yeon chae pianoreul chyeosseoyo ("I played piano with the window open.") could not be made with 고서는 since your playing of the piano is possible whether or not the window is open.

아/어/여 놓다/두다 (covered on page 257) is often used before (으)ㄴ 채(로). You can think of 채(로) as an extension of these two expressions: 아/어/여 놓다/두다 means that something was done and the result was kept or put aside, while 채(로) keeps going with that thought and tells you what was done with that result.

창문을 열<u>어 **두었어요**</u>. Changmuneul yeoreo dueosseoyo.

창문을 열<u>어 **놓았어요**</u>. Changmuneul yeoreo noasseoyo.

Both mean "I left the window open."

창문을 **연 채** 피아노를 쳤어요.
Changmuneul yeon chae pianoreul chyeosseoyo.

창문을 **열어 둔 채** 피아노를 쳤어요.
Changmuneul yeoreo dun chae pianoreul chyeosseoyo.

창문을 **열어 둔 채로** 피아노를 쳤어요.
Changmuneul yeoreo dun chaero pianoreul chyeosseoyo.

창문을 **열어 놓은 채** 피아노를 쳤어요.
Changmuneul yeoreo noeun chae pianoreul chyeosseoyo.

창문을 **열어 놓은 채로** 피아노를 쳤어요.
Changmuneul yeoreo noeun chaero pianoreul chyeosseoyo.

All mean "I played piano with the window open": taking the open window that the first two sentences told you about and continuing on to tell you what was done while that window was open.

EXAMPLE SENTENCES

늦을까 봐 양복을 입**은 채** 민수의 생일 파티에 갔어요.
Neujeulkka bwa yangbogeul ibeun chae minsuui saengil patie gasseoyo.

늦을까 봐 양복을 입**은 채로** 민수의 생일 파티에 갔어요.
Neujeulkka bwa yangbogeul ibeun chaero minsuui saengil patie gasseoyo.

I was worried I'd be late, so I hurried to Minsu's party while still wearing my suit.

아침을 먹지 않은 **채** 병원에 와 주세요.
Achimeul meokji aneun chae byeongwone wa juseyo.

아침을 먹지 않은 **채로** 병원에 와 주세요.
Achimeul meokji aneun chaero byeongwone wa juseyo.

Please come to the hospital without eating breakfast.

Progression: Almost, But Not Quite...

> **Speaking = Writing**
> ~(으)ㄹ 뻔하다 (eu)r ppeonhada   "~ almost happened"   ★★★★

회의가 너무 오래 걸려서 파티에 늦을 **뻔했어요**.
Hoeuiga neomu orae geollyeoseo patie neujeul ppeonhaesseoyo.
The meeting took a long time, so I was almost late for the party.

This expression is perfect for people who like to exaggerate. It's frequently used in sentences such as "I almost died!" Of course, you can also use it for more mundane things like almost being late, almost missing your train, and so on.

HOW IT'S CONJUGATED

		Past
Action verbs ending in a vowel	하다	할 뻔했다 hal ppeonhaetda
Action verbs ending in a consonant	먹다	먹을 뻔했다 meogeul ppeonhaetda

TAKE NOTE

There is another 뻔하다 which means "to be clear." The one in this expression will always follow an action verb and (으)ㄹ; the other one will not.

(으)려던 참이다 **(eu)ryeodeon chamida** (see the next section) is also used to talk about things almost happening, but it's used only with things that you intended to do. (으)ㄹ 뻔하다 is normally used when talking about things that were accidental and can be used to talk about yourself or anyone else. It's normally used for bad things, but doesn't have to be; if you want to say 복권에 당첨될 뻔했어요 **Bokgwone dangcheomdoel ppeonhaesseoyo** (I almost won the lottery) or talk about similar blessings that you just barely missed out on, that's fine.

The difference between 뻔하다 and (으)ㄹ락 말락 하다 **(eu)rrak mallak hada** (see page 265) is that 뻔하다 means that something could have happened, but didn't. You could have died in that car accident, but were spared. (으)ㄹ락 말락 하다 is more like wavering between doing A and not doing A, but ultimately not doing it. Also, (으)ㄹ락 말락 is normally used only in sentences where what almost happened is a result of the subject's will.

그 사고에서 죽을 **뻔했어요**. Geu sagoeseo jugeul ppeonhaesseoyo.
I could have died in that accident. (Maybe nothing happened to you at all in the end, or maybe you were seriously hurt but didn't die.)

그 사고에서 죽<u>을락 말락</u> 했어요. Geu sagoeseo jugeullak mallak haesseoyo.
I was hovering on the verge of death after that accident. (You were seriously injured and close to death, but ultimately survived.)

(으)ㄹ 뻔하다 is quite often used with words like 거의 **geoui** (almost) or 아마 **ama** (maybe). It also likes to hang out with hypothetical sentences such as "If I had…" Some common examples are 았/었/였다면 **at/eot/yeotdamyeon** (see page 289) and 았/었/였더 라면 **at/eot/yeotdeoramyeon** (see page 286).

EXAMPLE SENTENCES

눈 때문에 길이 참 미끄러워서 넘어**질 뻔했어요**.
Nun ttaemune giri cham mikkeureowoseo neomeojil ppeonhaesseoyo.
Because of the snow, the road is very slippery, so I almost fell.

오늘 아침에 지하철에서 사고가 났어요. 오늘 지하철을 탔으면 죽**을 뻔했어요**.
Oneul achime jihacheoreseo sagoga nasseoyo. Oneul jihacheoreul tasseumyeon jugeul ppeonhaesseoyo.
This morning, there was an accident on the subway. If I'd taken the subway today I could have died.

		Speaking > Writing
~(으)려던 참이다 (eu)ryeodeon chamida	"I was just about to ~"	★★★

현준: 엄마, 학교에 가**려던 참**이었어요.
Hyeonjun: Eomma, hakgyo garyeodeon chamieosseoyo.
Hyeonjun: Mom, I was just about to go to school.

Do you have a worried mother, an overbearing boss, or a nagging significant other? If so, you should learn this expression. It means you were just about to do something. Quite often it's said with a bit of an injured tone because you were about to go do the very thing someone just accused you of not doing.

HOW IT'S FORMED

(으)려 comes from (으)려고 하다 **(eu)ryeogo hada**, which is on page 215 and is used to talk about a plan. 던 is a past-tense marker, which in this case indicates that you had already made that plan. 참 has a few meanings; in this expression it means "on the point of" (I don't like this) and is followed by 이다, which means "you were."

HOW IT'S CONJUGATED

		Past	Present
Action verbs ending in a vowel	하다	하려던 참이었다 haryeodeon chamieotda	하려던 참이었다 하려던 참이다 haryeodeon chamida
Action verbs ending in a consonant	먹다	먹으려던 참이었다 meogeuryeodeon chamieotda	먹으려던 참이었다 먹으려던 참이다 meogeuryeodeon chamida

TAKE NOTE

This expression is used only in the first person and can't be used on its own to suggest or to command someone to do something. You can, however, say that you were about to do something and then use that as the basis for suggesting something to another person, perhaps by ending your A clause with ㄴ데 (A려던 참인데 **ryeodeon chaminde** B). This is often done when, for example, someone drops by your house just as you were about to eat and you invite them to join you.

If you use 참이었다 you are implying you had been planning the action for some time, while 참이다 means you were about to do it right that very second.

Sentences with (으)려던 참이다 very often use 안 그래도 **an geuraedo** or 그렇지 않아도 **geureochi anado** (even if you hadn't said that) or 마침 **machim** (as in "I was just about to").

Koreans use 참이다 and 참이었다 interchangeably, so just pick whichever one you like better for your sentence.

EXAMPLE SENTENCES

엄마: 현준아, 늦을 거야! 왜 학교에 아직 안 갔어?
Eomma: Hyeonjuna, neujeul geoya! Wae hakgyoe ajik an gasseo?

현준: 엄마, 학교에 가**려던 참이었어요**.
Hyeonjun: Eomma, hakgyoe garyeodeon chamieosseoyo.

엄마: 현준아, 늦을 거야! 왜 학교에 아직 안 갔어?
Eomma: hyeonjuna, neujeul geoya! Wae hakgyoe ajik an gasseo?

현준: 엄마, 학교에 가**려던 참이에요**.
Hyeonjun: Eomma, hakgyoe garyeodeon chamieyo.

Mom: Hyeonjun, you're going to be late! Why haven't you gone to school yet?
Hyeonjun: Mom, I was just about to go to school.

(Children in Korea often, though not by any means always, use 존댓말 when talking to their parents.)

A: 식사를 준비 하겠어요? Ga: Siksareul junbi hagesseoyo?
   Are you going to get dinner ready?

B: 안 그래도 준비하**려던 참이에요**.
   Na: An geuraedo junbiharyeodeon chamieyo.

   안 그래도 준비하**려던 참이었어요**.
   Na: An geuraedo junbiharyeodeon chamieosseoyo

   Even if you hadn't said that, I was just about to do it.

식사를 먹**으려던 참인**데 같이 먹을래요?
Siksareul meogeuryeodeon chaminde gachi meogeullaeyo?

식사를 먹**으려던 참이었는**데 같이 먹을래요?
Siksareul meogeuryeodeon chamieonneunde gachi meogeullaeyo?

I was just about to eat; would you like to join me?

| ~(으)ㄹ 지경이다 (eu)r jigyeongida | "On the verge of ~" | Speaking > Writing ★ |

짜증이 나서 죽을 **지경**이에요. Jjajeungi naseo jugeul jigyeongieyo.
I'm so annoyed! (so annoyed I could die)

Here's another expression that you can use to exaggerate. This one means "to be on the verge of ~."

HOW IT'S FORMED

(으)ㄹ is a future tense marker and 지경 is a noun which literally means "boundary."

HOW IT'S CONJUGATED

		Present
Action verbs ending in a vowel	하다	할 지경이다 hal jigyeongida
Action verbs ending in a consonant	먹다	먹을 지경이다 meogeul jigyeongida

TAKE NOTE

It's also possible to form a sentence using one of the other tense markers ([으]ㄴ/는) before 지경. In this case you are talking about a situation that actually happened or is happening, whereas (으)ㄹ 지경이다 is hypothetical.

> 그는 배고파서 죽은 **지경**이에요. Geuneun baegopaseo jugeun jigyeongieyo.
> He's starving to death. (He's so hungry he's dying.)

> 그는 배고파서 죽을 **지경**이에요. Geuneun baegopaseo jugeul jigyeongieyo.
> He's so hungry he's on the verge of dying.

(으)ㄹ 지경이다 and 아/어/여서 죽겠다 (see page 336) are interchangeable, but the latter is used quite often while the former is used only rarely.

지경 is used in many idiomatic expressions, of which the most common is 죽을 지경이다 (to be on the verge of dying). This can be used whether you actually are on the verge of dying or whether you're just milking the situation for sympathy.

지경이다 isn't used in the past tense.

EXAMPLE SENTENCES

오늘 너무 더워서 숨이 막힐 **지경**이에요.
Oneul neomu deowoseo sumi makil jigyeongieyo.
Today it's so hot I can't breathe. (It is so hot I'm on the verge of losing my breath – i.e., I almost cannot breathe).

그녀가 남자친구 때문에 **울 지경**이어서 갑자기 방에서 나갔어요.
Geunyeoga namjachingu ttaemune ul jigyeongieoseo gapjagi bangeseo
nagasseoyo.
Because of her boyfriend, she suddenly ran out of the room on the verge of tears.

	Speaking > Writing
A(으)ㄹ락 (eu)l-lak B(으)ㄹ락 하다 (eu)l-lak hada "~ almost happened"	★

지금 비가 **올락 말락 해요**. Jigeum biga ollak mallak haeyo.
Right now it's almost raining.

This is for people who are indecisive. It means that either something was wavering between A and B (A[으]ㄹ락 B[으]ㄹ락 하다) or was wavering between doing A or not doing
A (A[으]ㄹ락 말락 하다). It's also good for those days when the weather just can't seem to
make up its mind.

HOW IT'S FORMED

(으)ㄹ락—(으)ㄹ락 is the basis of the expression. It's like a grammatical seesaw, with the
sentence teetering between the verb before the first (으)ㄹ락 and the verb before the second
(으)ㄹ락. These verbs will be either opposites (A and B) or A and 말다 (which just means
the opposite of whatever was before it). Then 하다 is added at the end to tie it all together.

HOW IT'S CONJUGATED

		Past	Present
Action verbs ending in a vowel	하다	할락 말락 했다 hallak mallak haetda	할락 말락 하다 hallak mallak hada
Action verbs ending in a consonant	먹다	먹을락 말락 했다 meogeullak mallak haetda	먹을락 말락 하다 meogeullak mallak hada
Action verbs ending in ㄹ	들다	들락 말락 했다 deullak mallak haetda	들락 말락 하다 deullak mallak hada

TAKE NOTE

The difference between this expression and A등 B등 하다 **A dung B dung hada** is that the
ㄹ락s mean that something almost happened, but didn't. The 등s mean something almost
didn't happen, but did.

비가 **올락 말락 했어요**. Biga ollak mallak haesseoyo. It almost rained, but didn't.

비가 **오는 등 마는 등 했어요**. Biga oneun dung maneun dung haesseoyo.
It rained just a little.

If the situation that almost happened is accidental, it's far more common to say (으)ㄹ 뻔했다 (eu)l ppeonhaetda (see page 261). (으)ㄹ락 말락 is normally used in situations where what almost happened is a result of the subject's will. So the first example sentence is a "good" example of this grammar point, and the second, while technically correct, isn't quite natural.

EXAMPLE SENTENCES

갈락 말락 했지만 마지막 순간에 가영이 오지 않는다고 해서 저도 안 갔어요.
Gallak mallak haetjiman majimak sungane Kayoungi oji anneundago haeseo jeodo an gasseoyo.
I almost went, but at the last second Kayoung said she wasn't going, so I didn't go either.

그 사고에서 저는 **죽을락 말락 했어요**.
Geu sagoeseo jeoneun jugeullak mallak haesseoyo.
I almost died in that accident.

In the sentence above, the grammar is correct, but it's more natural to say 죽을 뻔했어요. Jugeul ppeon haesseoyo.

	Speaking > Writing
A는/(으)ㄹ 둥 neun/(eu)l dung B는/ (으)ㄹ 둥 하다 neun/(eu)l dung hada "Just barely A"	★

늦어서 식사를 먹는 둥 마는 둥 하고 나갔어요.
Neujeoseo siksareul meokneun dung maneun dung hago nagasseoyo.
I was late, so I barely ate and immediately left the house.

This can be used in two ways. One is when something almost, but didn't quite happen such as when you get to work and are hurried off to a meeting when you've only just turned on your computer, or when there are just a few flakes of snow coming down instead of steady snow. The other way is when someone is making poor excuses.

HOW IT'S FORMED

는 and (으)ㄹ are present and future tense markers. (으)ㄴ isn't used with this expression. 둥 doesn't really mean anything by itself.

HOW IT'S CONJUGATED

The first meaning (just barely A) works with action verbs. In this case A is what was just barely done and B is either 말다 or the opposite of A.

The second meaning (excuses) is used with descriptive or active verbs. Add (ㄴ/는)다는 둥 after each of A and B, which are two excuses that the person is making.

		Past	Present	Future
Action verbs ending in a vowel	하다	하는 둥 haneun dung (first meaning) 한다는 둥 handaneun dung (second meaning)	하는 둥 (first meaning) 한다는 둥 (second meaning)	할 둥 hal dung (first meaning) 한다는 둥 (second meaning)
Action verbs ending in a consonant	먹다	먹는 둥 meokneun dung (first meaning) 먹는다는 둥 meokneundaneun dung (second meaning)	먹는 둥 (first meaning) 먹는다는 둥 (second meaning)	먹을 둥 meogeul dung (first meaning) 먹는다는 둥 (second meaning)
Descriptive verbs (adjectives) ending in a vowel	예쁘다	예쁜 둥 yeppeun dung	예쁜 둥	예쁜 둥
Descriptive verbs (adjectives) ending in a consonant	작다	작은 둥 jageun dung	작은 둥	작은 둥

TAKE NOTE

The structure of this expression is rather similar to A(으)ㄹ락 B(으)ㄹ락 하다 (see page 265). The difference between the two is that the ㄹ락s mean something almost happened, but didn't. The 둥s mean something almost didn't happen, but did.

비가 **올락 말락 했어요**. Biga ollak mallak haesseoyo.
It almost rained, but didn't.

비가 **오는 둥 마는 둥 했어요**.
Biga oneun dung maneun dung haesseoyo.
It rained just a little.

Also, 둥 is normally used in sentences with negative connotations.
Don't get 둥 confused with 등; 등 means "etc." and is covered on page 48.
And definitely don't get 둥 confused with 똥.

EXAMPLE SENTENCES

■ First meaning (just barely A):

아이들이 제 말을 **듣는 둥 마는 둥 했어요**.
Aideuri je mareul deunneun dung maneun dung haesseoyo.
The children barely listened to what I was saying.

내 개가 아파요. 지금 **죽을 둥 말 둥** 해요.
Nae gaega apayo. Jigeum jugeul dung mal dung haeyo.
My dog is sick. He is about to die.

- Second meaning (making excuses):

그는 바쁘**다는 둥** 시간이 없**다는 둥** 핑계를 대면서 일을 거의 안 해요.
Geuneun bappeudaneun dung sigani eopdaneun dung pinggyereul daemyeonseo ireul geoui an haeyo.
He's always saying he's busy or doesn't have time, and so he hardly works.

Progression: Putting Things in Temporal Order

Focus: 다가 daga

다가 is the basis for many very commonly used expressions. They can be somewhat tricky to use and you can accidentally change the meaning of your sentences quite a bit with just a few minor mistakes, so you need to handle them with some care.

When you see 다가 in an expression, it essentially means "and then." All the expressions with 다가 have to do in some way with progression: A happens and then B happens. Of course, the nuances vary depending on which particular 다가 expression you use. 다가 all by itself means that A was interrupted by B; more ways of using it are shown in the chart.

Expression	Page	Meaning	Example
A다가 daga B	269	"A is interrupted by B"	학교에 가**다가** 교통 사고가 나서 늦었어요. Hakgyoe gadaga gyotong sagoga naseo neujeosseoyo. As I was going to school, there was a traffic accident, so I was late.
A아/어/여다가 a/eo/yeodaga B	270	"A is done, and then B is done on the basis of A"	늦을까 봐 선물을 빨리 찾**아다가** 파티에 갔어요. Neujeulkka bwa seonmureul ppalli chajadaga patie gasseoyo. I was afraid I'd be late, so I quickly bought a present and went to the party.
A았/었/였다가 at/eot/yeotdaga B	271	"A is finished and then B is done"	회의에 도착했**다가** 늦어서 죄송하다고 했어요. Hoeuie dochakaetdaga neujeoseo joesonghadago haesseoyo. After I got to the meeting, I apologized for being late.
A려다가 ryeodaga B	217	"I planned to A, but then B happened"	등산을 하려**다가** 비가 와서 집에 있었어요. Deungsaneul haryeodaga biga waseo jibe isseosseoyo. I planned to go hiking, but then it rained, so I stayed home.
A(으)ㄴ/는 데다(가) (eu)n/neun deda(ga) B	53	"B is added to A"	민수가 늦은 **데다가** 음식도 가지고 오지 않았어요. Minsuga neujeun dedaga eumsikdo gajigo oji anasseoyo. Minsu was late. He also didn't bring any food.
A에다(가) eda(ga) B	53	"B is added to A"	열**에다가** 스물을 더하면 서른이에요. Yeoredaga seumureul deohamyeon seoreunieyo. Ten plus twenty is thirty.
A다가는 daganeun B	210	"Unfortunately, if you do A, B might happen"	이렇게 천천히 준비하**다가는** 늦을 거예요. Ireoke cheoncheonhi junbihadaganeun neujeul geoyeyo. If you take your time getting ready, you'll be late.

Expression	Page	Meaning	Example
A다가도 dagado B	279	"A is (suddenly/dramatically) interrupted by B"	그녀는는 급하게 서두르**다가도** 항상 정신이 산만해져서 늦어요. Geunyeoneun geupage seodureudagado hangsang jeongsini sanmanhaejyeoseo neujeoyo. Even though she hurries, she always gets distracted and ends up being late.
A다(가) 보니 (까) da(ga) boni (kka) B	353	"After doing A for a long time, I noticed B"	친구 하고 길게 이야기를 하**다가 보니까** 수업에 늦게 됐어요. Chingu hago gilge iyagireul hadaga bonikka sueobe neutge dwaesseoyo. I was talking with my friend for a long time and suddenly noticed I was late for class.
A다(가) 보면 da(ga) bomyeon B	209	"If you keep on doing A, B will happen"	계속 이야기 하**다 보면** 늦을 거예요. Gyesok iyagi hada bomyeon neujeul geoyeyo. If you keep talking, you'll be late.
~다가 말다가 하다 daga maldaga hada	360	"Doing ~ on and off"	그렇게 준비를 하**다가 말다가** 하면 늦을 거예요. Geureoke junbireul hadaga maldaga hamyeon neujeul geoyeyo. If you keep on getting ready and then stopping like that, you'll be late.

			Speaking = Writing
A다가 daga B	"A is interrupted by B"		★★★★

학교에 가**다가** 교통 사고가 나서 늦었어요.
Hakgyoe gadaga gyotong sagoga naseo neujeosseoyo.
As I was going to school, there was a traffic accident, so I was late.

This is the expression you use when you were in the middle of something which was subsequently interrupted by something else. It's a good expression for those with children or younger siblings.

HOW IT'S CONJUGATED

Be careful not to put the verb in clause A into the past tense (for example, 했다가 haetdaga) because that changes the meaning (see page 271).

		All tenses
Action verbs ending in a vowel	하다	하다가 hadaga
Action verbs ending in a consonant	먹다	먹다가 meokdaga

TAKE NOTE

Since this expression is used in talking about actions, it is normally used only with action verbs. The subjects of clause A and clause B should be the same.

EXAMPLE SENTENCES

공부하**다가** 갑자기 잤어요. Gongbuhadaga gapjagi jasseoyo.
While studying, I suddenly fell asleep.

지하철을 타**다가** 거지에게 돈을 주었어요.
Jihacheoreul tadaga geojiege doneul jueosseoyo.
While taking the subway, I gave money to a beggar.

		Speaking > Writing
A아/어/여다(가) a/eo/yeoda(ga) B	"A is done, and then B is done on the basis of A"	★ ★ ★ ★

늦을까 봐 선물을 빨리 찾**아다가** 파티에 갔어요.
Neujeulkka bwa seonmureul ppalli chajadaga patie gasseoyo.
I was afraid I'd be late, so I quickly bought a present and went to the party.

Yeah, I had a hard time expressing this succinctly. Basically, in contrast to plain old 다가 which implies that A was interrupted, 아/어/여다가 means that A was done and the result was carried over and used in B. Think of making a snack and bringing it to a party. That's the situation where you would need 아/어/여다가.

HOW IT'S FORMED

Our old friends 아/어/여 are back to play with our new friend 다가. You may have noticed that when a verb takes 아/어/여 along with it, it usually means that verb is there in the sentence to stay: it will stick around and affect clause B. In other words, it means that whatever happened in clause A has a lasting effect. Think of all the helping verbs on page 31 or 아/어 있다. The 가 in 다가 is optional and is often omitted in longer 다가-type expressions: use it depending on which you think sounds better.

HOW IT'S CONJUGATED

		All tenses
Action verbs with 아/오	찾다	찾아다가 chajadaga
Action verbs with 어/우/으/이	먹다	먹다가 meokdaga
하다	하다	하다가 hadaga

TAKE NOTE

Since this expression is used in talking about actions, it is normally used only with action verbs. The subjects of clause A and clause B should be the same.

EXAMPLE SENTENCES

저 개를 잡**아다가** 보신탕을 만드세요.
Jeo gaereul jab**adaga** bosintangeul mandeuseyo.
Please catch the dog, and make dog meat stew out of it.

돈을 가져**와다가** 김밥을 샀어요. Doneul gajyeo**wadaga** kimbapeul sasseoyo.
I brought some money and bought kimbap.

김밥을 사**다가** 먹었어요. Kimbapeul sa**daga** meogeosseoyo.
I bought kimbap and ate it.

(In this case the expression with 아다가 looks the same as the expression with just 다가, so check the context carefully to determine which one is being used: 다가 by itself wouldn't make sense in this expression unless you started eating in the middle of buying kimbap, leaving your purchase unfinished).

A았/었/였다(가) at/eot/yeotda(ga) B	"A is finished and then B is done"	Speaking = Writing ★★★

회의에 도착**했다가** 늦어서 죄송하다고 했어요.
Hoeuie dochak**aetdaga** neujeoseo joesonghadago haesseoyo.
After I got to the meeting, I apologized for being late.

In order to use this expression, A must be completely finished. With 다가 by itself, A is interrupted, but 았/었/였이다가 is used only when two different actions follow each other without overlapping. If that's not entirely clear, a few examples (see below) should help.

HOW IT'S FORMED

The past tense marker 았/었/였 tells you A is finished and then 다가 comes along to arrange everything neatly and tells you when B, the next thing, happened. The 가 part of 다가 is optional.

HOW IT'S CONJUGATED

Because this expression is used only when A is completely finished, it is always in the past tense; if you're trying to write 하다가 or 해다가, you're using a different grammatical point (see pages 269 and 270).

		All tenses
Action verbs with 아/오	찾다	찾았다가 chajatdaga
Action verbs with 어/우/으/이	먹다	먹었다가 meogeotdaga
Action verbs ending in a vowel	하다	했다가 haetdaga

TAKE NOTE

Since this expression is used in talking about actions, it is normally used only with action verbs. The subjects of clause A and clause B should be the same. Although A is in the past tense form, you can still use the expression when talking about the present or future: just make sure your B verb uses the appropriate tense. A will have been finished by the time B happens, by definition.

EXAMPLE SENTENCES

Here I've compared the same sentences written with 다가 and with 았/었이다가 so that you can see the difference in meaning.

파티에 가**다가** 친구에게 전화했어요. **Patie gadaga chinguege jeonhwahaesseoyo.**
While going to the party, I (stopped and) called my friend.

파티에 갔**다가** 친구에게 전화했어요. **Patie gatdaga chinguege jeonhwahaesseoyo.**
After I went to the party, I called my friend.

TV를 보**다가** 잤어요. **Tibireul bodaga jasseoyo.**
While I was watching TV, I fell asleep.

TV를 **봤다가** 어머니한테 혼났어요. **Tibireul bwatdaga eomeonihante honnasseoyo.**
I watched TV and then my mother scolded me.

		Speaking = Writing
A고 나서 go naseo B	"A and then B"	★★★

저녁을 먹**고 나서** 담배를 피웠어요.
Jeonyeogeul meokgo naseo dambaereul piwosseoyo.
I ate dinner and then had a cigarette.

This basically just means "and then." It's a subset of 고서, but you can use 고 나서 only when the action in the first sentence is completely finished. All these sentences could also be made with 고서.

HOW IT'S FORMED

고 plus 나다 (to happen) plus 아/어/여서 (which means "then" here).

HOW IT'S CONJUGATED

		All tenses
Action verbs ending in a vowel	하다	하고 나서 hago naseo
Action verbs ending in a consonant	먹다	먹고 나서 meokgo naseo

TAKE NOTE

고 나서 can be used only with action verbs and only when the subjects of both clause A and clause B are the same.

EXAMPLE SENTENCES

영화를 보**고 나서** 집에 갔어요. Yeonghwareul bo**go naseo** jibe gasseoyo.
I watched a movie and then went home.

공부를 하**고 나서** 잤어요. Gongbureul ha**go naseo** jasseoyo.
I studied and then went to sleep.

A자마자 jamaja B	"B right after A"	★★★
A는 대로 neun daero B	"B right after A"	★★★
A자 ja B	"B right after A"	★★
A기(가) 무섭게 gi(ga) museopge B	"B right after A"	★

늦을까 봐 옷을 갈아입**자마자** 친구 집에 갔어요.
Neujeulkka bwa oseul garaip**jamaja** chingu jibe gasseoyo.

늦을까 봐 옷을 갈아입**는 대로** 친구 집에 갔어요.
Neujeulkka bwa oseul garaim**neun daero** chingu jibe gasseoyo.

I was afraid I'd be late, so I changed my clothes and then immediately went to my friend's house.

옷을 입**자** 전화가 왔어요. Oseul ip**ja** jeonhwaga wasseoyo.
As soon as I put on my clothes, the phone rang.

When life is happening quickly, these four expressions are here to help. They all mean that B happened right after A. However, each one has its own peculiarities. This section will compare the four expressions above and explain when you should or shouldn't use each one.

HOW IT'S FORMED

기 turns verbs into nouns; 무섭게 **museopge** is the well-known 무섭다 **museopda** (to be scary) but rather is unique to this expression. You can add the subject marker 가 after the verb with 기.

There's nothing special to note here about 자마자, 는 대로, or 자.

HOW IT'S CONJUGATED

		Past	Present	Future
Action verbs ending in a vowel	하다	하자마자 하자 하기(가) 무섭게	하자마자 hajamaja 하는 대로 haneun daero 하자 haja 하기(가) 무섭게 hagi(ga) museopge	하자마자 하는 대로 하기(가) 무섭게
Action verbs ending in a consonant	먹다	먹자마자 먹자 먹기(가) 무섭게	먹자마자 meokjamaja 먹는 대로 meokneun daero 먹자 meokja 먹기(가) 무섭게 meokgi(ga) museopge	먹자마자 먹는 대로 먹기(가) 무섭게

TAKE NOTE

자마자 can't be used when A is negative (a sentence with 안, 못, 않, etc.).

A는 대로 B, A기 무섭게 B, A자마자 B and A자 B can all be used interchangeably in some cases, but not in others. Let's compare.

는 대로 can normally be used interchangeably with 자마자 unless the sentence is in the past tense. 는 대로 can't be used in the past tense. 는 대로 can be used interchangeably with 자 in the present tense only. 는 대로 can't be used in the past tense and 자 can't be used in the future tense, so the two can only cross paths in the present. 는 대로 can always be changed to 기 무섭게.

기 무섭게 is completely interchangeable with all the other expressions here, but is far less common; in fact, I'm not sure I've ever heard or seen it used in the real Korean world. Nonetheless, if you want to impress people, are cramming for the TOPIK test, or are a completionist, it can be good to know.

자 by itself can be used interchangeably with 자마자 in statements, but not questions, commands, or imperatives. It also can't be used in the future tense. It can imply more time between A and B than 자마자 does.

There are several other ways of saying one thing happened after another: 고서 (see page 280), 고 나서 (see page 272), and some variations of 다가 (see page 268) – but none of them necessarily mean "immediately after." If it's important that your readers/listeners understand that one thing happened immediately after the other, you should use 자마자, 자, 는 대로, or 기 무섭게.

There is another expression, (으)ㄴ/는 대로, which looks exactly the same as the 는 대로 here, but is actually a variation of 는 대로 (see page 320). There's no really obvious way to tell them apart, so you'll mainly have to rely on context – the other one means "according to," so it will mainly appear in sentences such as "선생님 말하는 대로 **Seonsaengnim malhaneun daero**" ("According to what the teacher said"). It also sometimes takes (으)ㄴ instead of 는 or directly follows nouns such as 마음 **maeum**.

There are two more 자 expressions. One is the 반말 propositive 하자! **haja** ("Let's do it!") while the other, 자고 하다 **jago hada**, is the indirect speech propositive. The first will always appear at the end of a sentence while the 자 we're discussing here never will. The second will normally be followed by something else; 자고 **jago**, 자면 **jamyeon**, or 자는데 **janeunde** are examples. The 자 in this section, however, always likes to be the last syllable of whatever it's attached to, so it will never be followed by 고, 면, or anything else except the next clause in the sentence.

EXAMPLE SENTENCES

늦을까 봐 옷을 갈아입**자마자** 친구 집에 갔어요.
Neujeulkka bwa oseul garaipjamaja chingu jibe gasseoyo.
I was afraid I'd be late, so I changed my clothes and then immediately went to my friend's house.

(This sentence can also be written with 기 무섭게, but not 는 대로.)
늦을까 봐 옷을 갈아입**기 무섭게** 친구 집에 갔어요.
Neujeulkka bwa oseul garaipgi museopge chingu jibe gasseoyo.
늦을까 봐 옷을 갈아입**자** 친구 집에 갔어요.
Neujeulkka bwa oseul garaipja chingu jibe gasseoyo.

집에 돌아오**자마자** 저에게 전화해 주세요.
Jibe doraojamaja jeoege jeonhwahae juseyo.
Please call me as soon as you get home.

(This sentence can be written with 는 대로 and 기 무섭게, but not 자.)
집에 돌아오**는 대로** 저에게 전화해 주세요.
Jibe doraoneun daero jeoege jeonhwahae juseyo.
집에 돌아오**기 무섭게** 저에게 전화해 주세요.
Jibe doraogi museopge jeoege jeonhwahae juseyo.

저녁을 먹**자마자** 갈 거예요. Jeonyeogeul meokjamaja gal geoyeyo.
I'll come as soon as I eat dinner.

(This sentence can be written with 기 무섭게 and 는 대로, but not 자.)
저녁을 먹**는 대로** 갈 거예요. Jeonyeogeul meokneun daero gal geoyeyo.
저녁을 먹**기 무섭게** 갈 거예요. Jeonyeogeul meokgi museopge gal geoyeyo.

매일 일을 끝내**는 대로** 저녁을 먹어요.
Maeil ireul kkeunnaeneun daero jeonyeogeul meogeoyo.
I eat dinner as soon as I finish work every day.

(This sentence works with 자, 자마자 and 기 무섭게)
매일 일을 끝내**자** 저녁을 먹어요.
Maeil ireul kkeunnaeja jeonyeogeul meogeoyo.
매일 일을 끝내**자마자** 저녁을 먹어요.
Maeil ireul kkeunnaejamaja jeonyeogeul meogeoyo.
매일 일을 끝내**기 무섭게** 저녁을 먹어요.
Maeil ireul kkeunnaegi museopge jeonyeogeul meogeoyo.

		Speaking = Writing
A(으)ㄴ 지 (eu)n ji B	"Since A, B"	★★★
A(으)ㄴ 지 (eu)n ji B이/가 넘다/되다/지나다 i/ga neomda/doeda/jinada	"B has passed since A"	★
A(으)ㄴ 지 (eu)n ji B 만에 mane C	"C happened B after A"	★

집에서 출발<u>한 지</u> 2 시간 <u>**만에**</u> 친구 집에 도착했어요.
Jibeseo chulbalhan ji dusigan mane chingu jibe dochakaesseoyo.
Two hours after I left my house, I arrived at my friend's house.

한국에 <u>**온 지**</u> 3년이 <u>**지났어요**</u>. Hanguge on ji samnyeoni jinasseoyo.
It's been three years (three years have passed) since I came to Korea.

(으)ㄴ 지 forms the basis for two more expressions which we'll cover here: A(으)ㄴ 지 B이/가 넘다/되다/지나다, and A(으)ㄴ 지 B 만에 C. They're both ways to talk about how much time has passed since A.

HOW IT'S FORMED

(으)ㄴ 지 in this expression means "since."

There are many 만s in Korean, and the one in A(으)ㄴ 지 B 만에 is the one that means "full": in this case, "fully." So "fully B (a period of time) since A, C happened..."

넘다 means "to go over," 되다 means "to become," and 지나다 means "to pass"; in this case they're all interchangeable and mean that B (again, a period of time) has passed since A.

HOW IT'S CONJUGATED

In both expressions, B is a period of time, like 5년 **onyeon**, 두 달 **du dal**, 일주일 **iljuil**. It can also be a non-specific expression of time: 얼마 **eolma** or 오래 **orae**, for example. When making a sentence with 만에, you can leave out A if you don't need it, so the expression then becomes B만에 C B **mane** C: "After B, C happened."

C is an action that took place B (some period of time) since A.

		All tenses
Action verbs ending in a vowel	하다	한 지 han ji
Action verbs ending in a consonant	먹다	먹은 지 meogeun ji

TAKE NOTE

Watch out for all the other grammar points that use 지! Koreans seem to be quite fond of that syllable. Most of the other expressions with 지 use it before a negative: 지 못하다 ji motada, 지 않다 ji anta, and so on. There is also (으)ㄴ 지 알다/모르다 (eu)n ji alda/moreuda (see page 160) in which you will ever see only 지 followed by some conjugation of 알다 or 모르다. If you see 지 and then an expression of time, it's the (으)ㄴ 지 that means "since."

만 is another syllable that you'll see all over the place in different contexts. The 만 in this expression is always followed by 에. Any 만 that's not followed by 에 is another 만.

You can use (으)ㄴ 지 without 만에 or 넘다/되다/지나다; these are just two easy ways to talk about how much time has passed.

EXAMPLE SENTENCES

A: 집에서 출발**한 지** 얼마나 **됐어요**?
Ga: Jibeseo chulbalhan ji eolmana dwaesseoyo?
How long has it been since you left your house?

B: 집에서 출발**한 지** 벌써 2 시간이 **넘었어요**. 늦을 것 같아요.
Na: Jibeseo chulbalhan ji beolsseo dusigani neomeosseoyo. Neujeul geot gatayo.
I left my house two hours ago (two hours have passed since I left my house). It seems like I'll be late.

한국에 **온 지** 3년이 **됐어요**. Hanguge on ji samnyeoni dwaesseoyo
한국에 **온 지** 3년이 **넘었어요**. Hanguge on ji samnyeoni neomeosseoyo.
한국에 **온 지** 3년이 **지났어요**. Hanguge on ji samnyeoni jinasseoyo.
It's been three years (three years have passed) since I came to Korea.

한국에 **온 지** 3 년 **만에** 다시 고향에 돌아갔어요.
Hanguge on ji samnyeon mane dasi gohyange doragasseoyo.
Three years after I came to Korea, I went back to my home.

3년 **만에** 한국에 왔어요. Samnyeon mane hanguge wasseoyo.
I came to Korea three years ago.

한국에 **온 지** 1주일 **만에** 한글을 배웠어요.
Hanguge on ji iljuil mane hangeureul baewosseoyo.
I learned the Korean alphabet within a week of coming to Korea.

약을 먹**은 지** 세 시간이 **되었**는데 아직 머리가 아파요.
Yageul meogeun ji se sigani doeeonneunde ajik meoriga apayo.
It has been three hours since I took the medicine, and I still have a headache.

| A전에 jeone, 후에 hue, 뒤에 dwie B | "B (after the end of, before, after) A" | Speaking = Writing ★★★ |

수업 **전에** 저녁을 먹었어요. Sueop jeone jeonyeogeul meogeosseoyo.
I ate dinner before class.

수업 **후에** 저녁을 먹었어요. Sueop hue jeonyeogeul meogeosseoyo.
I ate dinner after class.

수업 **뒤에** 저녁을 먹었어요. sueop dwie jeonyeogeul meogeosseoyo.
I ate dinner after class.

The expressions above have to do with time and putting B and A in their temporal places. Let's look at each one:

A 전에 **A jeone:** before A
A 후에 **A hue:** after A
A 뒤에 **A dwie:** after A

HOW THEY'RE MADE

전, 뒤 and 후 are all changed into prepositions by the addition of 에.

HOW IT'S CONJUGATED

With all these expressions, A must include a measure of time—two years, five months, 얼마, 오래, or something that takes time or occurs at a point in time to which you are referring: 수업 **Sueop,** 결혼식 **gyeolhonsik,** 입학 **ipak,** etc. You can use it after an action verb if you conjugate the verb using 기 (for 전에) or (으)ㄴ (for 후에 and 뒤에).

		All tenses
Action verbs ending in a vowel	하다	하기 전에 hagi jeone 한 후에 han hue 한 뒤에 han dwie
Action verbs ending in a consonant	먹다	먹기 전에 meokgi jeone 먹은 후에 meogeun hue 먹은 뒤에 meogeun dwie
Nouns ending in a vowel	사고	사고 전에 sago jeone 사고 후에 sago hue 사고 뒤에 sago dwie
Nouns ending in a consonant	수업	수업 전에 Sueop jeone 수업 후에 sueop hue 수업 뒤에 sueop dwie

TAKE NOTE

All the above expressions have a variety of uses other than the one in question here: consult a dictionary or vocabulary guide for more information. Most commonly, all are used to put actions or events in temporal order and tell what happened before, after, or at the end of the sequence of events.

EXAMPLE SENTENCES

5년 **전에** 대학교를 졸업했어요. Onyeon jeone daehakgyoreul joreopaesseoyo.
Five years before, I graduated from college.

5년 **후에** 대학교를 졸업하겠어요. Onyeon hue daehakgyoreul joreopagesseoyo.
I will graduate from college after five years.

5년 **뒤에** 대학교를 졸업하겠어요. Onyeon dwie daehakgyoreul joreopagesseoyo.
I will graduate from college after five years.

30분 **전에** 시험이 끝났어요. Samsipbun jeone siheomi kkeunnasseoyo.
The test was over 30 minutes ago.

30분 **후에** 시험이 끝날 거예요. Samsipbun hue siheomi kkeunnal geoyeyo.
After 30 minutes, the test will be over.

30분 **뒤에** 시험이 끝날 거예요. Samsipbun dwie siheomi kkeunnal geoyeyo.
After 30 minutes, the test will be over.

아침 먹기 **전에** 샤워를 했어요. Achim meokgi jeone syaworeul haesseoyo.
Before eating breakfast, I took a shower.

아침 먹은 **후에** 샤워를 했어요. Achim meogeun hue syaworeul haesseoyo.
After eating breakfast, I took a shower.

아침 먹은 **뒤에** 샤워를 했어요. Achim meogeun dwie syaworeul haesseoyo.
After eating breakfast, I took a shower.

샤워를 하기 **전에** 아침을 먹을 거예요.
Syaworeul hagi jeone achimeul meogeul geoyeyo.
Before taking a shower, I'll eat breakfast.

샤워를 한 **후에** 아침을 먹을 거예요.
Syaworeul han hue achimeul meogeul geoyeyo.
After taking a shower, I'll eat breakfast.

샤워를 한 **뒤에** 아침을 먹을 거예요.
Syaworeul han dwie achimeul meogeul geoyeyo.
After taking a shower, I'll eat breakfast.

		Speaking = Writing
A다가도 dagado B	"A is interrupted by B"	★★

그녀는 급하게 서두르**다가도** 항상 정신이 산만해져서 늦어요. Geunyeoneun geupage seodureudagado hangsang jeongsini sanmanhaejyeoseo neujeoyo.
Even though she hurries, she always gets distracted and ends up being late.

This is much like 다가, but this expression implies a sudden and dramatic change in a situation.

HOW IT'S FORMED

다가 plus 도. 도 is used mostly in contrasting sentences (see page 104) and also has the effect of adding emphasis. 다가 by itself means only that the situation changed, but when you add 도 you're saying it changed.

HOW IT'S CONJUGATED

		All tenses
Action verbs ending in a vowel	하다	하다가도 hadagado
Action verbs ending in a consonant	먹다	먹다가도 meokdagado

TAKE NOTE

The subjects of both clauses should be the same.

EXAMPLE SENTENCES

슬프**다가도** 음악을 들으면 기분이 좋아져요.
Seulpeudagado eumageul deureumyeon gibuni joajyeoyo.
Even when I'm sad, I feel better if I listen to music.

자**다가도** 전화벨이 울리면 받아요. **Jadagado jeonhwaberi ullimyeon badayo.**
Even if he's asleep, he'll answer the phone if it rings.

		Speaking = Writing
A고서 goseo B	"A and then B"	★★

지하철을 타**고서** 늦었어요. **Jihacheoreul tagoseo neujeosseoyo.**
I took the subway and then I was late.

This shows that B happened after A, and sometimes at least partly because of A.

HOW IT'S FORMED

고 plus 서 (as in 아/어/여서), a combination of "and" and "so."

HOW IT'S CONJUGATED

		All tenses
Action verbs ending in a vowel	하다	하고서 hagoseo
Action verbs ending in a consonant	먹다	먹고서 meokgoseo

TAKE NOTE

고서 can be used only with action verbs and only when the subjects of both clause A and clause B are the same.

It's very similar to 고 나서 **go naseo** (see page 272) but can be used in a broader range of sentences.

EXAMPLE SENTENCES

저녁을 빨리 먹<u>고서</u> 영화를 봤어요.
Jeonyeogeul ppalli meokgoseo yeonghwareul bwasseoyo.
I ate dinner quickly and watched a movie.

저녁을 먹<u>고서</u> 담배를 피웠어요.
Jeonyeogeul meokgoseo dambaereul piwosseoyo.
I ate dinner and then had a cigarette.

		Speaking = Writing
A고서야 goseoya B	"A, then B"	★★

우리가 지하철을 타<u>고서야</u> 정시에 올 수 있었어요.
Uriga jihacheoreul tagoseoya jeongsie ol su isseosseoyo.
We took the subway and we were on time (at least partly because of taking the subway).

This is much like 고서 but requires that clause A be a condition of clause B. In other words, there's more of a causal relationship between A and B than there is with 고서. A happened before and helped bring about B. In other words, once you've done A, you can finally do B.

HOW IT'S FORMED

고 plus 서 (아/어/여서; so) plus 야 (아/어/여야 is an expression which means A must happen in order for B to happen). Put them all together and you get the meaning of this expression. In 고서야, unlike 아/어/여야, A is not a necessary condition for B, but it does help cause it.

HOW IT'S CONJUGATED

		All tenses
Action verbs ending in a vowel	하다	하고서야 hagoseoya
Action verbs ending in a consonant	먹다	먹고서야 meokgoseoya

TAKE NOTE

고서야 can be used only with action verbs and only when the subjects of both clause A and clause B are the same.

B should include an expression of possibility such as (으)ㄹ 수 있다 **(eu)r su itda** (see page 294).

EXAMPLE SENTENCES

공부를 열심히 안 하<u>고서야</u> 시험에 어떻게 합격할 수 있어요?
Gongbureul yeolsimhi an hagoseoya siheome eotteoke hapgyeokal su isseoyo?
If you don't study hard, how will you pass the test?

숙제를 하<u>고서야</u> 수업에 갈 수 있었어요.
Sukjereul hagoseoya sueobe gal su isseosseoyo.
I did my homework and then went to class (partly because I was finally ready).

Speaking = Writing

A고 보니(까)   "I did A and then noticed that B"   ★★
go boni(kka) B

지하철을 타<u>고 보니</u> 택시보다 더 느렸어요.
Jihacheoreul tago boni taeksiboda deo neuryeosseoyo.
I took the subway, but found it was slower than a taxi.

This expression is used to talk about something you noticed when you tried to do something else. A is something that was done, and B is what you observed after it was done.

HOW IT'S FORMED

고 plus 보다 (in this case, to notice or discover) plus 니(까) (so). The 까 part of 니까 is optional.

HOW IT'S CONJUGATED

		All tenses
Action verbs ending in a vowel	하다	하고 보니까 hago bonikka
Action verbs ending in a consonant	먹다	먹고 보니까 meokgo bonikka

TAKE NOTE

고 보니(까) is quite similar to another useful expression, 다(가) 보니(까) (see page 353). The difference between the two is that while the action in the A clause was repeated and is ongoing in 다가 보니까, it must be finished in order to be used with 고 보니까. So 아버지 되다가 보니까 **abeoji doedaga bonikka** ("I became a father and then noticed...") is an acceptable construction while 아버지 되고 보니까 **abeoji doego bonikka** is not because being a father is something that is ongoing. Likewise, you can say 사고가 나고 보니까

sagoga nago bonikka ("There was an accident and then I noticed") while 사고가 나다가 보니까 sagoga nadaga bonikka is ungrammatical because an accident happening is only a single, brief event.

고 보니까 can be used only with action verbs and only when the subjects of both clause A and clause B are the same.

EXAMPLE SENTENCES

이사할 집이 편리할 거라고 생각했는데 이사 하**고 보니까** 시끄럽기만 했어요.
Isahal jibi pyeollihal georago saenggakaenneunde isa hago bonikka sikkeureopgiman haesseoyo.
I thought the house I was moving to would be more conveniently located, but I found it was just noisy.

친구인 줄 알았는데 인사를 하**고 보니** 모르는 사람이었어요.
Chinguin jul aranneunde insareul hago boni moreuneun saramieosseoyo.
I thought he was my friend, but when I greeted him I found out he was someone I didn't know.

If: If

A(으)면 (eu)myeon B	"If A, then B"	Speaking = Writing ★★★★★

늦**으면** 전화해 주세요. Neujeumyeon jeonhwahae juseyo.
If you're late, please call me.

면 is the workhorse of the Korean conditional world, so learn it well. It simply means "if" and is not at all difficult to use. You'll see it all throughout this book in various other expressions. Here are a few:

Expression	Page	Meaning	Example sentence
A(으)면 B A (eu) myeon B	–	If A, then B	늦**으면** 전화해 주세요. Neujeumyeon jeonhwahae juseyo. If you're late, please call me.
A(이)라/(ㄴ/는)다/ 자면 B A (i)ra/(n/ neun)da/ jamyeon B	286	If A, then B	늦었**다면** 남자친구를 만나지 않았을 거예요. Neujeotdamyeon namjachingureul mannaji anasseul geoyeyo. If I'd been late, I wouldn't have met my boyfriend.
A았/었/였더라면 B A at/eot/ yeotdeoramyeon B	289	If only A, then B	택시를 타지 않았**더라면** 늦었을 거예요. Taeksireul taji anatdeoramyeon neujeosseul geoyeyo. If I hadn't taken a taxi, I would have been late.

Expression	Page	Meaning	Example sentence
A 같으면 B A gateumyeon B	293	If it were like A, then B	왜 이렇게 늦었어? 너가 내 아이 **같으면** 야단쳤을 거야. Wae ireoke neujeosseo? Neoga nae ai gateumyeon, yadanchyeosseul geoya. Why were you so late? If you were my child, I'd scold you.
A(이)라/(ㄴ/는)다/ (으)라/자고 하면 B A (i)ra/(n/neun)da/(eu) ra/jago hamyeon B	–	If you say A, then B	민수가 빨리 가자고 하면 서둘러요. Minsuga ppalli gajago hamyeon seodulleoyo. If Minsu suggested we go quickly, then let's hurry.
A에 의하면 B A e uihamyeon B	324	According to A, B	일기 예보에 **의하면** 내일 비가 올 거예요. Ilgi yeboe uihamyeon naeil biga ol geoyeyo. According to the weather forecast, it's going to rain tomorrow.
A 아니면 B A animyeon B	121	If not A, then B	늦을 거예요? **아니면** 시간에 맞출 거예요? Neujeul geoyeyo? Animyeon sigane matchul geoyeyo? Will you be late? Or will you arrive on time?
A에 비하면 B A e bihamyeon B	97	B, com- pared to A	가영에 **비하면** 민수가 더 늦었어요. Kayounge bihamyeon Minsuga deo neujeosseoyo. Minsu was later than Kayoung.
A(으)ㄴ/는가 하면 B A (eu)n/neunga hamyeon B	100	There's A, but there's also B	제 수업에 정시에 오는 사람들이 있**는가 하면** 늦게 오는 사람들도 있어요. Je sueobe jeongsie oneun saramdeuri inneunga hamyeon neutge oneun saramdeuldo isseoyo. In my class, there are some people who come on time and some who are late.
A(으)ㄹ 테면 B A (eu)r temyeon B	223	If you plan/ expect to do A, then B	어떤 얘기든 **할 테면** 그냥 하세요. Eotteon yaegideun hal temyeon geunyang haseyo. Whatever you want to say, just say it.
A(으)면 A(으)ㄹ수록 B A (eu)myeon A (eu) rsurok B	247	The more A, B	멀리 가**면 갈수록** 피곤해졌어요. Meolli gamyeon galsurok pigon-hae-jyeosseoyo. The farther I went, the more tired I became.
A다(가) 보면 B A da(ga) bomyeon B	209	If you do A, then B	계속 공부하**다가 보면** 유창해질 거예요. Gyesok gongbuhadaga bomyeon yuchanghaejil geoyeyo. If you keep studying, you'll become fluent.
~(으)면 되다/안 되다 ~(eu)myeon doeda/an doeda	200	~ is okay/ not okay	늦**으면 안 돼요**. Neujeumyeon an dwaeyo. It's not okay to be late.
~았/었/였으면 좋겠다/싶다/하다 ~at/eot/yeosseumyeon joketda/sipda/hada	178	It would be nice if ~	정시에 **왔으면 좋겠어요**. Jeongsie wasseumyeon jokesseoyo. It would have been better if you'd arrived on time.
~(으)면 뭘 해요? ~(eu)myeon mwol haeyo?	43	What's the point of ~?	왜 과속해요? 일찍 가**면 뭘 해요**? 안전이 제일 중요하지요. Wae gwasokaeyo? Iljjik gamyeon mwol haeyo? Anjeoni jeil jungyohajiyo. Why are you speeding? What's the point of getting there early? Safety is more important.

HOW IT'S CONJUGATED

		Past	Present	Future
Action verbs ending in a vowel	하다	했으면 haesseumyeon	하면 hamyeon	하면
Action verbs ending in a consonant	먹다	먹었으면 meogeosseumyeon	먹으면 meogeumyeon	먹으면
Descriptive verbs (adjectives) ending in a vowel	예쁘다	예뻤으면 yeppeosseumyeon	예쁘면 yeppeumyeon	예쁘면
Descriptive verbs (adjectives) ending in a consonant	작다	작았으면 jagasseumyeon	작으면 jageumyeon	작으면

TAKE NOTE

When using this expression in the past tense (했으면, 먹었으면), you can add 야 for emphasis. So 했으면 becomes 했으면야 **haesseumyeonnya**, 먹었으면 becomes 먹었으면야 **meogeosseumyeonnya**, etc. This means exactly the same thing as 했으면 and 먹었으면 by themselves, but emphasizes your regret or gratitude that you didn't A. See the examples below. In this case you normally end B with 았/었/였겠다 **at/eot/yeotgetda**, 았/었/였을 거예요 **ass/eoss/yeosseul geoyeyo** or 았/었/였을 텐데(요) **ass/eoss/yeosseul tende(yo)**.

EXAMPLE SENTENCES

비가 오**면** 꽃이 펴요. **Biga omyeon kkochi pyeoyo.** If it rains, the flowers bloom.

시간이 있었**으면** 왔을 거예요. **Sigani iss-eoss-eumyeon wasseul geoyeyo.**
If I'd had time I would have come.

사업을 했**으면** 지금쯤 부자가 됐을 거예요.
Saeobeul haesseumyeon jigeumjjeum bujaga dwaesseul geoyeyo.
If I'd started a business, I'd be rich by now.

사업을 했**으면야** 지금 부자가 됐을 거예요.
Saeobeul haess-eu-myeonnya jigeum bujaga dwaesseul geoyeyo.
If only I'd started a business, I'd be rich by now.

It can also be used with 그렇다 **geureota** to form 그러면 **geureomyeon**, which means "if so."

A: 늦을 텐데... **Neujeul tende...** I think we're going to be late
B: **그러면** 빨리 가세요. **Geureomyeon ppalli gaseyo.** Then hurry up.

A거든 geodeun B	"If A, then B"	Speaking > Writing ★★★★★

이 회의가 이렇게 중요하**거든** 늦지 마세요.
i hoeuiga ireoke jungyohageodeun neutji maseyo.
If this meeting is so important, then please don't be late.

거든 is similar to 면 **myeon** but can be used only when your A clause is the basis for a suggestion about your B clause.

HOW IT'S CONJUGATED

		Past	Present	Future
Action verbs ending in a vowel	하다	했거든 haetgeodeun	하거든 hageodeun	하거든
Action verbs ending in a consonant	먹다	먹었거든 meogeotgeodeun	먹거든 meokgeodeun	먹거든
Descriptive verbs (adjectives) ending in a vowel	예쁘다	예뻤거든 yeppeotgeodeun	예쁘거든 yeppeugeodeun	예쁘거든
Descriptive verbs (adjectives) ending in a consonant	작다	작았거든 jagatgeodeun	작거든 jakgeodeun	작거든
Nouns ending in a vowel	남자	남자였거든 namjayeotgeodeun	남자이거든 namjaigeodeun	남자이거든
Nouns ending in a consonant	물	물이었거든 murieotgeodeun	물이거든 murigeodeun	물이거든

TAKE NOTE

This one can be used only with suggestions, commands, or questions—no statements. Since it's used for things that will happen in the future such as suggestions, it can't be used with sentences in the past tense. The A clause can be in the past tense if that action is already finished, but B can't be.

거든 can also be used at the end of a sentence; in that case it has a somewhat different meaning; in fact, two different meanings depending on your intonation! See page 70 for how to use 거든 at the end of a sentence.

EXAMPLE SENTENCES

어머니 생신이**거든**, 어서 빨리 가서 선물을 사 드리세요.
Eomeoni saengsinigeodeun, eoseo ppalli gaseo seonmureul sa deuriseyo.
If it's your mother's birthday, then please hurry up and buy a present for her.

이 신발이 너무 작**거든** 큰 것으로 바꿔 줄게요.
I sinbari neomu jakgeodeun keun geoseuro bakkwo julgeyo.
If these shoes are too small, I'll give you a bigger size.

		Speaking = Writing
A(이)라/(ㄴ/는)다/자면 (i)ra/(n/neun)da/ jamyeon B	"If A were/had been true, then B"	★★★

늦었**다면** 남자친구를 만나지 않았을 거예요.
Neujeotdamyeon namjachingureul mannaji anasseul geoyeyo.
If I'd been late, I wouldn't have met my boyfriend.

Are you a daydreamer? Dislike reality? Here's an expression for you. This is much like 면, but can be used only to talk about either hypothetical situations contrary to what actually happened or situations in the future that haven't yet happened. In other words, reality has nothing to do with this one. If you imagine 면 and all the expressions that can be made with it as a giant circle, 라/다/ㄴ다/는다/자면 is a smaller circle within that big circle. All the sentences that use this expression could also be made with 면 and would mean the same thing, but the reverse is not true.

HOW IT'S FORMED

It uses the indirect speech particles 라/다/ㄴ다/는다/자, but has nothing to do with indirect speech; the part being "quoted" is just the situation that is being imagined or predicted. This is your A clause. B is what you think would happen if A were or had been true.

HOW IT'S CONJUGATED

자면 is used only after action verbs and is never used to talk about the past tense.

		Past	Present	Future
Action verbs ending in a vowel	하다	했다면 haetdamyeon	한다면 handamyeon 하자면 hajamyeon	할 거라면 hal georamyeon 하자면
Action verbs ending in a consonant	먹다	먹었다면 meogeotdamyeon	먹는다면 meokneundamyeon 먹자면 meokjamyeon	먹을 거라면 meogeul georamyeon 먹자면
Descriptive verbs (adjectives) ending in a vowel	예쁘다	예뻤다면 yeppeotdamyeon	예쁘다면 yeppeudamyeon	예쁠 거라면 yeppeulgeoramyeon
Descriptive verbs (adjectives) ending in a consonant	작다	작았다면 jagatdamyeon	작다면 jakdamyeon	작을 거라면 jageul georamyeon
Nouns ending in a vowel	남자	남자였다면 namjayeotdamyeon	남자라면 namjaramyeon	남자라면
Nouns ending in a consonant	물	물이었다면 murieotdamyeon	물이라면 muriramyeon	물이라면

TAKE NOTE

Keep reality out of it! Use this only for things that aren't true or that you're imagining or predicting. It should go with expressions that are also hypothetical such as ㄹ 것이다 **r geosi da**, ㄹ 텐데 **r tende** or 겠어요 **gesseoyo**.

Just like 았/었/였으면 **at/eot/yeosseumyeon** (see page 285), you can also add 야 after this expression (한다면야 **handamyeonnya**, 했다면야 **haetdamyeonnya**, 먹는다면야 **meokneunda-myeonnya**, 예쁘다면야 **yeppeudamyeonnya**, etc.), which emphasizes A and so conveys your feelings of regret or gratitude even more strongly. Compare the examples below.

자면 **jamyeon** is for hypothetical situations in the future and translates as "If you want to" (이)라면 **(i)ramyeon** and ([으]ㄴ/는)다면 **((eu)n/neun)damyeon** can be used in hypothetical situations in any tense.

Since this is essentially used to make recommendations, B normally (but not always) ends with an expression indicating duty or preference; 아/어/여야 하다/되다 a/eo/yeoya hada/doeda (see page 198) and 는 것이 좋다 neun geosi jota are common.

EXAMPLE SENTENCES

늦었**다면** 남자친구를 만나지 않았을 거예요.
Neujeotdamyeon namjachingureul mannaji anasseul geoyeyo.
If I'd been late, I wouldn't have met my boyfriend.

늦었**다면야** 남자친구를 만나지 않았을 거예요.
Neujeotdamyeonnya namjachingureul mannaji anasseul geoyeyo.
If I'd been late (and I'm really glad I wasn't), I wouldn't have met my boyfriend.

제가 부자**라면** 부모님께 큰 집을 사 드릴 거예요.
Jega bujaramyeon bumonimkke keun jibeul sa deuril geoyeyo.
If I were rich, I'd buy my parents a big house.

제가 부자**라면야** 부모님께 큰 집을 사 드릴 거예요.
Jega bujaramyeonnya bumonimkke keun jibeul sa deuril geoyeyo.
If only I were rich, I'd buy my parents a big house.

비가 왔**다면** 꽃이 필 거예요. Biga watdamyeon kkochi pil geoyeyo.
비가 왔**으면** 꽃이 필 거예요. Biga wasseumyeon kkochi pil geoyeyo.
If it had rained, the flowers would have bloomed.

In the last example above, both 다면 damyeon and 으면 eumyeon mean the same thing because the expression is in the past and it's now impossible for it to rain. As you can see, 다면 in this case implies some regret on the speaker's part. If a negative consequence was avoided, it can also convey a feeling of thanks. Below you can see how 면 and 다면 differ when used in the present tense.

비가 **온다면** 꽃이 필 거예요. Biga ondamyeon kkochi pil geoyeyo.
If it rains, the flowers will bloom. (Hypothetical; it's not raining now.)

비가 오**면** 꽃이 필 거예요. Biga omyeon kkochi pil geoyeyo.
If it rains, the flowers will bloom. (It may or may not be raining already.)

And a few examples with 자면:

정시에 도착하**자면** 집에서 일찍 출발해야 돼요.
Jeongsie dochakajamyeon jibeseo iljjik chulbalhaeya dwaeyo.
If you want to arrive on time, you should leave the house early.

돈을 많이 모으**자면** 투자를 하면 좋겠어요.
Doneul mani moeujamyeon tujareul hamyeon jokesseoyo.
If you want to save a lot of money, you should invest.

영어를 잘 배우**자면** 해외 여행을 가야 해요.
Yeongeoreul jal baeujamyeon haeoe yeohaengeul gaya haeyo.
If you want to learn English well, you must go overseas.

| A았/었/였더라면 at/ eot/yeotdeoramyeon B | "If only A, then B" | Speaking > Writing ★★★ |

택시를 타지 않**았더라면** 늦었을 거예요.
Taeksireul taji anatdeoramyeon neujeosseul geoyeyo.
If I hadn't taken a taxi, I would have been late.

This is a good expression to know if you're someone who always forgets things or doesn't plan ahead. It's even more hypothetical than 라/다/ㄴ다/는다면 ra/da/nda/neundamyeon and can be used only in hypothetical situations in the past tense, usually (but certainly not always) ones that had negative results in reality: "If only you had saved your money"; "If only you had asked that girl out."

HOW IT'S FORMED

The past tense marker 았/었/였 at/eot/yeot, plus 더라 deora, which is used for things that you personally experienced or heard, plus the conditional marker 면.

HOW IT'S CONJUGATED

		Past
Action verbs ending in a vowel	하다	했더라면 haetdeoramyeon
Action verbs ending in a consonant	먹다	먹었더라면 meogeotdeoramyeon
Descriptive verbs (adjectives) ending in a vowel	예쁘다	예뻤더라면 yeppeotdeoramyeon
Descriptive verbs (adjectives) ending in a consonant	작다	작았더라면 jagatdeoramyeon
Nouns ending in a vowel	남자	남자였더라면 namjayeotdeoramyeon
Nouns ending in a consonant	물	물이었더라면 murieotdeoramyeon

TAKE NOTE

Again, use this only when imagining the opposite of what really happened.
B often ends with (으)ㄹ 거예요 (eu)r geoyeyo, 겠어요 gesseoyo, or (으)ㄹ 텐데요 (eu)r tendeyo.

EXAMPLE SENTENCES

집에서 더 일찍 출발**했더라면** 늦지 않았을 텐데요.
Jibeseo deo iljjik chulbalhaetdeoramyeon neutji anasseul tendeyo.
If I'd left the house earlier, I wouldn't have been late.

병원에 가지 않**았더라면** 죽을 뻔했어요.
Byeongwone gaji anat**deoramyeon** jugeul ppeonhaesseoyo.
If he hadn't gone to the hospital, he would have died.

See page 261 for an explanation of (으)ㄹ 뻔했다 (eu)r ppeonhaetda. It goes well with 았/었/였더라면 at/eot/yeotdeoramyeon.

		Speaking = Writing
A(으)ㄴ/는/(으)ㄹ/의 경우에(는) (eu)n/neun/ (eu)r/ui gyeongue(neun) B	"If (in the case of) A, then B"	★★

저 같은 **경우에는** 그 보너스 받을 수 없어요.
Jeo gateun **gyeongueneun** geu boneoseu badeul su eopseoyo.
In cases like mine, I can't receive a bonus.

Here's a good expression to know if you're ever involved in disaster planning or if you just want to know how to talk about what could happen in different situations.

HOW IT'S FORMED

First, take the past, present, or future tense markers (으)ㄴ/는/(으)ㄹ. Then add 경우, which is a noun that means "case" or "occasion." 에는 simply means that whatever happens in B happens in the case of or occasion A. 는 may be dropped.

HOW IT'S CONJUGATED

		Past	Present	Future
Action verbs ending in a vowel	하다	한 경우에(는) han gyeongue(neun)	하는 경우에(는) haneun gyeongue(neun)	할 경우에(는) hal gyeongue(neun)
Action verbs ending in a consonant	먹다	먹은 경우에(는) meogeun gyeongue(neun)	먹는 경우에(는) meokneun gyeongue(neun)	먹을 경우에 (는) meogeul gyeongue(neun)
Descriptive verbs (adjectives) ending in a vowel	예쁘다	예쁜 경우에(는) yeppeun gyeongue(neun)	예쁜 경우에(는) yeppeun gyeongue(neun)	예쁠 경우에 (는) yeppeul gyeongue(neun)
Descriptive verbs (adjectives) ending in a consonant	작다	작은 경우에(는) jageun gyeongue(neun)	작은 경우에(는)	작을 경우에(는)
Nouns ending in a vowel	남자	남자의 경우에(는) namjaui gyeongue(neun)	남자의 경우에(는)	남자의 경우에(는)
Nouns ending in a consonant	물	물의 경우에(는) murui gyeongue(neun)	물의 경우에(는)	물의 경우에(는)

TAKE NOTE

This pattern can be changed to 면, but not vice versa.

There are a few commonly used expressions with 경우에는:

저 같은 **경우에는** jeo gateun gyeongueneun — In cases like mine

내 **경우에는** nae gyeongueneun — In my case

이 **경우에는** i gyeongueneun — In this case

그런 **경우에는** geureon gyeongueneun — In that case

어떠한 **경우에도** eotteohan gyeonguedo — In any case

어떤 **경우에는** eotteon gyeongueneun — In some cases

최악의 **경우에는** choeagui gyeongueneun — At worst (in the worst case)

모든 **경우에는** modeun gyeongueneun — In all cases

EXAMPLE SENTENCES

눈이 많이 **오는 경우에는** 길이 미끄러워져요.
Nuni mani oneun gyeongueneun giri mikkeureowojyeoyo.
If (in cases where) it snows a lot, the road will become slippery.

급한 일이 **생길 경우에는** 일찍 퇴근하지 마세요.
Geupan iri saenggil gyeongueneun iljjik toegeunhaji maseyo.
If anything urgent comes up, don't leave work early.

남자**의 경우에는** 오른쪽에 있는 화장실을 이용해 주세요.
Namjaui gyeongueneun oreunjjoge inneun hwajangsireul iyonghae juseyo.
Men should use the bathroom on the right side.

Speaking > Writing

A(으)ㄴ/는/(으)ㄹ 셈치(고)   "If we assume A, then B"   ★★
(eu)n/neun/(eu)r semchi(go) B

우리는 아주 늦을 거예요. 그러니까 우리는 없**는 셈 치고** 먼저 파티를 시작하세요.
Urineun aju neujeul geoyeyo. Geureonikka urineun eopneun sem chigo meonjeo patireul sijakaseyo.
We will be very late, so please assume we're not there and go ahead and start the party.

In this expression, you do B based on the assumption you make in A: you do B as if A were true.

HOW IT'S FORMED

셈 is a noun that means "supposition" and 치다 is the verb used to make that supposition. This expression is just the two words joined together plus whatever else you need to add to make the expression work.

HOW IT'S CONJUGATED

		Past	Present	Future
Action verbs ending in a vowel	하다	한 셈치고 han semchigo	하는 셈치고 haneun semchigo	할 셈치고 hal semchigo
Action verbs ending in a consonant	먹다	먹은 셈치고 meogeun semchigo	먹는 셈치고 meokneun semchigo	먹을 셈치고 meogeul semchigo
Descriptive verbs (adjectives) ending in a vowel	예쁘다	예쁜 셈치고 yeppeun semchigo	예쁜 셈치고	예쁠 셈치고 yeppeul semchigo
Descriptive verbs (adjectives) ending in a consonant	작다	작은 셈치고 jageun semchigo	작은 셈치고	작을 셈치고 jageul semchigo
Nouns ending in a vowel	남자	남자인 셈치고 namjain semchigo	남자인 셈치고	남자일 셈치고 namjail semchigo
Nouns ending in a consonant	물	물인 셈치고 murin semchigo	물인 셈치고	물일 셈치고 muril semchigo

TAKE NOTE

Don't confuse this with 셈이다 **semida** (see page 154); they're similar, but 셈이다 by itself means "seems like" whereas 셈치다 is used to consider a hypothetical situation: if we assume that A, then B follows from that.

셈치고는 is a different expression which means "for an A" or "considering that A." It's on page 86. Although it looks very much like 셈치고, the meaning is rather different.

셈치고 is probably the most common use of this expression, but 셈치다 can be conjugated with 고, 면, or whatever else you need, or it can just go at the end of a sentence.

EXAMPLE SENTENCES

속는 **셈치고** 믿어보세요.
Songneun semchigo mideoboseyo.
Take a chance and believe me this one time. (Even assuming you might be fooled again, just try to believe me this time.)

그 사람이 있는 **셈치고** 한 번 얘기해보세요.
Geu sarami inneun semchigo han beon yaegihaeboseyo.
Let's talk as if that person were here.

Speaking = Writing

A같으면 gateumyeon B   "If it were like A, then B"   ★

왜 이렇게 늦었어? 너가 내 아이 **같으면** 야단쳤을 거야.
Wae ireoke neujeosseo? neoga nae ai gateumyeon yadanchyeosseul geoya.
Why were you so late? If you were my child, I'd scold you.

Like 았/었/였더라면 at/eot/yeotdeoramyeon, 같으면 is used to imagine a situation contrary to reality: "If it were like ten years ago" (10년 전 같으면 sipnyeon jeon gateum-yeon) or "If that were my child" (내 아이 같으면).

HOW IT'S FORMED

같다 means "to be like" and is commonly seen in expressions like 같은 or 같이. In this expression it is combined with 면, which means "if." (see page 283).

HOW IT'S CONJUGATED

		Past	Present	Future
Nouns ending in a vowel	남자	남자 같았으면 namja gatasseumyeon	남자 같으면 namja gateumyeon	남자 같으면
Nouns ending in a consonant	물	물 같았으면 mul gatasseumyeon	물 같으면 mul gateumyeon	물 같으면

TAKE NOTE

If you want to talk about something that might be possible, you should use (이)라면 instead of 같으면. (이)라면 is on page 286. If you want to talk about a verb instead of a noun, use 았/었/였더라면 (see page 289).

EXAMPLE SENTENCES

옛날 **같았으면** 이렇게 빨리 갈 수 없어요.
Yennal gatasseumyeon ireoke ppalli gal su eopseoyo.
If it were like the old days, we wouldn't be able to go this fast.

한국 **같으면** 쉽게 할 수 있을 거예요.
Hangug gateumyeon swipge hal su isseul geoyeyo.
If this were like Korea, we could do it easily.

If: Possibility and The Lack Thereof

> **Speaking = Writing**
> ★★★★★
>
> ~(으)ㄹ 수 있다/없다   "can/can't ~"
> ~(eu)r su itda/eopda

한국어를 잘 **할 수 없어요**. Hangugeoreul jal hal su eopseoyo.
I can't speak Korean well.

한국어를 잘 **할 수 있어요**. Hangugeoreul jal hal su isseoyo.
I can speak Korean well.

This is one of the first expressions you'll learn while studying Korean. It's particularly helpful at the very beginning when you need to tell people you can't speak Korean. Later on you can mix things up a bit by getting into expressions like (으)ㄹ 수도 있다 or 는 수 있다/없다. It's pretty versatile and definitely worth knowing even if you never plan to take your Korean past the beginner level. ~(으)ㄹ 수 있다 means "can ~" while ~(ㅇ)ㄹ 수 없다 means "can't ~."

HOW IT'S FORMED

The future tense marker (으)ㄹ (see page 238) is followed by 수, which has quite a number of meanings; in this case it just means "possibility." Then 있다 (there is) or 없다 (there isn't) is added to show that there is or isn't the possibility of doing ~. Because 수 is a noun, you can add the subject marker 가 to it if you'd like; this doesn't really change the meaning, but it does put a little more emphasis on the fact that ~ is really possible or impossible. 는 is occasionally added to 수 as well, depending on the sentence, and also has the effect of emphasizing the possibility or impossibility of the statement, like so:

한국말을 잘 **할 수는 있어요**. Hangukmareul jal hal suneun isseoyo.
Here you can speak Korean well, but can't do anything else: for instance, your writing may be poor. So you're comparing your ability to speak Korean well against something else which may or may not be mentioned.

한국말을 잘 **할 수가 있어요**. Hangukmareul jal hal suga isseoyo.
This sentence means it's possible for you to speak Korean well.

HOW IT'S CONJUGATED

Descriptive verbs (adjectives) and nouns can't be conjugated with this expression, but you can turn them into action verbs (see page 25 for how to do that) and then use them with (으)ㄹ 수 있다/없다 if: for example, you want to say that a woman can become beautiful.

		Past	Present	Future
Action verbs ending in a vowel	하다	할 수 있었다 hal su iseotda 할 수 없었다 hal su eopseotda	할 수 있다 hal su itda 할 수 없다 hal su eopda	할 수 있겠다 hal su itgetda 할 수 없겠다 hal su eopgetda
Action verbs ending in a consonant	먹다	먹을 수 있었다 meogeul su iseotda 먹을 수 없었다 meogeul su eopseotda	먹을 수 있다 meogeul su itda 먹을 수 없다 meogeul su eopda	먹을 수 있겠다 meogeul su itgetda 먹을 수 없겠다 meogeul su eopgetda

TAKE NOTE

Another expression involving knowing and not knowing is ~(으)ㄹ 줄 알다/모르다 **~(eu) r jul alda/moreuda**. That one, however, means "to know how to do ~." ~(으)ㄹ 수 있다/ 없다 means "to be able to ~." In some cases, like 한국어를 할 수 있다/할 줄 알다 **Hangugeoreul hal su itda/hal jul alda**, you can use both; in others you can't.

There is also 못, which literally means "can't." This is a shorter way than (으)ㄹ 수 없다 to say you can't do something. You put it directly before the verb you can't do. It's interchangeable with (으)ㄹ 수 없다.

한국어를 잘 **못해요**. Hangugeoreul jal **motaeyo**. I can't speak Korean well.

알레르기 때문에 땅콩을 **못** 먹어요.
Allereugi ttaemune ttangkongeul mon meogeoyo.
Because of allergies, I can't eat peanuts.

There are a number of complicated expressions based on (으)ㄹ 수 있다/없다. They're useful to know but mostly not essential, so I'm putting them all in here rather than giving them their own sections because they're all essentially variations of (으)ㄹ 수 있다/없다.

■ ~는 수가 있다 ~neun suga itda

This expression uses the present tense marker 는 instead of the future tense marker (으) ㄹ before 수 있다. While (으)ㄹ 수 있다 only implies potential, 는 수가 있다 means that ~ is unusual but can and sometimes does happen. However, this event is not quite as possible as (으)ㄹ 수도 있다 **(eu)r sudo itda**.

보통 지하철 열차가 정시에 오지만 무슨 특별한 문제가 있으면 늦**는 수가 있어요**.
Botong jihacheol yeolchaga jeongsie ojiman museun teukbyeolhan munjega isseumyeon neunneun suga isseoyo.
Usually the subway trains are on time, but if there's a problem, they can also be late.

믿는 도끼에 발등 찍히**는 수가 있어요**.
Minneun dokkie baldeung jjikineun suga isseoyo.
The ax that you trust can also cut you. (a Korean proverb)

■ ~(으)ㄹ 수도 있다 ~(eu)r sudo itda

This is quite similar to ~기도 하다 ~gido hada, which you can find on page 352. ~기도 하다 is used to say that ~ also happens sometimes. Likewise, ~(으)ㄹ 수도 있다 means that ~ is also possible.

저녁에 비가 올 것 같아요. 눈이 **올 수도 있어요**.
Jeonyeoge biga ol geot gatayo. Nuni ol sudo isseoyo.
It seems like it'll rain this evening. It could also snow.

이 거리는 보통 안전하지만 사고가 **날 수도 있어요**.
I georineun botong anjeonhajiman sagoga nal sudo isseoyo.
This street is usually safe, but sometimes accidents do happen.

■ ~(으)ㄹ 수가 있어야지(요) ~(eu)r suga isseoyaji(yo)

This one is a little confusing. Take (으)ㄹ 수 있다 and add 가, which adds emphasis, and then 어야, which means "must" (see page 202), and then 지(요) which means "isn't it?" (see page 315). Instead of getting a really forceful confirmation of the possibility of ~, you get.~ is impossible. So this one means the opposite of what it looks like it should mean. A good English translation would be "How could (I/you/it/) possibly ~?"

차가 너무 밀려서 정시에 **올 수가 있어야지요**.
Chaga neomu millyeoseo jeongsie ol suga isseoyajiyo.
Traffic was too heavy, so I couldn't possibly arrive on time.

돈이 없어서 여행을 **갈 수가 있어야지요**.
Doni eopseoseo yeohaengeul gal suga isseoyajiyo.
I had no money, so how could I possibly travel?

■ ~(으)ㄹ 수 밖에 없다 ~(eu)r su bakke eopda

In this expression, you take (으)ㄹ 수 없다 (can't) and insert a 밖에 in the middle. The 밖에 means "outside of," making the whole expression "can't do anything except ~." So you had no choice but to ~.

그를 죽일 수 밖에 없었어요. Geureul jugil su bakke eopseosseoyo.
I had no choice but to kill him.

할 수 밖에 없었어요. hal su bakke eopseosseoyo. There was no choice.

■ ~는/(으)ㄹ 수 밖에 별 도리 없다 ~neun/(eu)r su bakke byeol dori eopda

Here we take (으)ㄹ 수 밖에 없다 (see above) and extend it a little more to add 별도리. 도리 means "way," "method," or "means," so this is just a slightly more elaborate way of saying "There was no choice but to."

갈 수 밖에 별 **도리가 없어요**. Gal su bakke byeol doriga eopseoyo.
I have no choice but to go.

그를 죽일 <u>수 밖에 도리 없었어요</u>. Geureul jugil su bakke dori eopseosseoyo.
I had no choice but to kill him.

EXAMPLE SENTENCES

수영 <u>할 수 있어요</u>? Suyeong hal su isseoyo? Can you swim?

수영 <u>할 수 없어요</u>. Suyeong hal su eopseoyo. I can't swim.

젓가락을 <u>쓸 수 있어요</u>. Jeotgarageul sseul su isseoyo. I can use chopsticks.

매운 음식을 <u>먹을 수 있어요</u>. Maeun eumsigeul meogeul su isseoyo.
I can eat spicy food.

~ 지 못하다 ji motada	"can't ~"	Speaking = Writing ★★★★★

정시에 <u>오지 못했어요</u>. Jeongsie oji motaesseoyo. I couldn't arrive on time.

Here's a very easy way to say you can't do something. This is also used to say you're not good at something: whether you can't sing or dance or speak Korean well, you can use 지 못하다 to explain this to people.

HOW IT'S FORMED

지 is a particle often used before negative expressions. 못 means "can't," and 하다 means "to do."

HOW IT'S CONJUGATED

		Past	Present	Future
Action verbs ending in a vowel	하다	하지 못했다 haji motaetda	하지 못하다 haji motada	하지 못할 것이다 haji motal geosida
Action verbs ending in a consonant	먹다	먹지 못했다 meokji motaetda	먹지 못하다 meokji motada	먹지 못할 것이다 meokji motal geosida

TAKE NOTE

This expression and (으)ㄹ 수 없다 (see page 294) are almost identical except that this one can also be used to say you're poor at doing something whereas (으)ㄹ 수 없다 generally means you can't do it at all.

EXAMPLE SENTENCES

노래를 <u>하지 못해요</u>. Noraereul haji motaeyo. I can't sing (well).

우리 반에 영어 **못하**는 아이들이 많아요.
Uri bane yeongeo motaneun aideuri manayo.
In our class there are many children who aren't good in English.

알레르기 때문에 생선을 먹**지 못 해**요.
Allereugi ttaemune saengseoneul meokji mot haeyo.
Because of allergies, I can't eat fish.

		Speaking > Writing
~기 쉽다/십상이다/어렵다 gi swipda/sipsangida/eoryeopda	"~ is easy/easy/ difficult"	★★★★★

정시에 **오기는 쉬워요**. Jeongsie ogineun swiwoyo.
정시에 **오기는 십상이에요**. Jeongsie ogineun sipsangieyo.
정시에 **오기는 어려워요**. Jeongsie ogineun eoryeowoyo.

Here are two ways to say something is easy and one to say it's difficult.

HOW IT'S FORMED

기 changes verbs to nouns. If you're familiar with 쉽다 and 어렵다, you'll know they usually do follow nouns. 십상이다 also means "easy" and is a good one for you TOPIK-takers to know.

HOW IT'S CONJUGATED

Add 기 after action verbs or add the verbs themselves directly after nouns. You can also conjugate verbs using 는 것(이), though this is somewhat less commonly done. Conjugate 쉽다/십상이다/어렵다 in any tense or any form you need.

		All tenses
Action verbs ending in a vowel	하다	하기 쉽다 hagi swipda 하기 십상이다 hagi sipsangida 하기 어렵다 hagi eoryeopda
Action verbs ending in a consonant	먹다	먹기 쉽다 meokgi swipda 먹기 십상이다 meokgi sipsangida 먹기 어렵다 meokgi eoryeopda
Nouns ending in a vowel	조사	조사(가) 쉽다 josa(ga) swipda 조사(가) 십상이다 josa(ga) sipsangida 조사(가) 어렵다 josa(ga) eoryeopda
Nouns ending in a consonant	시험	시험(이) 쉽다 siheom(i) swipda 시험(이) 십상이다 siheom(i) sipsangida 시험(이) 어렵다 siheom(i) eoryeopda

TAKE NOTE

쉽다 and 십상이다 both mean "easy," but aren't quite interchangeable; while 쉽다 simply means "easy," 십상이다 means "something is easy to find or see," or that there's a good chance of it. 어렵다, of course, is the opposite of both and means "difficult."

Watch out for 쉽다. It's an ㅂ-irregular verb, which means it changes to 쉬우 plus whatever you're adding. Don't get it confused with 쉬다, which means "to rest" and changes to 쉬 before being conjugated.

십상이다 isn't usually used with negative sentences. You should also be sure to mention a place when you use it. See the examples below.

EXAMPLE SENTENCES

한국어 듣**기가 쉬워요**.   Listening to Korean is easy.
Hangugeo deutgiga swiwoyo.

한국어 듣**기가 어려워요**.   Listening to Korean is difficult.
Hangugeo deutgiga eoryeowoyo.

코리아타운에서는 한국어를 듣**기 십상이에요**.
Koriatauneseoneun hangugeoreul deutgi sipsangieyo.
You can easily hear Korean in Korea Town.

금메달을 따**기는 쉽지 않아요**.   Getting a gold medal isn't easy.
Geummedareul ttagineun swipji anayo.

금메달을 따**기는 어렵지 않아요**.   Getting a gold medal isn't difficult.
Geummedareul ttagineun eoryeopji anayo.

올림픽에서 금메달을 따**기는 십상이에요**.
Ollimpigeseo geummedareul ttagineun sipsangieyo.
There's a good chance of getting a gold medal.

		Speaking > Writing
~(으)ㄹ 리(가) 있다/없다	"It's possible/	★★
(eu)l li(ga) itda/eopda	impossible that ~"	

정시에 도착했**을 리가 없어요**. Jeongsie dochakaesseul riga eopseoyo.
There's no way I could have arrived on time.

This is a good way to either emphatically deny something ([으]ㄹ 리 없다) or to ask if you have any chance at all ([으]ㄹ 리 있다/없다?). It's used to talk about whether or not the possibility of ~ exists.

HOW IT'S FORMED

리 literally means "possibility," so this expression is saying there is (있다) or isn't (없다) the possibility of ~. 가 is optional and serves to emphasize the impossibility of whatever is being discussed.

HOW IT'S CONJUGATED

		Past	Present	Future
Action verbs ending in a vowel	하다	했을 리(가) 있다 haesseul ri(ga) itda 했을 리(가) 없다 haesseul ri(ga) eopda	할 리(가) 있다 hal ri(ga) itda 할 리(가) 없다 hal ri(ga) eopda	할 리(가) 있다 hal ri(ga) itda 할 리(가) 없다 hal ri(ga) eopda
Action verbs ending in a consonant	먹다	먹었을 리(가) 있다 meogeosseul ri(ga) itda 먹었을 리(가) 없다 meogeosseul ri(ga) eopda	먹을 리(가) 있다 meogeul ri(ga) itda 먹을 리(가) 없다 meogeul ri(ga) eopda	먹을 리(가) 있다 meogeul ri(ga) itda 먹을 리(가) 없다 meogeul ri(ga) eopda
Descriptive verbs (adjectives) ending in a vowel	예쁘다	예뻤을 리(가) 있다 yeppeosseul ri(ga) itda 예뻤을 리(가) 없다 yeppeosseul ri(ga) eopda	예쁠 리(가) 있다 yeppeul ri(ga) itda 예쁠 리(가) 없다 yeppeul ri(ga) eopda	예쁠 리(가) 있다 yeppeul ri(ga) itda 예쁠 리(가) 없다 yeppeul ri(ga) eopda
Descriptive verbs (adjectives) ending in a consonant	작다	작았을 리(가) 있다 jagasseul ri(ga) itda 작았을 리(가) 없다 jagasseul ri(ga) eopda	작을 리(가) 있다 jageul ri(ga) itda 작을 리(가) 없다 jageul ri(ga) eopda	작을 리(가) 있다 jageul ri(ga) itda 작을 리(가) 없다 jageul ri(ga) eopda
Nouns ending in a vowel	남자	남자였을 리(가) 있다 namjayeosseul ri(ga) itda 남자였을 리(가) 없다 namjayeosseul ri(ga) eopda	남자일 리(가) 있다 namjail ri(ga) itda 남자일 리(가) 없다 namjail ri(ga) eopda	남자일 리(가) 있다 namjail ri(ga) itda 남자일 리(가) 없다 namjail ri(ga) eopda
Nouns ending in a consonant	물	물이었을 리(가) 있다 murieosseul ri(ga) itda 물이었을 리(가) 없다 murieosseul ri(ga) eopda	물일 리(가) 있다 muril ri(ga) itda 물일 리(가) 없다 muril ri(ga) eopda	물일 리(가) 있다 muril ri(ga) itda 물일 리(가) 없다 muril ri(ga) eopda

TAKE NOTE

(으)ㄹ 리 있어요 (eu)r ri isseoyo isn't used as a statement, only as a question. The form "~(으)ㄹ 리가 있겠어요?" "~(eu)r riga itgesseoyo?" is frequently used for this. If you want to say there's a possibility of something, use (으)ㄹ 수 있다 or one of its forms instead (see page 294). When used as a question, 리 있어요? (or 있겠어요?) is a bit rhetorical: it often means "How could there be any possibility of ~?", which is exactly the same meaning as 리 없어요. Consider the context to determine what someone means when they ask 리 있어요?

EXAMPLE SENTENCES

정시에 도착했을 **리가 없어요**. Jeongsie dochakaesseul **riga** eopseoyo.
There's no way I could have arrived on time.

정시에 도착했을 리가 있어요? Jeongsie dochakaesseul riga isseoyo?
How could I possibly have arrived on time?
or Was there any chance you could have arrived on time?

당신과 데이트를 **할 리가 없어요**. Dangsingwa deiteureul hal riga eopseoyo.
There's no way I would ever date you.

그녀가 너와 데이트를 **할 리가 있어**? Geunyeoga neowa deiteureul hal riga isseo?
Is there any chance she could ever date you?
or How could she possibly ever date you?

그는 진짜 여자**일 리가 있겠어요**? Geuneun jinjja yeojail riga itgesseoyo?
Could that really be a woman? or How could that possibly be a woman?

그는 진짜 여자**일 리 없어요**. Geuneun jinjja yeojail ri eopseoyo.
There's no way that could be a woman.

		Speaking = Writing
A고서는 goseoneun B, A아/어/ 여서는 a/eo/ yeoseoneun B	"While A, B (can't happen)"	★★

고기를 먹지 않**고서는** 푸딩을 받을 수 없어요.
Gogireul meokji ankoseoneun pudingeul badeul su eopseoyo.
고기를 먹지 않**아서는** 푸딩을 받을 수 없어요.
Gogireul meokji anaseoneun pudingeul badeul su eopseoyo.

If you don't eat your meat, you can't have any pudding.

Remember 고서? It's on page 280. 고서는 is the intersection of 고서 and (으)면 (see page 283): it's similar to both but more specific than either. It's a good one for moms or teachers: if you ever need to say, "If you don't eat your meat, you can't have any pudding!" in Korean, this is the expression you want.

HOW IT'S FORMED

고 plus 서 plus 는, which is an intensifier here. Alternately, 아/어/여 plus 서 plus 는.

HOW IT'S CONJUGATED

		Present
Action verbs with 오 or 아	잡다	잡아서는 jabaseoneun 잡고서는 japgoseoneun
Action verbs with 어, 우, 이 or 으	먹다	먹어서는 meogeoseoneun 먹고서는 meokgoseoneun
Action verbs ending in a vowel 하다	하다	해서는 haeseoneun 하고서는 hagoseoneun

	Present
Descriptive verbs with 오 or 아	짧다	짧아서는 **jjalbaseoneun**
Descriptive verbs with 어, 우, 이 or 으	넓다	넓어서는 **neolbeoseoneun**

TAKE NOTE

고 can be used only with action verbs and only when the subjects of both clause A and clause B are the same.

아/어/여서는 is very similar and can be used in most of the same places. However, 고서는 means "if," "while" or "after," and 아/어/여서는 can mean "if" or "after" but not "while."

고서는/아/어/여서는 can be changed to (으)ㄴ 채로 (see page 259), though the reverse is not always true.

신발을 신**은 채로는** 집에 들어올 수 없어요.
Sinbareul sineun chaeroneun jibe deureool su eopseoyo.

신발을 신**고서는** 집에 들어올 수 없어요.
Sinbareul singoseoneun jibe deureool su eopseoyo.

You can't come in the house while wearing your shoes.

B always ends with something negative: (으)ㄹ 수 없다 **(eu)l su eopda** is very common, but 지 않다 **ji anta** or **지 못 하다 ji mot hada** or other similar expressions are also possible.

EXAMPLE SENTENCES

신발을 신**고서는** 집에 들어올 수 없어요.
Sinbareul singoseoneun jibe deureool su eopseoyo.

신발을 신**어서는** 집에 들어올 수 없어요.
Sinbareul sineoseoneun jibe deureool su eopseoyo.

You can't come in the house while wearing your shoes.

티셔츠를 입**고서는** 그 클럽에 갈 수 없어요.
Tisyeocheureul ipgoseoneun geu keulleobe gal su eopseoyo.

티셔츠를 입**어서는** 그 클럽에 갈 수 없어요.
Tisyeocheureul ibeoseoneun geu keulleobe gal su eopseoyo.

You can't go to that club wearing a T-shirt.

(In both the above examples, 고서는 sounds much better).

아이들이 그렇게 작**아서는** 이 놀이터에서 놀면 안 돼요.
Aideuri geureoke jagaseoneun i noriteoeseo nolmyeon an dwaeyo.
Children that small aren't allowed to play on this playground.

(As this sentence uses an adjective to end A, it can't be written with 고서는 **goseoneun**).

A아/어/여서야	"If you A, how can you B?"	Speaking > Writing
a/eo/yeoseoya B		★

시간을 이렇게 많이 낭비**해서야** 어떻게 정시에 오겠어요?
Siganeul ireoke mani nangbi**haeseoya** eotteoke jeongsie ogesseoyo?
If you waste this much time, how are you going to get there on time?

What this one essentially means is that doing A makes B difficult or impossible. If you had a Korean mom, she might have used this expression to tell you that if you didn't do your homework you'd get a bad grade, or to ask you how you think you're going to get into college if you never studied.

HOW IT'S FORMED

A아/어/여서 B A a/eo/yeoseo B is a causative expression; if A, so then B. In 아/어/여서야 as well, there will be a causative relationship (usually negative) between A and B. 야 has to do with obligation and is featured in such expressions as 아/어/여야 하다/되다 **a/eo/yeoya hada/doeda** (see page 198) or all by itself as 아/어/여야 **a/eo/yeoya** (see page 202).

HOW IT'S CONJUGATED

		All tenses
Action verbs with 오 or 아	잡다	잡아서야 jabaseoya
Action verbs with 어, 우, 으 or 이	먹다	먹어서야 meogeoseoya
Action verbs ending in a vowel 하다	하다	해서야 haeseoya
Descriptive verbs (adjectives) with 오 or 아	작다	작아서야 jagaseoya
Descriptive verbs (adjectives) with 어, 우, 으 or 이	넓다	넓어서야 neolbeoseoya

TAKE NOTE

This expression is quite often used in questions such as "How can you have any pudding if you can't eat your meat?" In these cases, B often ends with a question such as 어떻게 ~겠어요? **eotteoke ~gesseoyo?** or 어디 ~겠어요? **eodi ~gesseoyo?** (In the latter case, 어디 does mean "where," but how: it's just a part of the expression). (으)ㄹ 수 없어요 **(eu)r su eopseoyo** is also a common ending for sentences with 아/어/여서야.

고서는 **goseoneun** and 아/어/여서야 **a/eo/yeoseoya** are very similar and can be used in most of the same places (see page 301 for more on this.) However, 고서는 means "if," "while," or "after," and 아/어/여서는 can mean "if" or "after" but not "while."

EXAMPLE SENTENCES

고기를 먹지 않**아서야** 어떻게 푸딩을 받을 수 있겠어요?
Gogireul meokji ana**seoya** eotteoke pudingeul badeul su itgesseoyo?
How can you have any pudding if you don't eat your meat?

이렇게 늦게 자**서야** 오늘 밤에 잘 수 없을 거예요. Ireoke neutge jaseoya oneul bame jal su eopseul geoyeyo.

If you sleep this late, you won't be able to sleep tonight.

Talking about What Others Have Said: Review of Reported Speech

This is something you absolutely need to know if you're planning to go any further than beginning Korean. Reported speech particles are used not just for indirect speech, but in an array of expressions, especially in situations where you are talking hypothetically or about an assumption you are or someone else is making. You can also use them when talking about things "people say" or "they say" ("They say it's going to be hot tomorrow") even if no one around at the time has said anything of the kind.

Reported speech particles look very intimidating at first and it took me a long time to get used to them. Korean grammar is normally relatively gentle compared to many other languages, but this particular case is a bit of an exception. With practice, all this will come naturally.

Let's take a look at the particles themselves first:

Particle	Example	When it's used	Example
라 ra	남자라 namjara	Nouns ending in vowels	벌써 8시**라고 했어요**. Beolsseo yeodeolsirago haesseoyo. He said it's already 8:00.
이라 ira	물이라 murira	Nouns ending in consonants	지각**이라고 했어요**. Jigagirago haesseoyo He called it tardiness.
ㄴ다 nda	한다 handa	Action verbs ending in vowels	늦게 온**다고 했어요**. Neutge ondago haesseoyo. He said we came late.
는다 neunda	먹는다 meokneunda	Action verbs ending in consonants	늦**는다고 했어요**. Neunneundago haesseoyo. He said we were late.
다 da	예쁘다 yeppeuda	Descriptive verbs (adjectives), past tense verbs with 았/었/였, 있다/없다	시간이 벌써 늦**다고 했어요**. Sigani beolsseo neutdago haesseoyo. He said it was already late.
자 ja	하자 haja	Suggestions	친구가 정시에 오**자고 했어요**. Chinguga jeongsie ojago haesseoyo. My friend suggested we come on time.
냐 nya	예쁘냐 yeppeunya	Questions using descriptive verbs or nouns ending in vowels to someone of lower status than you	벌써 8시**냐고 했어요**. Beolsseo yeodeolsinyago haesseoyo. He asked if it was already 8:00.

Particle	Example	When it's used	Example
이냐 inya	물이냐 murinya	Questions using nouns ending in consonants to someone of lower status than you	지각이냐고 했어요. Jigaginyago haesseoyo. He asked if it was tardiness.
으냐 eunya	작으냐 jageunya	Questions using descriptive verbs ending in consonants to someone of lower status than you	시간이 늦냐고 했어요. Sigani neunnyago haesseoyo. He asked if it was late.
느냐 neunya	하느냐 haneunya 먹었느냐 meogeonneunya	Questions using active and/or past tense verbs to someone of lower status than you	우리가 늦느냐고 했어요. Uriga neunneunyago haesseoyo. He asked if we were late.
라 ra	하라 hara	Commands ending in vowels	선생님이 정시에 오라고 했어요. Seonsaengnimi jeongsie orago haesseoyo. The teacher told us to come on time.
으라 eura	먹으라 meogeura	Commands ending in consonants	선생님이 우리에게 늦게 오라고 했어요. Seonsaengnimi uriege neutge orago haesseoyo. The teacher told us to come late.
어 달라다 eo dallada	먹어 달라다 meogeo dallada	Questions/commands to someone of higher status than you: 어, 우, 이 or 으	선생님께 늦으면 돼 달라고 했어요. Seonsaengnimkke neujeumyeon dwae dallago haesseoyo. I asked the teacher if it was okay to be late.
아 달라다 a dallada	잡아 달라다 jaba dallada	Questions/commands to someone of higher status than you: 아 or 오	선생님께 정시에 와 달라고 했어요. Seonsaengnimkke jeongsie wa dallago haesseoyo. I asked the teacher to please come on time.
여 달라다 yeo dallada	해 달라다 hae dallada	Questions/commands to someone of higher status than you: 하다	선생님께 좀 지각해 달라고 했어요. Seonsaengnimkke jom jigakae dallago haesseoyo. I asked the teacher to please come a little late.

For now, we're going to look at three kinds of expressions with these particles.

Adding 고 하다 to any of them, as in the examples above, is the basic way to say that someone else said something.

Because Koreans generally don't bother with pronouns, I've left them out here. Thus any of the translations above that don't mention a specific person could also mean something else. The first example, for instance, could mean that "he," "I," "you," "she," "they" or anyone called it tardiness.

늦다 is both an action verb and an adjective in Korean, as it is in English: to "be late" as in "to arrive late" is an action while to "be late" as in "it's late" is an adjective. That's why I can conjugate 늦다 using both the action verb and adjective forms. If this is confusing, don't worry; you'll have plenty of opportunities to see the different forms in action.

In the past tense, you can conjugate 하다 to 했어요. In the future tense, conjugate (으)ㄹ 것이다 (better known as (으)ㄹ 거예요 **(eu)r geoyeyo** or (으)ㄹ 거야) **(eu)r geoya** to (으)ㄹ 거라고 해요 **(eu)r georago haeyo** (or (으)ㄹ 거냐고 **(eu)r geonyago** or (으)ㄹ 거자고 **(eu)r geojago**).

내일 **갈 거라고 해요**. Naeil gal georago haeyo. He says he'll go tomorrow.

어제 **갔다고 해요**. Eoje gatdago haeyo. He says he went yesterday.

Another way to use the expression above is to drop the 하다 and just continue the sentence after 고. This is often done when quoting a proverb. Here are a couple of examples.

고생 끝에 낙이 **온다고** 나중에 좋은 일이 꼭 생길 거예요.
Gosaeng kkeute nagi ondago najunge joeun iri kkok saenggil geoyeyo.
Just like the proverb "At the end of sorrow, there's joy," something good is sure to happen later.
(고생 끝에 낙이 온다 Gosaeng kkeute nagi onda.: A Korean proverb that means "At the end of sorrow, there's joy.")

윗물이 맑아야 아랫물이 맑**다고** 윗사람이 질서를 잘 지키면 아랫사람도 잘 지킬 거예요.
Winmuri malgaya araenmuri makdago witsarami jilseoreul jal jikimyeon araetsaramdo jal jikil geoyeyo.
According to the proverb, "If the upper waters are clear, so are the lower waters": if people of higher status follow the rules, so will people of lower status.
(윗물이 맑아야 아랫물이 맑다 Winmuri malgaya araenmuri makda.: A Korean proverb that means "If the upper waters are clear, so are the lower waters.")

The particles plus 고 하다 can be shortened at the end of a sentence, as follows:

Particle	Short form	When it's used	Example
라고 해요 rago haeyo	래요 raeyo	Nouns ending in vowels	벌써 8시래요. Beolsseo yeodeolsiraeyo. He said it's already 8:00.
이라고 해요 irago haeyo	이래요 iraeyo	Nouns ending in consonants	지각이래요. Jigagiraeyo. He called it tardiness.
ㄴ다고 해요 ndago haeyo	ㄴ대요 ndaeyo	Action verbs ending in vowels	늦게 온대요. Neutge ondaeyo. He said we came late.
는다고 해요 neundago haeyo	는대요 neundaeyo	Action verbs ending in consonants	늦는대요. Neunneundaeyo. He said we were late.
다고 해요 dago haeyo	대요 daeyo	Descriptive verbs (adjectives), past tense verbs with 았/었/였, 있다/없다	시간이 벌써 늦었대요. Sigani beolsseo neujeotdaeyo. He said it was already late.

Particle	Short form	When it's used	Example
자고 해요 jago haeyo	재요 jaeyo	Suggestions	친구가 정시에 오재요. **Chinguga jeongsie ojaeyo.** My friend suggested we come on time.
냐고 해요 nyago haeyo	내요 nyaeyo	Questions using descriptive verbs or nouns ending in vowels to someone of lower status than you	벌써 8시내요. **Beolsseo yeodeolsinyaeyo.** He asked if it was already 8:00.
이냐고 해요 inyago haeyo	이내요 inyaeyo	Questions using nouns ending in consonants to someone of lower status than you	지각이내요. jigaginyaeyo He asked if it was tardiness.
으냐고 해요 eunyago haeyo	으내요 eunyaeyo	Questions using descriptive verbs ending in consonants to someone of lower status than you	시간이 늦으내요. sigani neujeunyaeyo He asked if it was late.
느냐고 해요 neunyago haeyo	늦내요 neunnyaeyo	Questions using active and/or past tense verbs to someone of lower status than you	우리가 늦느내요. **Uriga neunneunyaeyo.** He asked if we were late.
라고 해요 rago haeyo	래요 raeyo	Commands ending in vowels	선생님이 정시에 오래요. **Seonsaengnimi jeongsie oraeyo.** The teacher told us to come on time.
으라고 해요 eurago haeyo	으래요 euraeyo	Commands ending in consonants	선생님이 우리에게 늦으래요. **Seonsaengnimi uriege neujeuraeyo.** The teacher told us to come late.
어 달라다고 해요 eo dalladago haeyo	어 달래요 eo dallaeyo	Questions to someone of higher status than you: 어, 우, 이 or 으	지호가 선생님께 늦으면 **돼 달래요**. **Jihoga seonsaengnimkke neujeumyeon dwae dallaeyo.** Jiho asked the teacher if it was okay to be late.
아 달라다 a dallada	아 달래요 a dallaeyo	Questions to someone of higher status than you: 아 or 오	지호가 선생님께 정시에 **와 달래요**. **Jihoga seonsaengnimkke jeongsie wa dallaeyo.** Jiho asked the teacher to please come on time.
여 달라다 yeo dallada	여 달래요 yeo dallaeyo	Questions to someone of higher status than you: 하다	지호가 선생님께 좀 지각해 **달래요**. **Jihoga seonsaengnimkke jom jigakae dallaeyo.** Jiho asked the teacher to please come a little late.

Note that 래요 raeyo, 대요 daeyo, 재요 jaeyo, and the rest remain the same regardless of tense. Just like in English, it will normally be in the past tense unless you're talking about something someone always says.

Finally, you can conjugate the expressions using 는 if you want to construct a sentence such as "That crazy little thing called love" or "The thing the teacher said."

Particle	With 는	When it's used	Example
라고 해요 rago haeyo	라는 raneun	Nouns ending in vowels	수라는 남자 Suraneun namja a boy called Sue
이라고 해요 irago haeyo	이라는 iraneun	Nouns ending in consonants	사랑이라는 것 sarangiraneun geot a thing called love
ㄴ다고 해요 ndago haeyo	ㄴ다는 ndaneun	Action verbs ending in vowels	간다는 남자 gandaneun namja a man who is said to be going
는다고 해요 neundago haeyo	는다는 neundaneun	Action verbs ending in consonants	먹는다는 음식 meokneundaneun eumsik a food that is said to be eaten
다고 해요 dago haeyo	다는 daneun	Descriptive verbs (adjectives), past tense verbs with 았/었/였, 있다/없다	좋다는 결과 jotaneun gyeolgwa a result that is called good
자고 해요 jago haeyo	자는 janeun	Suggestions	친구가 하자는 운동 chinguga hajaneun undong an exercise my friend suggested

I've left out the rest of the table because you'll just about never hear 냐는 nyaneun, 라는 (as an order) or 달라는. If you really need to know, you can figure out the pattern from the examples above.

Talking about What Others Have Said: Combinations

Beyond the basic 라고 하다 **rago hada**, 라는 **raneun**, etc., you can also combine indirect speech with a number of other grammatical patterns to make your sentences more complex and more precise. These are often contractions of (다, 자, 라, etc.) 고 하다 plus whatever you're adding to it: for instance, 라고 하다 plus 기에 becomes 라기에 **ragie**, 는 다고 하다 **neundago hada** plus 기에 becomes 는다기에 **neundagie**, etc. In cases where this is done, I've written the contracted expressions; in cases where it's not normally done, I haven't. Even if an expression is normally contracted, you can still use it in its original form. 라고 하기에 **rago hagie** isn't wrong. However, if you go around doing this on a regular basis, you might well end up sounding as awkward as you would if you never used contractions in English.

If you're unsure about the differences between the different expressions (e.g. 던데 **deonde** vs. 는데 **neunde**, 어서 **eoseo** vs. 니까 **nikka**) then you can look them up in their respective sections – 던데 is on page 188, 는데 on page 69, 어서 on page 66 and 니까 on page 67. They normally don't change meaning when added to indirect speech particles.

Finally, a few of the expressions below work or are only commonly used only with 라고 and 다고 expressions. In these cases I've cut off the 자고 **jago**/냐고 **nyago**/달라고 **dallago** part of the table.

Here's a closer look at some of the patterns.

Particle	Plus	Equals	Meaning	Example
(이/으)라고 하다 (i/eu)rago hada	여요 yeoyo (see page 17)	~(이/으) 라고요 (i/eu) ragoyo	You said ~?	그것이 진짜라고요? Geugeosi jinjjaragoyo? You said that was true?
(ㄴ/는)다고 하다 (n/neun) dago hada	여요 (see page 17)	~(ㄴ/는) 다고요 (n/ neun)dagoyo	You said ~?	민수가 늦는다고요? Minsuga neunneundagoyo? You said Minsu is late?
자고 하다 jago hada	여요 (see page 17)	~자고요 ~jagoyo	You suggested ~?	민수가 빨리 가자고요? Minsuga ppalli gajagoyo? Minsu suggested we go quickly?
(이/으/느)냐고 하다 (i/eu/neu) nyago hada	여요 (see page 17)	~(이/으/느) 냐고요 (i/eu/ neu) nyagoyo	You asked ~?	민수가 언제 오냐고요? Minsuga eonje onyagoyo? Minsu asked when to come?.
(아/어/여) 달라고 하다 (a/eo/yeo) dallago hada	여요 (see page 17)	~아/어/여 달라고요 a/eo/yeo dallagoyo	You asked ~?	선생님께 6시에 와 달라고요? Seonsaengnimkke yeoseotsie wa dallagoyo? You asked the teacher to come at 6?

When using this in 반말, drop 요 and just use the 라고, 다고, 자고 etc. part of the question.

Particle	Plus	Equals	Meaning	Example
(이/으)라고 하다 (i/eu) rago hada	여서 yeoseo (see page 66)	A(이/으) 라고 해서 B A (i/eu)rago haeseo B	I heard that/ someone said A, so B	그것이 진짜라고 해서 믿었어요. Geugeosi jinjjarago haeseo mideosseoyo. I heard that was true, so I believed it.
(ㄴ/는)다고 하다 (n/neun) dago hada	여서 (see page 66)	A(ㄴ/는)다고 해서 B A (n/ neun)dago haeseo B	I heard that/ someone said A, so B	민수가 늦는다고 해서 나도 늦게 왔어요. Minsuga neunneundago haeseo nado neutge wasseoyo. They said Minsu is late, so I came late too.
자고 하다 jago hada	여서 (see page 66)	A자고 해서 B A jago haeseo B	I heard that/ someone suggested A, so B	민수가 빨리 가자고 해서 서둘렀어요. Minsuga ppalli gajago haeseo seodulleosseoyo. Minsu said to go quickly, so I hurried.
(이/으/느) 냐고 하다 (i/ eu/neu)nyago hada	여서 (see page 66)	A(이/으/느) 냐고 해서 B A (i/eu/neu) nyago haeseo B	I heard that/ someone asked A, so B	민수가 언제 오느냐고 해서 6시에 오라고 했어요. Minsuga eonje oneunyago haeseo yeoseotsie orago haesseoyo. Minsu asked when to come, so I told him to come at 6.
(아/어/여) 달라고 하다 (a/eo/yeo) dallago hada	여서 (see page 66)	A아/어/여 달라고 해서 B A a/eo/yeo dallago haeseo B	I heard that/ someone asked A, so B	선생님께 6시에 와 달라고 해서 나도 빨리 준비했어요. Seonsaengnimkke yeoseotsie wa dallago haeseo nado ppalli junbihaesseoyo. I asked the teacher to come at 6, so I had to get ready quickly too.

Particle	Plus	Equals	Meaning	Example
(이/으)라고 하다 (i/eu) rago hada	니(까) ni(kka) (see page 67)	A(이/으) 라니(까) B A (i/eu) rani(kka) B	I heard that/ someone said A, so B	그것이 진짜**라니까** 이것은 아마 가짜일 거예요. Geugeosi jinjjaranikka igeoseun ama gajjail geoyeyo. I heard that was true (or real), so I think this is fake.
(ㄴ/는)다고 하다 (n/ neun)dago hada	니(까) (see page 67)	A(ㄴ/는) 다니(까) B A (n/neun) dani(kka) B	I heard that/ someone said A, so B	민수가 늦**는다니**, 민수한테 전화해 주세요. Minsuga neunneundani, Minsuhante jeonhwahae juseyo. They said Minsu is late, so please call him.
자고 하다 jago hada	니(까) (see page 67)	A자니(까) B A jani(kka) B	I heard that/ someone suggested A, so B	민수가 빨리 가**자니까** 빨리 서두르세요. Minsuga ppalli gajanikka ppalli seodureuseyo. Minsu suggested to go quickly, so please hurry up.
(이/으/느) 냐고 하다 (i/eu/neu) nyago hada	니(까) (see page 67)	A(이/으/느) 냐니(까) B A (i/eu/neu) nyani(kka) B	I heard that/ someone asked A, so B	민수한테 언제 오**냐니까** 안 온다고 했어요. Minsuhante eonje onyanikka an ondago haesseoyo. I asked Minsu when he was coming, and he said he would not come.
(아/어/여) 달라고 하다 (a/eo/ yeo)dallago hada	니(까) (see page 67)	A아/어/여 달라니(까) B A a/eo/yeo dallani(kka) B	I heard that/ someone asked A, so B	선생님이 6시에 와 달라**니까** 빨리 준비하세요. Seonsaengnimi yeoseotsie wa dallanikka ppalli junbihaseyo. The teacher asked you to come at 6, so please get ready quickly.

(ㄴ/는)다니 (n/neun)dani is a particularly common expression. Don't confuse it with 더니 deoni (see page 190), which has to do with personal experience and is totally different.

You can also use ~(이)라니까(요) ~(i)ranikka(yo) and ~(ㄴ/는)다니까(요) ~(n/neun) danikka(yo) at the end of a sentence; in this case, use it when you want to repeat yourself in order to emphasize what you already said. It's the Korean equivalent of "I said, ~!"

Particle	Plus	Equals	Meaning	Example
(이/으)라고 하다 (i/eu) rago hada	는데 neunde (see page 69)	A(이/으)라고 하는데 B A (i/eu) rago haneunde B	I heard that/ someone said A; B	그것이 진짜라고 **하는데** 믿었어요. Geugeosi jinjjarago haneunde mideosseoyo. I heard that was true, so I believed it.
(ㄴ/는)다고 하다 (n/ neun)dago hada	는데 (see page 69)	A(ㄴ/는)다고 하는데/한데 B A (n/neun)dago haneunde/hande B	I heard that/ someone said A; B	민수가 늦**는다고 하는데** 전화해 주세요. Minsuga neunneundago haneunde jeonhwahaejuseyo. They said Minsu is late; please call him.

Particle	Plus	Equals	Meaning	Example
자고 하다 jago hada	는데 neunde (see page 69)	A자고 하는데B A jago haneunde B	I heard that/ someone suggested A; B	민수가 빨리 가자고 하는데 서둘러요. Minsuga ppalli gajago haneunde seodulleoyo. Minsu suggested we go quickly; let's hurry.
(이/으/느) 냐고 하다 (i/eu/neu)nyago hada	는데 (see page 69)	A(이/으/느) 냐고 하는데 B A (i/eu/neu)nyago haneunde B	I heard that/ someone asked A; B	민수가 언제 오냐고 하는데 저도 몰라서 아직 대답 할 수 없어요. Minsuga eonje onyago haneunde jeodo mollaseo ajik daedapal su eopseoyo. Minsu asked when to come; I don't know either, so I can't answer him yet.
(아/어/여) 달라고 하다 (a/eo/yeo) dallago hada	는데 (see page 69)	A아/어/여 달라고 하는데 B A a/eo/yeo dallago haneunde B	I heard that/ someone asked A; B	선생님께서 6시에 와 달라고 하는데 빨리 준비할래요. Seonsaengnimkkeseo yeoseotsie wa dallago haneunde ppalli junbihallaeyo. The teacher asked us to come at 6; let's get ready quickly.

Particle	Plus	Equals	Meaning	Example
(이/으)라고 하다 (i/eu) rago hada	여도 yeodo (see page 104)	A(이/으)라고 해도 B A (i/eu) rago haedo B	B even though someone says A	그것이 진짜라고 해도 정시에 와야 돼요. Geugeosi jinjjarago haedo jeongsie waya dwaeyo. Even if (you say) that's true, you still have to come on time.
(ㄴ/는)다고 하다 (n/neun)dago hada	여도 (see page 104)	A(ㄴ/는)다고 해도 B A (n/neun)dago haedo B	B even though someone says A	바쁘다고 해도 정시에 와야 돼요. Bappeudago haedo jeongsie waya dwaeyo. Even if (you say) you're busy, you still have to come on time.
자고 하다 jago hada	여도 (see page 104)	A자고 해도 B A jago haedo B	B even though someone suggests A	민수가 빨리 가자고 해도 그 일을 끝내 주세요. Minsuga ppalli gajago haedo geu ireul kkeunnaejuseyo. Even if Minsu suggested you leave quickly, please finish that job.
(이/으/느) 냐고 하다 (i/eu/neu) nyago hada	여도 (see page 104)	A(이/으/느) 냐고 해도 B A (i/eu/neu)nyago haedo B	B even though someone asks A	민수가 선물이 무엇이냐고 해도 알려 주지 마세요. Minsuga seonmuri mueosinyago haedo allyeojuji maseyo. Even if Minsu asks what the present is, please don't tell him.
(아/어/여) 달라고 하다 (a/eo/yeo)dallago hada	여도 (see page 104)	A아/어/여 달라고 해도 B A a/eo/yeo dallago haedo B	B even though someone asks A	선생님께서 6시에 와 달라고 해도 우리는 7시 까지 가요. Seonsaengnimkkeseo yeoseotsie wa dallago haedo urineun ilgopsi kkaji gayo. Even if teacher asked us to come at 6, let's go there by 7.

Particle	Plus	Equals	Meaning	Example
(이/으)라고 하다 (i/eu) rago hada	던데 deonde (see page 188)	A(이)라던데 B A (i) radeonde B	I heard that someone said A; B	그것이 진짜**라던데** 진짜예요? Geugeosi jinjjaradeonde jinjjayeyo? I heard that was true; is it?
(ㄴ/는)다고 하다 (n/neun) dago hada	던데 (see page 188)	A(ㄴ/는) 다던데 B A (n/neun) dadeonde B	I heard that someone said A; B	민수가 늦는다고 하던데 전화해 주세요. Minsuga neunneundago hadeonde jeonhwahaejuseyo. They said Minsu is late; please call him.

The expressions above are normally used in two situations. A reports a fact that you heard. B can either be a recommendation or suggestion based on that fact (as in the example for 라던데 **radeonde**) or a request for confirmation (진짜예요? **Jinjjayeyo?** 사실 이에요? **Sasirieyo?** 정말이에요? **Jeongmarieyo?**) as in the example for 다던데 **dadeonde**.

Particle	Plus	Equals	Meaning	Example
(이/으)라고 하다 (i/eu) rago hada	면 myeon (see page 283)	A(이/으) 라고 하면 B A (i/eu)rago hamyeon B	If (someone says) A, then B	그것이 진짜**라고 하면** 저도 믿을 거예요. Geugeosi jinjjarago hamyeon jeodo mideul geoyeyo. If you say that's true, then I'll believe it.
(ㄴ/는)다고 하다 (n/neun) dago hada	면 (see page 283)	A(ㄴ/는)다고 하면 B A (n/ neun)dago hamyeon B	If (someone says) A, then B	민수가 늦었**다고 하면** 민수가 벌금을 내야 돼요. Minsuga neujeotdago hamyeon Minsuga beolgeumeul naeya dwaeyo. If they say Minsu was late, he'll have to pay a fine.
자고 하다 jago hada	면 (see page 283)	A자고 하면 B A jago hamyeon B	If (someone suggests) A, then B	민수가 빨리 가**자고 하면** 서둘러요. Minsuga ppalli gajago hamyeon seodulleoyo. If Minsu suggested we go quickly, then let's hurry.
(이/으/ㄴ) 냐고 하다 (i/ eu/neu)nyago hada	면 (see page 283)	A(이/으/ㄴ) 냐고 하면 B A (i/eu/ neu)nyago hamyeon B	If (someone asks) A, then B	민수가 언제 와야 하**냐고 하면** 그냥 오지 말라고 하세요. Minsuga eonje waya hanyago hamyeon geunyang oji mallago haseyo. If Minsu asks when he needs to come, please tell him not to come.
(아/어/여) 달라고 하다 (a/eo/yeo) dallago hada	면 (see page 283)	A아/어/여 달라고 하면 B A a/eo/ yeodallago hamyeon B	If (someone asks) A, then B	선생님께서 6시에 와 달**라고 하면** 우리 빨리 서둘러요. Seonsaengnimkkeseo yeoseotsie wa dallago hamyeon uri ppalli seodulleoyo. If the teacher asks us to come at 6, then let's get ready quickly.

Particle	Plus	Equals	Meaning	Example
(이/으)라고 하다 (i/eu) rago hada	ㄹ 수 있다 r su itda (see page 194)	~(이)라고 할 수 있다 ~(i) rago hal su itda	It can be said that ~	그것은 진짜라고 할 수 있어요. Geugeoseun jinjjarago hal su isseoyo. That can be said to be true.
(ㄴ/는)다고 하다 (n/neun) dago hada	ㄹ 수 있다 (see page 194)	~(ㄴ/는)다고 할 수 있다 ~(n/ neun)dago hal su itda	It can be said that ~	그것은 너무 어렵다고 할 수 있어요. Geugeoseun neomu eoryeopdago hal su isseoyo. That can be said to be too difficult.

You can also use 할 수 없다 **hal su eopda** to express that something can't be said or 할 수도 있다 **hal sudo itda** to say that something else can be said.

그것이 진짜**라고 할 수 없어요**. Geugeosi jinjjarago hal su eopseoyo. That can't be said to be true.

A: 그것이 진짜**라고 할 수 있어요**. Geugeosi jinjjarago hal su isseoyo. That can be said to be true.

B: 이것이 진짜**라고 할 수도 있어요**. Igeosi jinjjarago hal sudo isseoyo. This can also be said to be true.

Particle	Plus	Equals	Meaning	Example
(이/으) 라고 하다 (i/eu)rago hada	기에 gie (see page 73)	A(이/으) 라기에 B A (i/eu) ragie B	Since I heard that A, (I did) B	친구가 그것은 진짜라기에 믿었어요. Chinguga geugeoseun jinjjaragie mideosseoyo. Since my friend said that was true, I believed it.
(ㄴ/는) 다고 하다 (n/neun) dago hada	기에 (see page 73)	A(ㄴ/는) 다기에 B A (n/neun) dagie B	Since I heard that A, (I did) B	민수가 늦는다기에 민수를 기다렸어요. Minsuga neunneundagie minsureul gidaryeosseoyo. Since I heard Minsu was late, I waited for him.
자고 하다 jago hada	기에 (see page 73)	A자기에 B A jagie B	Since someone suggested A, (I did) B	민수가 빨리 가자기에 서둘렀어요. Minsuga ppalli gajagie seodulleosseoyo. Since Minsu said to go quickly, I hurried.
(이/으/느) 냐고 하다 (i/eu/neu) nyago hada	기에 (see page 73)	A(이/으/ 느)냐기에 B A (i/eu/ neu)nyagie B	Since someone asked A, (I did) B	민수가 언제 오냐기에 가영한테 전화해서 물어봤어요. Minsuga eonje onyagie Kayounghante jeonhwahaeseo mureobwasseoyo. Since Minsu asked when to come, I called Kayoung and asked her.
(아/어/여) 달라고 하다 (a/eo/ yeo)dallago hada	기에 (see page 73)	A아/어/여 달라기에 B A a/eo/ yeodallagie B	Since someone asked A, (I did) B	선생님께서 6시에 와 달라기에 빨리 준비 해야 돼요. Seonsaengnimkkeseo yeoseotsie wa dallagie ppalli junbi haeya dwaeyo. Since I asked the teacher to come at 6, we need to get ready quickly.

Particle	Plus	Equals	Meaning	Example
(이/으)라고 하다 (i/eu) rago hada	더라 deora (see page 192)	~(이/으)라더라고요 ~(i/eu)radeoragoyo	I heard that ~	그것은 진짜<u>라더라고요</u>. Geugeoseun jinjjaradeoragoyo. I heard that was true.
(ㄴ/는)다고 하다 (n/neun) dago hada	더라 (see page 192)	~(ㄴ/는)다더라고요 ~(n/neun)dadeoragoyo	I heard that ~	민수가 늦었<u>다더라고요</u>. Minsuga neujeotdadeoragoyo. I heard Minsu was late.
자고 하다 jago hada	더라 deora (see page 192)	~자더라고요 ~jadeoragoyo	I heard that ~	민수가 빨리 가<u>자더라고요</u>. Minsuga ppalli gajadeoragoyo. I heard that Minsu suggested we go quickly.
(이/으/ㄴ)냐고 하다 (i/eu/neu)nyago hada	더라 (see page 192)	~(이/으/ㄴ)냐더라고요 ~(i/eu/neu)nyadeoragoyo	I heard that ~	민수가 언제 오<u>냐더라고요</u>. Minsuga eonje onyadeoragoyo. I heard that Minsu asked when to come.
(아/어/여)달라고 하다 (a/eo/yeo) dallago hada	더라 (see page 192)	~아/어/여달라더라고요 ~a/eo/yeo dalladeoragoyo	I heard that ~	선생님께서 6시에 <u>와 달라더라고요</u>. Seon-saeng-nim-kkeseo yeoseotsie wa dal-la-deoragoyo. I heard that the teacher asked you to come at six.

Note that the difference between 라더라고요 radeoragoyo (라더라 radeora in 반말) and the regular 라고 하다 rago hada is that when you add 더라고요 deoragoyo, you're specifically talking about your own personal experiences: a rumor or something that you heard. If you personally saw Minsu come in late, you'd use 늦었더라고요 neujeotdeoragoyo, but if Kayoung told you that Minsu came in late, you could say 늦었다더라고요 neujeotdadeoragoyo: you heard that Minsu came late even though you didn't personally see him enter.

Particle	Plus	Equals	Meaning	Example
(이/으)라고 하다 (i/eu) rago hada	지요 jiyo (see page 315)	~(이/으)라지요 (i/eu) rajiyo	I heard ~; is it true?	그것이 진짜<u>라지요</u>? Geugeosi jinjjarajiyo? I heard that was true; it is, isn't it?
(ㄴ/는)다고 하다 (n/neun) dago hada	지요 (see page 315)	~(ㄴ/는)다지요 (n/neun)dajiyo	I heard ~; is it true?	민수가 늦었<u>다지요</u>? Minsuga neujeotdajiyo? I heard Minsu was late; that's true, right?
자고 하다 jago hada	지요 (see page 315)	~자고 하지요 jago hajiyo	I heard ~; is it true?	민수가 빨리 가<u>자고 했지요</u>? Minsuga ppalli gajago haetjiyo? Minsu suggested we go quickly, didn't he?
(이/으/ㄴ)냐고 하다 (i/eu/neu)nyago hada	지요 (see page 315)	~(이/으/ㄴ)냐고 하지요 (i/eu/neu) nyago hajiyo	I heard ~; is it true?	민수가 언제 오<u>냐고 했지요</u>? Minsuga eonje onyago haetjiyo? Minsu asked when to come, didn't he?

Particle	Plus	Equals	Meaning	Example
(아/어/여) 달라고 하다 (a/eo/yeo) dallago hada	지요 (see page 315)	~아/어/여 달라고 하지요 ~a/eo/yeo dallago hajiyo	I heard ~; is it true?	선생님께서 6시에 <u>와 달라고 했지요</u>? Seonsaengnimkkeseo yeoseotsie wa dallago haetjiyo? The teacher asked us to come at 6, didn't he?

Particle	Plus	Equals	Meaning	Example
(이/으)라고 하다 (i/eu) rago hada	들 deul (see page 31)	~(이)라고들 하다 ~(i) ragodeul hada	They say that ~	그것이 진짜<u>라고들 해요</u>. Geugeosi jinjjaragodeul haeyo. They say that's true.
(ㄴ/는)다고 하다 (n/neun) dago hada	들 (see page 31)	~(ㄴ/는) 다고들 하다 ~(n/neun) dagodeul hada	They say that ~	야채가 건강에 좋<u>다고들 해요</u>. Yachaega geongange jotagodeul haeyo. They say vegetables are good for your health.

Talking about What Others Have Said: Spreading Rumors

Let's say you heard something from someone and want to confirm it. Here are some ways to do so.

> **Speaking > Writing**
> ~지요 jiyo?   "~, eh?"   ★★★★★

어제 늦었<u>지요</u>? **Eoje neujeotjiyo?** You were late yesterday, weren't you?

This ending has many uses. One of the most commonly used is to confirm information you expect the other person is also aware of, that is to check your facts. I liken it to the stereotypical Canadian use of "eh?" While speaking, it can be, and usually is, contracted to "죠."

You can also use it to offer to do something. When used in this way, it's not very forceful, much like when you offer to do something in English.

Finally, it can be used to make suggestions. When using it toward people of higher status than you, it translates as "Would you like to ~." If you use 지 alone toward people of lower status than you, it's a little more forceful and suggests they should really do ~. You'll hear this used all the time if you work in an elementary school or kindergarten. Below are examples of both uses:

HOW IT'S CONJUGATED

		Past	Present	Future
Action verbs ending in a vowel	하다	했지요? haetjiyo?	하지요? hajiyo?	하겠지요? hagetjiyo?
Action verbs ending in a consonant	먹다	먹었지요? meogeotjiyo?	먹지요? meokjiyo?	먹겠지요? meokgetjiyo?
Descriptive verbs (adjectives) ending in a vowel	예쁘다	예뻤지요? yeppeotjiyo?	예쁘지요? yeppeujiyo?	예쁘겠지요? yeppeugetjiyo?
Descriptive verbs (adjectives) ending in a consonant	작다	작았지요? jagatjiyo?	작지요? jakjiyo?	작겠지요? jakgetjiyo?
Nouns ending in a vowel	남자	남자였지요? namjayeotjiyo?	남자지요? namjajiyo?	남자겠지요? namjagetjiyo?
Nouns ending in a consonant	물	물이었지요? murieotjiyo?	물이지요? murijiyo?	물이겠지요? murigetjiyo?

TAKE NOTE

지 ji and 지요 jiyo have many uses, and it's important not to get them confused. This 지요 always goes at the end of a sentence, never before anything else, which distinguishes it from 지 말다 ji malda, 지 않다 ji anta and other negatives with 지.

As for telling 지요 (I'll) apart from 지요 (you should) and 지요 (isn't it?), that's mainly a matter of context.

EXAMPLE SENTENCES

오늘이 생일이**지요**? Oneuri saengirijiyo? Today's your birthday, isn't it?

오늘이 생일이**죠**? Oneuri saengirijyo? Today's your birthday, isn't it?

The two sentences above are the same, but the second form with 죠 is more common in spoken Korean.

축구를 좋아하**죠**? Chukgureul joahajyo? You like soccer, don't you?

감기 걸렸**죠**? Gamgi geollyeotjyo? You caught a cold, didn't you?

늦겠어요. 지금 출발하시**지요**. Neutgesseoyo. Jigeum chulbalhasijiyo. You'll be late. Why don't you go now?

Here's 지요, used to offer to do things:

제가 저녁을 사**지요**. Jega jeonyeogeul sajiyo. I'll buy dinner.

내일 보**지요**. Naeil bojiyo. I'll see you tomorrow.

제가 먼저 가**지요**. Jega meonjeo gajiyo. I'll go first.

And here it is to suggest things to people:

같이 가시**지요**. Gachi gasijiyo. Would you like to go together?

같이 가**지**. Gachi gaji. We really should go together.

비가 오는데 우산을 가지고 오시**지요**. Biga oneunde usaneul gajigo osijiyo.
You should bring an umbrella since it's raining.

이 떡을 먹어 보시**지요**. I tteogeul meogeo bosijiyo.
Would you like to try this rice cake?

얘들아! 떠들지 말**지**. Yaedeura! Tteodeulji malji.
Children! You shouldn't chatter.

숙제를 꼼꼼하게 하**지**. Sukjereul kkomkkomhage haji.
You should have done your homework carefully.

	Speaking > Writing
~(이)라/(ㄴ/는)다면서요 (i) ra/(n/neun)damyeonseoyo?	**"Is it true that~?"** **★★★**

어제 늦었**다면서요**? Eoje neujeotda-myeon-seo-yo?
I heard you were late yesterday. Is it true?

This is really an indirect speech combination (similar to the rest of pages 304 to 315), but it goes in this section because it's not versatile like the others and its meaning can't be deduced from just looking at it. It's really an expression unto itself. It's used to check your facts and confirm whether something you heard is true or fictitious.

HOW IT'S CONJUGATED

		Past	Present	Future
Action verbs ending in a vowel	하다	했다면서요 haetdamyeonseoyo	한다면서요 handamyeonseoyo	하겠다면서요 hagetdamyeonseoyo
Action verbs ending in a consonant	먹다	먹었다면서요 meogeotdamyeonseoyo	먹는다면서요 meokneundamyeonseoyo	먹겠다면서요 meokgetdamyeonseoyo
Descriptive verbs (adjectives) ending in a vowel	예쁘다	예뻤다면서요 yeppeotdamyeonseoyo	예쁘다면서요 yeppeudamyeonseoyo	예쁘겠다면서요 yeppeugetdamyeonseoyo

		Past	Present	Future
Descriptive verbs (adjectives) ending in a consonant	작다	작았다면서요 jagatdamyeonseoyo	작다면서요 jakdamyeonseoyo	작겠다면서요 jakgetdamyeonseoyo
Nouns ending in a vowel	남자	남자라면서요 namjaramyeonseoyo	남자라면서요	남자라면서요
Nouns ending in a consonant	물	물이라면서요 muriramyeonseoyo	물이라면서요	물이라면서요

EXAMPLE SENTENCES

오늘이 생일<u>이라면서요</u>? Oneuri saengiriramyeonseoyo?
I heard it's your birthday. Is it true?

축구를 좋아<u>한다면서요</u>? Chukgureul joahandamyeonseoyo?
I heard you like soccer. Is it true?

감기가 걸렸<u>다면서요</u>? Gamgiga geollyeotdamyeonseoyo?
I heard you caught a cold. Is it true?

Speaking > Writing

~(이)라는/(ㄴ/는)다는 말이다? ~(i)raneun/(n/neun) daneun marida?   "Are you saying that ~?"   ★★★

어제 늦었<u>다는 말이에요</u>? Eoje neujeotdaneun marieyo?
Are you saying you were late yesterday?

This ending is used to confirm, refute, or emphasize what someone said.

HOW IT'S FORMED

Indirect speech particles are used since you're talking about something you heard. They're conjugated with 는 (see page 23) which turns that part of the sentence into an adjective which describes 말, or "word." 이다 just means "it is."

HOW IT'S CONJUGATED

		Past	Present	Future
Action verbs ending in a vowel	하다	했다는 말이다 haetdaneun marida	한다는 말이다 handaneun marida	하겠다는 말이다 hagetdaneun marida
Action verbs ending in a consonant	먹다	먹었다는 말이다 meogeotdaneun marida	먹는다는 말이다 meokneundaneun marida	먹겠다는 말이다 meokgetdaneun marida
Descriptive verbs (adjectives) ending in a vowel	예쁘다	예뻤다는 말이다 yeppeotdaneun marida	예쁘다는 말이다 yeppeudaneun marida	예쁘겠다는 말이다 yeppeugetdaneun marida
Descriptive verbs (adjectives) ending in a consonant	작다	작았다는 말이다 jagatdaneun marida	작다는 말이다 jakdaneun marida	작겠다는 말이다 jakgetdaneun marida
Nouns ending in a vowel	남자	남자라는 말이다 namjaraneun marida	남자라는 말이다	남자라는 말이다
Nouns ending in a consonant	물	물이라는 말이다 muriraneun marida	물이라는 말이다	물이라는 말이다

EXAMPLE SENTENCES

오늘이 생일이**라는 말이에요**? Oneuri saengiriraneun marieyo?
Are you saying it's your birthday today?

축구를 좋아**한다는 말이에요**? 축구 잘 못한다고 하던데요.
Chukgureul joahandaneun marieyo? Chukgu jal motandago hadeondeyo.
Are you saying you like soccer? I heard you're not very good at it.

감기가 걸렸**다는 말이에요**? 거짓말인것 같은데요.
Gamgiga geollyeotdaneun marieyo? Geojin-marin-geot gateundeyo.
Are you saying you caught a cold? That doesn't seem true.

Speaking > Writing

~**다니요**/(이)**라니요**   "What do you mean, ~?"   ★★
daniyo/(i)raniyo?

어제 늦었**다니요**? Eoje neujeotdaniyo? What's this about being late yesterday?

This expression indicates surprise at something you just heard. If someone asks you about that class you're supposed to be teaching when you hadn't heard anything about any class, this is the expression for you. It's yet another way of repeating something that was said, but one that adds a touch of surprise or denial. Use this when someone is telling you something they've heard which you don't think is true; it's also useful in situations where you've been wrongly accused.

HOW IT'S CONJUGATED

A wonderful thing about this expression is that you don't have to worry as much about remembering which of the indirect speech verb endings to use with it because you just use 다니요 with all verbs, whether they're active or descriptive.

		Past	Present
Action verbs ending in a vowel	하다	했다니요 haetdaniyo	하다니요 hadaniyo
Action verbs ending in a consonant	먹다	먹었다니요 meogeotdaniyo	먹다니요 meokdaniyo
Descriptive verbs (adjectives) ending in a vowel	예쁘다	예뻤다니요 yeppeotdaniyo	예쁘다니요 yeppeudaniyo
Descriptive verbs (adjectives) ending in a consonant	작다	작았다니요 jagatdaniyo	작다니요 jakdaniyo
Nouns ending in a vowel	남자	남자라니요 namjaraniyo	남자라니요
Nouns ending in a consonant	물	물이라니요 muriraniyo	물이라니요

EXAMPLE SENTENCES

오늘이 생일이**라니요**? Oneuri saengiriraniyo?
Birthday? What's this about a birthday?

축구를 좋아하**다니요**? Chukgureul joahadaniyo? What do you mean I like soccer?

감기 걸렸**다니요**? Gamgi geollyeotdaniyo? Cold? What cold?

Talking about What Others Have Said: According to

		Speaking = Writing
A([으]ㄴ/는/[으]ㄹ [eu]n/ neun/[eu]l) 대로 daero B	"B according to A"	★★★★

늦게 오더라도 교통법규**대로** 운전하세요.
Neutge odeorado gyotongbeopgyudaero unjeonhaseyo.
Even if you're late, please obey the traffic rules.

Here's another way to say "according to."

HOW IT'S CONJUGATED

A can be a noun, in which case it's directly followed by 대로 with no space in between. It can also be a present tense action verb conjugated with 는 and followed by a space and then 대로. Descriptive verbs can't be used with 대로, though you can change them to action verbs using 아/어/여지다; see page 25 for how to do that.

		Past	Present	Future
Action verbs ending in a vowel	하다	한 대로 han daero	하는 대로 haneun daero	할 대로 hal daero
Action verbs ending in a consonant	먹다	먹은 대로 meogeun daero	먹은 대로	먹을 대로 meogeul daero
Nouns ending in a vowel	예보	예보대로 yebo daero	예보대로	예보대로
Nouns ending in a consonant	마음	마음대로 maeumdaero	마음대로	마음대로

TAKE NOTE

대로 **daero** can't be used with negative expressions. It can also never be used with adjectives except for 고 싶다 **go sipda**, 좋다 **jota** and 편하다 **pyeonhada**.

A는 대로 B also means that B immediately follows A; see page 273. There's really no way to tell the two apart except for context, so be careful.

A few commonly used words with 대로:

마음**대로** maeumdaero	as you wish
예상**대로** yesangdaero	as expected
시키는 **대로** sikineun daero	as ordered
얘기한 **대로** yaegihan daero	as said
되는 **대로** doeneun daero	as it happens (on its own, with no interference)
제멋**대로** jemeotdaero	as one likes

EXAMPLE SENTENCES

마음**대로** 했어요. Maeumdaero haesseoyo. I did as I wished.

좋을 **대로** 하세요. Joeul daero haseyo. Please do whatever is best.

그 책**대로** 연습했어요. Geu chaekdaero yeonseupaesseoyo.
I practiced according to what that book recommended.

| A에 **따라/따르면** e ttara/ ttareumyeon B | "According to A, B" | **Speaking < Writing**
★★★ |

민수**에 따르면** 가영이가 늦을 거예요.
Minsue ttareumyeon Kayoungiga neujeul geoyeyo.
According to Minsu, Kayoung will be late.

It's good to have opinions (see page 136), but it's even better to be able to back up your opinions with facts. Here's a good way to do that in Korean. It's very formal, which is great for those occasions when you want to sound good.

HOW IT'S FORMED

따르다 means "to follow" and can be conjugated as either 따라 or 따르면 to say "according to." Literally translated, it's "following A" or "if we follow A."

HOW IT'S CONJUGATED

A is a noun indicating your source: the newspaper, your mom, an expert in the subject, a drunk guy in a bar… B is what that person said.

		All tenses
Nouns ending in a vowel	남자	남자에 따라 namjae ttara 남자에 따르면 namjae ttareumyeon
Nouns ending in a consonant	신문	신문에 따라 sinmune ttara 신문에 따르면 sinmune ttareumyeon

TAKE NOTE

If you're using the expression to quote someone (other than the person giving you an order), then you should use 따르면 rather than 따라. 따라 and 따르면 can be used interchangeably when the meaning is "according to A" and A is a rule or an order.

엄마**에 따르면** 야채를 많이 먹어야 돼요.
Eommae ttareumyeon yachaereul mani meogeoya dwaeyo.
According to my mother, you have to eat a lot of vegetables.

엄마의 말**에 따라** 야채를 많이 먹었어요.
Eommaui mare ttara yachaereul mani meogeosseoyo.
Because my mother ordered me (according to my mother's orders), I ate a lot of vegetables.

법**에 따라** 처리하세요. **Beobe ttara cheorihaseyo.** Please deal with it lawfully (according to the law).

따르면 can normally be traded for 의하면 **uihamyeon** (see the next page), also interchangeably, except that 의하면 is normally not used if the person you're quoting is just anyone. If you're talking about a newspaper, an expert, a book, or something that carries some authority, you can use 의하면; however, if you're quoting your father or the aforementioned drunk guy at the bar, better go with 따르면.

일기 예보**에 따르면** 내일 비가 올 거예요.
Ilgi yeboe ttareumyeon naeil biga ol geoyeyo.
According to the weather forecast, it's going to rain tomorrow.

일기 예보**에 의하면** 내일 비가 올 거예요.
Ilgi yeboe uihamyeon naeil biga ol geoyeyo.
According to the weather forecast, it's going to rain tomorrow.

B will normally include an indirect speech particle (see page 304) if you're quoting a person.

따라 (and its parent 따르다) have a number of uses aside from "according to." For instance, you can talk about doing something "according to or depending on" A such as deciding whether or not to travel depending on your finances.

When 따르다 is used to mean "follow"; it normally follows an object with 을/를. When it means "according to," it follows 에.

엄마를 따랐어요. Eommareul ttarasseoyo. I followed my mother.

엄마에 따르면 야채를 많이 먹어야 돼요.
Eommae ttareumyeon yachaereul mani meogeoya dwaeyo.
According to my mother, you have to eat a lot of vegetables.

이 길**을 따라가면** 학교가 곧 보일 거예요.
I gireul ttaragamyeon hakgyoga got boil geoyeyo.
If you follow this street, you'll soon see the school.

이 길**에 따르면** 학교가 곧 보일 거예요.
I gire ttareumyeon hakgyoga got boil geoyeyo.
According to this street, you'll soon see the school. (nonsensical; applies only to a kind of fairy tale)

EXAMPLE SENTENCES

일기 예보**에 따르면** 내일 비가 올 거예요.
Ilgi yeboe ttareumyeon naeil biga ol geoyeyo.
According to the weather forecast, it's going to rain tomorrow.

대답은 상황**에 따라** 달라요. Daedabeun sanghwange ttara dallayo.
The answer is different, depending on the situation.

> | | Speaking < Writing |
> |---|---|
> | A에 **의하면** e uihamyeon B   "According to A, B" | ★★★ |

뉴스**에 의하면** 금년 장마가 늦게 올 거예요.
Nyuseue uihamyeon geumnyeon jangmaga neutge ol geoyeyo.
According to the news, the rainy season will be late this year.

Here's another way to say "according to."

HOW IT'S FORMED

의하다 means "according to" and is combined with 면 to get 의하면.

HOW IT'S CONJUGATED

A is your source: a newspaper, an expert, the weather report, and the like. B is what that source said.

		All tenses
Nouns ending in a vowel	전문가 jeonmunga	전문가에 의하면 jeonmungae uihamyeon
Nouns ending in a consonant	신문 sinmun	신문에 의하면 sinmune uihamyeon

TAKE NOTE

If you're talking about a newspaper, an expert, a book, or something that carries some authority, you can use 의하면; however, if you're quoting your father or some drunk guy at the bar, better go with 따라 or 따르면 (see page 322). For authoritative sources, 의하면, 따라 and 따르면 are all acceptable.

EXAMPLE SENTENCES

일기 예보**에 의하면** 내일 비가 올 거예요.
Ilgi yeboe uihamyeon naeil biga ol geoyeyo.
According to the weather forecast, it's going to rain tomorrow.

경제 전문가**에 의하면** 경제가 좋아질 거예요.
Gyeongje jeonmungae uihamyeon gyeongjega joajil geoyeyo.
According to an economist, the economy is going to improve.

> | | Speaking > Writing |
> |---|---|
> | A(으)ㄴ/는 **바** (eu)n/neun ba B   "According to A, B" | ★★★ |

뉴스에 나**온 바**에 의하면 금년 장마가 늦게 올 거예요.
Nyuseue naon bae uihamyeon geumnyeon jangmaga neutge ol geoyeyo.
According to the news, the rainy season will be late this year.

바 is somewhat different. It's what's called a dependent noun, which means it never appears on its own but only in the company of some friends, usually a statement that was said or shown earlier. 바 is mostly interchangeable with "것" and it normally follows (으)ㄴ (in the past) or 는 (in the present), and after that you can take it two ways. If you follow 바 with 에따르면 or 에 의하면, it means "according to A, B." You can also talk about 바가 있다/없다, and in this case it refers to an experience: something you did or didn't do. In this case it's interchangeable with (으)ㄴ 적 있다 (see page 187).

HOW IT'S CONJUGATED

		Past	Present
Action verbs ending in a vowel	하다	한 바 han ba	하는 바 haneun ba
Action verbs ending in a consonant	먹다	먹은 바 meogeun ba	먹는 바 meokneun ba

TAKE NOTE

Although 바 can be changed to 것, the reverse isn't always true. When it's used to mean "according to," 바 is used only in cases where something was discovered in some way. You'll see it used quite often to discuss survey results (조사한 바에 따르면 josahan bae ttareumyeon...)

EXAMPLE SENTENCES

일기 예보**한 바**에 의하면 내일 비가 올 거예요.
Ilgi yebohan bae uihamyeon naeil biga ol geoyeyo.
According to the weather forecast, it's going to rain tomorrow.

경제 전문가가 말**한 바**에 의하면 경제가 좋아질 거예요.
Gyeongje jeonmungaga malhan bae uihamyeon gyeongjega joajil geoyeyo.
According to an economist, the economy is going to improve.

김치를 먹**은 바**가 있어요. Kimchireul meogeun baga isseoyo.
I've eaten kimchi.

스키를 탄 바가 없어요. Seukireul ta baga eopseoyo.
I've never been skiing.

A기에 gie B	"From what was seen/ heard/said/known, B"	**Speaking < Writing** ★

가영이 듣**기에** 어제 민수가 또 늦었대요.
Kayoungi deutgie eoje Minsuga tto neujeotdaeyo.
From what Kayoung heard, yesterday Minsu was late again.

기에 is most commonly used to mean "since"; see page 73. However, it also has this slightly less useful function, which is to talk about something based on what you or someone else can see, hear, etc.

HOW IT'S CONJUGATED

A has to be a verb that's about gaining knowledge. 보다 **boda**, 생각하다 **saenggakada**, 알다 **alda**, and 듣다 **deutda** are common, but there are others as well. B is what is known from A.

		All tenses
Knowledge verbs ending in a vowel	보다	보기에 bogie
Knowledge verbs ending in a consonant	알다	알기에 algie

TAKE NOTE

Check the context carefully in order not to get this 기에 confused with the one that means "since." If in doubt, it's probably the other one.

You can also use 기에 **gie**, 기에는 **gieneun**, or 기로는 **gironeun**; the latter two just add emphasis.

EXAMPLE SENTENCES

제가 보**기에** 그 실수는 민수의 잘못이에요.
Jega bogie geu silsuneun Minsuui jalmosieyo.
From what I can see, this mistake was Minsu's fault.

제가 알**기에는** 그 실수를 민수의 잘못이에요.
Jega algieneun geu silsureul Minsuui jalmosieyo.
As far as I know, this mistake was Minsu's fault.

Speaking > Writing

A(으)로 **봐서는** (eu)   "B, as we can see through A…"   ★
ro bwaseoneun B

민수의 표정**으로 봐서는** 화가 많이 난 것 같아요. 다시 늦는가 봐요.
Minsuui pyojeongeuro bwaseoneun hwaga mani nan geot gatayo. Dasi neunneunga bwayo.
Looking at Minsu's expression, he seems to be very angry. It looks like he's late again.

This one is good for people who have to do research, presentations, and especially presentations based on their research. You can use it to explain the basis for a judgement, something that you can see through something else – like a fact that's obvious from a graph, or something you can guess from looking at a person's face.

HOW IT'S FORMED

(으)로 means "through" (see page 31). 보다 means "to look at" and it's conjugated here with 아서, which means "so" (see page 66). 는 emphasizes what you're saying.

HOW IT'S CONJUGATED

A should be a noun on its own or an action verb conjugated with 는 것. A is your source and B is what you've determined or are guessing based on A.

		Past	Present	Future
Action verbs ending in a vowel	하다	한 것으로 봐서는 han geoseuro bwaseoneun	하는 것으로 봐서는 haneun geoseuro bwaseoneun	할 것으로 봐서는 hal geoseuro bwaseoneun
Action verbs ending in a consonant	먹다	먹은 것으로 봐서는 meogeun geoseuro bwaseoneun	먹는 것으로 봐서는 meokneun geoseuro bwaseoneun	먹을 것으로 봐서는 meogeul geoseuro bwaseoneun
Nouns ending in a vowel	외모	외모로 봐서는 oemoro bwaseoneun	외모로 봐서는	외모로 봐서는
Nouns ending in a consonant	모양	모양으로 봐서는 moyangeuro bwaseoneun	모양으로 봐서는	모양으로 봐서는

TAKE NOTE

B is very often a guess, so it sounds natural to end it with one of the expressions for guessing: (으)ㄹ 것 같다 is a good one, or you can look through pages 136 to 156 to find more.

A is normally not something too specific. Rather than saying "I can see from his surprised expression that…" it would be more normal to simply say "I can see from his expression that…" Likewise, you wouldn't say "I can see from the 95% you got on this test that…" but rather "I can see from your test score that…"

EXAMPLE SENTENCES

시험 결과로 **봐서는** 듣기 실력이 많이 좋아졌어요.
Siheom gyeolgwaro bwaseoneun deutgi sillyeogi mani joajyeosseoyo.
Looking at your test results, I can see that your listening skills have really improved.

외모로 **봐서는** 미국인인 것 같아요.
Oemoro bwaseoneun miguginin geot gatayo.
From that person's appearance I'd guess he's an American.

Giving Explanations

~에 대하여 e daehayeo,   "about ~"   **Speaking = Writing**
~에 대해 e daehae,   ★★★★★
~에 대해서 e daehaeseo,
~에 대해서는 e daehaeseoneun,
~에 대한 e daehan

경제 문제<u>에 대해서</u> 알고 싶어요.
Gyeongje munjee daehaeseo algo sipeoyo.
I want to know more about the economic problem.

All of the above are ways to express talking about something.

HOW IT'S FORMED

대하다 daehada means "to be about or related to" and all the expressions above are variations of that. You can add ㄴ, 여, 여서, or 여서는. They all mean the same thing and can be used interchangeably except for 대한; see the "Take note" section for more information.

HOW IT'S CONJUGATED

		Past	Present	Future
Action verbs ending in a vowel	하다	한 것에 대해 han geose daehae 한 것에 대하여 han geose daehayeo 한 것에 대해서 han geose daehaeseo 한 것에 대한 han geose daehan	하는 것에 대해 haneun geose daehae 하는 것에 대하여 haneun geose daehayeo 하는 것에 대해서 haneun geose daehaeseo 하는 것에 대한 haneun geose daehan	할 것에 대해 hal geose daehae 할 것에 대하여 hal geose daehayeo 할 것에 대해서 hal geose daehaeseo 할 것에 대한 hal geose daehan
Action verbs ending in a consonant	먹다	먹은 것에 대해 meogeun geose daehae 먹은 것에 대하여 meogeun geose daehayeo 먹은 것에 대해서 meogeun geose daehaeseo 먹은 것에 대한 meogeun geose daehan	먹는 것에 대해 meokneun geose daehae 먹는 것에 대하여 meokneun geose daehayeo 먹는 것에 대해서 meokneun geose daehaeseo 먹는 것에 대한 meokneun geose daehan	먹을 것에 대해 meogeul geose daehae 먹을 것에 대하여 meogeul geose daehayeo 먹을 것에 대해서 meogeul geose daehaeseo 먹을 것에 대한 meogeul geose daehan

		Past	Present	Future
Nouns ending in a vowel	남자	남자에 대해 **namjae daehae** 남자에 대하여 **namjae daehayeo** 남자에 대해서 **namjae daehaeseo** 남자에 대한 **namjae daehan**	남자에 대해 남자에 대하여 남자에 대해서 남자에 대한	남자에 대해 남자에 대하여 남자에 대해서 남자에 대한
Nouns ending in a consonant	물	물에 대해 **mure daehae** 물에 대하여 **mure daehayeo** 물에 대해서 **mure daehaeseo** 물에 대한 **mure daehan**	물에 대해 물에 대하여 물에 대해서 물에 대한	물에 대해 물에 대하여 물에 대해서 물에 대한

TAKE NOTE

에 대한 is an exception. It turns your first clause into an adjective clause, which should then modify a noun. To put this in simpler terms: 대한 must be followed by a noun. "A story about Cinderella" becomes "신데렐라에 대한 이야기 **sinderellae daehan iyagi.**" "A discussion about politics" becomes "정치에 대한 토론 **jeongchie daehan toron.**"

All the other 대하다 expressions don't work like this and can simply be followed by whatever you need to add to them. Keep in mind that since 는 emphasizes the meaning, it sounds far more natural to use it while explaining a contrast; otherwise the emphasis isn't really necessary. See the examples below.

EXAMPLE SENTENCES

정치에 대한 토론을 들었어요. Jeongchie daehan toroneul deureosseoyo.

정치에 대하여 토론을 들었어요. Jeongchie daehayeo toroneul deureosseoyo.

정치에 대해 토론을 들었어요. Jeongchie daehae toroneul deureosseoyo.

정치에 대해서 토론을 들었어요. Jeongchie daehaeseo toroneul deureosseoyo.

I listened to a discussion about politics.

정치에 대한 토론을 못 들었어요. 그렇지만 경제에 대해서는 토론을 들었어요.
Jeongchie daehan toroneul mot deureosseoyo. Geureochiman gyeongjee daehaeseoneun toroneul deureosseoyo.
I couldn't understand the discussion about politics, but I understood the discussion about economics.

경제 문제<u>에 대하여</u> 알고 싶어요. Gyeongje munjee daehayeo algo sipeoyo.

경제 문제<u>에 대해</u> 알고 싶어요. Gyeongje munjee daehae algo sipeoyo.

경제 문제<u>에 대해서</u> 알고 싶어요. Gyeongje munjee daehaeseo algo sipeoyo.

I want to know more about the economic problem.

(This can't be written with 에 대한 because there's no noun following 대한).

정치<u>에 대해서</u> 관심이 없어요. 그렇지만 경제 문제<u>에 대해서는</u> 알고 싶어요.
Jeongchie daehaeseo gwansimi eopseoyo. geureochiman gyeongje munjee
daehaeseoneun algo sipeoyo.

I don't care about politics, but I want to know more about the economic problem.

~(이)랍니다/(ㄴ/는)답니다   "~, you know"   Speaking = Writing ★★★
(i)ramnida/(n/neun)damnida

옛날 옛날에는 백설공주라는 여자가 살았**답니다**.
Yennal yennareneun baek-seol-gong-juraneun yeojaga saratdamnida.
A long time ago, there lived a girl named Snow White.

This is a relatively formal and somewhat poetic ending that's used in three situations:

1) Introductions—of people or of facts you don't think your listener knows
2) Telling stories, as in in the example above
3) Talking about someone you're proud of

It's used to tell someone things that you know but don't think they do, and so it is often used by tour guides, storytellers, and proud moms. It's not often used toward someone you're close to unless that someone is a group of children to whom you're telling a story.

HOW IT'S FORMED

It's a contraction of the indirect speech forms (이)라고 합니다 (i)rago hamnida and (ㄴ/는) 다고 합니다 (n/neun)dago hamnida.

HOW IT'S CONJUGATED

This ending is always used at the end of a sentence.

		Past	Present	Future
Action verbs ending in a vowel	하다	했답니다 haetdamnida	한답니다 handamnida	할 거랍니다 hal georamnida
Action verbs ending in a consonant	먹다	먹었답니다 meogeotdamnida	먹는답니다 meokneundamnida	먹을 거랍니다 meogeul georamnida

	Past	Present	Future
Descriptive verbs (adjectives) ending in a vowel	예쁘다	예뻤답니다 yeppeotdamnida	예쁘답니다 yeppeudamnida	예쁠 거랍니다 yeppeul georamnida
Descriptive verbs (adjectives) ending in a consonant	작다	작았답니다 jagatdamnida	작답니다	작을 거랍니다
Nouns ending in a vowel	남자	남자랍니다 namjaramnida	남자랍니다	남자랍니다
Nouns ending in a consonant	물	물이랍니다 muriramnida	물이랍니다	물이랍니다

TAKE NOTE

I found it somewhat challenging to learn when to use this ending and sound natural with it. With enough exposure to the Korean language, it becomes much easier and being able to use it well in the right situations will make you sound quite fluent.

EXAMPLE SENTENCES

요즘 맞벌이 하는 부부들이 많**답니다**.
Yojeum matbeori haneun bubudeuri mantamnida.
These days there are many dual-income couples, you know.

우리 첫손자가 민수**랍니다**. **Uri cheotsonjaga Minsuramnida.**
My first grandchild is named Minsu.

우리 딸 가영이 다음 달에 대학교를 졸업**한답니다**.
Uri ttal Kayoungi daeum dare daehakgyoreul joreopandamnida.
My daughter Kayoung is going to graduate university next month, you know.

		Speaking = Writing
A(이)란 (i)ran B	"A is B"	★★★
A기란 giran B	"A is difficult"	★

지각**이란** 늦게 오는 것인데요. **Jigagiran neutge oneun geosindeyo.**
Tardiness means "coming late."

한국에서 일찍 퇴근하**기란** 하늘의 별 따기이에요.
Hangugeseo iljjik toegeunhagiran haneurui byeol ttagiieyo.
In Korea, leaving work early is as difficult as picking a star from the sky.

These two expressions have similar forms and similar meanings, but they are used in totally different ways. However, they're not that difficult to understand. (이)란 is used to define words just like in a dictionary. If you want to talk about what love is or what it is to be a leader, use (이)란. 기란 is used to talk about things that are difficult?).

HOW IT'S FORMED

기 turns verbs into nouns. (이)란/기란 are contractions of (이)라는 것/기라는 것.

HOW IT'S CONJUGATED

(이)란 follows only nouns. 기란 follows only action verbs.

		All tenses
Action verbs ending in a vowel	하다	하기란 hagiran
Action verbs ending in a consonant	먹다	먹기란 meokgiran

		All tenses
Nouns ending in a vowel	남자	남자란 namjaran
Nouns ending in a consonant	물	물이란 muriran

TAKE NOTE

When using 기란, B must be a sentence which explains that A is difficult. Here are some examples:

쉬운 일이 아니다 swiun iri anida	isn't easy
힘든 일이다 himdeun irida	is difficult
여간 어렵지 않다 yeogan eoryeopji anta	is difficult
하늘의 별 따기이다 haneurui byeol ttagiida	is like picking a star from the sky (a Korean proverb)

EXAMPLE SENTENCES

■ 기란 giran

새로운 언어를 배우**기란** 쉬운 일이 아니에요.
Saeroun eoneoreul baeugiran swiun iri anieyo.
Learning a new language isn't easy.

아침에 일찍 일어나**기란** 여간 어렵지 않아요.
Achime iljjik ireonagiran yeogan eoryeopji anayo.
Waking up early is really difficult.

■ 이란 iran

사랑**이란** 희생인데요. **Sarangiran huisaengindeyo.** Love is sacrifice.

희생**이란** 무엇인가요? **Huisaengiran mueosingayo?** What is sacrifice?

~(으)ㄹ 만하다 (eu)l manhada   "~ is worthwhile"

Speaking = Writing
★★

그 콘서트에 밴드가 다 좋아서 정시에 맞춰 **갈 만해요**.
Geu konseoteue baendeuga da joaseo jeongsie matchwo gal manhaeyo.
All the bands at that concert are good, so it's worth arriving on time.

This is a way to say that something is worth doing (or seeing or eating or reading or listening to, etc.). If you use this expression, you're recommending ~ to a listener but are probably not wildly excited about it. It's worth the time, but not more than that.

HOW IT'S FORMED

만하다 in this case means "to be worth."

HOW IT'S CONJUGATED

		All tenses
Action verbs ending in a vowel	하다	할 만하다 hal manhada
Action verbs ending in a consonant	먹다	먹을 만하다 meogeul manhada

TAKE NOTE

만하다 by itself without the (으)ㄹ in front is used to compare the size of two things, mostly in idiomatic expressions. 만하다 will always follow nouns, never verbs.

기만 하다 **giman hada** means to do one thing and one thing only. It will always follow 기, never (으)ㄹ.

There are also a number of expressions with 만 **man**: 만에 **mane**, 만 못하다 **man motada**, 만 해도 **man haedo**, and just plain 만. You can look them up in their appropriate sections on pages 276, 134, 99 and 31 respectively if you like. They mostly involve 만, which means "only" and aren't followed by 하다.

EXAMPLE SENTENCES

그 새로 나온 책은 **읽을 만해요**.
Geu saero naon chaegeun ilgeul manhaeyo.
That new book is worth reading.

여행을 하고 싶다니 제주도가 가 **볼 만해요**.
Yeohaengeul hago sipdani jejudoga ga bol manhaeyo.
Since you said you wanted to travel, I think Jeju do is worth seeing.

Location

		Speaking = Writing
A(으)ㄴ/는/(으)ㄹ 데 (eu)n/neun/(eu)l de B	"B happens at A"	★★

점심을 먹은 데에서 만날래요? Jeomsimeul meogeun deeseo mannallaeyo?
Let's meet at the place we had lunch.

데 means place and is used in conjunction with A, which explains what exactly that place is and (maybe) why the listener should care. This expression sets up A as "the place where B happens."

HOW IT'S FORMED

The tense markers (으)ㄴ/는/(으)ㄹ are there to help you explain A, while 데, as stated above, is simply a noun that means "place."

HOW IT'S CONJUGATED

		Past	Present	Future
Action verbs ending in a vowel	하다	한 데 han de	하는 데 haneun de	할 데 hal de
Action verbs ending in a consonant	먹다	먹은 데 meogeun de	먹는 데 meokneun de	먹을 데 meogeul de
Descriptive verbs (adjectives) ending in a vowel	예쁘다	예쁜 데 yeppeun de	예쁜 데	예쁠 데 yeppeul de
Descriptive verbs (adjectives) ending in a consonant	작다	작은 데 jageun de	작은 데	작을 데 jageul de

TAKE NOTE

A can't be 이, 그, or 저. In this case you can use 곳 **got** instead of 데.

Don't confuse 데 and 때. 때 **ttae** means "time" and is commonly used in the expression "(으)ㄹ 때," which means "while." 데 means "place."

A(으)ㄴ/는 데 B is another expression which is used to talk about effectiveness (see page 170). It's never used with (으)ㄹ. Otherwise, you can tell the two apart by context: the other 는 데 will always be followed by a sentence indicating effectiveness (효과적이다 **hyogwa-jeogida**, 필수적이에요 **pilsujeonieyo**, etc.) or lack thereof, while this one will always have to do with places.

EXAMPLE SENTENCES

큰 TV를 <u>놓을 데</u>가 없어요. Keun tibireul noeul dega eopseoyo.
I have no place to put a big TV.

운동하<u>는 데</u>가 아주 시끄러워요. Undonghaneun dega aju sikkeureowoyo.
The place I exercise in is very noisy.

Limits and Excess

| ~(기)만 하다 (gi)man hada | "only do ~" | Speaking > Writing
★★★★ |

어제 숙취가 심했어요. 하루 종일 누워있기만 했어요.
Eoje sukchwiga simhaesseoyo. Haru jongil nuwoitgiman haesseoyo.
I had a bad hangover yesterday. I did nothing but lie down.

This expression is for addicts and people who have to talk about them. It means to do a certain thing, and only that thing, repeatedly.

HOW IT'S FORMED

기 turns a verb into a noun. 만 means "only" and is added to nouns.

HOW IT'S CONJUGATED

It works with action verbs plus 기. If you want to use a noun which has been turned into a verb by the addition of 하다 (examples are 운동하다 undonghada, 야구하다 yaguhada, 운전하다 unjeonhada), then you can drop the 하다 and follow the noun by itself with 만 하다. It's not necessary to say 운동하기만 했다 undonghagiman haetda, for example.

		Past	Present	Future
Action verbs ending in a vowel	하다	하기만 했다 hagiman haetda	하기만 하다 hagiman hada	하기만 할 것이다 hagiman hal geosida
Action verbs ending in a consonant	먹다	먹기만 했다 meokgiman haetda	먹기만 하다 meokgiman hada	먹기만 할 것이다 meokgiman hal geosida
Nouns ending in a vowel	야구	야구만 했다 yaguman haetda	야구만 하다 yaguman hada	야구만 할 것이다 yaguman hal geosida
Nouns ending in a consonant	게임	게임만 했다 geimman haetda	게임만 하다 geimman hada	게임만 할 것이다 geimman hal geosida

TAKE NOTE

기만 하다 and (으)ㄹ 뿐이다 **(eu)l ppunida** (on next page) are similar, but 기만 하다 specifically means to do one thing repeatedly while (으)ㄹ 뿐이다 can be used in a much greater variety of situations.

만 하다 has two other uses. One is to talk about something "worth doing." That's covered on page 333 and can be differentiated because it always follows a verb conjugated with (으) ㄹ. The 만 하다 we're talking about here follows only either verbs with 기 or nouns. The other use of 만 하다 is to compare sizes (see page 135). That one's a bit trickier to distinguish, but one key is that it's normally used to talk about objects, while this 만 하다 is used to talk mostly about people and what they're (only) doing. Other than that, check the context.

EXAMPLE SENTENCES

민수가 게임**만 해요**. Minsuga geimman haeyo.
Minsu does nothing but play games.

아주 피곤해서 내일 자**기만 할 거예요**.
Aju pigonhaeseo naeil jagiman hal geoyeyo.
I'm very tired, so tomorrow I'm only going to sleep.

~아/어/여서 죽겠다　　　"I'm so ~ I could die"　　**Speaking > Writing**
a/eo/yeoseo jukgetda　　　　　　　　　　　　　　★★★★

민수가 또 늦어요. 짜증나**서 죽겠어요**.
Minsuga tto neujeoyo. Jjajeungnaseo jukgesseoyo.
Minsu's late again. I'm so annoyed I could just die.

Drama queens, rejoice! Here's the perfect Korean expression if you're prone to exaggerate. It literally translates as "I'm so ~ I could die" and means that ~ is really bad: the cold, the boredom, the hunger, or whatever minor inconvenience is bothering you that day.

HOW IT'S FORMED

아/어/여서 means "so" (see page 66). 죽겠다 is 죽다 (to die) conjugated in the future tense to suggest that while you're not dead yet, you might be soon.

HOW IT'S CONJUGATED.

		All tenses
Action or descriptive verbs with 아 or 오	잡다	잡아서 죽겠다 jabaseo jukgetda
Action or descriptive verbs with 어, 우, 으 or 이	먹다	먹어서 죽겠다 meogeoseo jukgetda
하다	피곤하다	피곤해서 죽겠다 pigonhaeseo jukgetda

TAKE NOTE

While 아/어/여서 죽겠다 is normally used only with bad things, you can use it for good things as well: "That baby is so cute I could just die!" can be translated almost exactly into Korean.

EXAMPLE SENTENCES

오늘 추<u>워서 죽겠어요</u>. Oneul chuwoseo jukgesseoyo. It's cold today!

배가 고<u>파서 죽겠어요</u>. Baega gopaseo jukgesseoyo. I'm hungry!

너무 많이 먹<u>어서 죽겠어요</u>. Neomu mani meogeosseo jukgesseoyo.
I ate too much!

| ~([으]ㄹ [eu]l) 뿐이다 ppunida | "only ~" | Speaking > Writing
★★★ |

제가 벌써 회의에 늦어서 걱정**할 뿐이에요**.
Jega beolsseo hoeuie neujeoseo geokjeonghal ppunieyo.
I'm already late for the meeting, so all I'm doing is worrying.

This expression, useful for very modest people or those who like to downplay a fact, means that the situation is or was limited to "~ and only ~." It be used for sentences such as "We're just friends," "All I did was sleep," or "Nonsense, I was only doing what any other person would have done."

HOW IT'S FORMED

뿐 is a noun which means "only." And yes, that's an adverb in English.

HOW IT'S CONJUGATED

		Past	Present
Action verbs ending in a vowel	하다	했을 뿐이다 haeseul ppunida	할 뿐이다 hal ppunida
Action verbs ending in a consonant	먹다	먹었을 뿐이다 meogeosseul ppunida	먹을 뿐이다 meogeul ppunida
Descriptive verbs (adjectives) ending in a vowel	예쁘다	예뻤을 뿐이다 yeppeoseul ppunida	예쁠 뿐이다 yeppeul ppunida
Descriptive verbs (adjectives) ending in a consonant	작다	작았을 뿐이다 jagasseul ppunida	작을 뿐이다 jageul ppunida
Nouns ending in a vowel	남자	남자였을 뿐이다 namjayeosseul ppunida 남자 뿐이다 namja ppunida	남자일 뿐이다 namjail ppunida 남자 뿐이다
Nouns ending in a consonant	물	물이었을 뿐이다 murieosseul ppunida 물 뿐이다 mul ppunida	물일 뿐이다 muril ppunida 물 뿐이다

TAKE NOTE

A commonly used expression based on 뿐 is A([으]ㄹ) 뿐만 아니라 B ([eu]l) ppunman anira B, which means "not just A, but also B" (see page 55).

(으)ㄹ 뿐이다 and 기만 하다 (see page 335) are quite similar, but 기만 하다 can be used when only one action was done repeatedly. (으)ㄹ 뿐이다 can be used much more widely.

You can add 만 or 기만 to A if you want to make your expression even more emphatic.

나는 잠 잤**을 뿐이에요**. Naneun jam jasseul ppunieyo. I did nothing but sleep.

나는 잠만 잤**을 뿐이에요**. Naneun jamman jasseul ppunieyo.
No, really, ALL I did was sleep.

뿐이다 and 따름이다 ttareumida (see page 346) are interchangeable except that you can use 뿐이다 directly after nouns, while 따름이다 follows only verbs (or nouns with 이).

EXAMPLE SENTENCES

그녀는 개성이 없어요. 예쁠 **뿐이에요**.
Geunyeoneun gaeseongi eopseoyo. Yeppeul ppunieyo.
She doesn't have any personality. She's just beautiful (and there's nothing more to her than that).

저 사람은 제 남자친구 아닌데요. 친구일 **뿐이에요**.
Jeo sarameun je namjachingu anindeyo. Chinguil ppunieyo.
That person isn't my boyfriend. We're just friends.

확실하지 않아요. 소문으로 들었**을 뿐이에요**.
Hwaksilhaji anayo. Somuneuro deureosseul ppunieyo.
I'm not sure. I just heard a rumor.

		Speaking = Writing
A(으)ㄴ/는 한 (eu)n/neun han B	"B as far as/as long as A"	★★

늦게 퇴근하지 않**는 한** 비행기를 놓치지 않을 거예요.
Neutge toegeunhaji anneun han bihaenggireul nochiji aneul geoyeyo.
As long as you don't leave work late, you won't miss your flight.

You can use this expression to say that as long as A happens, B will happen.

HOW IT'S FORMED

한 is a noun which literally means "limit," and it can be used on its own as that noun. In this expression 는 is added to an action verb to turn A into an adjective clause modifying the noun 한.

HOW IT'S CONJUGATED

		Past	Present	Future
Action verbs ending in a vowel	하다	한 한 han han	하는 한 haneun han	할 한 hal han
Action verbs ending in a consonant	먹다	먹은 한 meogeun han	먹는 한 meokneun han	먹을 한 meogeul han
Descriptive verbs (adjectives) ending in a vowel	예쁘다	예쁜 한 yeppeun han	예쁜 한	예쁜 한
Descriptive verbs (adjectives) ending in a consonant	작다	작은 한 jageun han	작은 한	작은 한
Nouns ending in a vowel	남자	남자인 한 namjain han	남자인 한	남자인 한
Nouns ending in a consonant	물	물인 한 murin han	물인 한	물인 한

TAKE NOTE

아/어/여야, as covered on page 202, is another expression where A is required for B. In this case A must happen in order for B to happen; with 한, A is not always a necessity, but B will happen as long as A is going on.

EXAMPLE SENTENCES

건강하게 먹<u>는 한</u> 다이어트에 성공할 수 있어요.
Geonganghage meokneun han daieoteue seonggonghal su isseoyo.
As long as you eat healthy, you can succeed in your diet.

다른 수트 케이스가 작<u>은 한</u> 비행기 안으로 가지고 들어갈 수 있을 거예요.
Dareun suteu keiseuga jageun han bihaenggi aneuro gajigo deureogal su isseul geoyeyo.
You will be able to bring a suitcase into an airplane as long as it's a small one.

Speaking = Writing

A에 한해서 e hanhaeseo B   "B is limited to A"   ★★

무료 입장이 12시 이후<u>에 한해서</u> 가능해요.
Muryo ipjangi yeoldusi ihue hanhaeseo ganeunghaeyo.
Free entry is available only after twelve.

Here's a good one for tour guides or amusement park owners. It's a way to say that B is limited or only available to A: For example, free entry is limited to senior citizens only or an offer is limited to today.

HOW IT'S FORMED

한 is a noun that means "limit." Here it's made into a verb using 하다 and then conjugated using 여서 (see page 66) to mean "something is limited to A, so B."

HOW IT'S CONJUGATED

		All tenses
Nouns ending in a vowel	남자	남자에 한해서 namjae hanhaeseo
Nouns ending in a consonant	물	물에 한해서 mure hanhaeseo

TAKE NOTE

This is similar to 는 한 in some ways, but 는 한 follows verbs while 한하다 follows nouns.

EXAMPLE SENTENCES

이 표는 한 사람 한 표에 <u>**한해요**</u>. I pyoneun han saram han pyoe hanhaeyo.
This ticket is good only for one person.

이 제공은 한국 시민<u>**에 한해서**</u> 외국인들은 받을 수 없어요.
I jegongeun hanguk simine hanhaeseo oegugindeureun badeul su eopseoyo.
This offer is limited to Korean citizens, so foreigners can't take advantage of it.

		Speaking < Writing
~조차 jocha, ~마저 majeo, ~까지 kkaji, ~도 do	"even ~"	★★

민수가 어찌나 늦었는지 청소부조차 퇴근했어요.
Minsuga eojjina neujeonneunji cheongsobujocha toegeunhaesseoyo.

민수가 어찌나 늦었는지 청소부까지 퇴근했어요.
Minsuga eojjina neujeonneunji cheongsobukkaji toegeunhaesseoyo.

민수가 어찌나 늦었는지 청소부마저 퇴근했어요.
Minsuga eojjina neujeonneunji cheongsobumajeo toegeunhaesseoyo.

민수가 어찌나 늦었는지 청소부도 퇴근했어요.
Minsuga eojjina neujeonneunji cheongsobudo toegeunhaesseoyo.

Minsu was so late that even the cleaning lady had gone home.

These expressions are good to use if you should find yourself in an extreme situation such as final exams.

도 is absolutely essential and Koreans use it all the time, so be sure to learn it well.

조차 is a very negative word which can't be translated exactly, but which appears in sentences like "not even a genius could pass this test," "not even his own mother could love him," or "it's freezing cold, the heater is broken and I even forgot to wear a sweater today."

까지 should be one of the first particles you need to learn in Korean; it means "to," as you probably know well by now. That meaning carries over to this use of 까지, which expresses that something goes really far: as far as ~, which is a little extreme for the situation.

마저 is an expression that only the TOPIK makers seem to care about. If you've found yourself in this section because you are taking the TOPIK, don't worry. 마저 is easy to learn.

HOW IT'S CONJUGATED

		All tenses
Action verbs ending in a vowel	하다	할 수조차 없다 hal sujocha eopda
Action verbs ending in a consonant	먹다	먹을 수조차 없다 meogeul sujocha eopda
Nouns ending in a vowel	남자	남자조차 namjajocha 남자까지 namjakkaji 남자마저 namjamajeo 남자도 namjado
Nouns ending in a consonant	물	물조차 muljocha 물까지 mulkkaji 물마저 mulmajeo 물도 muldo

TAKE NOTE

조차 is choosy and cannot just be used anywhere. First of all, it's always used in negative sentences: B will normally (but not always) include a word like 못, 아, or 지 않다. If your sentence is already about something bad happening, you may not need these expressions. You can use 조차 with a verb by putting the verb into an expression with (으)ㄹ 수조차 없다 (see page 294). Descriptive verbs, however, can't be used with any of the particles; either rearrange your sentence or rearrange your descriptive verb by adding 어/아지다 to it (see page 25 shows you how to do that).

Secondly, 조차, 마저, 까지 (only in negative uses of 까지) and 도 are normally interchangeable, though 조차 makes things out to be slightly worse than any of the other three. If you're using 조차, the situation is really bad, at least in your own eyes, if no one else's. 까지 can be used for positive as well as negative situations, while **마저** and 조차 can't.

Finally, a couple of expressions that go well with these are 얼마나/어찌나 A(으)ㄴ/는지 B **eolmana/eojjina A(eu)n/ neunji B** (see page 343) and ~은/는 커녕 **~eun/neun keonyeong** (see page 41). Look at the examples to learn how to use these together with 조차, 까지, and 마저.

EXAMPLE SENTENCES

어제 얼마나 더운지 에어컨**조차** 소용이 없었어요.
Eoje eolmana deounji eeokeonjocha soyongi eopseosseoyo.

어제 어찌나 더운지 에어컨**조차** 소용이 없었어요.
Eoje eojjina deounji eeokeonjocha soyongi eopseosseoyo.

어제 얼마나 더운지 에어컨**까지** 소용이 없었어요.
Eoje eolmana deounji eeokeonkkaji soyongi eopseosseoyo.

어제 어찌나 더운지 에어컨**까지** 소용이 없었어요.
Eoje eojjina deounji eeokeonkkaji soyongi eopseosseoyo.

어제 얼마나 더운지 에어컨**마저** 소용이 없었어요.
Eoje eolmana deounji eeokeonmajeo soyongi eopseosseoyo.

어제 어찌나 더운지 에어컨**마저** 소용이 없었어요.
Eoje eojjina deounji eeokeonmajeo soyongi eopseosseoyo.

어제 얼마나 더운지 에어컨**도** 소용이 없었어요.
Eoje eolmana deounji eeokeondo soyongi eopseosseoyo.

어제 어찌나 더운지 에어컨**도** 소용이 없었어요.
Eoje eojjina deounji eeokeondo soyongi eopseosseoyo.

Yesterday it was so hot not even the air conditioning could help.

피자 한판은 커녕 한 조각**조차** 먹을 수 없어요.
Pija hanpaneun keonyeong han jogakjocha meogeul su eopseoyo.

피자 한판은 커녕 한 조각**까지** 먹을 수 없어요.
Pija hanpaneun keonyeong han jogakkkaji meogeul su eopseoyo.

피자 한판은 커녕 한 조각**마저** 먹을 수 없어요.
Pija hanpaneun keonyeong han jogangmajeo meogeul su eopseoyo.

피자 한판은 커녕 한 조각**도** 먹을 수 없어요.
Pija hanpaneun keonyeong han jogakdo meogeul su eopseoyo.

I can't even eat one slice, let alone an entire pizza.

가영이 테니스뿐만 아니라 수영**까지** 잘 해요.
Kayoungi teniseuppunman anira suyeongkkaji jal haeyo.

가영이 테니스뿐만 아니라 수영**도** 잘 해요.
Kayoungi teniseuppunman anira suyeongdo jal haeyo.

Kayoung is not only good at tennis, but swimming as well.

(Can't be used with 마저 or 조차 since they can't be used for positive expressions.)

어찌나/얼마나 eojjina/eolmana
A(으)ㄴ/는지 B (eu)n/neunji

"So A that B"

Speaking > Writing
★★

Here's another expression you can use to talk about extremes. This one means that something was "so A that B."

HOW IT'S FORMED

어찌나 means "so." 얼마나 means "how much" or "how many." (으)ㄴ/는지 is an expression which turns a phrase into a into a noun clause.

HOW IT'S CONJUGATED

Nouns are a little complicated; you can use them with these expressions, but only if you add an adjective before them and an 이 after them. So 어찌나 남자인지 doesn't work, but 어찌나 좋은 남자인지 does.

		Past	Present	Future
Action verbs ending in a vowel	하다	어찌나 했는지 eojjina haenneunji 얼마나 했는지 eolmana haenneunji	어찌나 하는지 eojjina haneunji 얼마나 하는지 eolmana haneunji	어찌나 할지 eojjina halji 얼마나 할지 eolmana halji
Action verbs ending in a consonant	먹다	어찌나 먹었는지 eojjina meogeonneunji 얼마나 먹었는지 eolmana meogeonneunji	어찌나 먹는지 eojjina meokneunji 얼마나 먹는지 eolmana meokneunji	어찌나 먹을지 eojjina meogeulji 얼마나 먹을지 eolmana meogeulji
Descriptive verbs (adjectives) ending in a vowel	예쁘다	어찌나 예뻤는지 eojjina yeppeonneunji 얼마나 예뻤는지 eolmana yeppeonneunji	어찌나 예쁜지 eojjina yeppeunji 얼마나 예쁜지 eolmana yeppeunji	어찌나 예쁠지 eojjina yeppeulji 얼마나 예쁠지 eolmana yeppeulji
Descriptive verbs (adjectives) ending in a consonant	작다	어찌나 작았는지 eojjina jaganneunji 얼마나 작았는지 eolmana jaganneunji	어찌나 작은지 eojjina jageunji 얼마나 작은지 eolmana jageunji	어찌나 작을지 eojjina jageulji 얼마나 작을지 eolmana jageulji
Nouns ending in a vowel	남자	어찌나 좋은 남자였는지 eojjina joeun namjayeonneunji 얼마나 좋은 남자였는지 eolmana joeun namjayeonneunji	어찌나 좋은 남자인지 eojjina joeun namjainji 얼마나 좋은 남자인지 eolmana joeun namjainji	어찌나 좋은 남자일지 eojjina joeun namjailji 얼마나 좋은 남자일지 eolmana joeun namjailji
Nouns ending in a consonant	물	어찌나 좋은 물이었는지 eojjina joeun murieonneunji 얼마나 좋은 물이었는지 eolmana joeun murieonneunji	어찌나 좋은 물인지 eojjina murinji 얼마나 좋은 물인지 eolmana murinji	어찌나 좋은 물일지 eojjina murilji 얼마나 좋은 물일지 eolmana murilji

TAKE NOTE

얼마나 and 어찌나 are interchangeable in the expressions above.

Action verbs are often used together with adverbs. So rather than 얼마나 먹었는지, you'd say:

<u>얼마나</u> 많이 먹었<u>는지</u> eolmana mani meogeonneunji   I ate so much that...

<u>얼마나</u> 자주 먹었<u>는지</u> eolmana jaju meogeonneunji   I ate so often that...

<u>얼마나</u> 잘 먹었<u>는지</u> eolmana jal meogeonneunji   I ate so well that...

or something similar.

얼마나 A(으)ㄴ/는지 is featured in another rather common expression: 얼마나 A(으)ㄴ/는지 모르다/모르겠다. **Eolmana A (eu)n/neunji moreuda/moreugetda.** It means "I don't even know how A it is/was," which implies that something was A.

오늘 날씨가 **얼마나** <u>추운지</u> 모르겠어요.
Oneul nalssiga eolmana chuunji moreugesseoyo.

오늘 날씨가 **얼마나** <u>추운지</u> 몰라요.
Oneul nalssiga eolmana chuunji mollayo.

It's freezing cold out today.

내일 날씨가 얼마나 <u>추울지</u> <u>모르겠어요</u>.
Naeil nalssiga eolmana chuulji moreugesseoyo.
I don't know how cold it will be tomorrow.

EXAMPLE SENTENCES

어제 **어찌나** 많이 먹었<u>는지</u> 나중에 배가 아팠어요.
Eoje eojjina mani meogeonneunji najunge baega apasseoyo.

어제 **얼마나** 많이 먹었<u>는지</u> 나중에 배가 아팠어요.
Eoje eolmana mani meogeonneunji najunge baega apasseoyo.

Yesterday I ate so much that I got a stomachache.

민수가 **어찌나** 늦었<u>는지</u> 연극이 벌써 끝났어요.
Minsuga eojjina neujeonneunji yeongeugi beolsseo kkeunnasseoyo.

민수가 **얼마나** 늦었<u>는지</u> 연극이 벌써 끝났어요.
Minsuga eolmana neujeonneunji yeongeugi beolsseo kkeunnasseoyo.

Minsu was so late that the show had already finished.

가영이 **어찌나** 좋은 학생<u>인지</u> 항상 시험에서 만점을 받아요.
Kayoungi eojjina joeun haksaenginji hangsang siheomeseo manjeomeul badayo.

가영이 **얼마나** 좋은 학생<u>인지</u> 항상 시험에서 만점을 받아요.
Kayoungi eolmana joeun haksaenginji hangsang siheomeseo manjeomeul badayo.

Kayoung is such a good student that she always gets a 100% on tests.

~(이)야말로 (i)yamallo   "~ is perfect/exactly right"

Speaking > Writing
★★

늦으면 이번에**야말로** 전화할 거예요.
Neujeumyeon ibeoneyamallo jeonhwahal geoyeyo.
This time I'll definitely call you if I'm late.

(이)야말로 is used to say that one particular thing, among many, is just right. For instance, if your friend has only a day in New York and wants to know that one thing that cannot be missed, you could use (이)야말로 to recommend the Statue of Liberty. You could also use (이)야말로 if you've finally met the man or woman of your dreams, are adopting a pet from an animal shelter, are buying shoes, or are in any situation where one thing is definitely much better than all the rest. You can also use it to say "definitely" or "without fail," as in "This time I'll definitely do it" or "That's definitely the right one."

HOW IT'S CONJUGATED

		All tenses
Nouns ending in a vowel	남자	남자야말로 namjayamallo
Nouns ending in a consonant	물	물이야말로 muriyamallo

TAKE NOTE

This is often used together with 뭐니 뭐니 해도 **mwoni mwoni haedo** ("above all else" or "regardless of anything else").

EXAMPLE SENTENCES

한국 음식 중에 김치**야말로** 대표적인 한국 음식이에요.
Hanguk eumsik junge kimchiyamallo daepyojeogin hanguk eumsigieyo.

뭐니 뭐니 해도 한국 음식 중에 김치**야말로** 대표적인 한국 음식이에요.
Mwoni mwoni haedo hanguk eumsik junge kimchiyamallo daepyojeogin hanguk eumsigieyo.

Kimchi is the representative food of Korea. (Among Korean food, kimchi is representative of Korean food.)

이 역할은 가영**이야말로** 잘 할 거예요.
I yeokareun Kayoungiyamallo jal hal geoyeyo.
Kayoung is perfect for this role.

~(으)ㄹ 따름이다 (eu)l ttareumida   "nothing but ~"

Speaking = Writing
★

제가 벌써 회의에 늦어서 걱정**할 따름이에요**.
Jega beolsseo hoeuie neujeoseo geokjeonghal ttareumieyo.
I'm already late for the meeting, so all I'm doing is worrying.

Here's another useful expression for either putting people down or minimizing your own accomplishments. It means "nothing but ~."

HOW IT'S CONJUGATED

		Past	Present	Future
Action verbs ending in a vowel	하다	했을 따름이다 haesseul ttareumida	할 따름이다 hal ttareumida	할 따름이다
Action verbs ending in a consonant	먹다	먹었을 따름이다 meogeosseul ttareumida	먹을 따름이다 meogeul ttareumida	먹을 따름이다
Descriptive verbs (adjectives) ending in a vowel	예쁘다	예뻤을 따름이다 yeppeosseul ttareumida	예쁠 따름이다 yeppeul ttareumida	예쁠 따름이다
Descriptive verbs (adjectives) ending in a consonant	작다	작았을 따름이다 jagasseul ttareumida	작을 따름이다 jageul ttareumida	작을 따름이다
Nouns ending in a vowel	남자	남자였을 따름이다 namjayeosseul ttareumida	남자일 따름이다 namjail ttareumida	남자일 따름이다
Nouns ending in a consonant	물	물이었을 따름이다 murieosseul ttareumida	물일 따름이다 muril ttareumida	물일 따름이다

TAKE NOTE

따름이다 and 뿐이다 (see page 337) are interchangeable except that you can use 뿐이다 directly after nouns, while 따름이다 follows only nouns with 이 added to turn them into verbs.

EXAMPLE SENTENCES

그녀는 개성이 없어요. 예**쁠 따름이에요**.
Geunyeoneun gaeseongi eopseoyo. Yeppeul ttareumieyo.
She doesn't have any personality. She's just beautiful (and there's nothing more to her than that).

저 사람은 제 남자친구 아닌데요. 친구**일 따름이에요**.
Jeo sarameun je namjachingu anindeyo. Chinguil ttareumieyo.
That person isn't my boyfriend. We're just friends.

확실하지 않아요. 소문으로 들었**을 따름이에요**.
Hwaksilhaji anayo. Somuneuro deureosseul ttareumieyo.
I'm not sure. I just heard a rumor.

> **Speaking > Writing**
> A만으로는 maneuroneunB   "A alone isn't enough"   ★

생각**만으로는** 정시에 올 수 없어요. 서둘러야겠죠.
Saenggangmaneuroneun jeongsie ol su eopseoyo. Seodulleoyagetjyo.
You won't get there on time just by thinking about it. You have to hurry.

Here's an expression for all you managers. This is a way to say that something on its own just isn't enough for whatever you're trying to accomplish.

HOW IT'S FORMED

만 means "only" (see page 31). 으로 means "through" (see page 31), and 는 is optional: it simply adds emphasis: "through only A."

HOW IT'S CONJUGATED

Action verbs can be changed to nouns using 는 것.

		Past	Present	Future
Action verbs ending in a vowel	하다	한 것만으로는 han geonmaneuroneun	하는 것만으로는 haneun geonmaneuroneun	할 것만으로는 hal geonmaneuroneun
Action verbs ending in a consonant	먹다	먹은 것만으로는 meogeun geonmaneuroneun	먹는 것만으로는 meokneun geonmaneuroneun	먹을 것만으로는 meogeul geonmaneuroneun
Descriptive verbs (adjectives) ending in a vowel	예쁘다	예쁜 것만으로는 yeppeun geonmaneuroneun	예쁜 것만으로는	예쁜 것만으로는
Descriptive verbs (adjectives) ending in a consonant	작다	작은 것만으로는 jageun geonmaneuroneun	작은 것만으로는	작은 것만으로는
Nouns ending in a vowel	남자	남자만으로는 namjamaneuroneun	남자만으로는	남자만으로는
Nouns ending in a consonant	물	물만으로는 mulmaneuroneun	물만으로는	물만으로는

TAKE NOTE

B should be an expression like 부족하다 **bujokada** or 하기가 힘들다 **hagiga himdeulda** which indicates that A isn't enough by itself.

만으로는 and 만 by itself are quite similar, but 만으로는 is used a little more specifically to say that something isn't enough by itself.

EXAMPLE SENTENCES

한국어 잘 배우기 위해서 문법 공부**만으로** 부족해요. 한국 사람과 대화를 해야 돼요.

Hangugeo jal baeugi wihaeseo munbeop gongbumaneuro bujokaeyo. Hanguk saramgwa daehwareul hae ya dwaeyo.

Studying grammar alone isn't enough to learn Korean well. You also need to have conversations with Koreans.

노력**만으로는** 그 일을 끝내기가 힘들어요. 도움이 필요해요.

Noryeongmaneuroneun geu ireul kkeunnaegiga himdeureoyo. Doumi piryohaeyo.

It'll be difficult to finish that job just by trying. You need help.

		Speaking > Writing
A(기)도 (gi)do A(이) 지만 (i)jiman B	"A is all fine and well, but B is more important"	★

A: 저는 살을 빼고 싶으니까 운동을 해야겠어요.

    Jeoneun sareul ppaego sipeunikka undongeul haeyagesseoyo.

    I want to lose weight, so I'll have to exercise.

B: 운동**도** 운동**이지만** 패스트 푸드부터 먹지 마세요.

    Undongdo undongijiman paeseuteu pudeubuteo meokji maseyo.

    Exercise is all fine and well, but you should start by not eating fast food.

This is for people who need to give advice to friends who are headed off in the wrong direction. Let's say your friend wants to lose weight and says they're going to start exercising. This is a good plan, but you think they'd be better off if they'd just stop eating fast food three meals a day. That's the kind of situation in which you'd use this expression.

HOW IT'S FORMED

기 turns verbs into nouns. 도 means "too." 이 turns nouns into verbs, while 지만 means "but."

HOW IT'S CONJUGATED

Add 기 to verbs to turn them into nouns before putting them before 도.

		Past	Present	Future
Action verbs ending in a vowel	하다	하기도 했지만 hagido haetjiman	하기도 하지만 hagido hajiman	하기도 할 거지만 hagido hal geojiman
Action verbs ending in a consonant	먹다	먹기도 먹었지만 meokgido meogeotjiman	먹기도 먹지만 meokgido meokjiman	먹기도 먹을 거지만 meokgido meogeul geojiman

		Past	Present	Future
Descriptive verbs (adjectives) ending in a vowel	예쁘다	예쁘기도 예쁘지만 yeppeugido yeppeujiman	예쁘기도 예쁘지만	예쁘기도 예쁘지만
Descriptive verbs (adjectives) ending in a consonant	작다	작기도 작지만 jakgido jakjiman	작기도 작지만	작기도 작지만
Nouns ending in a vowel	남자	남자도 남자이지만 namjado namjaijiman	남자도 남자이지만	남자도 남자이지만
Nouns ending in a consonant	물	물도 물이지만 muldo murijiman	물도 물이지만	물도 물이지만

EXAMPLE SENTENCES

A: 가영이 정말 예쁘지요? Kayoungi jeongmal yeppeujiyo?
Kayoung is really pretty, isn't she?

B: 예쁘**기도** 예쁘**지만** 성격이 나빠서 가영을 싫어요.
Yeppeugido yeppeujiman seonggyeogi nappaseo Kayoungi sireoyo.
Beauty is all fine and well, but she has a bad personality so I don't like her.

A: 한국어를 잘 하고 싶어서 요즘 문법을 열심히 배워요.
Hangugeoreul jal hago sipeoseo yojeum munbeobeul yeolsimhi baewoyo.
I want to speak Korean well, so these days I'm learning grammar.

B: 문법도 문법이지만 한국 사람과 대화를 했으면 좋겠어요.
Munbeopdo munbeobijiman hanguk saramgwa daehwareul haesseumyeon jokesseoyo.
Learning grammar is all fine and well, but you also have to talk to Koreans.

Habits

	Speaking > Writing
~곤/고는 하다 gon/goneun hada "habitually do ~"	★★★★

민수가 대학교 때 자주 수업에 늦게 **오곤 했어요**. Minsuga daehakgyo ttae jaju sueobe neutge ogon haesseoyo.
During university, Minsu was habitually late for class.

곤 하다, a good grammatical pattern for those who like to live their lives according to a consistent schedule, means "to do something repeatedly or as a habit." It's used in sentences such as "I always have toast and jam for breakfast" or "I often go to that bar after work."

HOW IT'S CONJUGATED

		Past	Present
Action verbs ending in a vowel	하다	하곤 했다 hagon haetda 하고는 했다 hagoneun haetda	하곤 하다 hagon hada 하고는 하다 hagoneun hada
Action verbs ending in a consonant	먹다	먹곤 했다 meokgon haetda 먹고는 했다 meokgoneun haetda	먹곤 하다 meokgon hada 먹고는 하다 meokgoneun hada

TAKE NOTE

곤 하다 and 고는 하다 are interchangeable, but 곤 하다 is somewhat more common.

곤/고는 하다 is used to describe a habit rather than something that always happens without fail. So if you want to talk about eating toast and jam for breakfast most mornings, you could use 곤 하다, but it would be strange to use it to describe your alarm clock going off every single day at 7:00.

곤 하다 and 기 일쑤이다 gi ilssuida (see page 356) are interchangeable when the sentence is negative. 기 일쑤이다 isn't usually used with positive sentences.

아/어/여 대다 a/eo/yeo daeda (see page 357) means to do something repeatedly, but not necessarily as a habit. If your ex-boyfriend or ex-girlfriend calls you all day long the day after you've broken up with him or her, you can use 아/어/여 대다 to describe the action, but not 곤 하다 because the calling is done repeatedly but is not habitual. If that same ex-boyfriend or ex-girlfriend calls you every day for months on end, then you could use 곤 하다.

EXAMPLE SENTENCES

남자친구와 헤어진 후에 그는 몇일 동안 계속 저에게 전화하**곤 했어요**.
Namjachinguwa he-eo-jin hue geuneun myeochil dongan gyesok jeoege jeonhwahagon haesseoyo.
After I broke up with my boyfriend, he kept on calling me for several days.

퇴근한 후에 맥주 두세잔 마시**곤 해요**.
Toegeunhan hue maekju dusejan masigon haeyo.
After work I usually drink a few glasses (two or three glasses) of beer.

~(으)ㄴ/는 편이다 (eu)n/neun pyeonida	"tends to ~"	Speaking = Writing ★★★

민수가 또 늦었어요. 그는 자주 늦**는 편이지요**?
Minsuga tto neujeosseoyo. Geuneun jaju neunneun pyeonijiyo?
Minsu's late again. He often tends to be late, doesn't he?

This can be used to talk about someone or something which tends to be a certain way.

HOW IT'S FORMED

편 means "side," so this expression literally means "on the side of ~."

HOW IT'S CONJUGATED

		Past	Present
Action verbs ending in a vowel	하다	하는 편이었다 haneun pyeonieotda	하는 편이다 haneun pyeonida
Action verbs ending in a consonant	먹다	먹는 편이었다 meokneun pyeonieotda	먹는 편이다 meokneun pyeonida
Descriptive verbs (adjectives) ending in a vowel	예쁘다	예쁜 편이었다 yeppeun pyeonieotda	예쁜 편이다 yeppeun pyeonida
Descriptive verbs (adjectives) ending in a consonant	작다	작은 편이었다 jageun pyeonieotda	작은 편이다 jageun pyeonida

TAKE NOTE

편이다 can never be used in the future tense.

It's not used to talk about objectively verifiable facts: for example, "He tends to be a man." You could, however, say that "He tends to be manly."

> 그는 남자**인 편이에요**. Geuneun namjain pyeonieyo. He tends to be a man. (ungrammatical)

> 그는 남자다**운 편이에요**. Geuneun namjadaun pyeonieyo. He tends to be manly. (just fine)

Action verbs are normally used in conjunction with adverbs like 자주 jaju, 가끔 gakkeum, and so on.

A similar expression is ~(으)ㄴ/는 축에 들다 (eu)n/neun chuge deulda (see page 359). There's a very slight difference in meaning between the two. Think of 편이다 as placing the subject on a scale between 0 and 100. Let's say 0 is 제일 작은 jeil jageun and 100 is 제일 큰 jeil keun. If the subject rates over 50 on that scale, 큰 편이다 keun pyeonida. With 축에 들다 chuge deulda, rather than a scale, you're dividing people into groups and saying which group they belong in: the big group or the small group. It's more often used when comparing yourself to family or colleagues, rather than the entire human population. 편이다 compares you to everyone. Another difference is that 편이다 is rather more formal. 축에 들다 shouldn't be used toward elders.

EXAMPLE SENTENCES

저는 라면을 좋아해요. 라면을 자주 먹**는 편이에요**.
Jeoneun ramyeoneul joahaeyo. Ramyeoneul jaju meokneun pyeonieyo.
I like ramen. I tend to eat ramen a lot.

저 학생은 작<u>은</u> **편**이라서 다른 학생보다 더 작은 책상이 필요해요.
Jeo haksaengeun jageun pyeoniraseo dareun haksaengboda deo jageun chaeksangi piryohaeyo.
That student is small (for his grade), so he needs a smaller desk than the other students.

Speaking > Writing

~**기도 하다** gido hada   "~ sometimes happens/   ★★★
~ happens, too"

수업에 정시에 오**기도 하**고 늦**기도 해요**.
Sueobe jeongsie ogido hago neutgido haeyo.
I sometimes come to class on time and sometimes I come late.

This is a way to talk about things that are known to occur from time to time.

HOW IT'S FORMED

기 turns a verb into a noun. 도 in this case means "too," and 하다 means "to occur" here.

HOW IT'S CONJUGATED

It follows action verbs. 하다 can be conjugated to express the past tense or the future tense.

		Past	Present	Future
Action verbs ending in a vowel	하다	하기도 했다 hagido haetda	하기도 하다 hagido hada	하기도 할 것이다 hagido hal geosida
Action verbs ending in a consonant	먹다	먹기도 했다 meokgido haetda	먹기도 하다 meokgido hada	먹기도 할 것이다 meokgido hal geosida

TAKE NOTE

This expression and ~(으)ㄹ 수도 있다 **~(eu)l sudo itda** are similar, but ~기도 하다 means that ~ actually does happen while ~(으)ㄹ 수도 있다 means that ~ has the potential to happen, whether or not it actually does.

기도하다 or 기도 하다 by itself means "to pray" or "to attempt." 기도 하다 directly following another verb means "~ sometimes happens." Don't get them confused.

You can repeat 기도 하다 in the middle of your sentence and again at the end to say that sometimes you do one thing and sometimes you do another. See the examples.

EXAMPLE SENTENCES

어제 주로 비가 왔어요. 그래도 눈이 오**기도 했어요**.
Eoje juro biga wasseoyo. Geuraedo nuni ogido haesseoyo.
Yesterday it mainly rained, but occasionally it snowed.

점심에 밥을 먹곤 하지만 라면을 먹**기도 해요**.
Jeomsime babeul meokgon hajiman ramyeoneul meokgido haeyo.
I usually eat rice for lunch, but sometimes I eat ramen.

어떤 날은 잘 자**기도 하**지만 어떤 날은 잘 못 자요.
Eotteon nareun jal jagido hajiman eotteon nareun jal mot jayo.
Some days I sleep well, but some days I don't.

A다(가) 보니(까) da(ga) boni(kka) B	"After doing A for a while, I noticed B"	Speaking > Writing ★★★

친구 하고 길게 이야기를 하**다가 보니까** 수업에 늦게 됐어요.
Chingu hago gilge iyagireul hadaga bonikka sueobe neutge dwaesseoyo.
I was talking with my friend for a long time and suddenly noticed I was late for class.

You know how sometimes you get carried away doing something for a long time and suddenly you notice something has changed? For example you've been studying Korean for a long time and then suddenly you realize you're able to understand most of what's going on around you? That's what this expression is for.

HOW IT'S FORMED

다가 plus 보다 plus (으)니까. 보다, as you know, means to watch or see; in this expression it means to discover or to notice. 니까, as we saw on page 67, means "so." Put it all together and you (sort of) get, "After A, I noticed that B." 가 and 까 are both optional, and so A다가 보니까 B, A다 보니까 B, A다가 보니 B, and A다 보니 are all variations of this expression. You can use them interchangeably.

HOW IT'S CONJUGATED

		All tenses
Action verbs ending in a vowel	하다	하다가 보니까 hadaga bonikka
Action verbs ending in a consonant	먹다	먹다가 보니까 meokdaga bonikka

TAKE NOTE

A is an action that is repeated and/or lasts for some time. If you studied Korean just once and then noticed some improvement, you can't use this expression (but you can use 고 보니 instead.; see page 282). If you've been studying for a while, this expression is perfect. It can't be used in the future or with imaginary situations.

As it's an expression used to talk about something that changed, the B clause usually ends with an expression indicating change such as ~어/아지다 eo/ajida or ~게 되다 ge doeda.

A다가 보면 B is related; it means that if you keep doing A for a long time, B will happen. It's in the section on warnings and can be found on page 209.

돈을 그렇게 많이 쓰**다 보면** 돈이 다 없어질 거예요.
Doneul geureoke mani sseuda bomyeon doni da eopseojil geoyeyo.
If you keep spending that much money, you won't have any left.

EXAMPLE SENTENCES

한국어 공부하**다 보니** 쓰기 능력이 훨씬 더 좋아졌어요.
Hangugeo gongbuhada boni sseugi neungnyeogi hwolssin deo joajyeosseoyo.
After studying Korean (for some time), my writing ability greatly improved.

몇 시간 동안 축구를 하**다 보니까** 다리가 아파졌어요.
Myeot sigan dongan chukgureul hada bonikka dariga apajyeosseoyo.
After playing soccer for several hours, he hurt his leg.

	Speaking < Writing
~(으)ㄴ/는 법이다 (eu)n/neun beobida "~ is natural"	★★★
기/게 마련이다 gi/ge maryeonida	★★

빨리 세운 계획은 실패하**는 법이다**.
Ppalli seun gyehoegeun silpaehaneun beobida.

빨리 세운 계획은 실패하**기 마련이다**.
Ppalli seun gyehoegeun silpaehagi maryeonida.

빨리 세운 계획은 실패하**게 마련이다**.
Ppalli seun gyehoegeun silpaehage maryeonida.

A plan that's made quickly is bound to fail.

No, not natural like organic oatmeal. Natural like people losing weight if they eat that same organic oatmeal, or gaining weight if they eat only junk food. (으)ㄴ/는 법이다 and 기/게 마련이다 are two interchangeable ways to say that something occurs naturally or is only to be expected.

HOW IT'S FORMED

(으)ㄴ/는 are present tense markers for action verbs and adjectives. 법 means "law," so this expression means that it's "a kind of law that ~."

기 is a way to change a verb into a noun. 게 is a short form of 것이, which is another way to make a noun. 마련이다 is another way to say something is natural.

HOW IT'S CONJUGATED

		Past	Present	Future
Action verbs ending in a vowel	하다	하는 법이었다 haneun beobieotda 하기 마련이었다 hagi maryeonieotda 하게 마련이었다 hage maryeonieotda	하는 법이다 haneun beobida 하기 마련이다 hagi maryeonida 하게 마련이다 hage maryeonida	하는 법일 것이다 haneun beobil geosida 하기 마련일 것이다 hagi maryeonil geosida 하게 마련일 것이다 hage maryeonil geosida
Action verbs ending in a consonant	먹다	먹는 법이었다 meokneun beobieotda 먹기 마련이었다 meokgi maryeonieotda 먹게 마련이었다 meokge maryeonieotda	먹는 법이다 meokneun beobida 먹기 마련이다 meokgi maryeonida 먹게 마련이다 meokge maryeonida	먹는 법일 것이다 meokneun beobil geosida 먹기 마련일 것이다 meokgi maryeonil geosida 먹게 마련일 것이다 meokge maryeonil geosida
Descriptive verbs (adjectives) ending in a vowel	예쁘다	예쁜 법이었다 yeppeun beobieotda 예쁘기 마련이었다 yeppeugi maryeonieotda 예쁘게 마련이었다 yeppeuge maryeonieotda	예쁜 법이다 yeppeun beobida 예쁘기 마련이다 yeppeugi maryeonida 예쁘게 마련이다 yeppeuge maryeonida	예쁜 법일 것이다 yeppeun beobil geosida 예쁘기 마련일 것이다 yeppeugi maryeonil geosida 예쁘게 마련일 것이다 yeppeuge maryeonil geosida
Descriptive verbs (adjectives) ending in a consonant	작다	작은 법이었다 jageun beobieotda 작기 마련이었다 jakgi maryeonieotda 작게 마련이었다 jakge maryeonieotda	작은 법이다 jageun beobida 작기 마련이다 jakgi maryeonida 작게 마련이다 jakge maryeonida	작은 법일 것이다 jageun beobil geosida 작기 마련일 것이다 jakgi maryeonil geosida 작게 마련일 것이다 jakge maryeonil geosida
Nouns ending in a vowel	남자	남자인 법이었다 namjain beobieotda 남자이기 마련이었다 namjaigi maryeonieotda 남자이게 마련이었다 namjaige maryeonieotda	남자인 법이다 namjain beobida 남자이기 마련이다 namjaigi maryeonida 남자이게 마련이다 namjaige maryeonida	남자인 법일 것이다 namjain beobil geosida 남자이기 마련일 것이다 namjaigi maryeonil geosida 남자이게 마련일 것이다 namjaige maryeonil geosida
Nouns ending in a consonant	물	물인 법이었다 murin beobieotda 물이기 마련이었다 murigi maryeonieotda 물이게 마련이었다 murige maryeonieotda	물인 법이다 murin beobida 물이기 마련이다 murigi maryeonida 물이게 마련이다 murige maryeonida	물인 법일 것이다 murin beobil geosida 물이기 마련일 것이다 murigi maryeonil geosida 물이게 마련일 것이다 murige maryeonil geosida

TAKE NOTE

마련하다 means to prepare or arrange; 마련이다 means "to be natural." Be careful with these two.

The expression ~(으)ㄹ 법하다 is similar, but in this case the use of the future (으)ㄹ denotes a general rule which is then contradicted by the situation at hand. It means, "Normally A, but in this case B."

프로 야구 선수들이 야구를 잘 **할 법한**데 오늘 실수만 해요.
Peuro yagu seonsudeuri yagureul jal hal beopande oneul silsuman haeyo.
Normally professional baseball players are pretty good, but today they're doing nothing but making mistakes.

EXAMPLE SENTENCES

과로하면 피곤**한 법이다**. Gwarohamyeon pigonhan beobida.

과로하면 피곤하**기 마련이다**. Gwarohamyeon pigonhagi maryeonida.

과로하면 피곤하**게 마련이다**. Gwarohamyeon pigonhage maryeonida.

If you work too much, of course you'll be tired.

건강하게 먹으면 살이 빠지**는 법이다**.
Geonganghage meogeumyeon sari ppajineun beobida.

건강하게 먹으면 살이 빠지**기 마련이다**.
Geonganghage meogeumyeon sari ppajigi maryeonida.

건강하게 먹으면 살이 빠지**게 마련이다**.
Geonganghage meogeumyeon sari ppajige maryeonida.

If you eat healthily, you're bound to lose weight.

~기(가) 일쑤이다 gi(ga) ilssuida   "habitually do ~"

Speaking > Writing
★★

민수가 대학교 때 자주 수업에 늦게 오**기 일쑤였다**.
Minsuga daehakgyo ttae jaju sueobe neutge ogi ilssuyeotda.
During university, Minsu was habitually late for class.

This is another, slightly less common way to talk about doing something habitually.

HOW IT'S CONJUGATED

		Past	Present	Future
Action verbs ending in a vowel	하다	하기(가) 일쑤였다 hagi(ga) ilssuyeotda	하기(가) 일쑤이다	하기(가) 일쑤일 것이다 hagi(ga) ilssuilgeotsida
Action verbs ending in a consonant	먹다	먹기(가) 일쑤였다 meokgi(ga) ilssuyeotda	먹기(가) 일쑤이다	먹기(가) 일쑤일 것이다 meokgi(ga) ilssuilgeotsida

TAKE NOTE

곤 하다 (see page 349) and 기 일쑤이다 are interchangeable when the sentence is negative. 기 일쑤이다 isn't usually used with positive sentences.

EXAMPLE SENTENCES

남자친구와 헤어진 후에 그는 며칠 동안 계속 저에게 전화하**기 일쑤였다**.
Namjachinguwa heeojin hue geuneun myeochil dongan gyesok jeoege
jeonhwahagi ilssuyeotda.
After I broke up with my boyfriend, he kept on calling me for several days.

가영이는 거짓말하**기 일쑤이다**. Kayoungineun geojinmalhagi ilssuida.
Kayoung always lies.

		Speaking > Writing
~아/어/여 대다 a/eo/yeo daeda	"repeatedly do ~"	★★

개가 계속 짖어 대서 짜증 났어요. Gaega gyesok jijeo daeseo jjajeung nasseoyo.
The dog kept barking, so I was annoyed.

This expression is good for people with roommates or those who have to deal with babies crying or dogs barking all night long, or any other situation where someone or something continues to do something annoying.

HOW IT'S CONJUGATED

		Past	Present	Future
Action verbs with 오 or 아	잡다	잡아 댔다 jaba daetda	잡아 대다 jaba daeda	잡아 댈 것이다 jaba dael geosida
Action verbs with 어, 우, 으 or 이	먹다	먹어 댔다 meogeo daetda	먹어 대다 meogeo daeda	먹어 댈 것이다 meogeo dael geosida
하다	하다	해 댔다 hae daetda	해 대다 hae daeda	해 댈 것이다 hae dael geosida

TAKE NOTE

대다 has a number of meanings outside of this expression: "to put," "to touch," "to provide," "to pay," "to park," "to make an excuse." In these cases, 대다 follows either 을/를 or 에. To distinguish this expression from the others, keep an eye out for the 아/어/여 before 대다 and the context.

아/어/여 대다 is normally used in sentences with negative connotations.

곤 하다 means to do something habitually. If your ex-boyfriend or ex-girlfriend calls you all day long the day after you've broken up with him or her, you can use 아/어/여 대다 to describe the action, but not 곤 하다 because the calling is repeatedly done but is not habitual. If the same ex-boyfriend or ex-girlfriend calls you every day for months on end, then you could use 곤 하다.

EXAMPLE SENTENCES

여자친구가 계속 잔소리를 **해 대**는데 헤어질까요?
Yeojachinguga gyesok jansorireul hae daeneunde heeojilkkayo?
My girlfriend always nags me; should I break up with her?

선거 때문에 하루 종일 선거 운동원들이 스피커로 소리를 질**러 대요**.
Seongeo ttaemune haru jongil seongeo undongwondeuri seupikeoro sorireul jilleo daeyo.
Because of the election, campaigners are yelling through speakers all day long.

~는 것이(게) 보통이다 neun geosi(ge) botongida	"Normally, ~"	Speaking > Writing ★★

민수가 늦**는 것이 보통이**에요. Minsuga neunneun geosi botongieyo.
민수가 늦**는 게 보통이**에요. Minsuga neunneun ge botongieyo.
It's normal for Minsu to be late.

Some things are just not that exciting. Here's how you can talk about something that's normal or usual.

HOW IT'S FORMED

는 것 changes a verb into a noun. You can use 는 게 instead; it's just a contraction of 는 것이. 보통 means "normal" or "usual." So ~ is normal, commonplace, or to be expected.

HOW IT'S CONJUGATED

		Past	Present	Future
Action verbs ending in a vowel	하다	하는 것이 보통이었다 haneun geosi botongieotda 하는 게 보통이었다 haneun ge botongieotda	하는 것이 보통이다 haneun geosi botongida 하는 게 보통이다 haneun ge botongida	하는 것이 보통이 것이다 haneun geosi botongil geosida 하는 게 보통일 것이다 haneun ge botongil geosida
Action verbs ending in a consonant	먹다	먹는 것이 보통이었다 meokneun geosi botongieotda 먹는 게 보통이었다 meokneun ge botongieotda	먹는 것이 보통이다 meokneun geosi botongida 먹는 게 보통이다 meokneun ge botongida	먹는 것이 보통일 것이다 meokneun geosi botongil geosida 먹는 게 보통일 것이다 meokneun ge botongil geosida

TAKE NOTE

보통 all by itself can mean normal (as in this expression) but also mediocre or average—if you review a date by saying 그 사람은 보통이에요 **Geu sarameun botongieyo**, it means the person was normal in the sense that they were mediocre, nothing special, and you probably aren't too excited about the possibility of going out with them again.

EXAMPLE SENTENCES

이렇게 높은 점수를 얻<u>는 것이 보통이</u> 아니에요.
Ireoke nopeun jeomsureul eonneun geosi botongi anieyo.

이렇게 높은 점수를 얻<u>는 게 보통이</u> 아니에요.
Ireoke nopeun jeomsureul eonneun ge botongi anieyo.

It's not often that someone gets this high a test score.

저기 온도가 −30도 이하가 되<u>는 것이 보통이</u>에요.
Jeogi ondoga maineoseu samsipdo ihaga doeneun geosi botongieyo.

저기 온도가 −30도 이하가 되<u>는 게 보통이</u>에요.
Jeogi ondoga maineoseu samsipdo ihaga doeneun ge botongieyo.

The temperature there is often lower than -30 degrees.

~(으)ㄴ/는 축에 들다   "tends to be ~"   **Speaking > Writing**
(eu)n/neun chuge deulda   ★

민수가 또 늦었어요. 그는 학생 중에서 자주 늦<u>는 축에 들</u>지요?
Minsuga tto neujeosseoyo. Geuneun haksaeng jungeseo jaju neunneun chuge deuljiyo?
Minsu's late again. He tends to be later than most of the other students, doesn't he?

This expression, similar to (으)ㄴ/는 편이다 (eu)n/neun pyeonida, means "tends to."

HOW IT'S FORMED

축 means "axis," like on a graph. 들다 means "to belong to."

HOW IT'S CONJUGATED

		Past	Present
Action verbs ending in a vowel	하다	하는 축에 들었다 haneun chuge deureotda	하는 축에 들다 haneun chuge deulda
Action verbs ending in a consonant	먹다	먹는 축에 들었다 meokneun chuge deureotda	먹는 축에 들다 meokneun chuge deulda
Descriptive verbs (adjectives) ending in a vowel	예쁘다	예쁜 축에 들었다 yeppeun chuge deureotda	예쁜 축에 들다 yeppeun chuge deulda
Descriptive verbs (adjectives) ending in a consonant	작다	작은 축에 들었다 Jageun chuge deureotda	작은 축에 들다 jageun chuge deulda

TAKE NOTE

This expression shouldn't be used in the future tense.

When using 축에 들다 with action verbs, always add an adverb such as 자주 jaju or 드물게 deumulge.

Just like 편이다, 축에 들다 isn't used to talk about objectively verifiable facts: for instance, "he tends to be a man." You could, however, say that he tends to be manly.

> 그는 남자인 축에 들어요.　　　　　He tends to be a man. (ungrammatical)
> Geuneun namjain chuge deureoyo.

> 그는 남자다운 축에 들어요.　　　　He tends to be manly. (just fine)
> Geuneun namjadaun chuge deureoyo.

A similar expression is ~(으)ㄴ/는 편이다 (see page 350). There's a very slight difference in meaning between the two. Think of 편이다 as placing the subject on a scale between 0 and 100. Let's say 0 is 제일 작은 and 100 is 제일 큰. If the subject rates over 50 on that scale, 큰 편이다. With 축에 들다, rather than a scale, you're dividing people into groups and saying which group they belong in: the big group or the small group. It's more often used when comparing yourself to family or colleagues, rather than the entire human population. 편이다 compares you to everyone. Another difference is that 편이다 is rather more formal. 축에 들다 shouldn't be used toward elders.

If you want to use 축에 들다 to compare yourself to others, you can use an expression like 제 가족 중에서 je gajok jungeseo or 제 친구 중에서 je chingu jungeseo. See the examples below.

EXAMPLE SENTENCES

> 저는 라면을 매일 먹어요. 제 가족 중에서 라면을 자주 먹**는 축에 들어요**.
> Jeoneun ramyeoneul maeil meogeoyo. Je gajok jungeseo ramyeoneul jaju meokneun chuge deureoyo.
> I eat ramen every day. Compared to the rest of my family, I eat ramen a lot.

> 저 학생은 다른 학생보다 작**은 축에 들**어서 더 작은 책상이 필요해요.
> Jeo haksaengeun dareun haksaengboda jageun chuge deureoseo deo jageun chaeksangi piryohaeyo.
> That student is small compared to the others, so he needs a smaller desk.

		Speaking > Writing
~다가 말다가 하다 daga maldaga hada	"Doing ~ on and off"	★

> 그렇게 준비를 하**다가 말다가** 하면 늦을 거예요.
> Geureoke junbireul hadaga maldaga hamyeon neujeul geoyeyo.
> If you keep on getting ready and then stopping like that, you'll be late.

Are you someone who cannot commit to something, such as having trouble keeping New Year's resolutions? If so, this expression's for you.

HOW IT'S FORMED

다가 plus 말다. 말다 basically means "to not be that way" and is used much in expressions indicating indecision: for example, 하거나 말거나 **hageona malgeona** (see page 61) or 하는 둥 마는 둥 **haneun dung maneun dung** (see page 266). So the literal meaning of this expression is "to do ~ and then not do ~ and then." It's normally used for something that is done intermittently. 가 is optional.

HOW IT'S CONJUGATED

		Past	Present	Future
Action verbs ending in a vowel	하다	하다가 말다가 했다 hadaga maldaga haetda	하다가 말다가 하다 hadaga maldaga hada	하다가 말다가 할 것이다 hadaga maldaga hal geosida
Action verbs ending in a consonant	먹다	먹다가 말다가 했다 meokdaga maldaga haetda	먹다가 말다가 하다 meokdaga maldaga hada	먹다가 말다가 할 것이다 meokdaga maldaga hal geosida

TAKE NOTE

The subjects of clause A and clause B should be the same.

EXAMPLE SENTENCES

운동을 하**다가 말다가** 하면 근육에 무리가 갈 거예요.
Undongeul hadaga maldaga hamyeon geunyuge muriga gal geoyeyo.
If you keep exercising on and off like that, it will be too stressful for your muscles.

공부하**다가 말다가** 해서 시험 준비를 잘 못했어요.
Gongbuhadaga maldaga haeseo siheom junbireul jal motaesseoyo.
I studied on and off, so I wasn't well-prepared for the test.

Faking it

~(으)ㄴ/는 척하다/체하다	"Pretend to ~"	Speaking > Writing
(eu)n/neun cheokada/chehada		★ ★ ★ ★

정말 늦게 가고 있어서 다른 약속이 있**는 척할** 거예요.
Jeongmal neutge gago isseoseo dareun yaksogi inneun cheokal geoyeyo.

정말 늦게 가고 있어서 다른 약속이 있**는 체할** 거예요.
Jeongmal neutge gago isseoseo dareun yaksogi inneun chehal geoyeyo.

I'm really late, so I'm going to pretend I have another appointment.

These two expressions go together because they're totally interchangeable. They're good for con men and women out there because they're both used to talk about pretending to do or be something.

HOW IT'S CONJUGATED

		Past	Present	Future
Action verbs ending in a vowel	하다	한 척했다 han cheokaetda 한 체했다 han chehaetda	하는 척하다 haneun cheokada 하는 체하다 haneun chehada	하는 척 할 것이다 haneun cheok hal geosida 하는 체 할 것이다 haneun che hal geosida
Action verbs ending in a consonant	먹다	먹은 척했다 meogeun cheokaetda 먹은 체했다 meogeun chehaetda	먹는 척하다 meokneun cheokada 먹는 체하다 meokneun chehada	먹는 척 할 것이다 meokneun cheok hal geosida 먹는 체 할 것이다 meokneun che hal geosida
Descriptive verbs (adjectives) ending in a vowel	예쁘다	예쁜 척했다 yeppeun cheokaetda 예쁜 체했다 yeppeun chehaetda	예쁜 척하다 yeppeun cheokada 예쁜 체하다 yeppeun chehada	예쁜 척 할 것이다 yeppeun cheok hal geosida 예쁜 체 할 것이다 yeppeun che hal geosida
Descriptive verbs (adjectives) ending in a consonant	작다	작은 척했다 jageun cheokaetda 작은 체했다 jageun chehaetda	작은 척하다 jageun cheokada 작은 체하다 jageun chehada	작은 척 할 것이다 jageun cheok hal geosida 작은 체 할 것이다 jageun che hal geosida
Nouns ending in a vowel	남자	남자인 척했다 namjain cheokaetda 남자인 체했다 namjain chehaetda	남자인 척하다 namjain cheokada 남자인 체하다 namjain chehada	남자인 척 할 것이다 namjain cheok hal geosida 남자인 체 할 것이다 namjain che hal geosida
Nouns ending in a consonant	학생	학생인 척했다 haksaengin cheokaetda 학생인 체했다 haksaengin chehaetda	학생인 척하다 haksaengin cheokada 학생인 체하다 haksaengin chehada	학생인 척 할 것이다 haksaengin cheok hal geosida 학생인 체 할 것이다 haksaengin che hal geosida

TAKE NOTE

A(으)ㄴ/는 채 B means to be in a certain state. Aside from the different spelling, you can tell it apart from 체 here because 채 isn't followed by 하다 but rather by a sentence explaining what was done while in the state of A. 체 as seen in this section will always be followed by 하다.

알다 and 모르다 are very commonly used with 척하다.

> 아는 척하다 aneun cheokada to pretend to know
>
> 모르는 척하다 moreuneun cheokada to pretend not to know

EXAMPLE SENTENCES

> 민수가 싫으니까 거리에서 봤을 때 모르는 **척했어요**.
> Minsuga sireunikka georieseo bwasseul ttae moreuneun cheokaesseoyo.
>
> 민수가 싫으니까 거리에서 봤을 때 모르는 **체했어요**.
> Minsuga sireunikka georieseo bwasseul ttae moreuneun chehaesseoyo.
>
> 민수가 싫으니까 거리에서 봤을 때 **모른 척했어요**.
> Minsuga sireunikka georieseo bwasseul ttae moreun cheokaesseoyo.
>
> 민수가 싫으니까 거리에서 봤을 때 **모른 체했어요**.
> Minsuga sireunikka georieseo bwasseul ttae moreun chehaesseoyo.

I don't like Minsu, so when I saw him in the street I pretended not to recognize him.

> 할인 받고 싶어서 학생**인 척했어요**.
> Harin batgo sipeoseo haksaengin cheokaesseoyo.
>
> 할인 받고 싶어서 학생**인 체했어요**.
> Harin batgo sipeoseo haksaengin chehaesseoyo.

I wanted to get a discount, so I pretended I was a student.

3 Frequently Seen Word Parts

~답다 dapda "typical of ~"

답다 is used to talk about qualities like manliness, womanliness, etc.: qualities that are typical of a certain noun. The most well-known example is 아름답다 (to be beautiful), but you can also add 답다 to any other noun you want.

Add 답다 to the end of the noun which describes the category. The rest of your sentence should describe how ~ is typical or not typical of that category.

| 남자 | 남자**답다** namjadapda |
| 아름 | 아름**답다** areumdapda |

Note that 답다 can't be used to describe something that isn't already ~. For instance, you can't call a man 여자답다 yeojadapda. If you do want to talk about a girly man, try 스럽다 seureopda (see the next expression on this page). You can call a man 남자답다 if you think he has all the qualities that make him a perfect specimen of a man. Alternatively, you can say he's 남자답지 않다 namjadapji anta if he's not at all manly.

가영이 자주 쇼핑을 가요. 정말 여자**다워요**.
Kayoungi jaju syopingeul gayo. Jeongmal yeojadawoyo.
Kayoung goes shopping a lot. She's really a typical girl.

제 남자친구는 늘 예쁜 것을 사주고 문을 열어줘요. 신사**답**지요?
Je namjachinguneun neul yeppeun geoseul sajugo muneul yeoreojwoyo.
Sinsadapjiyo?
My boyfriend always buys me pretty things and opens doors for me. He's really gentlemanly, don't you think?

이번 방학 때 아름**다운** 곳에 가고 싶어요
Ibeon banghak ttae areumdaun gose gago sipeoyo.
This vacation, I want to go somewhere beautiful.

~스럽다 seureopda "appears to be ~"

스럽다 is all about appearances. It means that something appears to be a certain way. You'll see it used all the time as part of certain words in 자연스럽다, 어른스럽다, etc..

자연	자연**스럽다** jayeonseureopda	to be natural
어른	어른**스럽다** eoreunseureopda	to be mature
걱정	걱정**스럽다** geokjeongseureopda	to be worried

| 사랑 | 사랑<u>스럽다</u> sarangseureopda | to be loving |
| 자랑 | 자랑<u>스럽다</u> jarangseureopda | to be proud |

Unlike 답다, you can't use 스럽다 to describe something that actually ~. For example, you can't use 어른스럽다 to describe an actual adult, but you can use it to describe a child. If you want to say an adult is especially adult-like, use 답다 instead (see the previous page).

민수 때문에 걱정**스러워요**. 요즘 늦은 밤에 집에 돌아오곤 해요.
Minsu ttaemune geokjeongseureowoyo. Yojeum neujeun bame jibe doraogon haeyo.
I'm really worried about Minsu. These days he usually comes home late at night.

우리 딸이 1등상을 받았어요. 얼마나 자랑**스러워요**.
Uri ttari ildeungsangeul badasseoyo. Eolmana jarangseureowoyo.
My daughter got first prize. I'm so proud!

그는 여성스러운 남자일 뿐이에요. Geuneun yeoseongseureoun namjail ppuni-eyo. He's nothing but a girly man.

~롭다 ropda "to be ~"

롭다 is similar to 스럽다 (see just above), but it's used only after certain nouns ending with vowels.

자유	자유롭다 jayuropda	to be free
새	새롭다 saeropda	to be new
향기	향기롭다 hyanggiropda	to be fragrant
해	해롭다 haeropda	to be harmful
명예	명예롭다 myeongyeropda	to be honorable

자유롭게 살고 싶어요. Jayuropge salgo sipeoyo. I want to live freely.

어제 새로운 가방을 샀어요. Eoje saeroun gabangeul sasseoyo.
Yesterday I bought a new bag.

그 예쁜 꽃이 놀랍게도 향기**롭**지 않아요.
Geu yeppeun kkochi nollapgedo hyanggiropji anayo.
Surprisingly, that beautiful flower doesn't smell good.

~거리다 georida "does ~ repeatedly"

There are a number of verbs which end in 거리다. In these cases, 거리다 means "to do repeatedly." You'll see it used with many motion verbs and onomatopoeic verbs.

| 깜빡**거리다** kkamppakgeorida | to flicker |
| 덜렁**거리다** deolleonggeorida | to jingle |

중얼**거리다** jungeolgeorida   to mutter

비실**거리다** bisilgeorida   to stagger

씩씩**거리다** ssikssikgeorida   to gasp, pant

낄낄**거리다** kkilkkilgeorida   to giggle

등산할 때 씩씩**거렸**어요. Deungsanhal ttae ssikssikgeoryeosseoyo.
While mountain-climbing, I was panting.

선생님이 보지 않을 때 아이들이 다 중얼**거리**고 있어요.
Seonsaengnimi boji aneul ttae aideuri da jungeolgeorigo isseoyo.
While the teacher isn't looking, the children are whispering.

촛불이 깜빡**거리**고 있어요. Chotburi kkamppakgeorigo isseoyo.
The candle is flickering.

Talking about People

You'll have noticed that Koreans use different words that all essentially mean "person." There are a couple of reasons for this, and they have to do with both the Korean language's hanja roots and with the great importance the language places on people's ranks.

- 인, 자, 사, 원, 가, 부, 관 in, ja, sa, won, ga, bu, gwan

These words are all derived from hanja.

인 (人) is used all over the place, and it simply means "person." It's never used by itself and only rarely as a job title.

외국인 **oegugin**   foreigner

한국인 **hangugin**   Korean (person)

부인 **buin**   wife

군인 **gunin**   soldier

자 (者) also simply means person. It's sometimes used as a job title.

기술자 **gisulja**   engineer, technician

저자 **jeoja**   writer

피해자 **pihaeja**   victim

기자 **gija**   reporter

사 (師) means "master" or "teacher." It's used for professions that require some level of mastery.

교사 **gyosa**	teacher
사진사 **sajinsa**	photographer
의사 **uisa**	doctor
간호사 **ganhosa**	nurse
기사 **gisa**	driver

원 (員) means "member" and is used for situations where the person is a member of some organization.

회사원 **hoesawon**	office worker
사무원 **samuwon**	office worker, clerk
직원 **jigwon**	employee
은행원 **eunhaengwon**	bank teller

가 (家) has quite a few different meanings such as "house" (it's also the 가 in 가족) and "shop," but when it's used to talk about people it also implies some level of expertise or specialization.

화가 **hwaga**	painter
작가 **jakga**	writer
전문가 **jeonmunga**	expert

부 (夫) is also the male 부 in 부부 (couple). It means "man," but when applied to jobs it's used for either a man or a woman. Jobs ending in 부 tend to be of the blue-collar kind.

어부 **eobu**	fisherman
농부 **nongbu**	farmer
광부 **gwangbu**	miner
청소부 **cheongsobu**	cleaner
배달부 **baedalbu**	deliveryman

관 (官) is also used to talk about government buildings. It's used to describe people in government positions or official capacities.

경찰관 **gyeong-chal-gwan**	police officer
소방관 **sobanggwan**	firefighter

■ 꾼, 쟁이, 뱅이, 꾸러기, 광 kkun, jaengi, baengi, kkureogi, gwang

These words have nothing to do with hanja. They're pure, 100% Korean. With the exception of 꾼, they're not usually used to describe job titles, but just people who do a certain thing a lot. There's not much difference between them, but they're paired with different words. You just have to remember which ending follows which words.

일꾼 ilkkun	laborer
나무꾼 namukkun	lumberjack
노름꾼 noreumkkun	gambler
사냥꾼 sanyangkkun	hunter
누리꾼 nurikkun	habitual Internet user (Netizen)
점쟁이 jeomjaengi	fortuneteller
멋쟁이 meotjaengi	fashionable person
무식쟁이 musikjaengi	ignorant person
겁쟁이 geopjaengi	coward
욕심쟁이 yoksimjaengi	greedy person
게으름뱅이 geeureumbaengi	lazy person
가난뱅이 gananbaengi	poor person
주정뱅이 jujeongbaengi	drunk
비렁뱅이 bireongbaengi	beggar, hobo
장난꾸러기 jangnankkureogi	someone who always plays
잠꾸러기 jamkkureogi	someone who always sleeps
말썽꾸러기 malsseongkkureogi	someone who always makes trouble
심술꾸러기 simsulkkureogi	a cynic, grumpy person
스포츠광 seupocheugwang	sports fan
낚시광 naksigwang	fishing maniac
살인광 saringwang	homicidal maniac
영화광 yeonghwa-gwang	movie buff

■ 사람, 명, 분, 인분 saram, myeong, bun, inbun

These are all just different words that mean "person." 사람 is general and can be used in almost any situation. 명 and 분 are counting markers for people, so you'll talk about 한명, 세명, 네명 hanmyeong, semyeong, nemyeong, and so on. 분 is very formal while 명 is much less so. You'd use 명 to talk about how many people are in your own party while the waiter would use the more polite 분 to talk about that same party. 인분 actually means "servings" (or "excrement") and maybe the two aren't that far apart in certain restaurants.... Thus, you use it when you order food: steak for three people would be 스테이크 삼 인분 주세요. **Seuteikeu sam inbun juseyo.**

Prefixes

Prefix	Meaning	Example Words
외 oe	the only one	외톨이 **oetori** (loner), 외아들 **oeadeul** (only son), 외딸 **oettal** (only daughter)
되 doe	again	되찾다 **doechatda** (to recover), 되묻다 **doemutda** (to ask again), 되돌아가다 **doedoragada** (to go back again)
날 nal	raw, uncooked	날생선 **nalsaengseon** (raw fish), 날고기 **nalgogi** (raw meat), 날계란 **nalgyeran** (raw egg)
풋 put	unripe	풋사랑 **putsarang** (puppy love), 풋사과 **putsagwa** (unripe apple), 풋고추 **putgochu** (unripe pepper)
군 gun	unnecessary, useless	군침 **gunchim** (drooling, e.g. at the smell of food), 군살 **gunsal** (extra weight), 군말 **gunmal** (useless chatter)
헛 heot	unnecessary, useless	헛기침 **heotgichim** (fake cough), 헛걸음 **heotgeoreum** (fool's errand), 헛소문 **heotsomun** (baseless rumor)
덧 deot	in addition, plus	덧붙이다 **deotbuchida** (to append), 덧칠 **deotchil** (to paint over), 덧셈 **deotsem** (addition)
맨 maen*	bare	맨발 **maenbal** (barefoot), 맨얼굴 **maeneolgul** (without makeup), 맨손 **maenson** (empty-handed)

* This isn't the same as the 맨 that means "most" (맨 위에 **maen wie**, 맨 뒤에 **maen dwie**, etc.). This one is placed directly in front of the word it modifies.

Appendix 1:
How to Sound Like a Native

Adverbs of Time

Most adverbs are made using 게 or 히; see page 24 to find out how that works. However, there are a significant number of very useful adverbs that don't follow these patterns. They're summarized below.

일찍 iljjik	early
일단 ildan	once, first of all
비로소 biroso	at last, for the first time
돌연 dolyeon	suddenly
갑자기 gapjagi	suddenly
별안간 byeolangan	suddenly
느닷없이 neudateopsi	suddenly
뚝 dduk	(something was done) suddenly
어느덧 eoneudeot	before we knew it
어느새 eoneuse	before we knew it
냉큼 naengkeum	immediately
당장 dangjang	immediately
얼른 eolleun	quickly, promptly, eagerly
빨리 ppali	quickly, promptly, eagerly
급히 geupi	quickly, promptly, eagerly
즉시 jeuksi	quickly, promptly, eagerly, immediately
곧 got	quickly, promptly, eagerly, immediately
금세 geumse	instantly, at once
금방 geumbang	instantly, at once
바로 baro	at once, immediately, directly, straight, right, exactly
새로 sero	newly

이미 **imi**	already
벌써 **beolsseo**	already
간밤 **ganbam**	last night
어제 **eoje**	yesterday
오늘 **oneul**	today
그저께 **geujeokke**	the day before yesterday
내일 **naeil**	tomorrow
모레 **more**	the day after tomorrow
당일 **dangil**	the same day
동시에 **dongsie**	simultaneously
한꺼번에 **hankkeobeone**	simultaneously, all at once
확 **hwak**	(to do something) completely, all at once
뜬금없이 **tteungeumeopsi**	all of a sudden
마지막 **majimak**	the last
드디어 **deudieo**	finally
마침내 **machimne**	finally
결국 **gyeolguk**	eventually
계속 **gyeosok**	continuously
당분간 **dangbungan**	for the time being
한참 **hancham**	for some time
슬슬 **seulseul**	gradually, taking one's time
여태 **yeote**	still, so far, yet
아직 **ajik**	still, so far, yet
여전히 **yeojeonhi**	still, as ever
아까 **akka**	a while ago
막 **mak**	just now
방금 **banggeum**	just now
이제 **ije**	now
지금 **jigeum**	now

Adverbs of Frequency

평소(에) pyeongso(e)	usually, ordinarily, always
늘 neul	always
항상 hangsang	always
언제나 eonjena	always
언제쯤 eonjejjeum	always
계속 gyesok	continuously
끊임없이 ggeunimeopsi	continuously
자꾸 jakku	often, incessantly, persistently
빈번히 binbeoni	frequently
자주 jaju	often
수시로 susiro	frequently, often
가끔 gakkeum	sometimes
간혹 ganhok	sometimes, occasionally
이따금 ittageum	sometimes
종종 jongjong	sometimes, often
띄엄띄엄 ttuieomttuieom	occasionally
드문드문 deumundeumun	sometimes, occasionally
틈틈이 teumteumi	at spare moments
드물게 deumulge	rarely
한때 hantte	once
결코 gyeolko	never, by no means
절대로 jeoldero	never, by no means

Adverbs of Degree

■ None

전혀 jeonhyeo	not at all
절대로 jeoldero	never, absolutely not
도무지 domuji	entirely, never (with negatives)
통 tong	entirely, never (with negatives)

■ Not much

오직 ojik	only
적어도 jeokeodo	at least
그리 geuri	not much
그다지 geudaji	not much
좀처럼 jomcheoreom	rarely, not easily (usually with negative expressions)
살며시 salmyeosi	furtively, secretly
빠듯이 ppadeutsi	barely, narrowly
번쩍 beonjjeok	lightly
겨우 gyeou	hardly
덜 deol	not much, less than
여간 yeogan	rarely, not much (used with the opposite of whatever you're really trying to say)

■ Some

| 적당히 jeokdanghi | somewhat |

■ A lot

더 deo	more
흔히 heunhi	commonly
꽤 ggue	fairly, much
푹 ggwae	(to rest) deeply, soundly
특히 teuki	especially
무척 mucheok	very
어찌나 eojjina	so
훨씬 hweolssin	greatly, by far, much
맨 maen	first, most, very

유난히 yunanhi	especially
하도 hado	too
깊이 gipi	deeply
워낙 wonak	originally, very, by nature
원래 wonre	originally, very, by nature
무려 muryeo	as much as

■ Almost entirely

거의 geoui	almost
대충 daechung	roughly, in general

■ Entirely

완전히 wanjeonhi	completely
수없이 sueopsi	innumerably
온통 ontong	all, entirely
가득 gadeuk	full
잔뜩 jantteuk	full
정성껏 jeonseongkkeot	with all one's heart
실컷 silkeot	to one's heart's content, as much as possible
마음껏 maeumkkeot	to one's heart's content

Giving Your Opinion and Sounding Smart

Should you ever find yourself in a serious debate or having to write a serious essay in Korean, here are a few expressions you can use to state your opinion.

First of all, ~(이)라고/(ㄴ/는)다고 보다 and 생각하다 are expressions you can use to end a sentence that states what you think. They are on page 147.

Secondly, many variants of 그렇다 are commonly used when starting sentences (see the next page).

~말할 나위도 없다 **malhal nawido eopda** it goes without saying that ~

A뒤에는 B이/가 있다 **A dwuieneun B i/ga itda** B is behind A

A(으)로 하여금 B게 하다 **A (eu)ro hayeogeum B ge hada** make A do B

A이/가 B~에 영향을 주다/미치다 **A i/ga B ye yeonghyangeul juda/michida**
   A influences B

A(으)ㄹ 겸 해서 B **A (eu)r gyeom haeseo B** A is one of many possible causes for B

A(으)ㄴ/는 반면에 B **A (eu) n/neun banyeone B** B, as opposed to A

~에 맞서(서) **e matseo (seo)** in opposition to ~

A은/는 B에 비해서/비하면 **A eun/neun B e bihaeseo/bihamyeon** A, compared to B

다른 어느 ~보다 **dareun eoneu ~ boda** more than any other ~

~(으)로 여기다 **(eu)ro yeogida** consider/deem as ~

~게/것이 분명하다 **ge/gutsi bunmyeonghada** it is obvious that ~

A면서 B(이)가 C게 되다 **A myeonseo B(i)ga C ge doeda**
   as A happens, B becomes C

~(이)라/(ㄴ/는)다니까요 **(i)ra (n/neun) danikkayo**
   re-emphasizes ~ (something the speaker already said) forcefully

A의 입장에서는 B **A eui ipjangeseoneun B** B, from A's point of view

~에 의해서/의하면 **e euihaeseo/euihamyun** according to ~

~에서 보는 바와 같이 **eseo boneun bawa gachi** as you can see in ~

A(이)란/(ㄴ/는)단 말이 나왔으니까 B **A(i)ran/(n/neun)dan mali nawasseunikka B**
   having mentioned A, B

다음과 같은 **daeumgwa gateun** like the following

위에서 (앞에서) 언급했듯이 **wieseo (apeseo) eongeuphaetdeusi**
   as I mentioned before/above

앞서 제시했던 것과 같이 **apseo jesihaetdeon geotgwa gachi** as I mentioned earlier

이상에서 알 수 있는 것과 같이 **isangeseo al su itneun geotgwa gachi**
   as we can learn from the above

~(이)라/(ㄴ/는)다고 할 수 있다 (i)ra/(n/neun) dago hal su itda you can say that ~

적게는 A에서 많게는 B까지 jeokgeneun A eseo mankeneun B kkaji
  from at least A to a maximum of B

제가 보기에는 jega bogieneun From what I've seen

제 생각으로는/제 생각에는 je saenggakeuroneun/je saenggakeneun I think

제가 말씀드리고 싶은 것은 jega malsseumdeurigo sipeun geoseun
  What I want to say is that

저는 이렇게 생각합니다 jeoneun ireoke saenggakhapnida This is what I think.

제 말의 의미는 je malui uimineun What I mean is that

저는 ~씨와 생각이 같습니다 jeoneun ~ssiwa saenggaki gatseubnida
  I agree with ~

How to Deal with 그렇다

그렇다, which means "to be like that," can be used to mean many things that may not be immediately obvious. It's quite often used to take a break in the middle of a long sentence. Just as you might drone on in English, pause for a second and then start again with "However" or "Therefore," you can use 그렇다 for similar purposes in Korean. It can be conjugated just like any other descriptive verb. Here are some useful words with 그렇다.

그래(요) geure(yo) Yes/I agree/Uh-huh

그렇구나/그렇군요 geureotkuna/geureotkunyo Oh, really!/Oh, I see!

그렇지(요) geureotchi(yo) Yes/Absolutely/Uh-huh/That's true, isn't it!

그렇고말고(요) geureotkomalgo(yo) Of course!/Absolutely!/Definitely!/Obviously!

그래서 geureseo Therefore/so

그러니까 geureonikka Therefore/so

그러므로 geureomeuro Therefore

그러하다 geureohada So, like that

그러면 geureomyeon If so, then

그렇다고 geureotago If you say so, then

그렇지만 geureochiman But

그러나 geureona But

그래도 geuredo In spite of that

그렇지 않아도 geureochi anado Even if you hadn't said/done that

Appendix 2:
Useful Korean Language Resources

■ Beginning Level

If you're not quite ready for this book yet or you want to review basic grammar, there are a few resources that I found invaluable.

The *Talk to Me in Korean* website does a fantastic job of explaining different expressions, how to form them, and how to use them. It also has much information about real-life Korean language, including vocabulary, useful hanja characters, and stories in Korean. The website is http://www.talktomeinkorean.com/

Another good website is Sogang's free online class. The website is http://korean.sogang.ac.kr and it has various activities and lessons for beginning levels. Activities are quite good in helping you review, especially if you're studying on your own.

Stephen Revere's book *Survival Korean* is another great beginning level book. He's very good at explaining things in ways that make sense, and he makes the concepts easy to remember. Revere, Stephen. *Survival Korean.* Nexus, 2005.

Finally, if you are a little more advanced 가나다, *Wild Korean* by 안상현, is a very good book to help you speak Korean in various everyday situations. It has a list of useful vocabulary for each section along with grammar points and expressions to help you. If you want to learn how to speak Korean when you go to the hospital, to the supermarket, to the bank, and so on, this is the book for you. Ahn Sanghyun. *Wild Korean,* BookShelf Publishing

■ Intermediate Level

Obviously I'm going to recommend this book…

■ Advanced Level

If this book is not enough, there are two comprehensive reference guides I frequently referred to while writing this grammar reference book.

한국어 문법 사전 (translated roughly as *Korean Grammar Dictionary* [by Hangukeo Munbeop Sajeon]) covers just about anything you'd ever need. It's all in Korean, so you need to know your grammatical terms if you want to look anything up. But it's all there, and the author does a very good job of explaining when and how each expression can be used.

Finally, if you're very serious about learning grammar, *A Reference Grammar of Korean* is exactly what it claims to be. However, it's a thick book, is difficult to understand, and uses a strange Romanization system instead of actual Korean characters. It's really intended more for linguists than for students of Korean, but it is about the most comprehensive resource available and there is much additional material on hanja, North and South Korean dialects, and many other topics. Martin, Samuel E. *A Reference Grammar of Korean,* Tuttle Publishing, 2006.

■ Textbook Series

The best series I've seen to date is *Korean Grammar in Use*. It goes from beginning through intermediate levels at the time of writing this book. It organizes everything by purpose, just like I did, and compares different expressions so you know when to say what. *Korean Grammar in Use* is published by 다락원.

Index

Using the Index: An Introduction

The index lists grammatical points alphabetically using the Korean alphabet. In cases where an expression changes forms depending on whether it follows a consonant or vowel, the vowel form is used. For example, let's say you want to look up 먹을 거예요 **meogeul geoyeyo**. You can tell that the grammatical point 을 거예요 **eur geoyeyo** follows the verb 먹다, and you can guess that 을 probably wouldn't follow a vowel and that the vowel form of this expression is probably ㄹ 거예요. And you're right!

Tips

Parentheses indicate that a part of an expression is not always used. When you see (으)ㄹ 거예요, this means that sometimes the expression is used as 을 거예요 **eur geoyeyo** and sometimes as ㄹ 거예요 **r geoyeyo**.

이 and 으 are the usual vowels used when an expression changes forms to follow a consonant, so if you want to look up something starting with one of those, try starting with the letter right after the 이 or 으 (e.g. for (이)라고 **(i)rago**, look up 라고).

In cases where expressions change at the beginning in other ways (e.g. the many that begin with (으)ㄴ, 는 or (으)ㄹ), I've listed all the forms separately so you can easily find them without having to guess which variations are applicable to the particular expression you want to learn about.

In some cases, the ends of expressions may look different depending on the level of politeness or dictionary form versus the form used in speech. For example, the (으)ㄹ 거예요 above is actually (으)ㄹ 것이다 **(eu)r geosida** in its dictionary form. In cases like that which can be confusing, I've tried to list both forms; however, if you don't see what you're looking for but see something similar, try looking it up to see if it's what you're after. With a couple of unique exceptions, all levels of politeness of expressions are NOT listed here – you will not find (으)ㄹ 거야 **(eu)r geoya** or (으)ㄹ 겁니다 **(eu)r geomnida**, respectively the familiar and super-polite forms of (으)ㄹ 거예요). This is simply because it would make the index really long and because changes in level of politeness are usually consistent and done at the end of the sentence anyway, so as long as you can find the beginning of the expression, you can usually make an educated guess about whether or not it matches what you want to find.

Combinations of expressions are not usually listed or covered in this book, simply because there are too many and it would make the book very long and repetitive. So if, for example, you want to find something like 라고 해서 **rago haeseo**, and you don't see it in the index but you do see 라고 하다, look that up first and then look up the second part 여서. (In fact, reported speech combinations such as that one have their own section on page 309; other combinations, however, do not.)

Finally, if you need a refresher, here's the order of the South Korean alphabet:

ㄱ ㄲ ㄴ ㄷ ㄸ ㄹ ㅁ ㅂ ㅃ ㅅ ㅆ ㅇ ㅈ ㅉ ㅊ ㅋ ㅌ ㅍ ㅎ
ㅏ ㅐ ㅑ ㅒ ㅓ ㅔ ㅕ ㅖ ㅗ ㅘ ㅙ ㅚ ㅛ ㅜ ㅝ ㅞ ㅟ ㅠ ㅡ ㅢ ㅣ

Syllables are very important in alphabetical order. For example, the syllable 게 **ge** comes before 겠 **gess** alphabetically, so an expression like 게 하다 **ge hada** comes before 겠다 **gessda** even though ㅎ follows ㅆ in the alphabet.